EVE'S APPLE TO THE LAST SUPPER

EVE'S APPLE TO THE LAST SUPPER

PICTURING FOOD IN THE BIBLE

C.M. KAUFFMANN

THE BOYDELL PRESS

First published 2017
The Boydell Press, Woodbridge

ISBN 978 1 78327 137 5

The Boydell Press is an imprint of Boydell & Brewer Ltd
PO Box 9, Woodbridge, Suffolk IP12 3DF, UK
and of Boydell & Brewer Inc.
668 Mount Hope Ave, Rochester, NY 14620–2731, USA
website: www.boydellandbrewer.com

A catalogue record for this title is available
from the British Library

This publication is printed on acid-free paper

Designed by BBR, Sheffield

CONTENTS

ACKNOWLEDGEMENTS

This text is intended to bridge the gap between 'popular' and 'academic' writing. While it is centred on the illustrations, it provides a fuller introduction and context for the subject than is to be found in a picture book, while not offering the amount of detailed exposition expected of academic publications. To take just one example, footnotes have been kept to a minimum.

Thanks are due to Michelle Brown for initial encouragement to proceed with this project and to numerous friends for help and advice. Ronald Lightbown and John Mallet, former Victoria and Albert Museum colleagues, offered expertise on different kinds of table ware and settings, and Lesley Smith provided illuminating references to medieval biblical commentaries. Without Mireille Galinou, the illustrations would never have been listed or assembled. Bonnie Cullen simplified and improved the text at numerous points. As always, Martin Kauffmann was a stern, questioning and constructive reader whose suggestions elicited many improvements. Finally, heartfelt thanks are due to the Warburg Institute for its Library and Photographic Collection where much of the work was done.

BIBLE TEXTS

The Latin Vulgate, St Jerome's translation from the Greek, was the principal text in medieval Western Europe. Its closest English version is the Douai-Reims translation of 1582/1609, but, as this is no longer easily available, the biblical quotations are taken from the *Holy Bible New Revised Standard Version* (2007). Thanks are due to the Rev. Callan Slipper for his advice.

INTRODUCTION

Given that food is perhaps the most basic feature in our lives, it is hardly surprising that it figures so prominently in the Bible. From Eve's fruit to the Last Supper and the pilgrims' Supper at Emmaus, meals play a major part in key events in both the Old and the New Testament. Less widely realised is the sheer number of meals mentioned as part of the narrative. Hardly a page goes by without a reference to a meal of some kind. Metaphors referring to food, from the land of milk and honey (Exod. 3.8) to 'my cup overflows' (Psalm 23), are equally omnipresent.

Of literally hundreds of meals mentioned in the Bible, relatively few were ever illustrated. Even so, some richly illuminated medieval manuscripts show plenty of meals, some of them relatively obscure. The Old Testament picture book produced in Paris in about 1250 illustrates, in a formulaic way, some fifteen meals and it contains only Genesis to Kings.[1] Here we shall discuss the most frequently illustrated scenes, ten from the Hebrew Bible and a round dozen from the Gospels, most of them made for a Christian audience.[2] As we shall see, they were not all equally popular throughout the whole period to be covered here, from 300 to 1700, and their importance as images at different times will be linked with their place both in biblical interpretation and in the historical circumstances in which they were produced.

These pictorial representations paid attention to the seated guests and their surroundings, but on the whole there is not much variety of food to be seen on the table. The Bible itself is sparse in its descriptions of food and its preparation. Only occasionally does it examine the process of cooking. For example, the meal at Gilgal prepared for Elisha (II Kings 4.38–41) is described in some detail, but it does not appear to have been illustrated. On the whole in the earlier Middle Ages the dress of the diners is broadly based on the classical model of long tunics and cloaks, in contrast with the three-quarter-length tunics worn by the servants. Only from about 1300 do the dresses usually reflect contemporary costume. In other ways the setting can also reflect contemporary usage. For example, some of the earliest images show the semi-circular tables and reclining guests of the late classical period (**126**). The round table remained common in Byzantine depictions until the twelfth century, but in Western art it is more often replaced by oblong tables in the early Middle Ages.

This raises the question of how far such compositions reflect contemporary usage and to what extent they are bound by pictorial tradition. To a considerable extent, medieval artists based their compositions on earlier models, particularly for religious subjects. Cult images such as the Crucifixion changed relatively rarely over the centuries. Abraham's three guests are seated at an oblong table in the fifth- and sixth-century mosaics in Rome and Ravenna (**14**, **15**), so that it is reasonable to assume that the continued appearance of the round table in religious imagery, particularly in pictures of the Last Supper, is due more to pictorial tradition than to contemporary usage. From the eleventh century the long oblong table, always covered by a table cloth, becomes the standard furniture, but the round table still appears occasionally in the fifteenth century and the pictorial evidence does not really tell us when and to what extent it went out of fashion.

It is the utensils on the table that provide more evidence of contemporary usage. In the early Middle Ages the jugs and bowls are portrayed in simple, standard forms. The lack of cutlery, except for knives, indicates that food was eaten from the fingers, but this is only rarely depicted (for example, **51**, **119**, **131**). We know from texts on table manners that spoons were in use in the twelfth century, but they hardly ever appear in the biblical illustrations to be discussed.[3] Increasingly, from the thirteenth century, the dishes and vessels are more clearly contemporary objects. Bowls and plates were brought by servants, goblets and cups placed on the table. As we shall see, in the Psalter commissioned by Sir Geoffrey Luttrell in Lincolnshire in the 1330s the illustration of a secular family meal shows a greater opulence and variety of dishes than the compositionally similar depiction of the Last Supper in the same manuscript. This difference is clearly due to the greater austerity and asceticism given to the religious subject (**137**). In the later fourteenth and fifteenth centuries, with the growing naturalism of pictorial representation, the table settings, dishes and utensils provide a precise reflection of contemporary usage. The actual food depicted remains sparse, but the settings indicate upper-class life, most spectacularly in sixteenth-century banquet scenes. Images of peasants eating are few and far between (**48**).

The popularity of the roughly twenty scenes to be discussed derives partly from their importance in the Bible's narrative but even more so from the interpretations in biblical commentaries. Abraham providing a splendid meal for his three visitors is a major event in the narrative of Genesis, but the frequent appearance of the scene in Christian art is more due to the identification of the three guests as Old Testament forerunners, or types, of the Holy Trinity. Above all, as we shall see, some of the most frequently illustrated meals in both the Old and the New Testament were those that had been interpreted as forerunners of the Last Supper.

THE BASIC FEATURES

BREAD, WINE, FISH AND TABLE FELLOWSHIP

Through the Last Supper and the central importance of the Eucharist as symbolising the body and blood of Christ, bread and wine are the fundamental biblical foods. They had, of course, always been staple foods. The cultivation of wheat and barley has been traced back to the eighth millennium BCE and bread was a common component of diet in the Hebrew Bible, of which the Pentateuch, the first five books, compiled from different literary sources, was probably written in the eighth to sixth centuries BCE, perhaps about a millennium after the period of the patriarchs it describes. To take one example, which will be discussed in detail, the Book of Ruth – the date of which remains obscure – tells how Ruth's kinsman Boaz, impressed by her hard work in the field, invites her to sit with the reapers: 'come here and eat some bread and dip your morsel in sour wine' (Ruth 2.14). In Jewish liturgy the ceremony of Kiddush, held on the Sabbath and on festivals from the fifth century BCE, centred on reciting a blessing over wine and bread in gratitude for the sustenance God has provided. In contrast with the Christian belief from the time of the Last Supper, the food itself does not become holy. In the Gospels bread first appears in the devil's temptation of Jesus: 'If you are the Son of God, command these stones to become loaves of bread' (Matt. 4.3; Luke 4.3). Thereafter it remains the staple food – indeed, given the relative scarcity of meat once Canaan was under cultivation, it has been estimated that bread made up as much as 50 per cent of the calorific intake in Palestine during the Roman period.[1] It figures in the most common metaphors, as in: 'I am the bread of life. Whoever comes to me will never be hungry' (John 6.35) and 'Man shall not live by bread alone' (Matt. 4.4; Luke 4.4), to quote just two examples.

Wheat and barley headed the list of seven foods which the Israelites were to receive in the Promised Land; the others are vines, figs, pomegranates, olives and honey (Deut. 8.8). These are shown in a wickerwork basket in the recently discovered floor mosaic in the fifth-century CE synagogue at Sepphoris (Zippori) in northern Israel, near Nazareth (**1**). The basket is referred to in Deuteronomy 26.2–4 with the command to bring the first fruits to the priest to be placed before the altar: 'and you shall put it in a basket and go to the place that the Lord your God will choose as a dwelling for his name'. All these fruits are obviously of historic importance, but it is the history of wine that is almost as ancient and all-pervasive as that of bread.[2] The transformation from the wild grape to the cultivated vineyard is thought to have taken place at about 3000 BCE and, certainly, grapes figure prominently in Egyptian

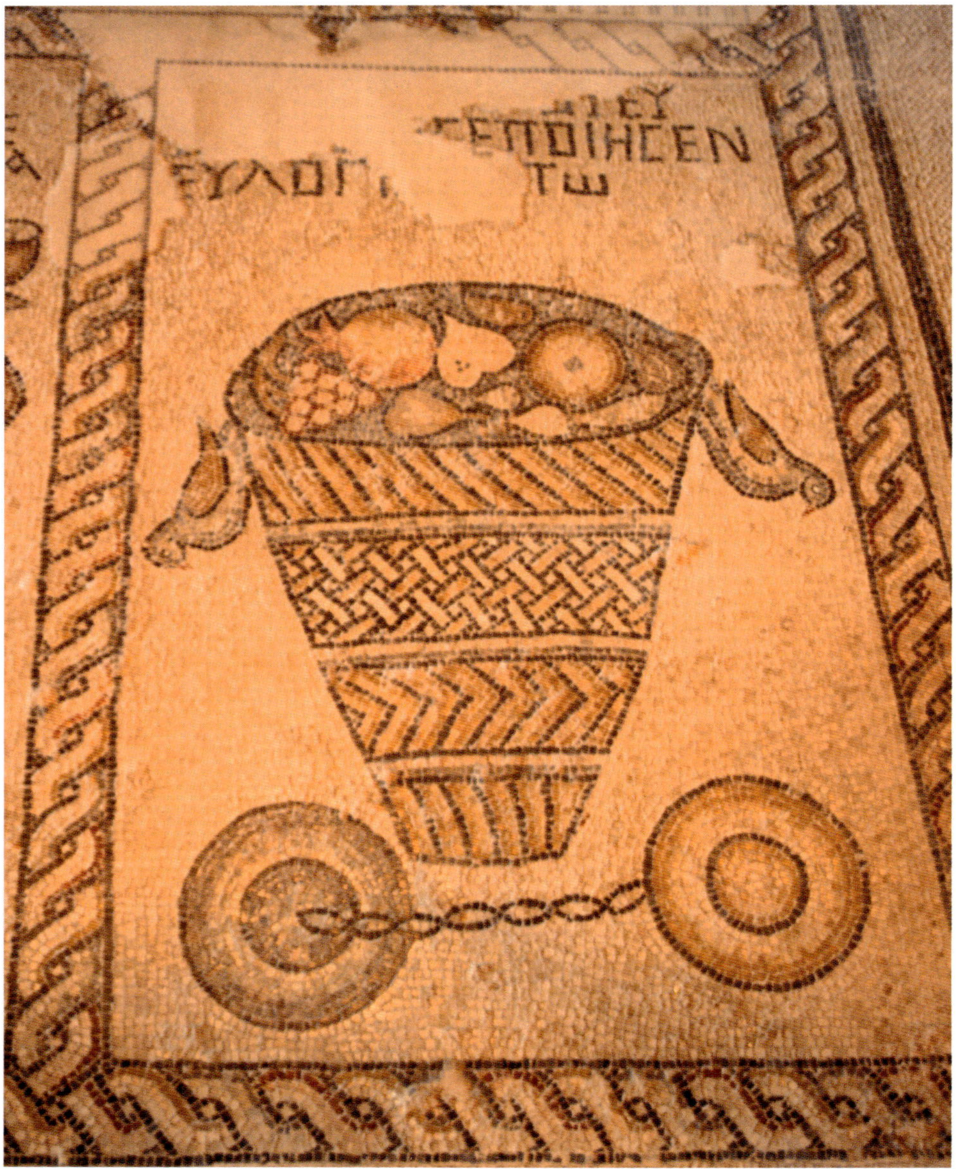

1. Basket containing the seven fruits of the Promised Land, as described in Deuteronomy. Floor mosaic, Sepphoris synagogue, Israel, fifth century.

and Mesopotamian art. Moses' spies in the land of Canaan brought back a cluster of grapes so large that it had to be carried on a staff between the shoulders of two men (Numbers 13.23). The power of intoxicants was recognised as important to religious experience in many cultures, not least in the veneration of Dionysus by the Greeks. The son of Zeus, he was the god of wine and intoxication, the hero of Euripides' *Bacchae* (408–406 BCE) and of the Roman cult of Bacchus. His death at the hands of titans and his resuscitation forms a parallel with the Passion and Resurrection of Christ. The dangers of intoxication were signalled in the Hebrew Bible by the drunkenness of Noah, shamed by his sons (Gen. 20–24), and of Lot, seduced by his daughters (Gen. 19.30–38). Yet wine was also interpreted as the inspired words of God both by Isaiah in his 'Song of the Vineyard' (Is. 5.1–17) and by Jeremiah: 'I am like a drunken man, like a man overcome by wine, because of the Lord and because of his holy words' (Jer. 23.9). Most famously, the special place of wine is confirmed by Jesus, speaking to his apostles: 'I am the true vine … you are the branches' (John 15.1–5).

The first connection between bread and wine in the Bible occurs at Genesis 14.18–20, when Melchizedek, king of Salem and priest, brought them out as refreshment for Abraham, who was returning from battle. Melchizedek was the first priest

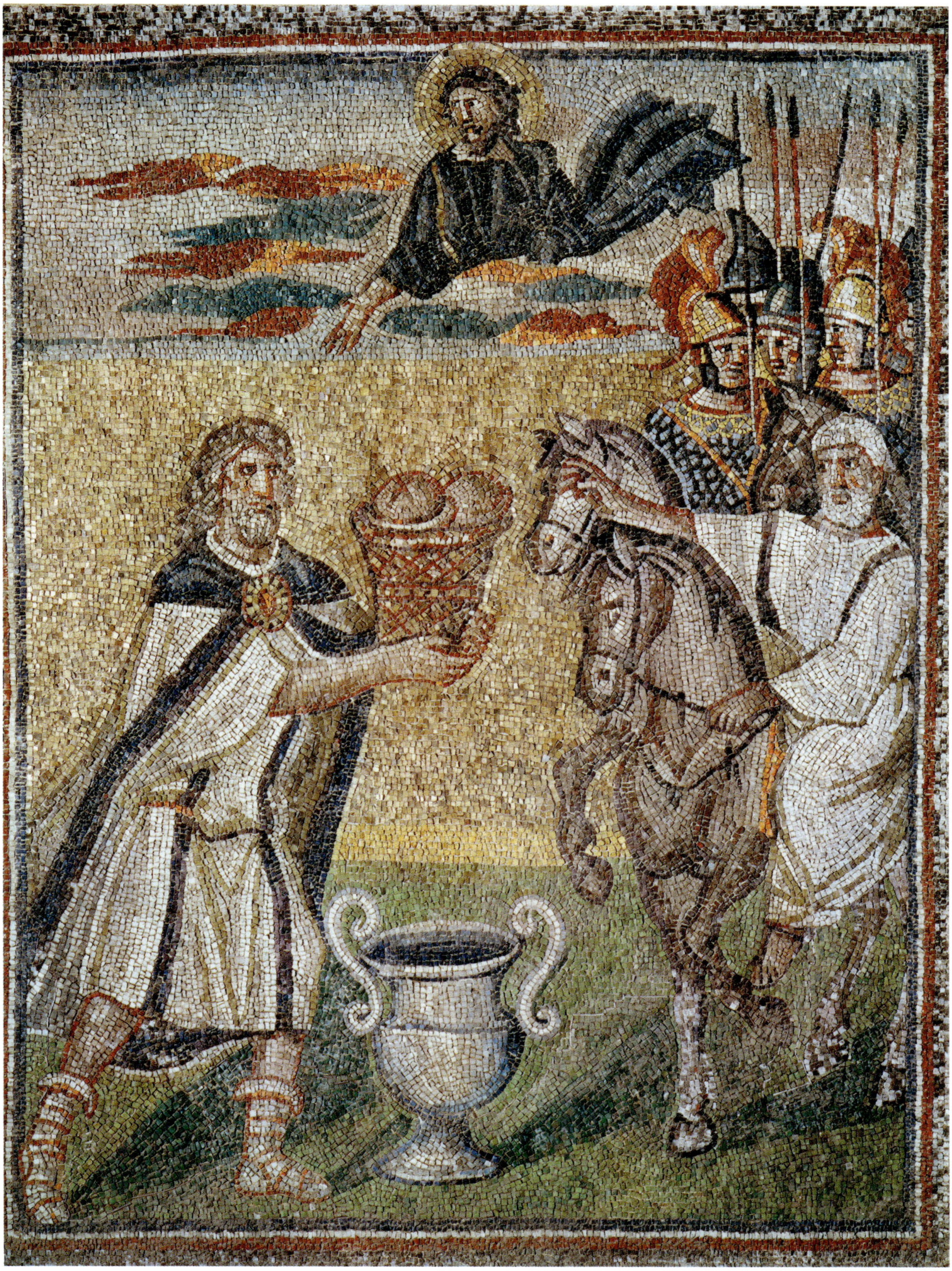

2. Melchizedek offering bread and wine to Abraham; interpreted as a forerunner of the Eucharist. Mosaic, Rome, Santa Maria Maggiore, c.430.

3. The fish as symbol of Christ. Funerary inscription, monument of Licinia, Thermae Museum, Rome, third century.

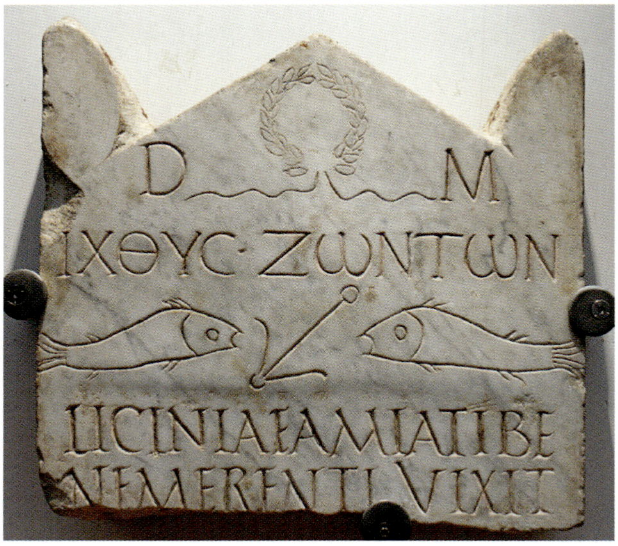

4. Fish and bread. Wall painting, Callixtus catacomb, Rome, third century.

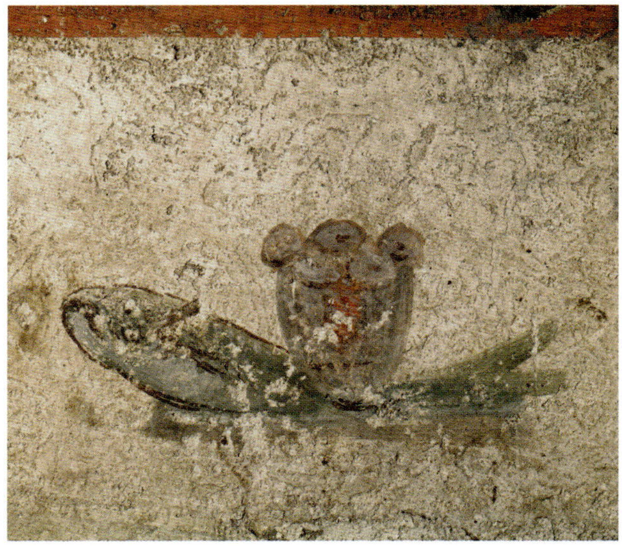

mentioned in the Bible and he was subsequently seen as a forerunner of Jesus in the Epistle to the Hebrews (ch. 7). It was the Church Fathers Ambrose (c.339–97; bishop of Milan) and Augustine (354–430; bishop of Hippo, in north Africa) who interpreted Melchizedek's offering of bread and wine as a forerunner of the sacrament of the Eucharist. This gave the story a considerable importance and it was frequently illustrated either showing Melchizedek alone with his offering at the altar or together with Abraham, as in the fifth-century mosaic in the nave of Santa Maria Maggiore in Rome (**2**). In the sky above, God the Father points at Melchizedek with his right hand, providing visual evidence for the Eucharistic interpretation for this Old Testament event.

As we shall see in the illustrations of biblical meals, fish was as ubiquitous as bread and wine. 'Come ye after me and I will make you fishers of men' (Matt. 4.19) is only one example of the common motif of Jesus fishing for the souls of believers that recurs throughout the Gospels. More specifically, the fish itself becomes the symbol of Christ with the interpretation of the Greek word for fish – Ichthys – as an acrostic for Iesus Christos Theou Huios Soter (Jesus Christ son of God, Saviour).[3] This was first expressed in the third century by Tertullian, the north African Church Father who wrote in his treatise on baptism (ch. 1.3): 'But we little fish, like our Ichthys Jesus Christ, are born in water, and it is only by remaining in water that we are safe.' This interpretation was certainly well known by the fourth century and in the *City of God* (1.xviii.c.23) St Augustine gives both the Greek of the acrostic and its Latin translation.

Evidence for the Christian belief in fish as a holy food has been provided by a tomb inscription dating to before 216 CE. This was the tomb of one Abercius, found at Hieropolis near Synnada (Turkey) and now in the Lateran Museum in Rome. 'Fish from the source' is linked with wine and bread as holy food, though the precise meaning of the inscription has never been clarified. Yet the meaning of the fish as a badge of Christian affiliation depicted on numerous other tombs (**3**), with or without the Ichthys inscription, is clear, and it probably also explains the fish and bread still life painted in the Callixtus catacomb in Rome (**4**). More generally, fish was seen as preferable to meat and the Jewish practice of eating fish on Fridays was emulated by the Christians.

Eating is essential for life, but there is more to meals than just seeking nourishment. As Roland Barthes proposed: 'It is also at the same time a system of communication, a body of images, a protocol of usages, mode of life and behaviour.'[4] Rites connected

5. *Agapé*, communal meal of Christian believers. Wall painting, SS Marcellino e Pietro catacomb, Rome, fourth century.

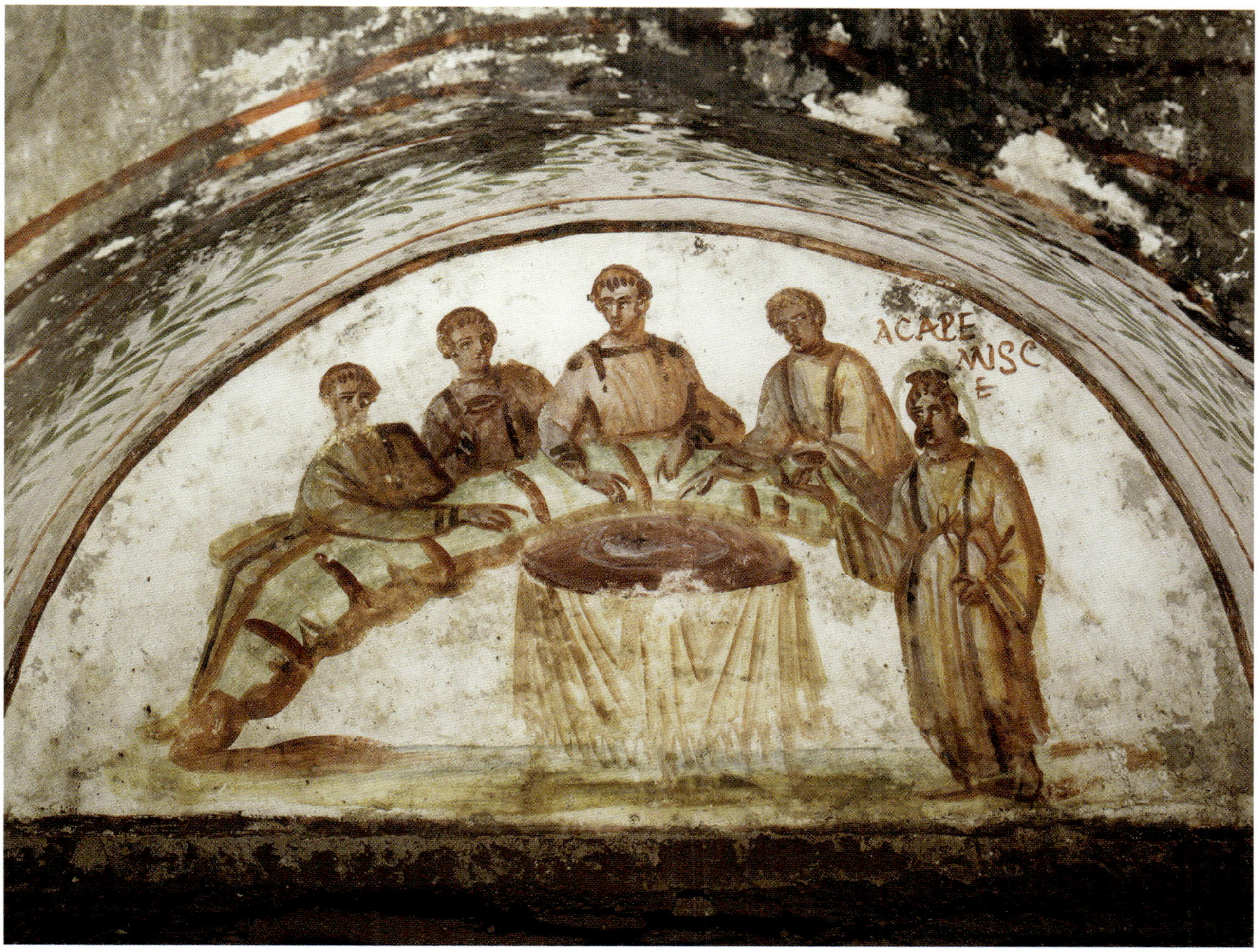

with holy meals are known in most religions and they occur frequently in the Old Testament. In the time of King Saul, for instance, Samuel had to prepare the sacrificial meal so that the people could enjoy re-unification with God: 'for the people will not eat until he comes, since he must bless the sacrifice; afterwards those eat who are invited' (1 Samuel 9.13). Communal meals forge social bonds and, from the time of Plato, the Greek and Roman *symposium* – literally, dining party – glorified these convivial and intellectually meaningful gatherings. The concept of the communal meal of Christian believers is first expressed in the description of 'breaking the bread' and then 'eating food with glad and generous hearts' (Acts 2.46). In the second-century Epistle of Jude the believers' communal meal is described as God's 'love feast' (Jude 12). It became known as *Agapé*, a word actually inscribed on one of the depictions of such meals in the Roman catacombs (**5**). God's blessing was an integral part of the occasion, but, more broadly, table fellowship was synonymous with fellowship in all aspects of life.[5]

THE OLD TESTAMENT

It was the Old Testament, the adapted version of the Hebrew Bible, which contained the instruction 'You shall not make for yourself an idol' (Exod. 20.4). This is the second of the ten Commandments and it is quite specific in forbidding any kind of pictorial image. These were seen at the time as the preserve of heathen religions, which used them as the central part of their worship. The prohibition was maintained in principle, though with numerous exceptions, by the Jewish religion, but it was abandoned by Christians from the third century. By that time it had become apparent that images could play an important part in spreading the concepts of a missionising religion. The doctrinal justification for this change was that as Jesus had become a man in his Incarnation, so depictions of him as a man were permitted. The Old Testament, particularly the narrative books, were frequently illustrated in Christian art and the most popular subjects were those that were interpreted as forerunners or types of the events of the Gospels.[1] We have seen, for example, that Melchizedek bringing bread and wine to Abraham was interpreted as a type of the Last Supper, and the same kind of connection occurs in several of the examples discussed. Throughout this book each section is preceded by the relevant biblical text and, as we shall see, it remains important to keep these quotations in mind when viewing the images.[2]

I
ADAM AND EVE: THE FALL

But the serpent said to the woman, 'you will not die; for God knows when you eat of it your eyes will be opened, and you will be like God, knowing good and evil'. So when the woman saw that the tree was good for food, and that it was a delight for the eyes, and that the tree was to be desired to make one wise, she took of its fruit and ate; and she also gave some to her husband, who was with her, and he ate. (Gen. 3.4–6).

The fundamental contrast between mankind's original sin in taking the fruit from the tree of knowledge of good and evil and the story of salvation through Jesus Christ provides the reason for the popularity of depictions of the Fall in Christian art from the earliest times. In the wall paintings of catacombs – underground burial chambers – and on the reliefs of sarcophagi the implication is clear. The deceased who died because of Adam's sin will enter paradise through Jesus Christ. The moral is drawn in visual terms in the earliest depictions, such as the wall painting in the Christian baptistery at Dura Europos in Syria (early third century), where the figure of the Good Shepherd, the personification of Jesus, stands immediately above the Fall.[3] In most of the early examples, such as the fourth-century wall painting in the catacomb of Pietro and Marcellino in Rome (**6**) and the carving on the sarcophagus of the Roman official Junius Bassus (d.359) (**7**), Adam and Eve, hiding their nakedness, stand symmetrically round the tree on which the serpent is entwined. Most of the images invented for Christian art in these early years were adapted from Greco-Roman compositions and the Fall was no exception. Poseidon and Athena, contenders for the office of patron of Athens, appear on coins and on cameos surrounding a tree entwined by a serpent, while Hercules is frequently shown standing next to a tree with a serpent entwined as he guards the apples of the Hesperides.[4]

In these early illustrations of the Fall there is usually a sense of approximate equality between Adam and Eve. They appear in identical or at any rate similar postures even when Eve is shown moving towards the tree. However, in the Byzantine Octateuchs – illustrated texts of the first eight books of the Bible – the blame on Eve is reinforced by adding a separate scene showing her persuading Adam to accept the fruit.[5] On the bronze doors of

6. Wall painting. SS Marcellino e Pietro catacomb, Rome, fourth century. The basic composition that has remained standard.

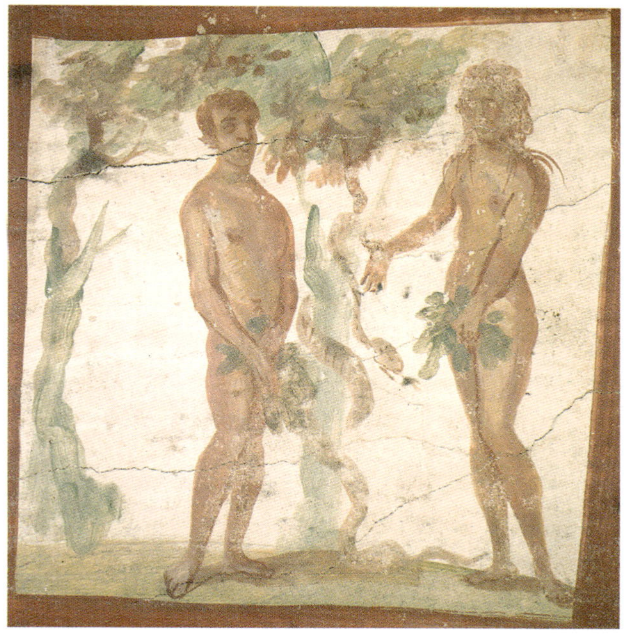

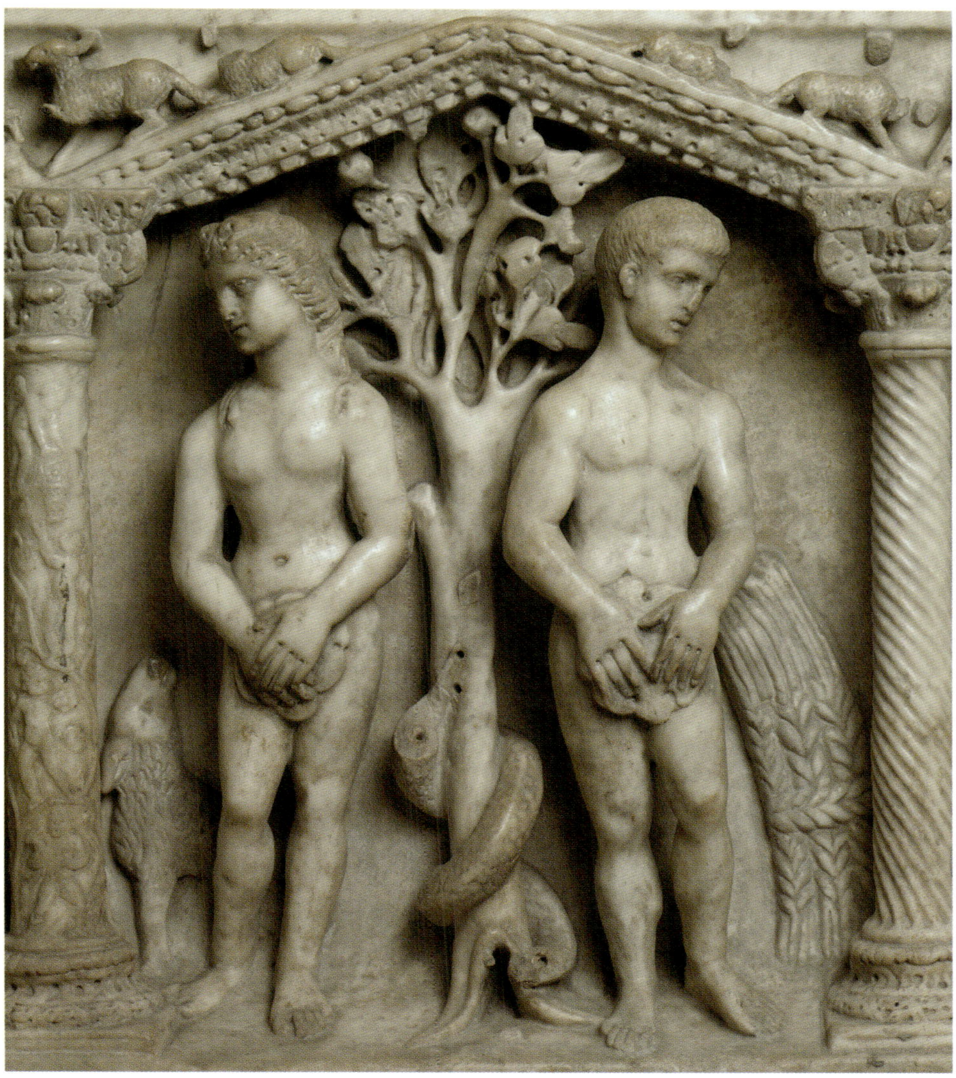

7. Stone relief. Sarcophagus of Junius Bassus (d.359), Vatican, Treasury Museum. The tree appears to be a fig tree.

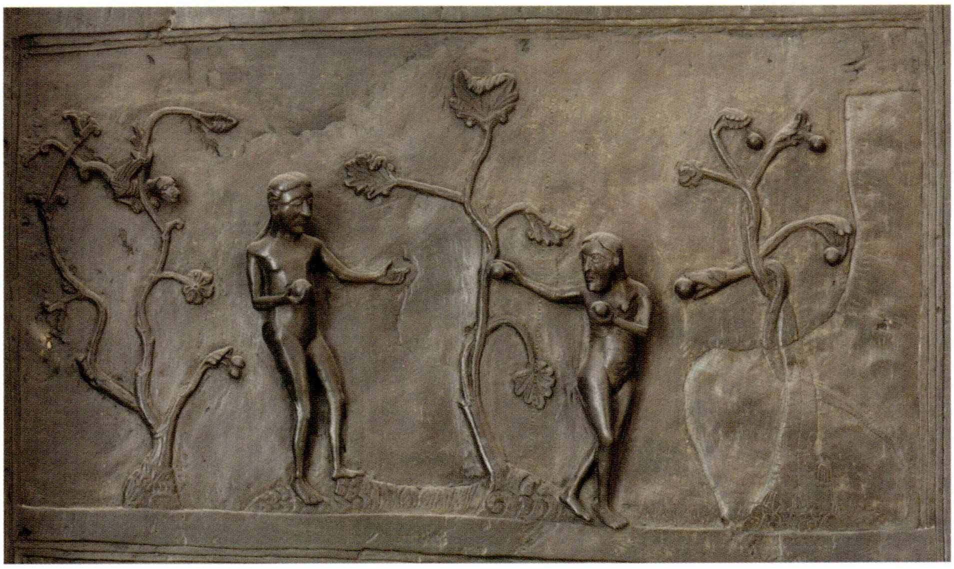

8. Bronze doors, Hildesheim Cathedral (c.1007–15). Eve's apple replaces her breast.

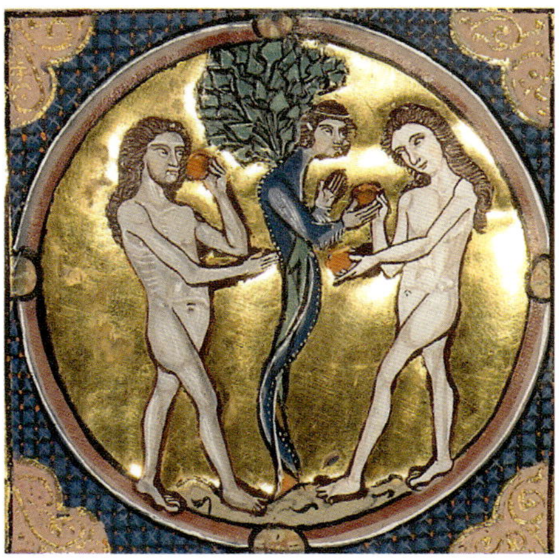

9. *Bible moralisée*, c.1235. The serpent has a woman's face. Oxford, Bodleian Library, MS Bodl.270b, fol. 7v.

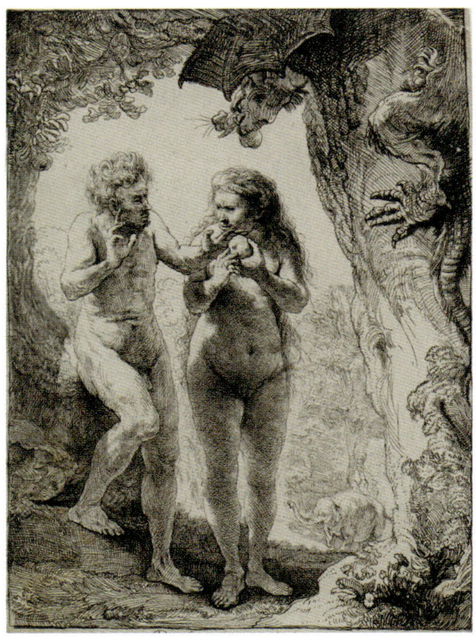

10. Rembrandt (1606–69), etching dated 1638. Adam and Eve are shown as equally involved. London, British Museum.

the cathedral at Hildesheim (c.1007–15) the image of Eve has been described as charged with sexual tension, her body twisted sinuously while the apple she holds obscures and therefore replaces her breast (**8**).[6] More generally in the West, her sin is increasingly emphasised as she takes the fruit from the serpent's mouth and, from the late twelfth century, the serpent is often shown with a woman's face (**9**). In his commentary on Genesis, the theologian Petrus Comestor (d.1179) describes Eve as talking to the serpent in which she saw her own form reflected. This misogynist interpretation remained popular in the later Middle Ages and Renaissance and it was not until the time of Rembrandt's etching of the subject (1638 (**10**)) that relative equality between Adam and Eve was restored. Even Cranach, who had returned to a more traditional snake, shows Adam in doubt as Eve presses the fruit upon him (**11**).

Such changes in the pictorial tradition hardly affect our basic concern with food. According to popular belief, Eve gave Adam an apple, yet there is no such identification in the Bible. As we have seen, 'fruit' is

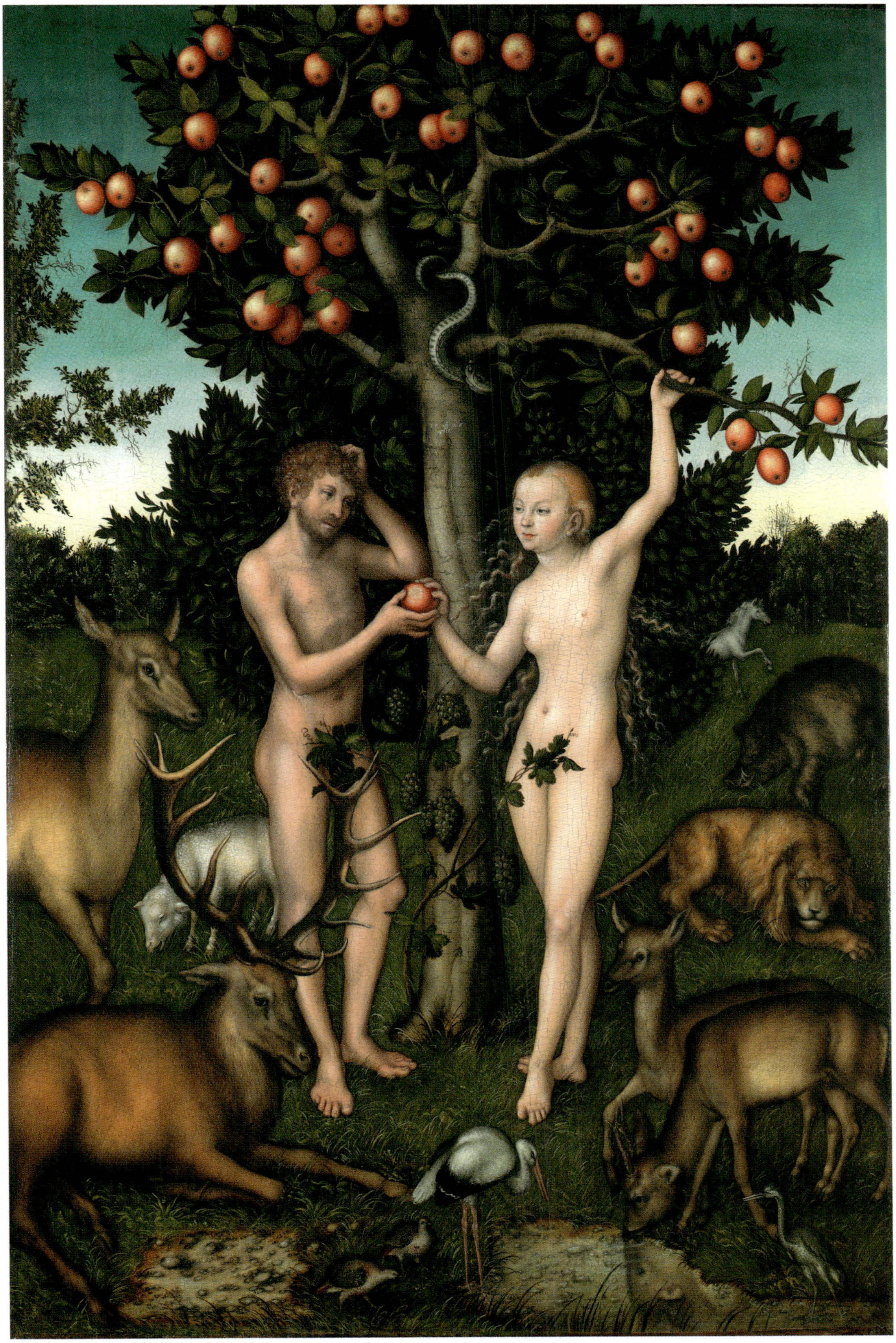

11. Lucas Cranach (1472–1553). Dated 1526. The apples are clearly identified as such. London, Courtauld Institute Gallery.

the only description given. In Jewish commentaries the forbidden fruit had been identified with a fig, a grape, an apple, wheat and a nut,[7] but the Early Christian theologians took no interest in such speculation. We know that there was a fig tree in the Garden of Eden, as Adam and Eve 'sewed fig leaves together and made themselves aprons' immediately after the Fall (Gen. 3.7). Fig trees have been identified on some fourth-century Roman sarcophagi reliefs (**7**) but in later periods they are more common in Byzantine art. There are Byzantine texts from the fifth century, such as that of Isidore of Pelusium in Egypt, identifying the tree of the knowledge of good and evil as a fig.[8] The clearest depiction of a fig tree may be seen in the Genesis mosaics in the atrium of the cathedral of St Mark in Venice (**12**). These date from about 1260, but they have been shown to have some links with a Greek manuscript of about 500, the badly damaged Cotton Genesis in the British Library. We have, therefore, evidence for the continued depiction of the fig tree in images of the Fall in Byzantine art of the Early Christian and medieval periods.[9]

The origin of the identification of the apple as Eve's fruit in Christian art is more difficult to pin down. The fruit shown in catacomb paintings and on sarcophagus reliefs have been widely interpreted as apples and, indeed, they may well have been intended as such, but the identification is far from clear. For example, the small fruit in the painting of the Fall in cell 77 of the Domitilla Catacomb in Rome may be reasonably interpreted as an apple;[10] the slightly larger fruit in the Greek manuscript of Genesis in the Austrian National Library in Vienna (c.500) has been identified as a pomegranate (**13**).

At any rate, for the earliest period of such representation, covering the third to the early fifth

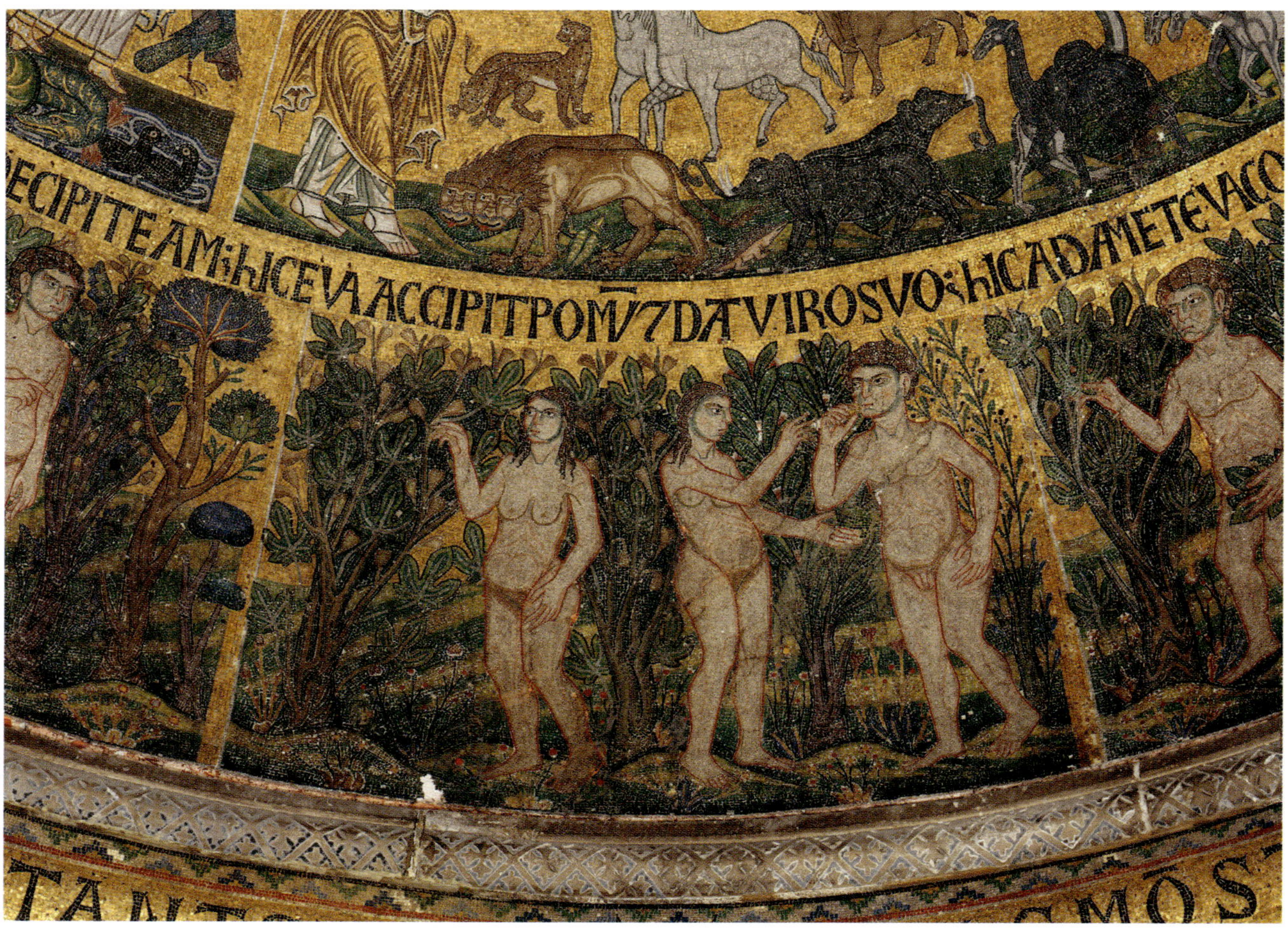

12. Cupola mosaic, Venice, Cathedral of St Mark, atrium, c.1260. A clear example of the fruit as figs.

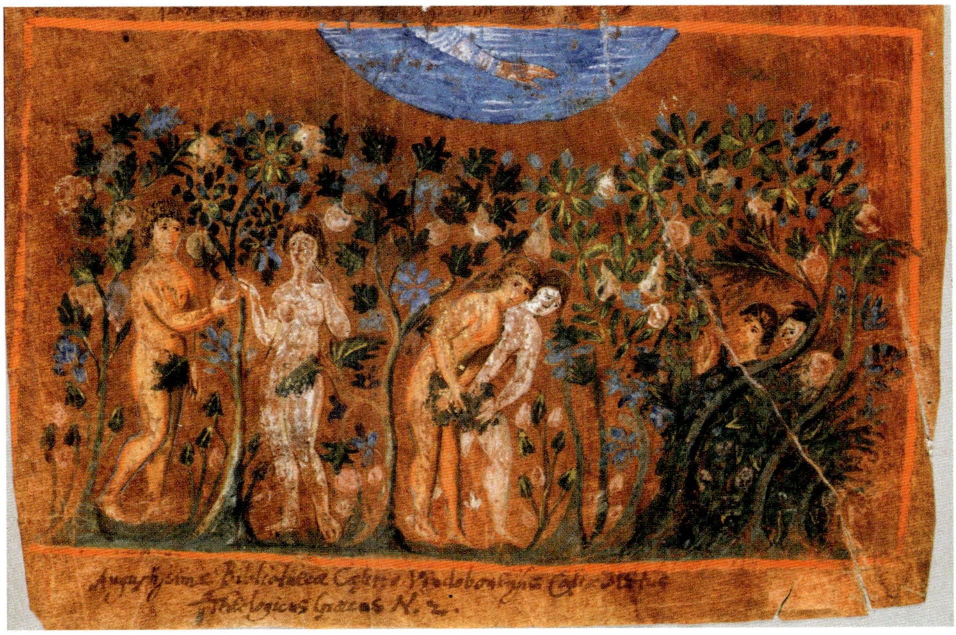

13. Manuscript of Genesis, Byzantine, c.500. The fruit has been identified as pomegranates. Vienna, Austrian National Library, Cod. Vindob. Theol. Gr. 31, fol. 1.

centuries, we are entirely dependent on the visual depictions, as there are no literary references to the identity of the paradisiacal fruit as an apple at the time. The earliest extant is contained in the early fifth-century *Heptateuchos*, a poetic paraphrase of biblical texts by Cyprianus Gallicus, who identified the tree of knowledge of good and evil as the 'extremely noxious apple'. He probably came from Gaul, as the name implies, or possibly from northern Italy. This identification also appears in the poetic commentary of Alcimus Avitus of Vienne in about 500.[11]

We are left with the problem of why the apple tree was depicted long before there were any written texts supporting such identification. There may have been earlier texts that have disappeared, but in any case the lack of clear evidence has led to a variety of suggested sources for the identification. Jewish commentaries may have played a part, but, as we have seen, they contained several other suggested fruits. In classical literature the apple had been a symbol of love and fruitfulness and, as such, an attribute of Aphrodite (Venus), very different from the symbol of temptation and sin that it became in Christianity.[12] Yet the link of the apple with paradise has been traced back to Greek mythology. The apple of the Hesperides takes its name from the maidens who guarded the golden apples that earth gave to Hera on her marriage to Zeus. Apart from focusing on such links with classical concepts of the fruit of paradise, it has been suggested that the apple emerged in this context as the result of a play on words. The Latin *malum* is an apple, but it is also the word for evil or the evil one and, therefore, a symbol of sin, which it remained in Eve's hand. These are all reasonable suggestions and they should be taken into account, but it must be admitted that they are not supported by tangible evidence.

It has also been argued that the dominance of the apple in the area of the Western Church has less to do with classical parallels than with popular belief.[13] Both of the early texts in which the identification is found were probably written in France and, while apples were also popular in Italy, it was in France and northern Europe that they were most widely available. At any rate, their prevalence could help to explain the growth of this popular belief in the identity of the paradisiacal tree in western Europe, in contrast with the areas of the Byzantine empire in which the fig provided the more common interpretation. This may well be a rare case where botany and agriculture hold the clue in the absence of early theological texts.

2
ABRAHAM AND THE THREE ANGELS

The Lord appeared to Abraham by the oaks of Mamre … He looked up and saw three men standing near him. When he saw them he ran … to meet them and bowed down to the ground. He said 'My lord if I find favour with you, do not pass by your servant … Let me bring a little bread, that you may refresh yourselves'. And Abraham hastened into the tent to Sarah and said, 'Make ready quickly three measures of choice flour, knead it and make cakes'. Abraham ran to the herd, and took a calf, tender and good, and gave it to the servant, who hastened to prepare it. Then he took curds and milk and the calf that he had prepared and set it before them; and he stood under the tree while they ate. (Gen. 18.1–8)

Subsequently, Sarah listened in the tent as the guests told Abraham that she would bear a son within a year despite her advanced age.

These events were frequently illustrated in Christian art largely because the three visitors were interpreted as representing the Holy Trinity. The Egyptian theologian Origen, writing his *Homilies on Genesis* in about 230 CE, stressed the central importance of Abraham 'meeting three men and adoring only one',[14] and his words were endorsed two centuries later by no less an authority than St Augustine (*Contra Maximianus Arianorum*). Meanwhile, St Ambrose, in his treatise on Abraham (c.375–8), had firmly stated that it was the Trinity that the patriarch saw and this remained the Christian interpretation.[15]

In very few biblical meals is the food described in as much detail as we have here. As Origen already noted, the variety and quality of the items described demonstrated Abraham's concern to provide a warm welcome to his visitors. The calf selected had to be 'tender and good'; in other words, only the best was good enough. So much is clear; the trouble arises over the multitude of translations of some of the food described. Sarah is asked to bake 'cakes', a reasonable translation of the Latin *panes* except that the word is now generally applied to a sweetened substance. To avoid that misunderstanding, some translations have preferred 'loaves', which is closest to the Hebrew original. Perhaps, in current parlance, 'bread rolls' would be most appropriate. The good and tender calf is described as being 'cooked' (*coxit*) in the Latin Vulgate

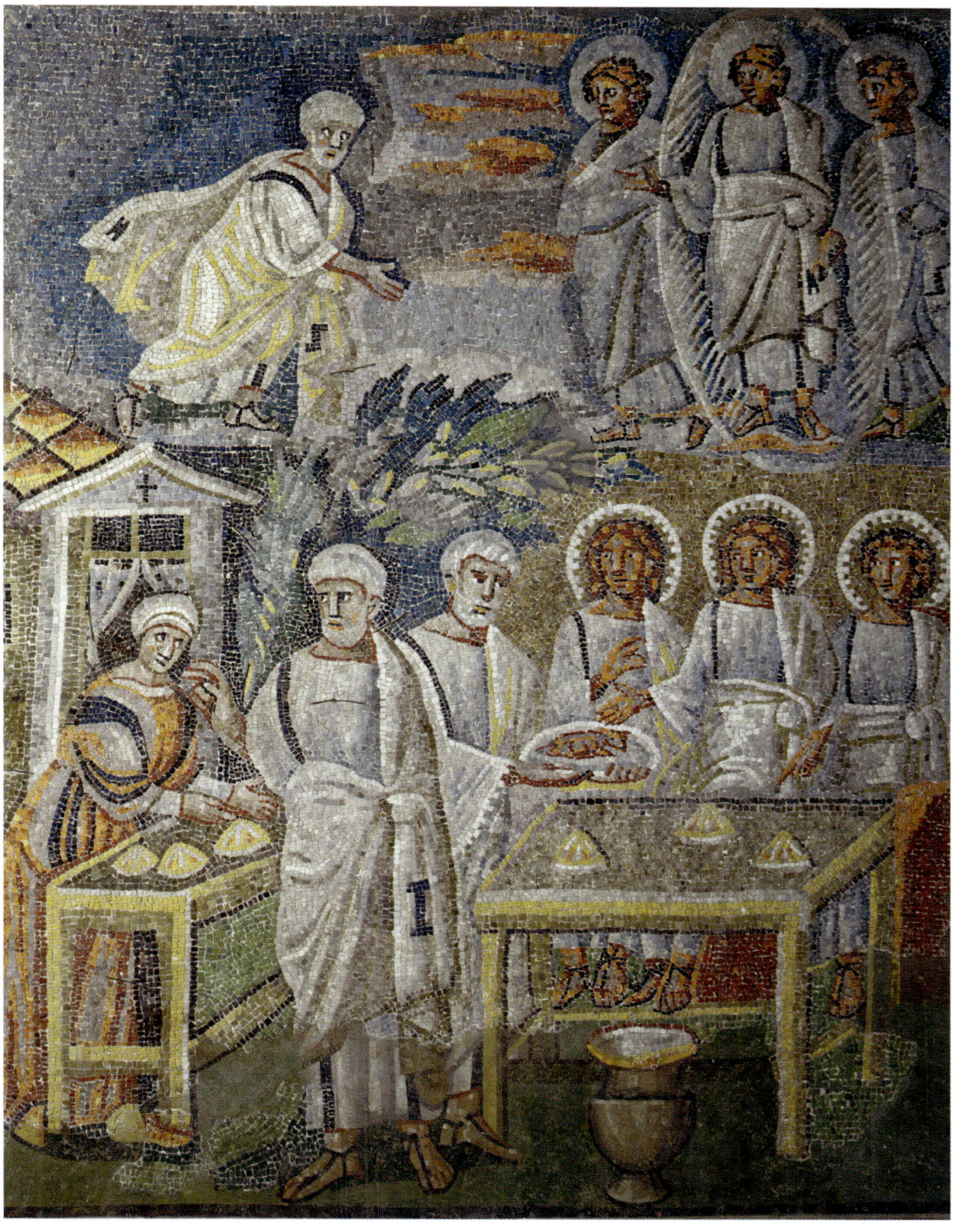

14. Nave mosaic, Rome, Santa Maria Maggiore, c.432–40. Abraham greets the three visitors at the top; below, Abraham instructs Sarah and then serves the food to the visitors.

and variously 'dressed', 'prepared' and 'boiled' in different translations. Similarly, the Vulgate's *butyrum* appears as 'curds' and 'cream' as well as 'butter' in the English versions. These variations are due partly to the multiplicity of biblical texts written in three ancient languages over a long period of time and tackled by different generations of translators. To some extent they also reflect the increased vocabularies of modern European languages. Perhaps future translators will be justified in converting *panes* into rolls.

The earliest surviving depiction of the scene, a fourth-century wall painting in the catacomb under the Via Latina in Rome, shows Abraham greeting the three men. There is a calf standing at his side, but the meal is not pictured.[16] Limiting the illustration to the greeting alone remains common in the Middle Ages; the story is often abbreviated while retaining the essential Trinitarian symbolism. Even so, the majority of depictions of Genesis 18 show the three visitors at the table, with or without the scene of their arrival. The earliest of these is the mosaic in the nave of Santa Maria Maggiore in Rome, dating from c.432–40 (**14**). In the upper register Abraham bows before the three visitors, each of whom has a halo, while the central

15. Chancel mosaic, Ravenna, San Vitale, c.540–47. The scene of Abraham and the three visitors is followed by the Sacrifice of Isaac.

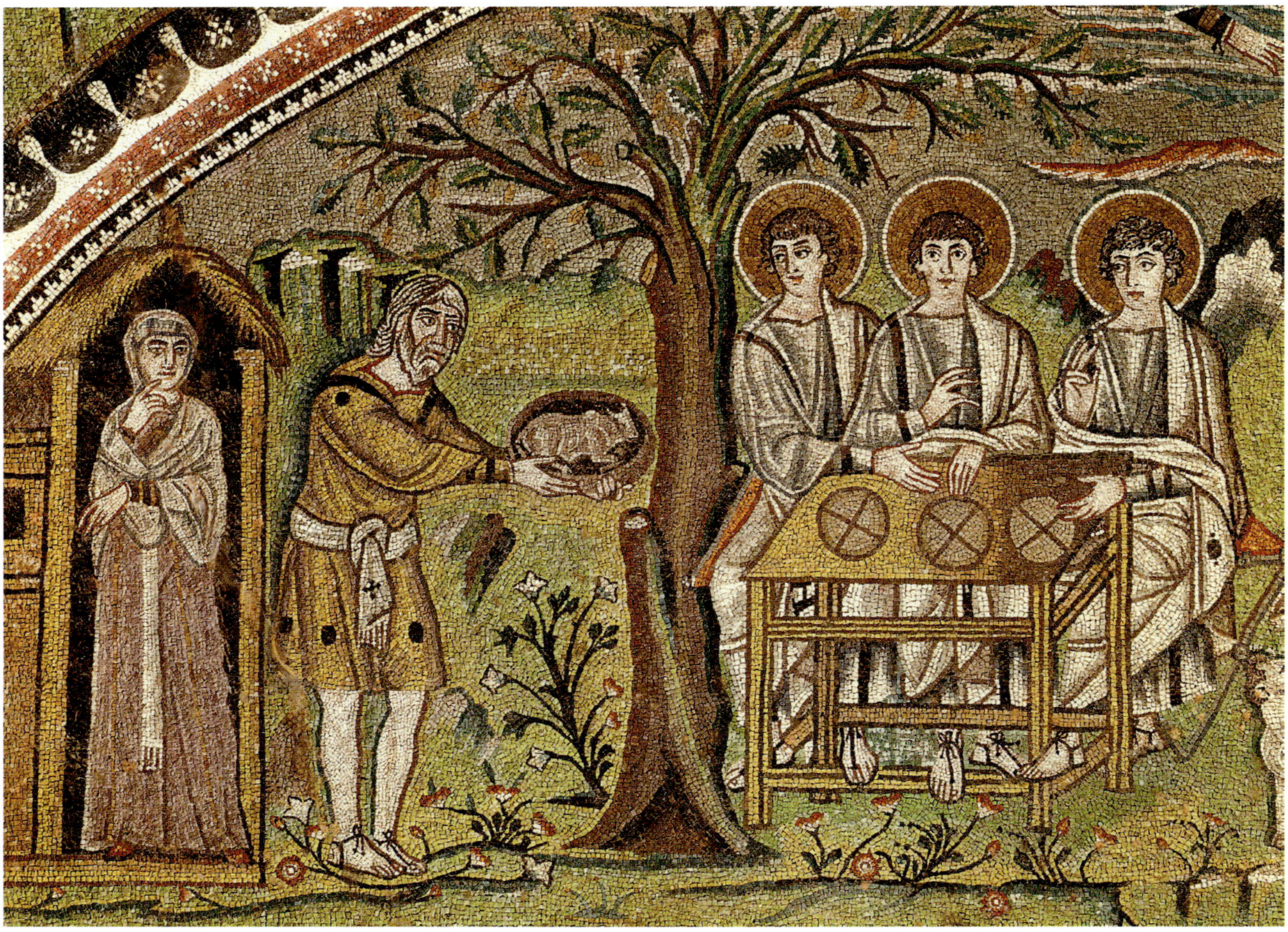

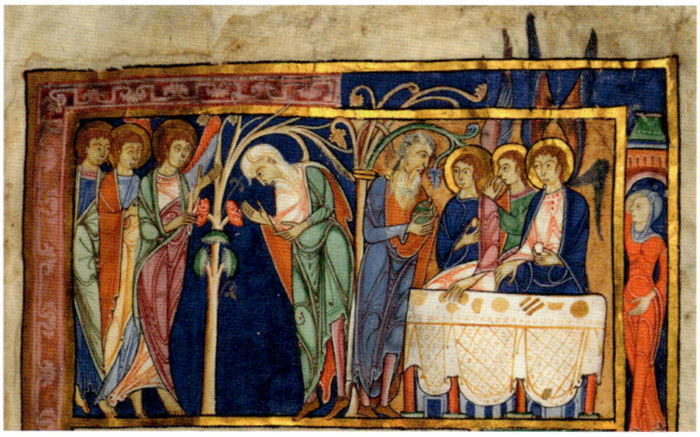

16. Genesis miniature, upper register, Bible, probably from Canterbury, c.1150. The three visitors are now clearly shown as angels. London, Lambeth Palace Library, MS 3, fol. 6.

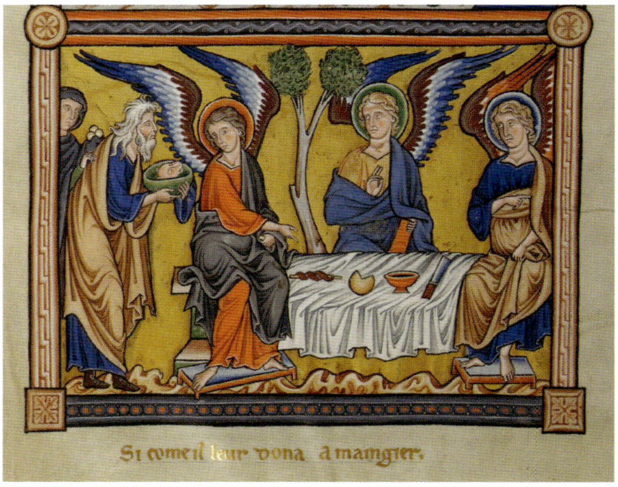

17. Psalter of Queen Ingeborg, north-eastern France, c.1210. Abraham's dish contains a calf's head; the table has a knife, a bowl, bread and an entwined breadstick. Chantilly, Musée Condé, MS 1695, fol. 10v.

one stands within the rays of an oval aureole, the symbol of Christ. The high rank of both Abraham and his visitors is confirmed by the classical garb of white tunic and cloak in which they are dressed. The two registers are joined by the branches of the great oak tree of Mamre, where the scene is set. In the lower register Abraham appears twice: on the left instructing Sarah, who is preparing the bread, and on the right bringing a dish containing the calf to the three visitors, now sitting at the table. Three loaves are on the table and a wine jar stands below, but there is no sign of the curds and milk mentioned in the text. The Christian symbolism of the scene is reinforced by the cross clearly marked on the tympanum above the door of the house, where Sarah is standing.[17]

Another early version of the scene is the mid-sixth-century mosaic in the chancel of San Vitale in Ravenna, where it is portrayed next to the Sacrifice of Isaac (**15**) and opposite the sacrifices of Abel and of Melchizedek. The meal is shown in a composition very similar to that in Santa Maria Maggiore, except that Abraham appears only once and Sarah, no longer active in preparing the meal, stands as an observer in the doorway. Abraham is bringing the dish containing the tiny calf to the table on which the three loaves have already been placed. The emphasis on the identical size and appearance of the three large loaves, each marked with a cross, is probably intended to indicate the equality in rank of the three visitors, following the interpretation put forward by Petrus Chrysologus, archbishop of Ravenna, a century earlier.[18]

The heavenly nature of the three visitors is indicated by the aureole in Santa Maria Maggiore, but neither there nor in San Vitale are they shown as angels. Their earliest appearance with wings is in the badly damaged Cotton Genesis of c.500.[19] In subsequent centuries they are invariably shown as angels. Indeed, in the so-called Lambeth Bible, probably produced at Canterbury in c.1150, the wings are of such importance that they are allowed to penetrate above the picture frame (**16**). Only from the time of the Raphael school painting in the Vatican Logge – which shows only the greeting, not the meal – are the visitors returned to purely human form.[20] In general terms, the composition remains standard, as does the food. Very occasionally, the body of the small calf on Abraham's dish is transformed into a calf's

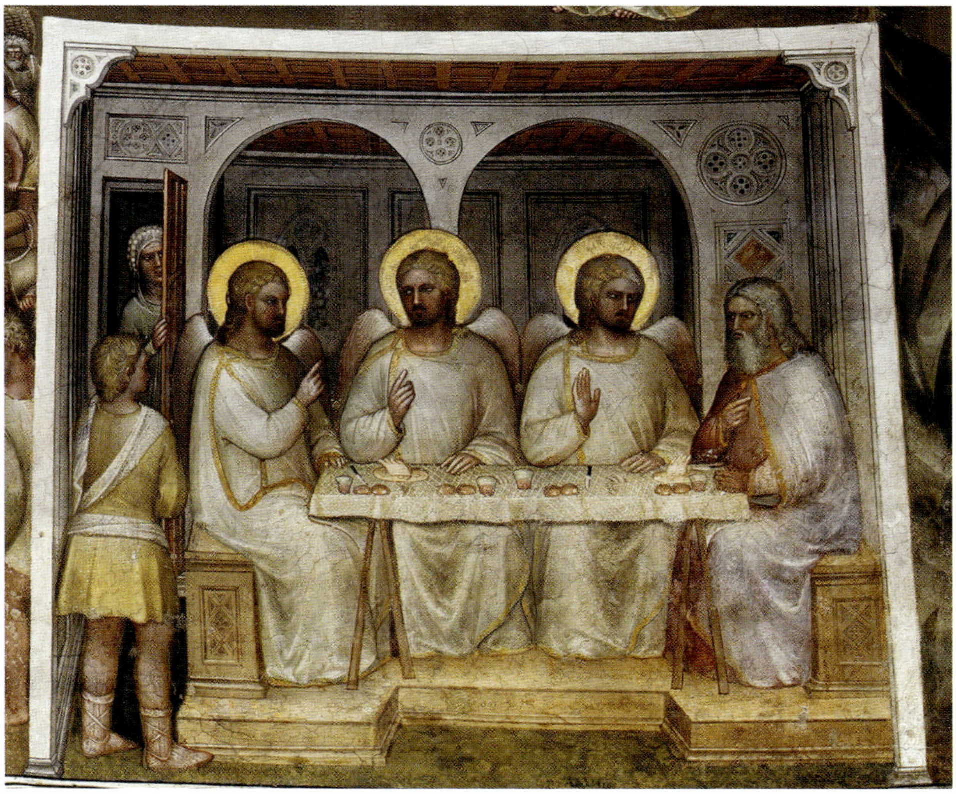

18. Giusto da Menabuoi (active c.1363–93), wall painting, Padua Baptistery, c.1375. Unusually, the meal is transferred to an interior setting.

head, as in the psalter of Queen Ingeborg, a northern French manuscript of about 1210 (**17**). Occasionally, in fourteenth-century Italy, the meal is transferred into an interior setting, as in a wall painting in the Baptistery at Padua, where Abraham is seated next to the angels (**18**). While the interior setting is most unusual, the artist, Giusto da Menabuoi, has taken care to show the food on the table: the calf, curds in a jar and small loaves are all clearly rendered.

The scene was relatively rarely depicted in the Renaissance, but became popular again in the seventeenth century, above all in Holland. This may seem surprising, given that religious imagery was, on the whole, discouraged in Protestant countries, where the fear of idolatry had been the cause of much destruction at the time of the Reformation. However, Old Testament illustrations were more readily tolerated than those of the life of Christ and in Holland such 'history' subjects were taken up by the upper levels of the bourgeoisie as prestige art.

Biblical subjects were usually given a naturalistic setting, and this description could be applied to the painting of 1656 by Gerbrand van den Eeckhout, who was Rembrandt's favourite pupil and close friend (**19**). Abraham, shown in oriental costume with a turban, is greeting the three angels, equipped with huge

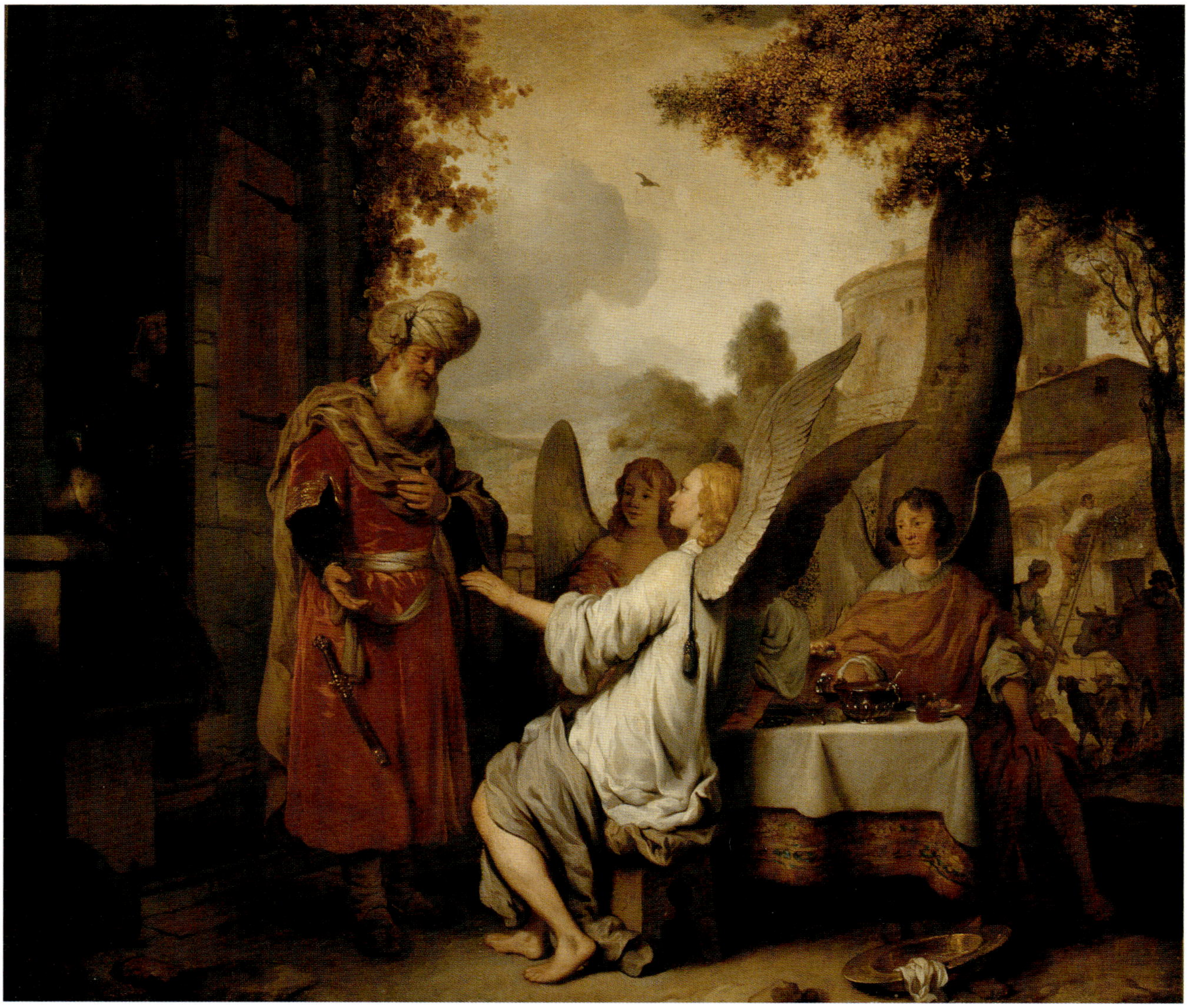

19. Gerbrand van den Eeckhout (Amsterdam, 1621–74), painting dated 1656, showing the scene in a naturalistic setting. St Petersburg, Hermitage.

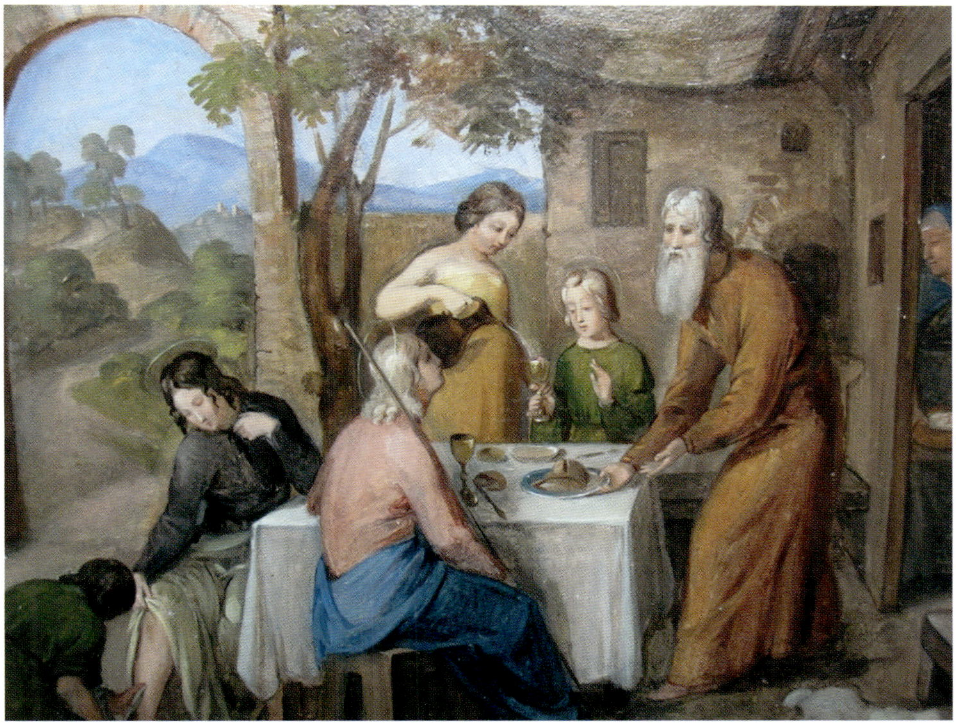

20. Moritz Oppenheim (1800–82), German-Jewish artist working in Rome. Oil sketch, 1824–25. The composition is traditional except for the figure washing the feet of the angel on the left. Private collection.

wings, who are already seated at the table. Sarah, her lined face indicating her advanced age, stands in the doorway, as she had done in the earliest depictions of the scene. The oak tree of Mamre remains dominant, while the scene is given a naturalistic background of farmyard and landscape. There is some bread and a silver bowl on the table, but no other food is shown. Indeed, given that the composition combines the welcome and the meal, it is likely that the food has not yet been served.

As an addendum, to provide an example of the increasing depiction of biblical subjects by Jewish artists in the nineteenth century, there is a version of this scene by Moritz Oppenheim dating from about 1824 (**20**). Oppenheim belonged to the first generation of Jews released from the ghetto by Napoleonic rule in Germany. From 1811 he was able to attend the municipal grammar school in Hanau, near Frankfurt, and then the local art academy. He completed his studies in Rome, where he was in close contact with the German 'Nazarenes', a group of artists who painted religious subjects in the style of the early Italian renaissance.

Oppenheim worked on several biblical themes during his stay in Rome in 1822–25.[21] Here he has followed the traditional iconography, with Abraham serving the calf while Sarah is indoors preparing more food. As in the Early Christian versions (**14**), the three visitors have haloes but not wings. The central guest appears to be blessing the bread and wine, providing a clear reference to the Last Supper. Another unusual addition to the meal is the figure washing the feet of the angel on the left, a literal reference to Abraham's words when he meets the three visitors: 'Let a little water be brought and wash your feet' (Gen. 18.4).

3
ESAU SELLING HIS BIRTHRIGHT; ISAAC BLESSING JACOB

Prior to the story of Isaac blessing Jacob, the younger of his twin sons, we are told how one day Esau, the elder son, 'came in from the field and was famished. 'Let me eat some of that red stuff, for I am famished'. Jacob said, 'First sell me your birthright' … So he swore to him and sold his birthright to Jacob. Then Jacob gave Esau bread and lentil stew, and he ate and drank, and rose and went away. Thus Esau despised his birthright. (Gen. 25.29–34)

The red pottage was apparently made from Egyptian red lentils. Lentils have generally been seen as the food of the poor in all countries where they are grown, often spurned when better food is obtained. Classical authors, such as Pliny the elder, describe lentils as the food of the poorer classes in Egypt, and it was widespread also among the Israelites. Clearly, the dish is specified in this biblical scene to stress Esau's action as giving away something valuable, his inheritance, in exchange for something particularly valueless, a dish of lentils.

The scene is rarely illustrated in the Early Christian or medieval periods, so the very full treatment in the Ashburnham Pentateuch (named after its nineteenth-century owner) comes as a surprise. This is a Latin manuscript with large full-page illustrations usually dated to the sixth century and placed in Syria, but recently thought to have been produced in Rome in the fifth century (**21**).[22] The three scenes illustrating this story show Jacob, with a pot on the oven, in discussion with Esau, on the right, and then offering the dish of lentils to Esau seated at the table. This provides a striking example of the fuller narratives pictured in medieval illuminated manuscripts as compared with the later versions, which usually condense the story into a single scene. The lentils, though somewhat large, are clearly depicted and more recognisable than most of the food in the illustrations to be discussed. The scene also appears in a simplified form in the Byzantine Octateuchs from the eleventh century (**22**). Jacob, identified by his halo, is shown stirring the stew in a pot over the fire when Esau returns from the hunt and subsequently, on the right, offering the bowl to his brother. Again, more of the cooking is depicted than is usual in biblical illustrations.

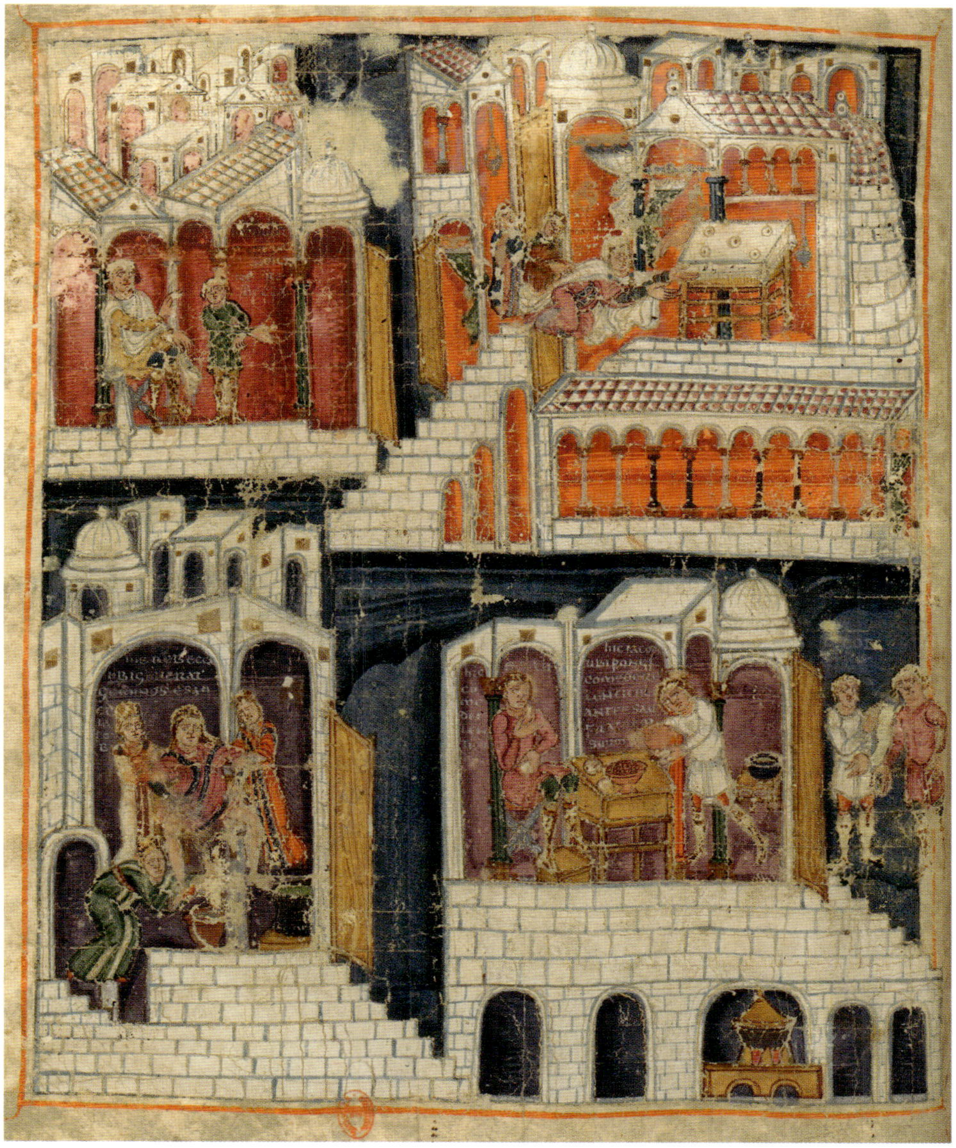

21. Jacob and Esau, 'Ashburnham Pentateuch', illuminated manuscript, fifth or sixth century. Jacob meeting Esau on the lower right; the pot on the oven, and Jacob serving the lentils to Esau on the left. Paris, Bibliothèque Nationale, MS n.acq.lat. 2334, fol. 22v.

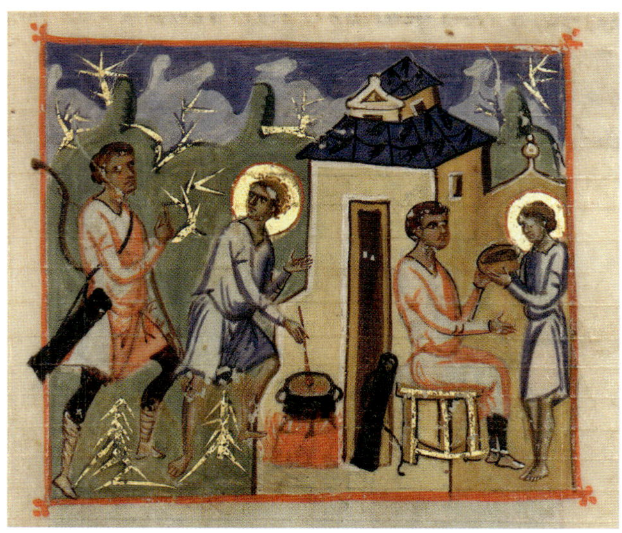

22. Jacob and Esau, Byzantine Octateuch, c.1075. Jacob is cooking and then offering the lentils to Esau. Vatican Library, MS Vat. Gr. 747, fol. 47.

ISAAC BLESSING JACOB

Esau had already sold his birthright to Jacob for a meal of bread and lentil stew when the following events occurred. 'When Isaac was old and his eyes were dim so that he could not see he called his elder son Esau … and said 'now then take your weapons, your quiver and your bow and go into the field and hunt game for me. Then prepare for me savoury food, such as I like, and bring it to me to eat, so that I may bless you before I die' … Rebekah said to her son Jacob … Go to the flock and get me two choice kids so that I may prepare from them savoury food for your father … His mother prepared savoury food … and she put the skins of the kids on his hands and on the smooth part of his neck. Then she handed the savoury food and the bread that she had prepared to her son Jacob … Jacob said to his father, 'I am Esau your firstborn. I have done as you told me; now sit up and eat of my game' … Isaac did not recognise him because his hands were hairy like his brother Esau's hands; so he blessed him … Then he said 'bring it to me, so that I may eat of my son's game and bless you'. So he brought it to him, and he ate; and he brought him wine, and he drank. Then his father Isaac blessed him. (Gen. 27.1–29)

Esau's arrival and Isaac's discovery of Jacob's deception is described in Genesis 27.30–40.

Tertullian, the north African Church Father, writing in about 207 CE, was the first theologian to identify Jacob, the younger but preferred son, as prefiguring the Christians, whereas Esau, a huntsman and the elder son, represented the Jews. This interpretation was expanded by St Ambrose, among others. Rebekah, the figure of the Church, gave Jacob, representing the Christian people, the vestments of the Old Testament because the Jews were not capable of using them. This interpretation accounts for Jacob's halo in some of the illustrations (**22**) and for the frequent depiction of the subject in the Early Christian period.[23]

The earliest surviving representations of the scene are the two in the catacomb under the Via Latina in Rome dating from about 315–30.[24] They are not in good condition but it is clear that one of them (cubiculum A) was adapted for the mosaic in Santa Maria Maggiore a century later. The second version of the scene in the Via Latina catacomb – in cubiculum B – has Isaac lying on the bed, Jacob arriving holding the kid, while Esau, with bow and arrow, is going off to hunt. The kid is shown as a hand-held animal, underlining Rebekah's insistence that Jacob should fetch a kid from the herd. Presumably she made the choice as goat's meat would be more similar to lamb in texture and taste than the venison that Esau was hunting. Both cubiculum A and B contain only Old Testament scenes and the subject of Isaac blessing Jacob was presumably chosen for its typological interpretation as representing the blessing received by the Christians.

The fullest illustration appears in the Ashburnham Pentateuch, in which the story is told in haphazardly arranged scenes rather than sequential registers (**23**). It begins in the top left corner with Isaac sending Esau out for game, followed by Rebekah persuading Jacob to offer Isaac a meal. Below left, Jacob brings her two black kids, while the rest of the herd is shown below. Rebekah then cooks the meat, which is in a saucepan on a wooden table. Then, moving to the top right-hand corner, Isaac, seated, tests Jacob's arms and Jacob brings him the kid in a dish. Below right, Esau returns from the hunt and cooks a meal for his father. Pieces of meat are on the table, while the black saucepan is on the fire. Finally, in the centre, Esau offers game to Isaac who is, again, seated, while Jacob is sent away to his uncle Laban. This sequence of scenes in the Ashburnham Pentateuch remains unique; no forerunners or successors have been found for this full and literal illustration of the biblical text.

Subsequently, the story is told more succinctly in one or two scenes as part of an Old Testament narrative. The Byzantine Octateuchs of the eleventh

23. Ashburnham Pentateuch, fifth or sixth century. The story told in seven scenes beginning top left, with Isaac sending Esau out to hunt, and then Rebekah sending out Jacob, followed by Rebekah cooking, below. Paris, Bibliothèque Nationale, MS n.acq.lat. 2334, fol. 25.

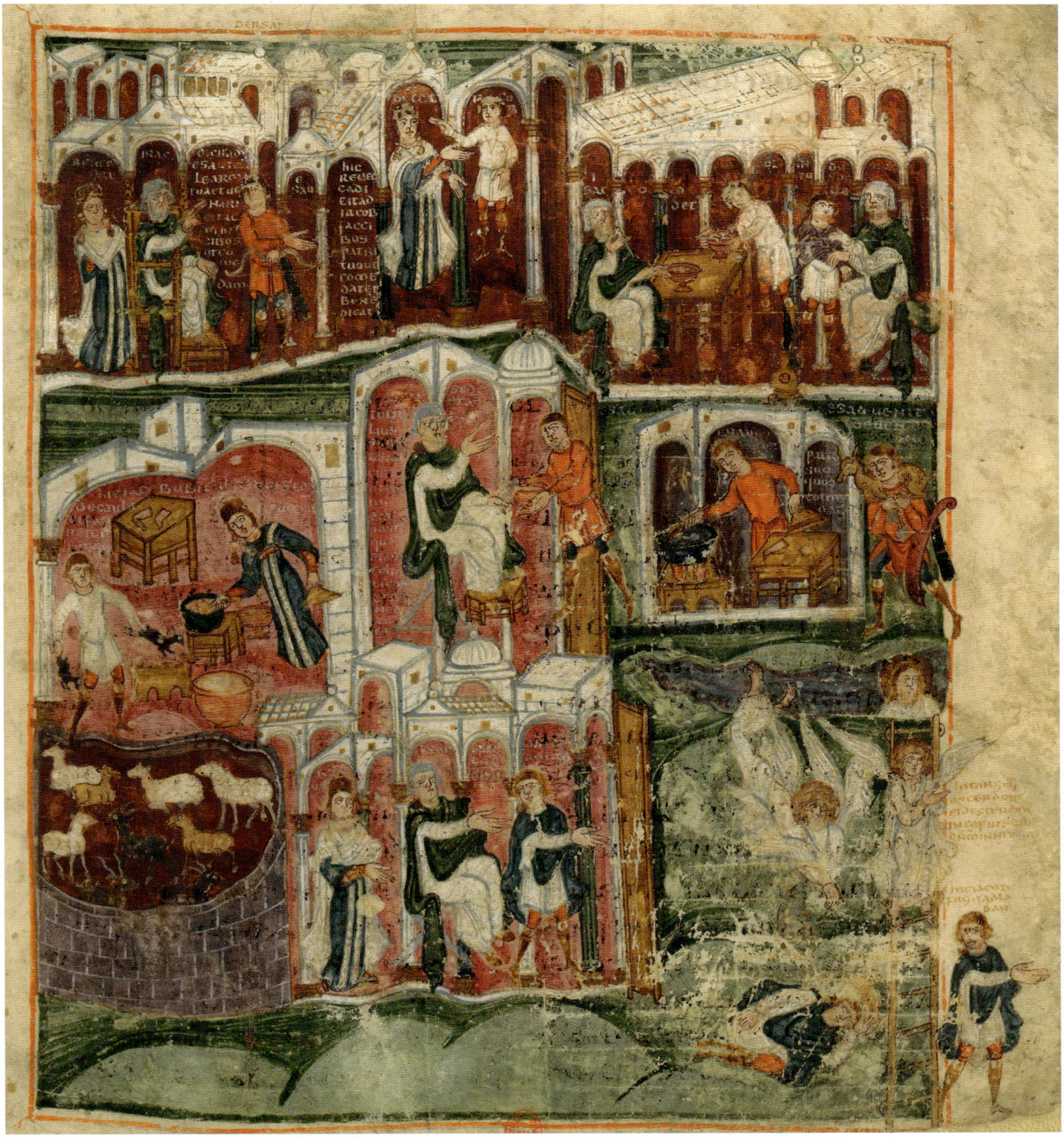

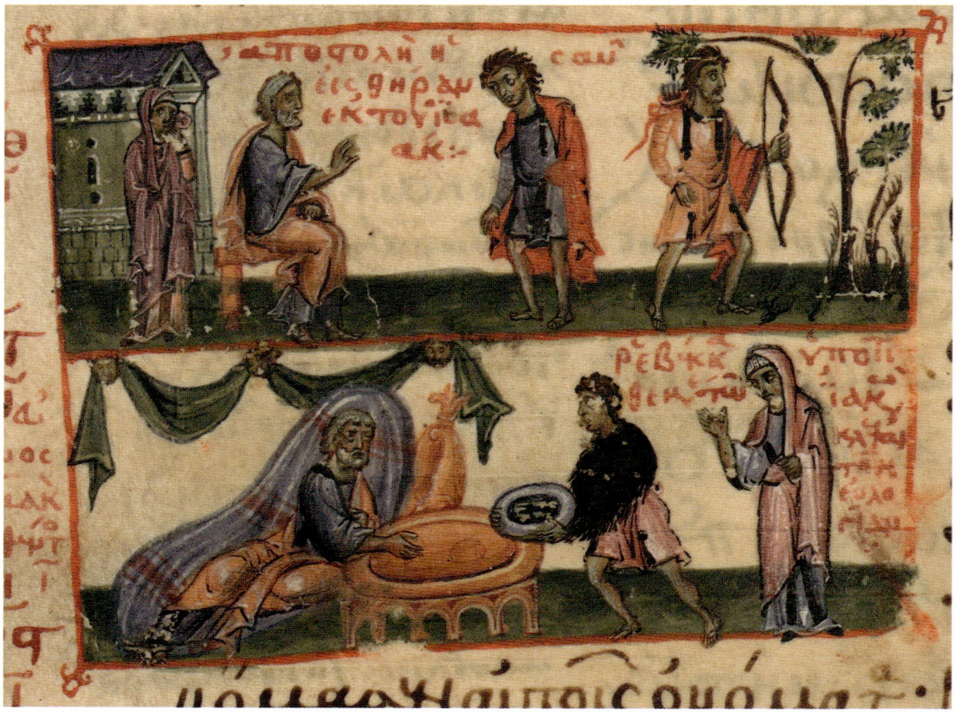

24. Byzantine Octateuch, c.1125–55, Isaac sends Esau out for venison, above. Below, Jacob offers the dish to Isaac. Vatican Library, MS Vat. gr. 746, fol. 92v.

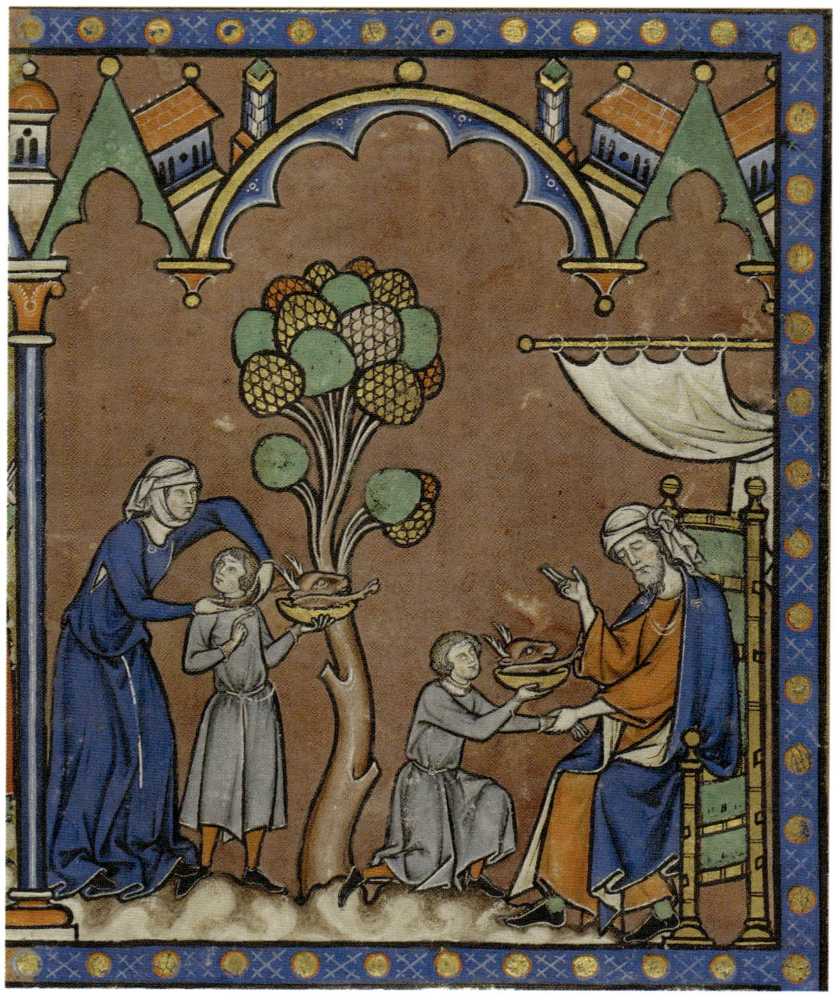

25. Picture Bible, Paris, c.1250. The kid's head is shown protruding from the dish held by Jacob. New York, Pierpont Morgan Library, M. 638, fol. 4.

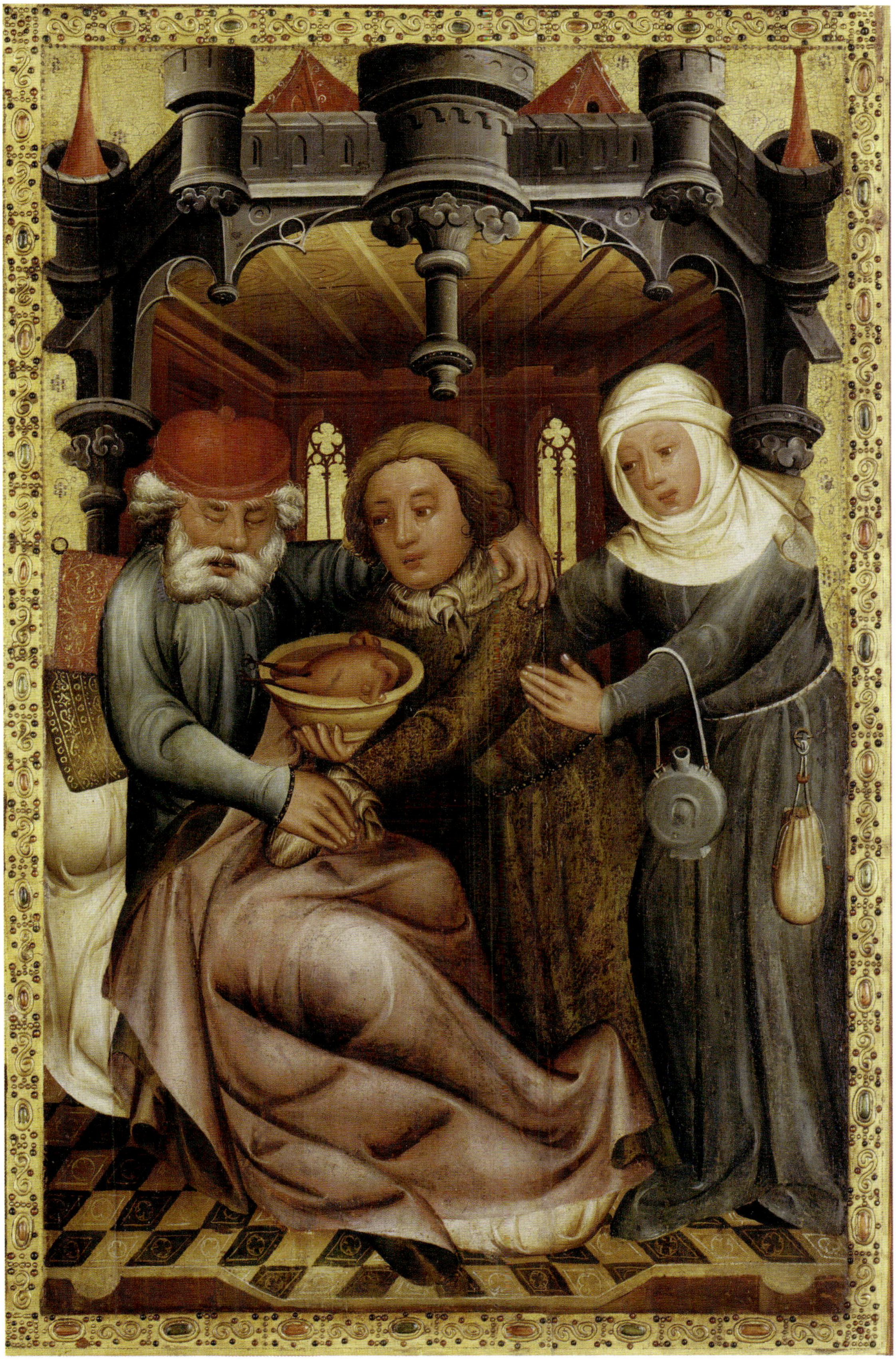

26. Master Bertram (c.1340–1415), panel from the altarpiece from St Peter's Church, Hamburg, c.1380. The artist has ignored the biblical text and transformed the kid into a fowl. Hamburg, Kunsthalle.

and twelfth centuries show Isaac reclining on the bed, in the manner of the Santa Maria Maggiore mosaic, while Jacob brings him the kid on a dish (**24**). In the West, Isaac is often seated on a chair rather than reclining, as in the mid-thirteenth-century French Old Testament picture book in the Morgan Library in New York. Here, Jacob, encouraged by his mother, presents Isaac with a kid, of which the head is shown protruding from the dish (**25**). The German artist Master Bertram painted an emotionally expressive version of the scene in his altar-piece of c.1380 from St Peter's Church, Hamburg, in which the kid has been transformed into a fowl (**26**). Clearly the artist was more concerned with the biblical narrative than with the details of the food described. The Renaissance composition of c.1520 by a follower of Raphael in the Vatican Logge returns us essentially to the Early Christian depiction in Santa Maria Maggiore a millennium earlier (**27**).

Outstanding among the relatively few seventeenth-century versions of the scene is that by Jusepe de Ribera dated 1637 (**28**, **29**). Ribera was originally trained in Valencia but lived most of his life in Italy, particularly in Naples, which was under Spanish rule. He painted only a few Old Testament subjects, concentrating instead on classical mythology, on

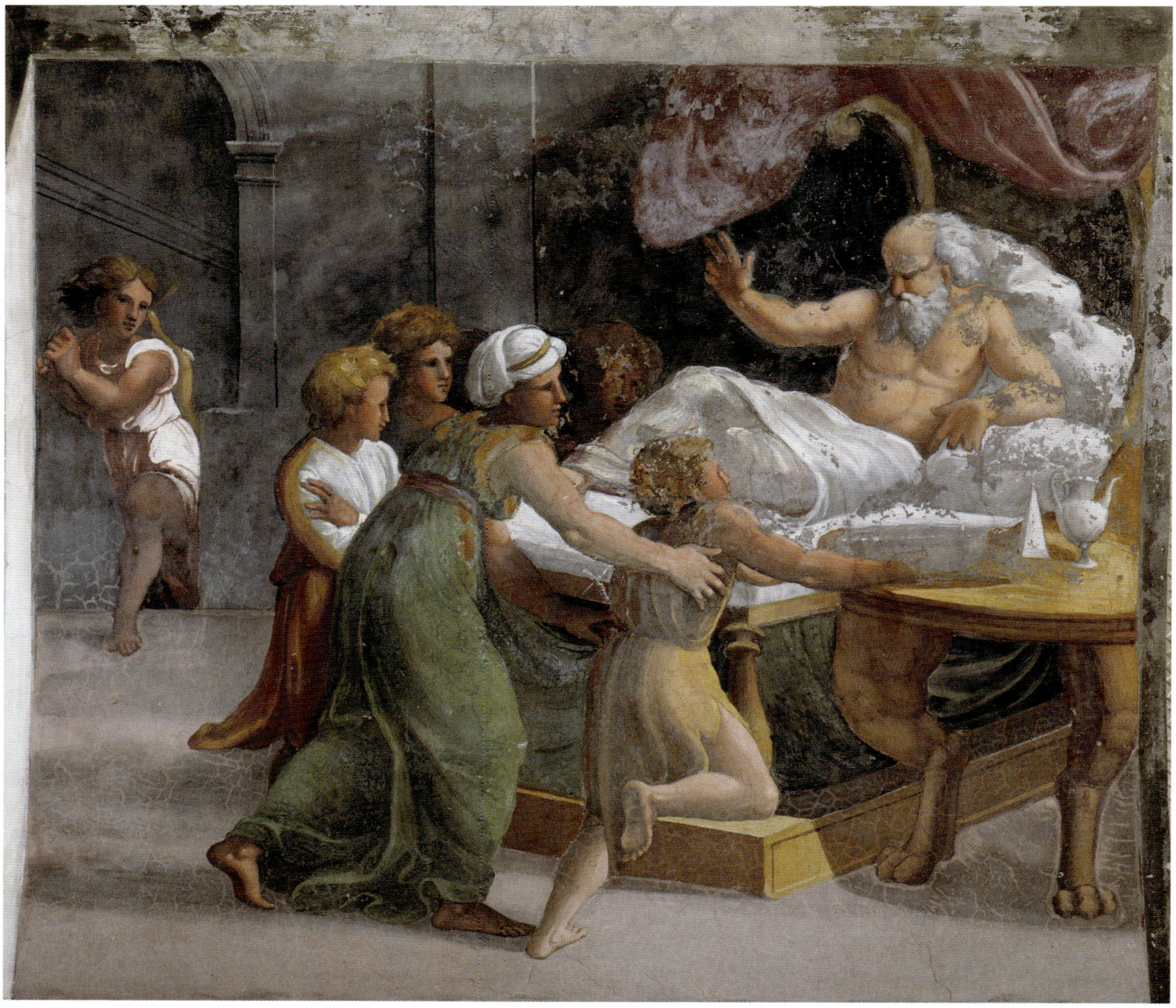

27. Follower of Raphael, wall painting c.1520, Vatican Logge. In essence, a similar composition to the one in S. Maria Maggiore, a millennium earlier.

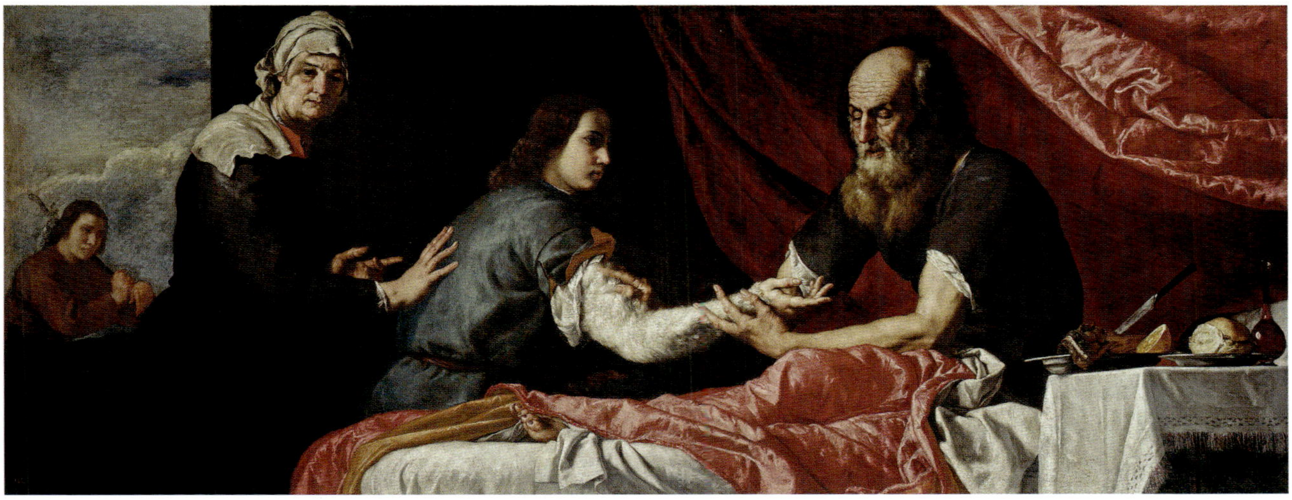

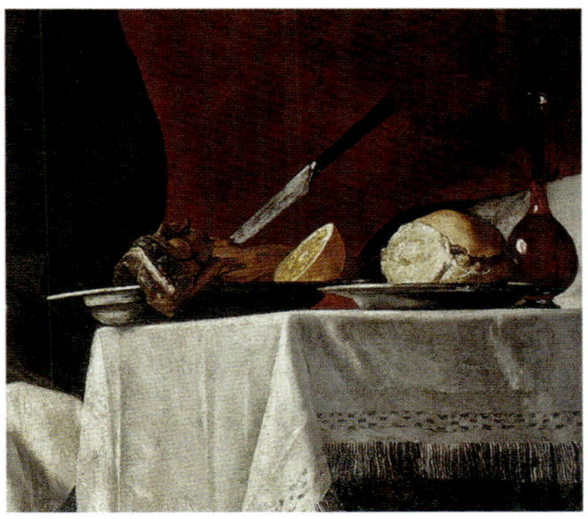

28, 29. Jusepe de Ribera (1591–1652), oil painting dated 1637. The food is clearly depicted: a joint, half a lemon on a dish, with bread and a carafe of wine. Madrid, Museo del Prado.

the life of Christ and, above all, on saints' lives. His *Isaac blessing Jacob* was in the Spanish royal collection possibly from the seventeenth century, but the details of the commission are not known.

The strong contrast of light and shade embodies the influence of Caravaggio, who was in Naples a few years before Ribera's arrival in 1616 and who remained the principal influence on his work. The central emphasis is on Jacob's hairy arm, seemingly covered in white fur, but the principal strength of the painting lies in the facial expressions, particularly Rebekah's mixture of excitement and anxiety. The food on the table on the right constitutes a beautiful still life: a joint with half a lemon on a dish, with bread and a carafe of wine. The lemon is a relatively recent addition in the depiction of biblical meals. Lemons are not mentioned in the Hebrew Bible; they were unknown to the ancient Greeks and Romans and entered Europe only in the twelfth or thirteenth centuries, when they were introduced by the Arabs into Spain. By 1369 they are to be found in a Dutch cookery book, but, like oranges, they remained rarities and, as far as customs records show, they were first imported into England as late as 1495. Lemons were clearly commonplace as flavouring by the time Ribera painted this picture, but this should not conceal the fact that they were unknown to the early illustrators of the Bible.

4
THE PASSOVER MEAL

Immediately before the tenth plague and the Israelites' departure from Egypt, the Lord instructed Moses to institute a meal of remembrance to be observed in the future. 'Tell the whole congregation of Israel that on the tenth of this month they are to take a lamb for each family … your lamb shall be without blemish, a year old male; you may take it from the sheep or from the goats'.

The Israelites must slaughter the sheep on the fourteenth day of the month and place some blood on the doorposts and lintels of their houses. 'They shall eat the lamb that same night and they shall eat it roasted over the fire with unleavened bread and bitter herbs … This is how you shall eat it: your loins girded, your sandals on your feet and your staff in your hands and you shall eat it hurriedly. It is the Passover of the Lord … When I see blood, I will pass over you and no plague shall destroy you when I strike the land of Egypt.' (Exod.12.3–14)

Surprisingly, given its biblical importance, the Passover meal is seldom depicted in the Old Testament narrative cycles of the Early Christian and early medieval periods. Even when the subject is indicated in such illustrations, as in the Byzantine Octateuchs, it is only the slaughter of the lambs that is shown. The meal itself appears in the Old Testament picture series in the mid-thirteenth-century psalter of St Louis, king of France (**30**). At God's command Moses instructs his followers to slaughter the lambs, the lintels are marked with their blood and, within the house, the meal is being eaten. The lamb is in a pot over the fire; the two men at the meal are standing and holding their staves, ready to depart. Moses is wearing the peaked hat which had become the usual mode of dress to denote Jews by this time. In 1215 the fourth Lateran Council ruled that Jews had to wear a distinguishing mark as part of their clothing in order to limit intercourse between Jews and Christians, and such hats were accepted as an identifying sign even though they were not compulsory until local regulations were enforced in the later fourteenth century. A printed Bible, published by Steffen Arndes in Lübeck in 1494 and illustrated with 152 woodcuts, contains what had become the standard depiction of the scene (**31**). Men and women stand beside the round table holding

30. Psalter of St Louis, Paris, c.1254–70. The lamb is slaughtered, the lintel marked with its blood, it is cooked over a fire and eaten by the Israelites who stand, holding their staves, ready to depart. Paris, Bibliothèque Nationale, MS lat. 10525, fol. 32.

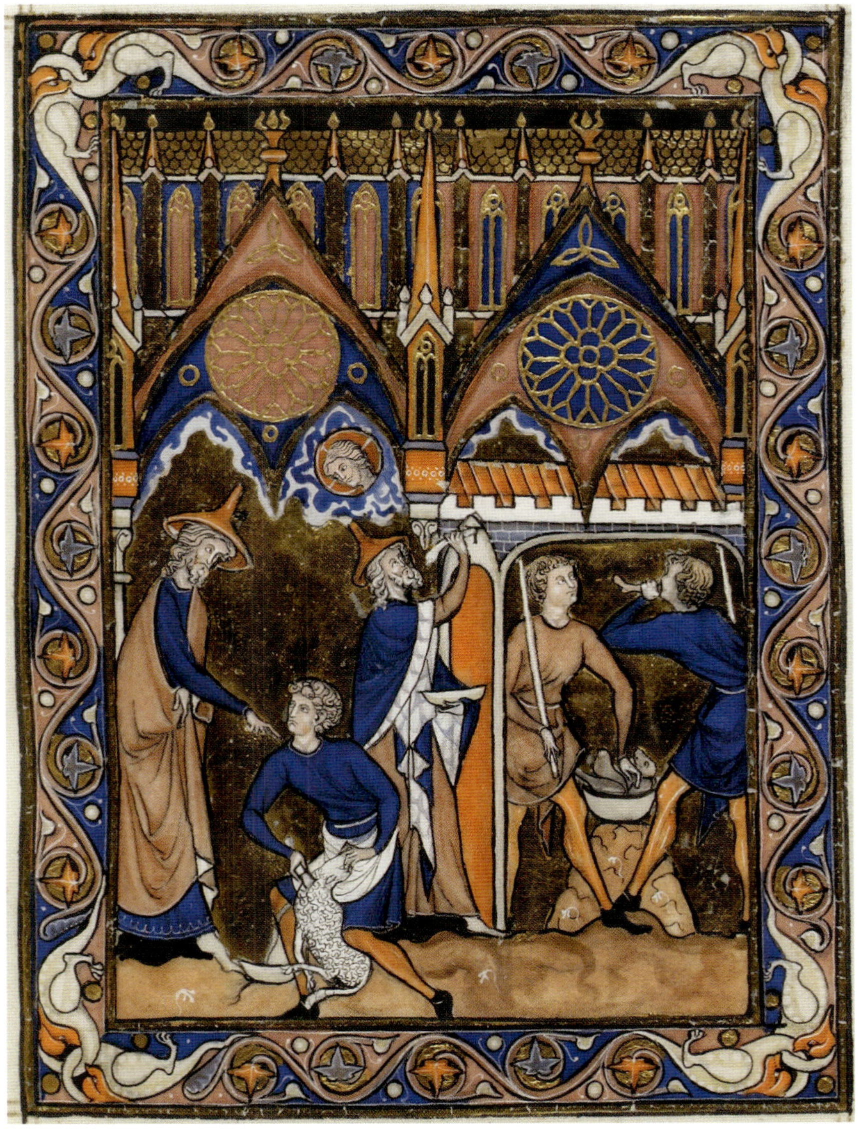

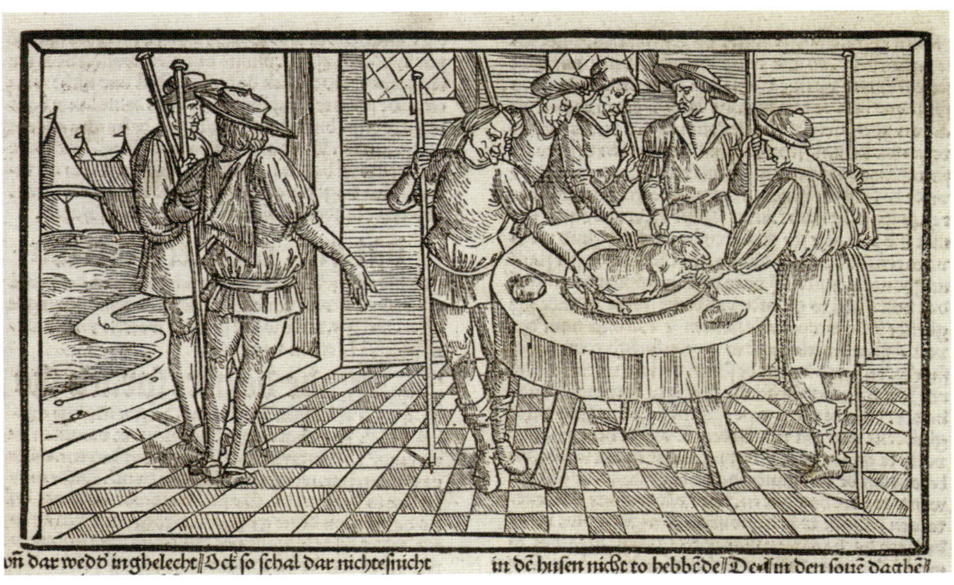

31. Woodcut from a printed Bible published by Stefan Arndes in Lübeck in 1494. The departing Israelites help themselves from a dish containing a whole lamb.

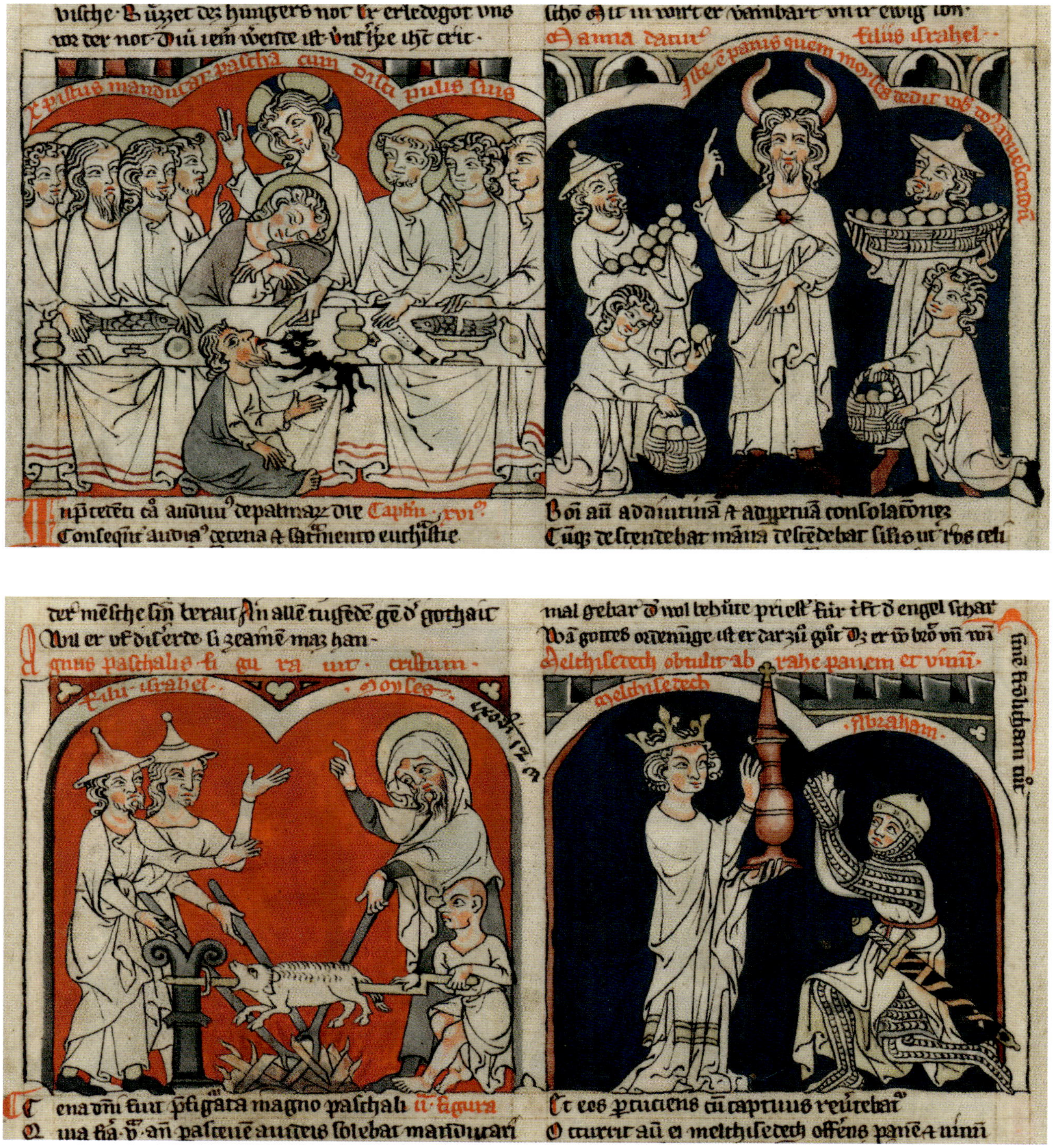

32. Manuscript of the *Speculum Humanae Salvationis* (Mirror of Human Salvation), fourteenth century. The Last Supper is compared with three Old Testament types: the Gathering of Manna, the lamb roasted on a spit for the Passover meal, and Abraham and Melchizedek. Austria, Kremsmünster Stiftsbibliothek, MS 243, fols 21v–22.

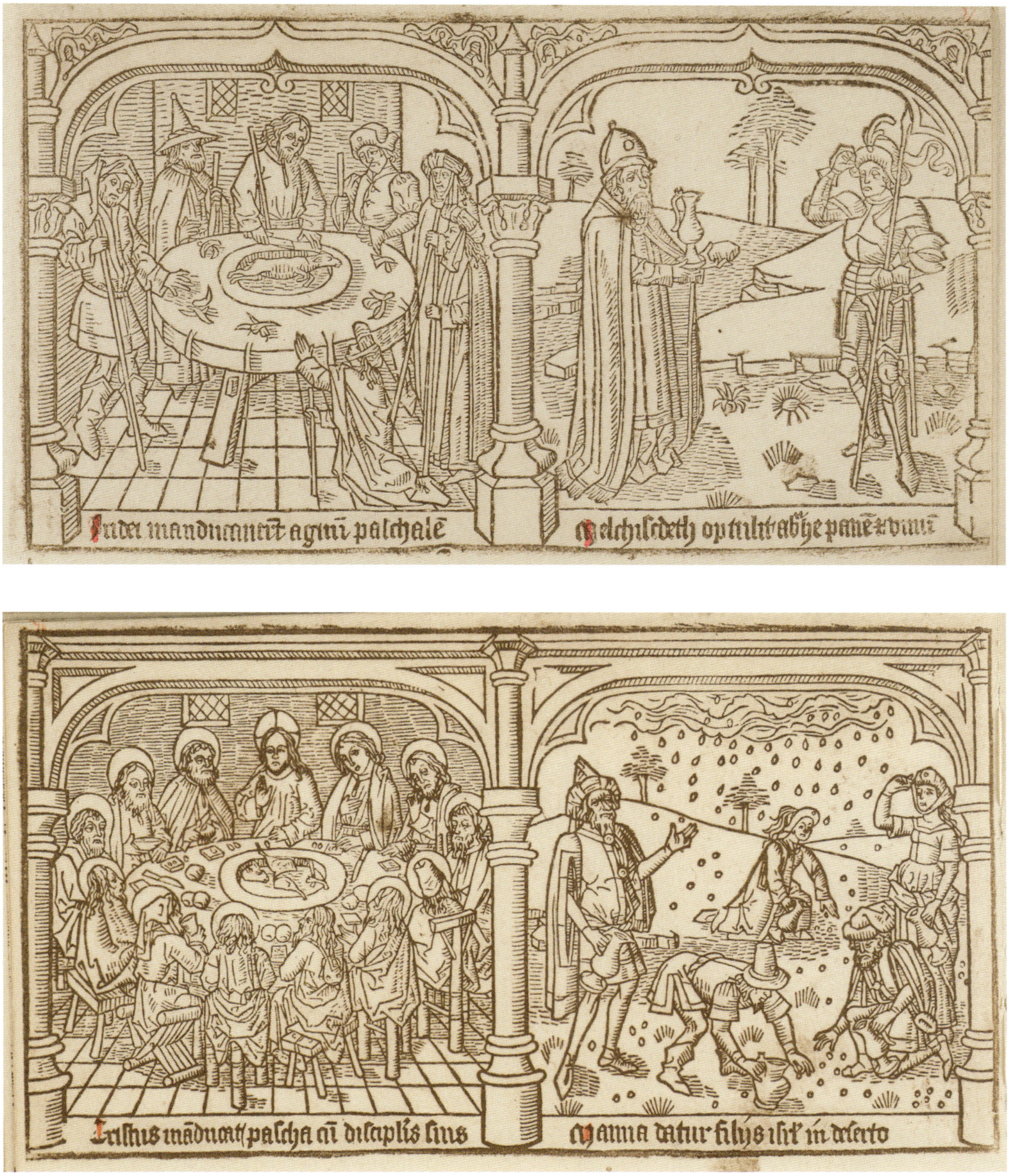

33. Woodcuts from a printed Mirror of Human Salvation, Netherlandish, c.1475. The same four scenes, but the Passover meal is shown in a more traditional composition.

their staves to indicate their imminent departure. On the dish is a whole lamb, which seems to mark a conflict between making clear the nature of the animal and depicting it as it would be eaten.

In contrast with its rare appearance in narrative cycles, the Passover meal was frequently figured as an Old Testament type of the Last Supper. From the earliest Christian commentaries, the Resurrection of Christ was closely linked with the Jewish Passover. Just as the unction of blood on the lintels and columns of the Israelites' doors leads to the first born inside the house being spared, so God spares those marked with the blood of Christ. As early as the second century the theologian Justin Martyr asserted that, just as the lambs' blood saved the Jews in Egypt, so it is a sign of the salvation of sinners who have been marked by baptism.[25]

The prefiguration of the Paschal meal for the Last Supper originated in the Gospels. Christ wants to have the apostles at the Passover commemorative meal in Jerusalem: 'I have eagerly desired to eat this Passover with you before I suffer ...' (Luke 22.15).[26] The symbolism of the Paschal meal for the Eucharist was emphasised by several Early Christian theologians from the time of St Hyppolytus (c.170–c.236). Both meals celebrate future salvation.

From the thirteenth century the parallel between the two is quite often illustrated. Among the typological roundels making up the stained glass windows in the choir of Meissen Cathedral, the Paschal meal is directly paired with the Last Supper. Three Jews, wearing their prominent peaked hats, are standing behind the table holding their staves and about to eat the lamb lying in a large dish. Its feet are tied, emphasising its sacrificial function. The elderly bearded man in the middle is probably Moses, a comparison with the central figure of Christ at the table in the nearby Last Supper roundel.

The most numerous images of the Passover meal are those in the manuscripts of the *Speculum Humanae Salvationis* (Mirror of Human Salvation), a book of New Testament scenes with their Old Testament types. Composed for both clergy and laity in about 1300 with early manuscripts from Italy and southern Germany, it was enormously popular for the next 200 years. Close on 400 copies still exist – some with texts translated into German, French and English – of which about 150 are illustrated. The standard comparisons for the Last Supper are with the Gathering of Manna on the right, and the Paschal meal and Abraham and Melchizedek on the opposite page (**33**). Within this layout, the individual compositions vary. In the fourteenth-century manuscript from the abbey of Kremsmünster in Austria, for example, the meal is replaced by a scene of the Israelites roasting a lamb on a spit at Moses's instruction (**32**).[27] More usually, the scene is shown as it was in other contexts, with the Israelites standing round the table and preparing to eat the lamb. From the 1460s the *Speculum Humanae Salvationis* became even more widely available in printed copies with woodcut illustrations. In a printed edition published in the Netherlands in about 1475, the woodcut has the standard composition but differs from most of the earlier examples in showing women at the table, one of whom is, most unusually, kneeling in an attitude of supplication.

In his well-known altar-piece, painted at the request of the Confraternity of the Holy Sacrament for the Church of S. Pierre in Louvain (Leuven) in 1464–67, Dieric Bouts followed the layout of the *Speculum* except that the Last Supper has become the centrepiece (see below, p. 147, and **34**). For the Paschal meal the food is more clearly identified than in the earlier examples. Apart from the lamb on a dish in the centre of the table, each diner is supplied with bread, bitter herbs in the form of horse radish (maror) leaves, a wine glass and a knife. The dish itself is clearly metal, demonstrating its symbolic identity as the paten of the Eucharist. Bouts was one of the leading Netherlandish painters of his time and this composition is remarkable not only for the depiction of the room and the variety of the male and female costumes but for the deeply moving expressions of thoughtfulness and anxiety on the part of the diners.

It was also in the context of the Eucharist that the Paschal meal was occasionally illustrated in Books of Hours, the principal prayer book of the later Middle Ages. It appears, for example, in somewhat different forms, in the Book of Hours of Catherine of Cleves (New York, Morgan Library, M 917), a Netherlandish manuscript of about 1440, and that of Alfonso of Aragon, duke of Calabria, produced in Naples in about 1470 (**35**). In both cases it provided the illustration for the office of Corpus Christi,

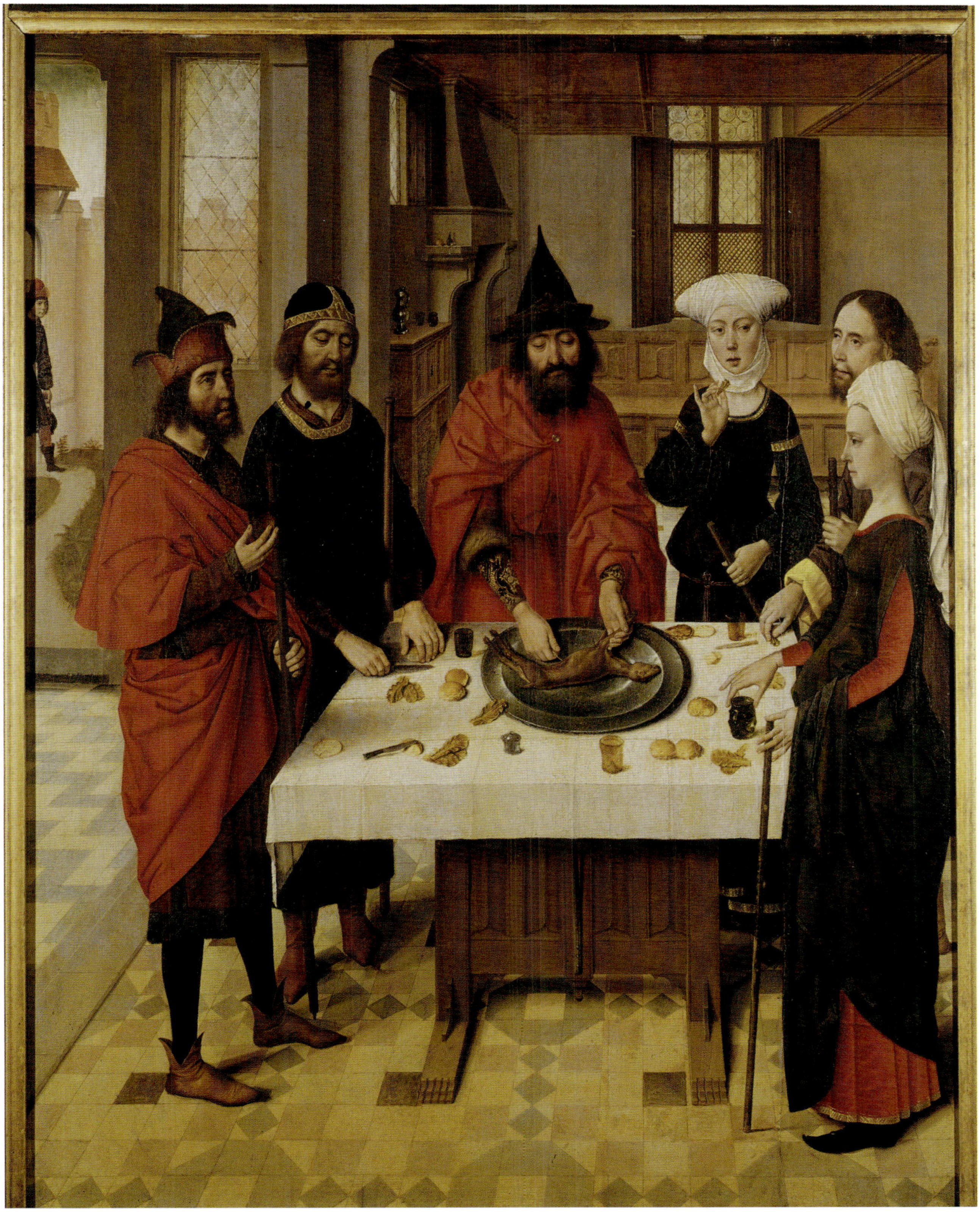

34. Dieric Bouts (d.1475), panel from the Last Supper altarpiece in St Peter's Church, Louvain, 1464–67. Unusually, the food is clearly identified, including lamb in a dish, bread and horseradish leaves.

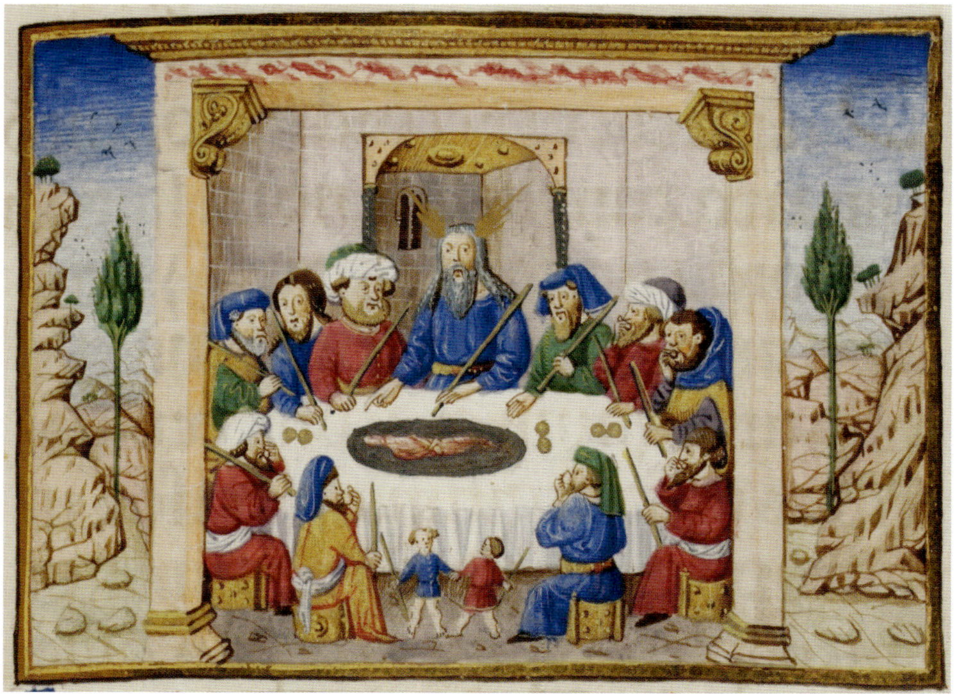

35. Book of Hours of Alphonso of Aragon, Naples c.1470. The Last Supper is shown in a roundel below. London, Victoria and Albert Museum, MS L. 2387–1910, fol. 341.

the feast commemorating the institution of the Holy Eucharist observed in the Western Church, since the second half of the thirteenth century, on the Thursday after Trinity Sunday. Indeed, in the Neapolitan manuscript the Paschal meal is accompanied by the Last Supper in a roundel in the lower margin. Moses, shown with two golden rays emanating from his head and accompanied by twelve followers, is directly paired with Christ and the twelve Apostles at the Last Supper below. A century later the subject is again paired with the Last Supper in Tintoretto's ceiling painting in the Scuola di San Rocco in Venice (**154**).

As a postscript to this discussion of the original Passover meal, it should be added that the annual meal of remembrance which the Jews were instructed to observe in the future (Exod. 12.14) and which is described in detail in Deuteronomy 16.1–8 is also depicted. Such illustrations occur in Hebrew prayer books, particularly in the Haggadah, the service book for the festival of Passover Eve (Seder), celebrated twice on two consecutive nights. In the second Commandment (Exod. 20.4) the Israelites were forbidden to make images for fear of idolatry, but the rule was not always strictly observed and in the fourteenth century a number of richly illuminated manuscripts were produced, particularly in north-eastern Spain and in the Rhineland.[28] One of the best-known of these, the so-called Sarajevo Haggadah, probably produced in Catalonia in about 1330–40, has three scenes relating to the Passover festival. One miniature shows the distribution of *charoset*, a mixture of apples, nuts, spices and wine, which symbolises the mortar used by the Israelites during their servitude in Egypt, as well as the distribution of unleavened bread (*matzah*). The meal itself is shown in a separate miniature (**36**). At the end of a long table, on which there are gilt dishes, one of them full of eggs, and a bottle of wine, sits the host with his left arm resting on a cushion as tradition demanded. He raises his glass to his young son, who traditionally asks his father 'wherein is this night different from all other nights?' Unusually, a black woman sits on the other side of the table, probably a servant who has converted to Judaism and is accepted for the family celebration. At any rate she is not working; it is the hostess who is carving the food.

More idiosyncratic is the Birds' Head Haggadah, probably produced in Mainz in about 1300 and so called because all the biblical Israelites and contemporary Jews were shown with long-beaked birds' heads. The manuscript's patron presumably

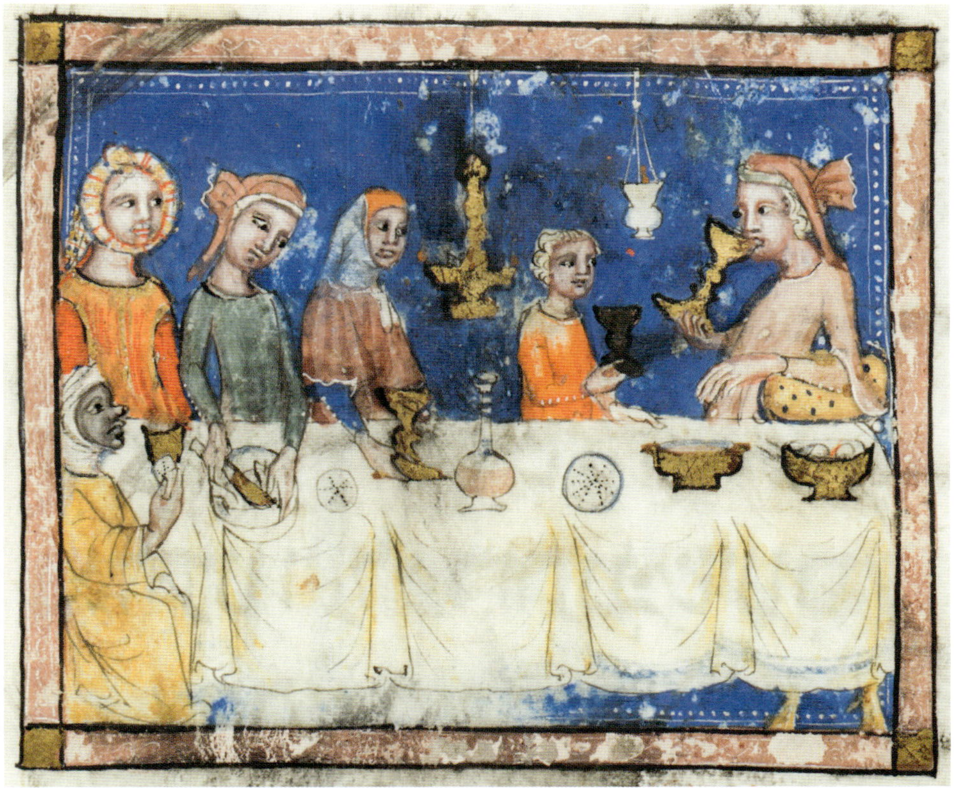

36. Manuscript of the Haggadah (Hebrew prayer book for the festival of Passover), Catalonia, c.1330–40. The father raises his glass to his younger son. One of the gilt dishes on the table contains eggs. Sarajevo, National Museum of Bosnia and Herzegovina.

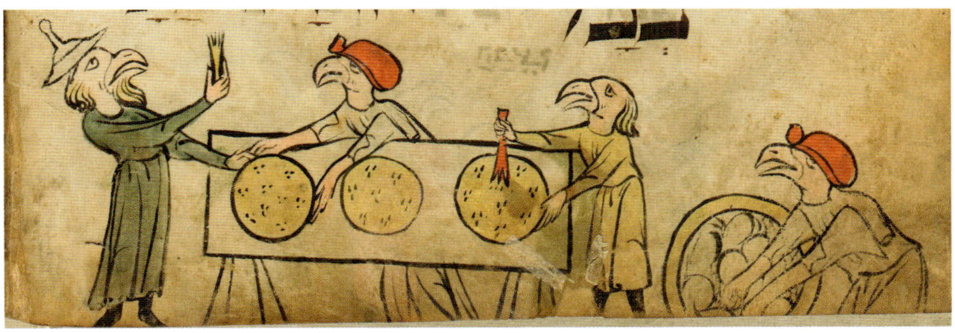

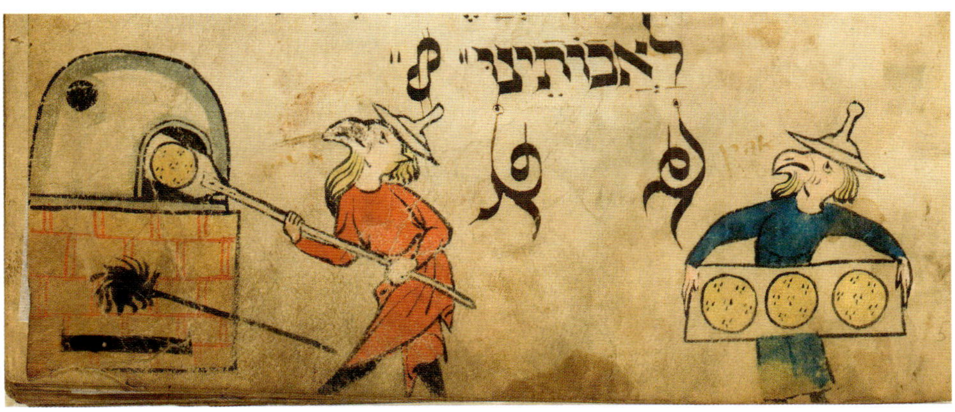

37, 38. Birds' Head Haggadah, South Germany (? Mainz) c.1300, so named because because the heads of the figures depicted have bird-like features. Matza prepared and placed in the oven. Jerusalem, Israel Museum, MS 180/57, fols 25v–26.

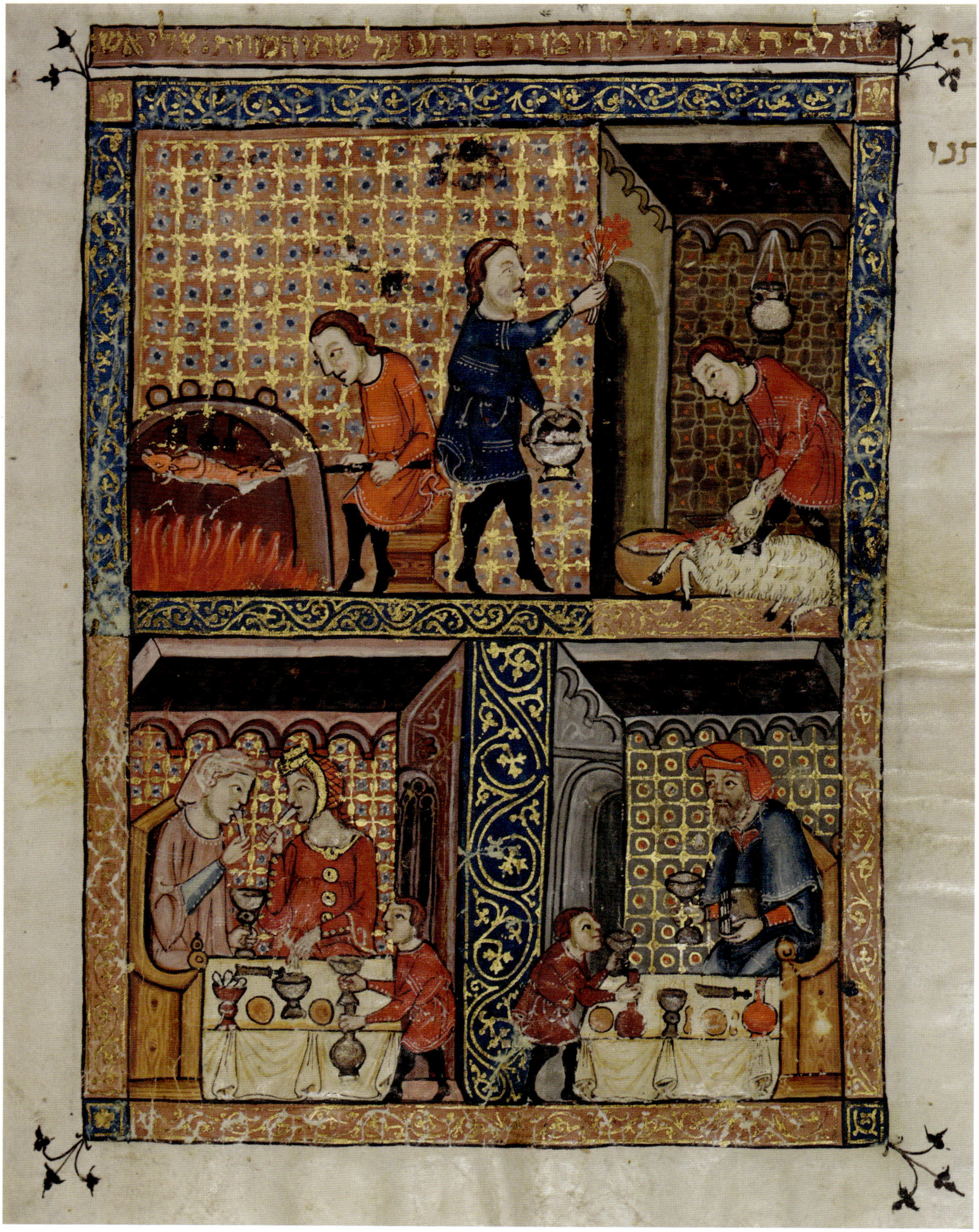

39. Manuscript of the Haggadah, Catalonia, c.1330–40. The lamb slaughtered, the doorposts struck with a bundle of hyssop soaked in the lamb's blood, then the lamb is roasted on a spit in the oven. Below, the meal, with the head of the household and his son at one table and the women at another. Manchester, Rylands Library, MS Heb.6, fol. 19v.

specified that the depiction of human features was to be avoided in order to obey the prohibition on the making of images. Like the illustrations of the Catalonian manuscripts of the Haggadah, the Birds' Head Haggadah includes scenes from Exodus as well as of the Passover meal and its preparation. Unusually, it concentrates on the making of matzah (**37**, **38**). In the first scene, a man wearing a peaked hat, like all the other Jewish men portrayed in the book, is instructing a woman, wearing a red turban, and a bare-headed child, on the pricking of the dough. The following scene shows two men engaged in the baking of the matzah in the oven. It has been suggested that this emphasis on the making of matzah was to demonstrate the totally innocent nature of the process in the face of accusations concerning the Eucharist against the Jews. It was generally believed that Jesus' Last Supper was a Passover meal. Increasingly, in the thirteenth century, the Eucharist was firmly identified not as a memorial but as a real and continuing presence of God. As the Eucharist became a real presence, the Haggadah's description of matzah – 'this is the bread of affliction' – when imposed on the Last Supper, could be seen as host desecration. Whether or not these precise illustrations of the preparation of matzah in the Birds' Head Haggadah can be seen as a reply to such accusations, they remain the most detailed descriptions among surviving Haggadah illustrations.

Typically of the Catalonian manuscripts, the Haggadah in the Rylands Library in Manchester, c.1330–40, has one full-page miniature to illustrate the Seder meal and its preparation (**39**). The scenes are to be read from right to left, as in the Hebrew text. First, the lamb is slaughtered and its blood collected in a bowl. Then the doorposts are struck with a bundle of hyssop soaked in the lamb's blood. This was in accordance with Moses' instruction to the Israelites (Exod. 12.21–28) and differs from the depiction in Christian art, where the emphasis is on the mark of the T cross, symbolic of the Crucifixion. Finally, in the upper register, the lamb is roasted on a spit in the oven.

Below, the meal is shown in two sections. At one table the head of the household raises his glass, looking at his young son, while the women sit at another table. They are eating roasted shank bones, which symbolise the paschal offering and which formed a prominent part of the service. Also on their table are two round pieces of *matzah*, the *maror* or bitter herbs, the *charoset* and eggs in a bowl reminiscent of the Temple offering. Not surprisingly, these depictions of what was a contemporary celebration demonstrate a greater variety of content and attention to detail than the Christian illustrations of the biblical Passover meal.

5
QUAILS AND MANNA

In the second month after leaving Egypt, the Israelites, inhabiting the wilderness of Sin between Elim and Sinai, complained of hunger to Moses and Aaron. 'Then the Lord said to Moses 'I am going to rain bread from heaven for you and each day the people shall go out and gather enough for that day'. Subsequently, as Moses and Aaron were speaking to the Israelites, 'The glory of the Lord appeared in the cloud. The Lord spoke to Moses and said 'I have heard the complaining of the Israelites; say to them "at twilight you shall eat meat, and in the morning you shall have your fill of bread, then you shall know that I am the Lord your God". In the evening quails came up and covered the camp; and in the morning there was a layer of dew around the camp. When the layer of dew lifted, there on the surface was a fine flaky substance, as fine as frost on the ground … Moses said to them it is the bread that the Lord has given you to eat.' (Exod. 16.4–15)

'The house of Israel called it manna; it was like coriander seed, white, and the taste of it was like wafers made with honey.' Moses told Aaron to keep some in a jar as a memorial. 'The Israelites ate manna for forty years until they came to a habitable land' (Exod. 16.31–35). These events were immediately followed by the story of Moses striking water from the rock (Exod. 17.1–7).

The gathering of manna is also described briefly in two psalms:

He rained down on them manna to eat
and gave them the grain of heaven.
Mortals ate of the bread of angels;
He rained flesh upon them like dust.
Winged birds like the sand of the seas.
(Psalm 77 (78).24–27)

They asked, and he brought quails,
And gave them food from heaven in
abundance. (Psalm 104 (105).40)

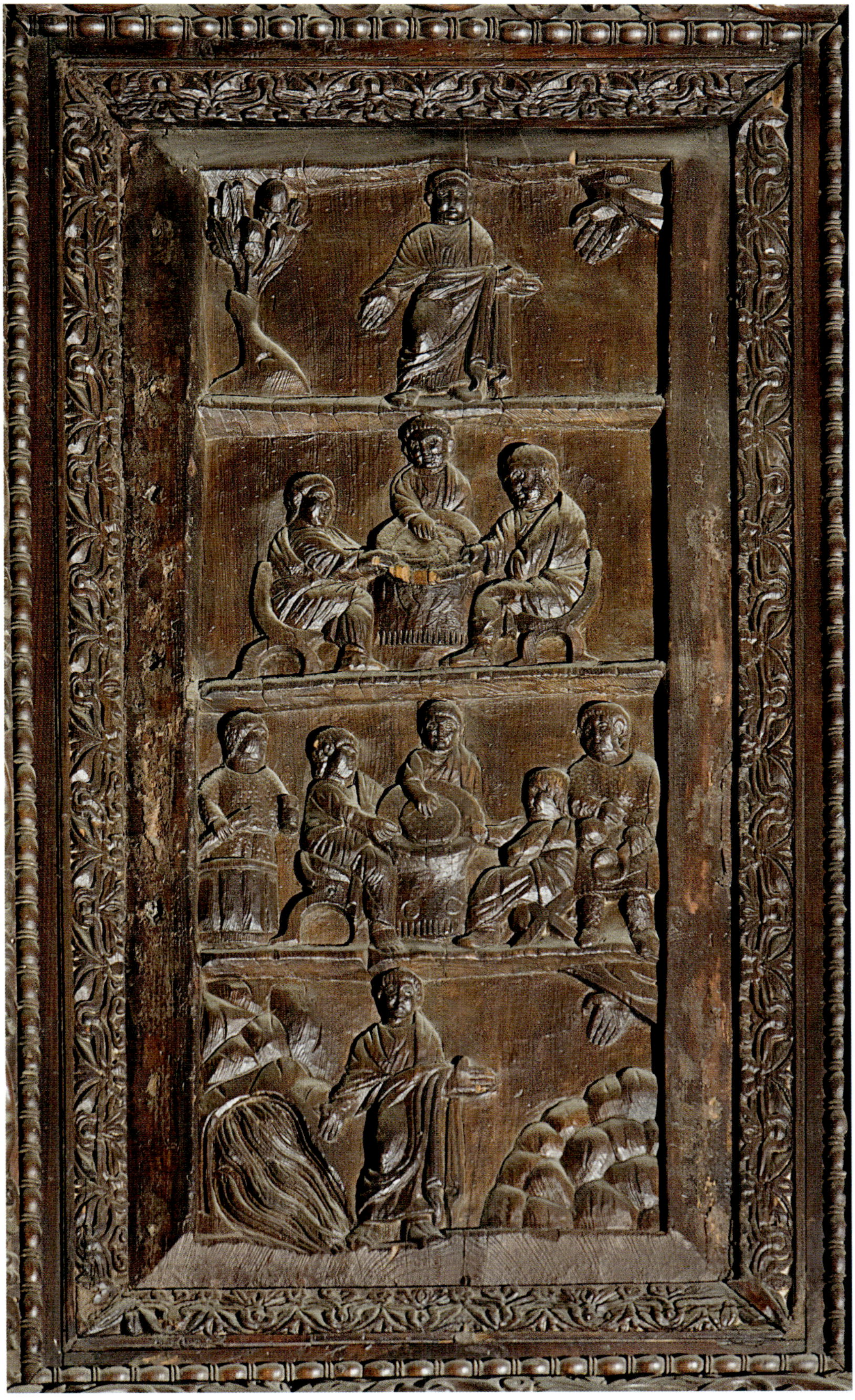

40. Wooden doors of Santa Sabina, Rome, c.430. Quails and Manna eaten at table, which appears opposite the comparable Multiplication of the Loaves and Fishes carved on the right door.

The arrival of the quails is clearly described but there is a degree of confusion in the biblical narrative concerning manna. On the one hand, the Lord announces his intention to 'rain bread from heaven'; on the other, manna is described as a 'layer of dew' which melts into a 'fine flaky substance'. The more succinct text of Psalm 77 (78) leaves no room for doubt: 'he rained down on them manna to eat'. This concept of manna raining down remained standard in verbal descriptions and visual images.

Various 'scientific' suggestions were put forward to provide an explanation of this miracle. The most popular was that manna was the sweet substance exuded by the tamarix tree (mannifera), but this could provide only small quantities, hardly enough to feed all the Israelites daily for forty years. Yet such natural explanations were still common a century ago; more recently there has been less desire to convert biblical miracles into scientifically explained phenomena.

Christian interpretations, on the other hand, have been straightforward. Manna was seen as a symbol of the Old Testament overtaken by the story of salvation through Jesus Christ and, more specifically, as a type of the Eucharist. John's Gospel describes Jesus telling the Jews 'I am the bread of life. Your ancestors ate the manna in the wilderness and they died' and, in contrast, 'I am the living bread that came down from heaven. Whoever eats of this bread will live for ever, and the bread I will give for the life of the world is my flesh' (John 6.48–51). The parallel between manna and the body of Jesus is visually depicted in the illustration to Psalm 77 (78) in the ninth-century Byzantine psalters, where Jesus addressing a group of Jews appears just above the Israelites gathering manna.

More rarely, the miracle of manna was interpreted as a forerunner of Christ's miracles connected with the provision of food. On the carved reliefs on the wooden doors of the Church of Santa Sabina in Rome (c.430) the eating of quails and then manna, in the form of meals at table, is shown opposite the multiplication of the loaves and fishes and Christ turning water into wine (**40**).

As far as surviving monuments allow one to judge, depictions of the rain of manna are relatively rare in the Early Christian period. A fourth-century wall painting in the Cyriaca catacomb in Rome is much damaged, but the group of four or five figures standing amidst the descending rain remain recognisable.[29] A sarcophagus relief of the same period in the museum at Arles shows the Israelites with arms outstretched awaiting the quails in a scene next to that of Moses striking water from the rock.

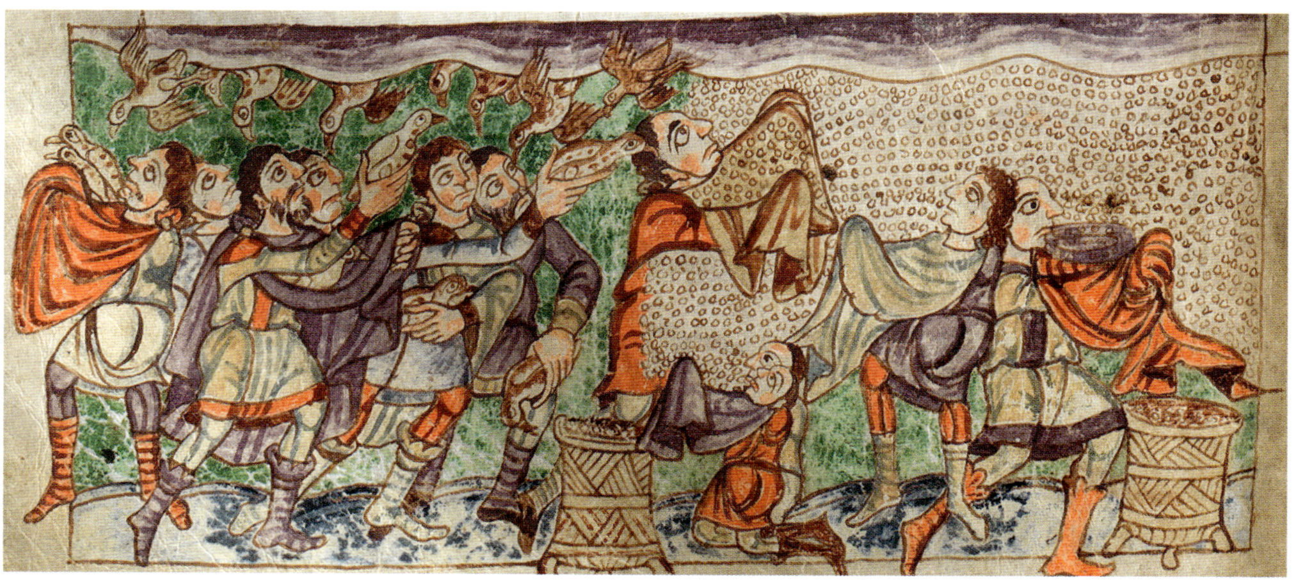

41. Psalter illustration (at Psalm 77), S. Germain-des-Près, c.820–30. The quails on the left are followed by the fall of manna. Stuttgart, Württembergische Landesbibliothek, Biblia Folio 23, fol. 91v.

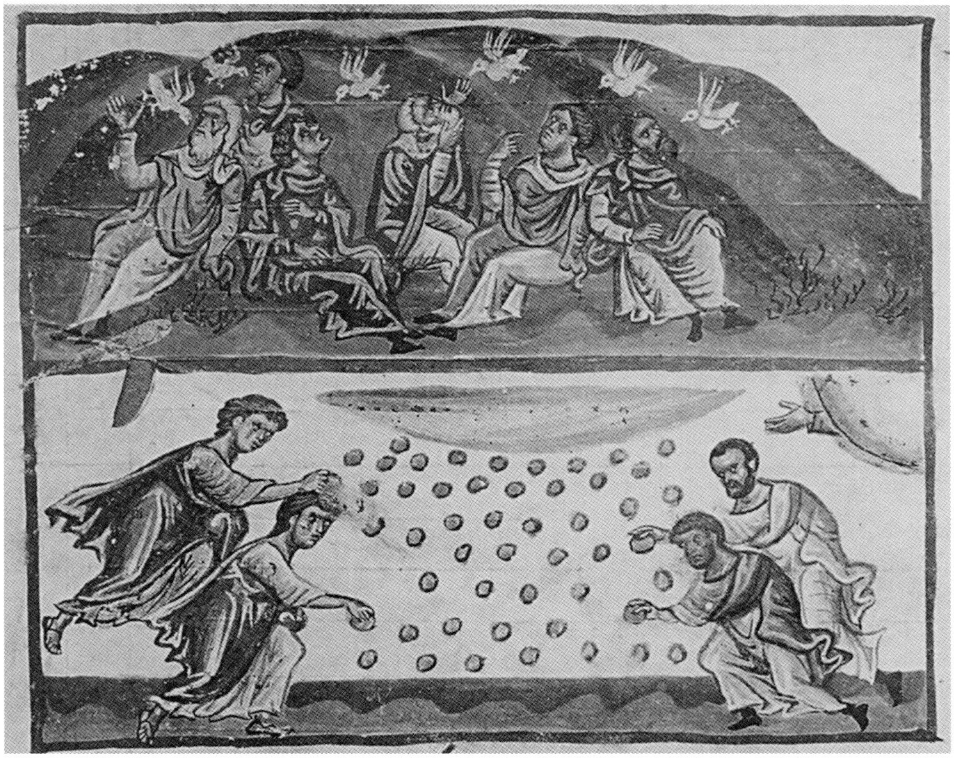

42. Byzantine Octateuch, c.1125–55.Miracle of the quails; Israelites gather manna. Istanbul, Top Kapi Sarayi Museum, MS gr.8, fol. 203.

The scene's earliest appearance in an Old Testament narrative sequence is in the nave mosaics in Santa Maria Maggiore (c.432–40) where the miracle is limited to the quails which immediately precede the arrival of the manna in the biblical text.

To judge from the surviving manuscripts, it was in the period from the ninth to the eleventh centuries that a fairly standard illustration was developed both in Byzantium and in Western Europe. The Carolingian psalter of about 820–30 in the library at Stuttgart depicts the scene at Psalm 77 (78) (**41**). On the left, quails fly in above the Israelites while, on the right, manna, in the form of small circles, falls from heaven, to be gathered up and placed in baskets. A similar version appears in the Byzantine Octateuchs. It also shows the quails apparently flying towards the mouths of the seated men in the upper register, while manna from heaven is gathered by the Israelites below (**42**). This is broadly similar to the Stuttgart Psalter composition, but the story continues with a separate illustration for the scene of Moses ordering Aaron to place some manna in a pot as a memorial to the miracle.

A somewhat different series of scenes appears in a group of Byzantine psalters at Psalm 77 (78), in which the illustrations are placed in the margins around the text.[30] In the psalter dated 1066, the manna is shown falling and being gathered in the right margin, while at the foot of the page an angel with large flowing wings and a halo is offering bread to an old man who holds out his hands to receive it: clearly another reference to the bread of the Eucharist (**43**, **44**). On the next page, the quails are caught and then roasted on a spit held just above the flames to illustrate verse 29 of the Psalm: 'and they ate and were well filled, for he gave them what they craved'.

The scene of the Israelites roasting quails in these Byzantine psalters reappears in large-scale public art in a mosaic of about 1260 in a cupola in the atrium of St Mark's in Venice (**45**). Moses kneels in the centre while quails fly down and manna falls from heaven. The figures in the foreground are all men, but the quail-roasting episode has become more domestic, with a couple in front of a tent which separates them from the rest of the composition. The woman, assisted by one of the man's hands, holds two spits to roast the quails in leaping flames. Scenes of such domesticity are rare in medieval biblical imagery.

In western art of the later Middle Ages the tendency is to simplify the illustration by omitting the quails and showing only the rain of manna. The French mid-thirteenth-century picture Bible in the Morgan Library concentrates on the manna falling in large flakes, which the Israelites are gathering up and eating from bowls (**46**). Two hundred years later, in a Netherlandish oil painting of 1464–67, the landscape has become more naturalistic and the women, fashionably dressed, more prominent among the gatherers (**148**). This is one of the four side panels surrounding the altarpiece of the Last Supper in the Church of St Peter at Louvain, the masterpiece of Dieric Bouts. As we have seen, all four side panels are Old Testament types of the Last Supper.

Our next example is the work of an unknown Dutch artist of about 1470, who is named after this painting as the Master of Manna Gathering (**47**). One of the two wings of a larger altarpiece – the other is of the *Fire offering of the Jews* (Museum Boymans-van Beuningen, Rotterdam) – the panel was destroyed in the museum at Douai during the bombardment of 1944. The artist has been described as a follower of Albert van Ouwater of Haarlem, whose elaborate costumes are very similar to those of the manna gatherers here. The Manna Master has arranged his figures in a circular ground plan, with a man in the centre holding a bowl above his head as though it were a chalice at the Mass. The manna

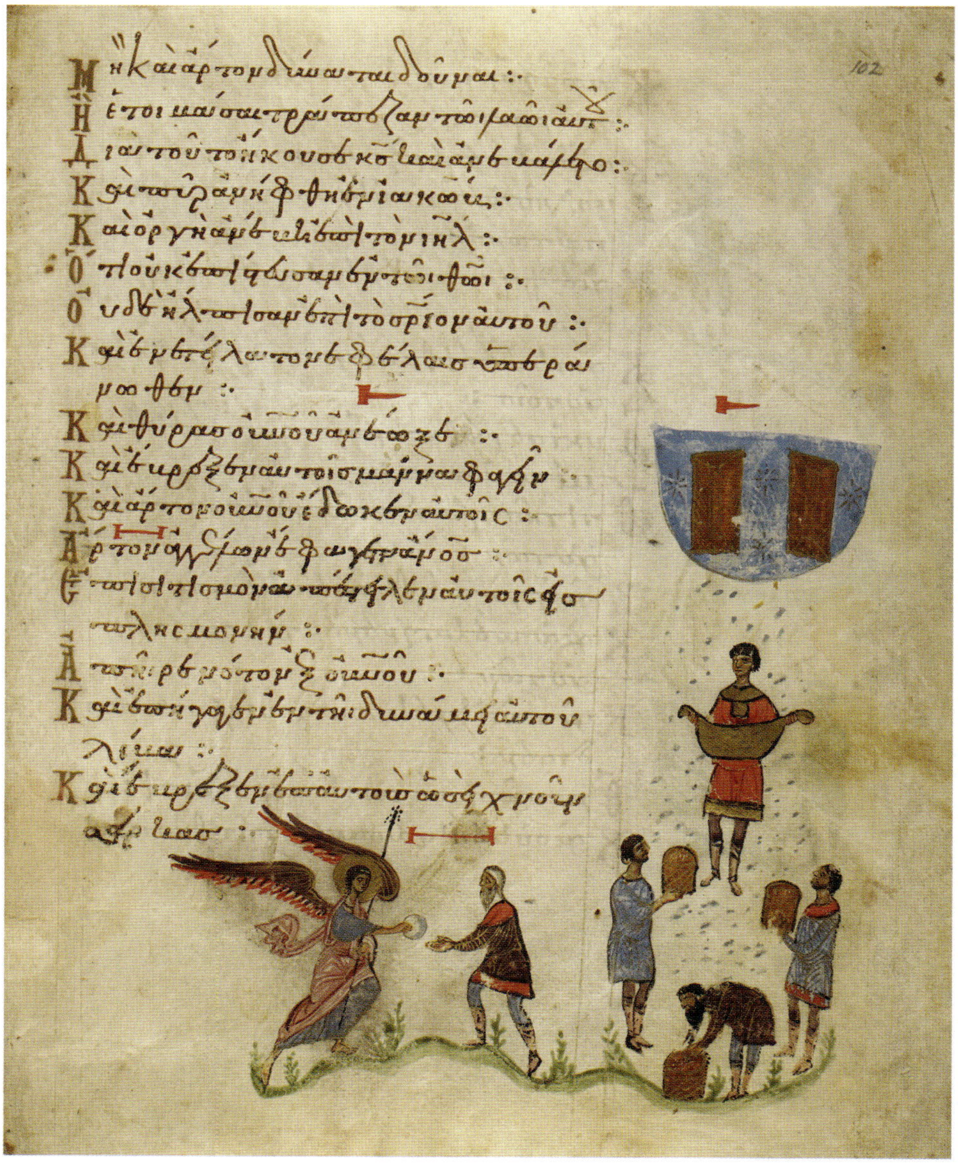

43, 44. Byzantine Psalter (at Psalm 77), dated 1066. At the foot of the page an angel is offering bread to an old man, linking the fall of manna with the bread of the Eucharist. The opposite page shows the slaughter and roasting of the quails. London, British Library, MS Add. 19352, fols 102, 102v.

itself, in the form of wafers, is also reminiscent of the unleavened bread of the Holy Communion. The large conical hats are variants of the peaked hats typical of the Jewish costume we have already discussed. More explicit anti-semitic prejudice, common in fifteenth-century imagery, is expressed in the men's dark skins, prominent noses and angry or greedy expressions. Only the fashionably dressed woman in the foreground is allowed to remain calm and beautiful as she picks up the wafers fallen from heaven.

The *Gathering of Manna* remained a popular subject, but the composition was fairly standard until the appearance of Jacopo Tintoretto's painting on the ceiling of the Sala Superiore in the Scuola Grande di San Rocco in Venice (1576–81) (**151**). This was a confraternity founded in 1478 with the aim of helping the needy and the sick, especially during epidemics. Tintoretto was a member of the confraternity and spent nearly twenty-five years painting large canvases to decorate the walls and ceilings of the new building. The programme of the sala superiore was strictly typological. The ten Gospel scenes were placed on the walls and the twenty-one Old Testament forerunners on the ceiling above.

Not surprisingly, the Manna miracle was the largest of the types of the Last Supper, with a central position at the east end of the ceiling. Tintoretto's

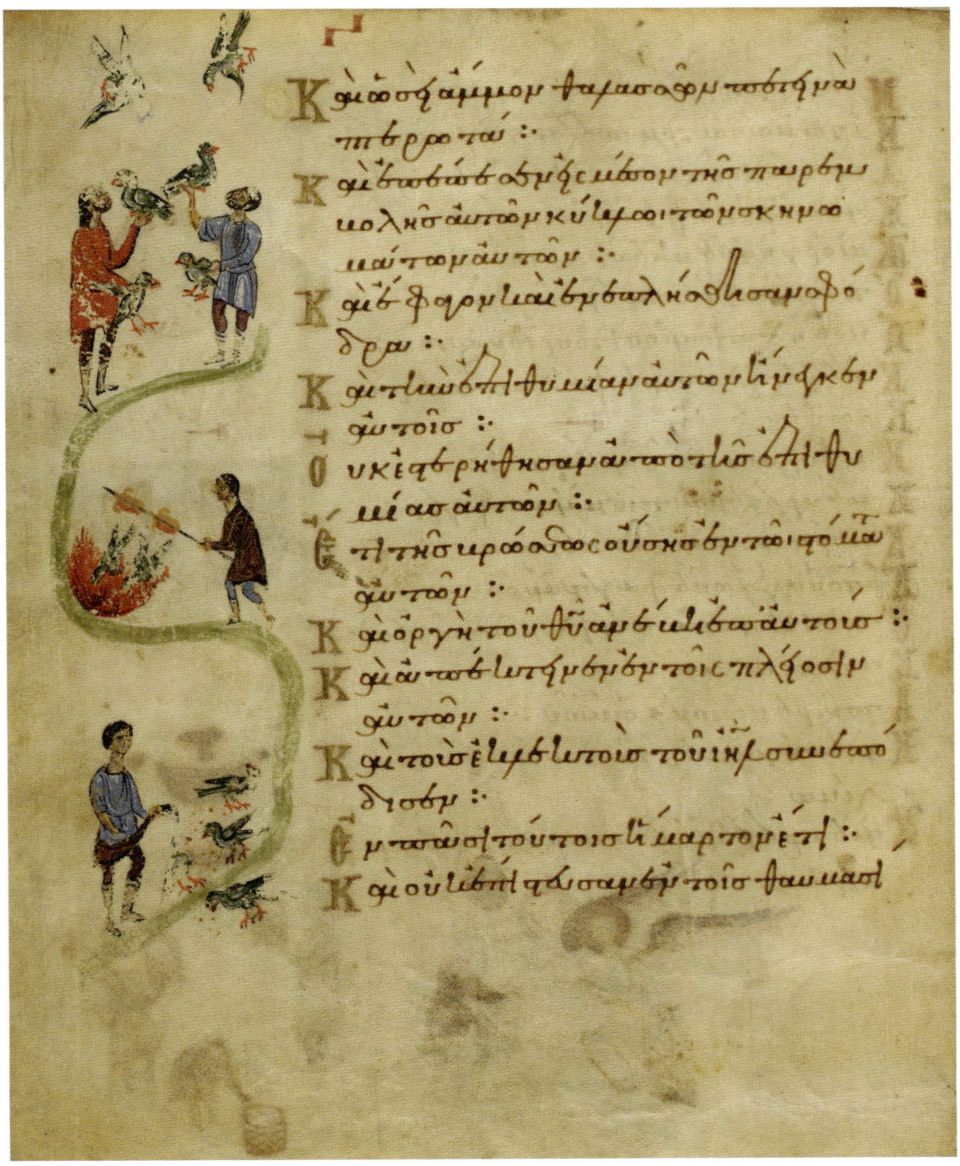

45. Atrium cupola mosaic, St Mark's Venice, c.1260. Moses kneels while the couple on the left are roasting the quails.

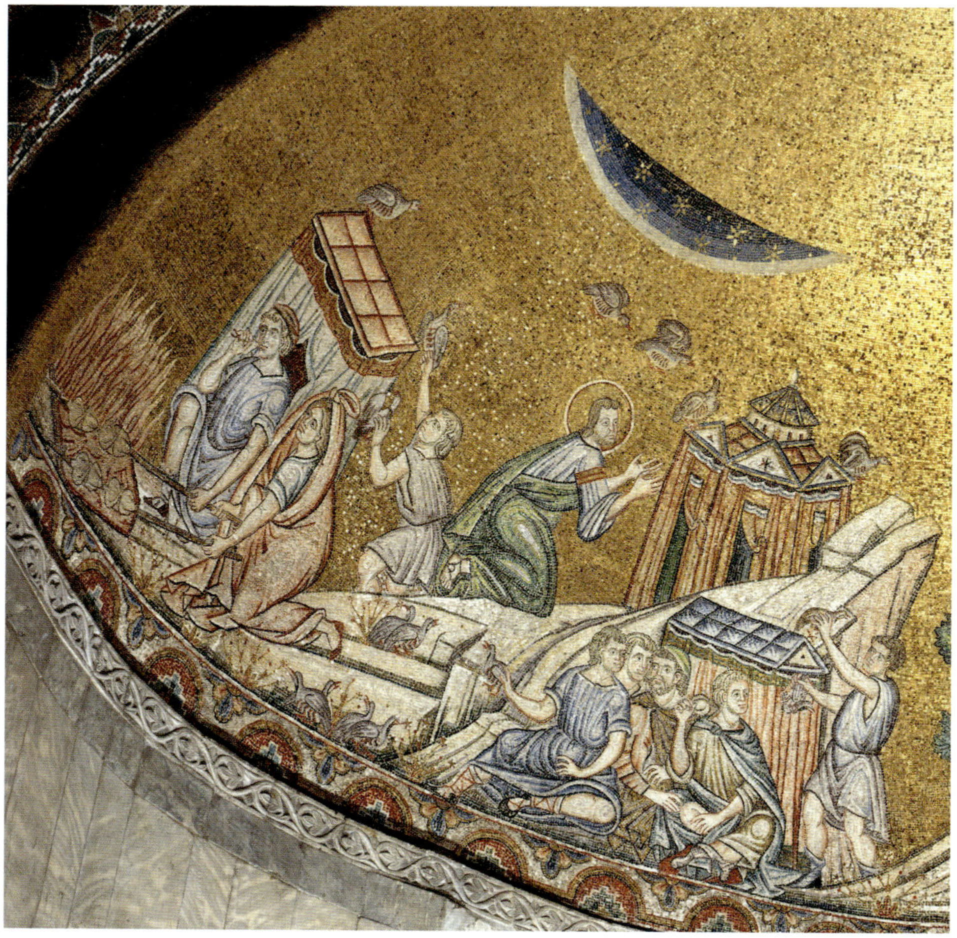

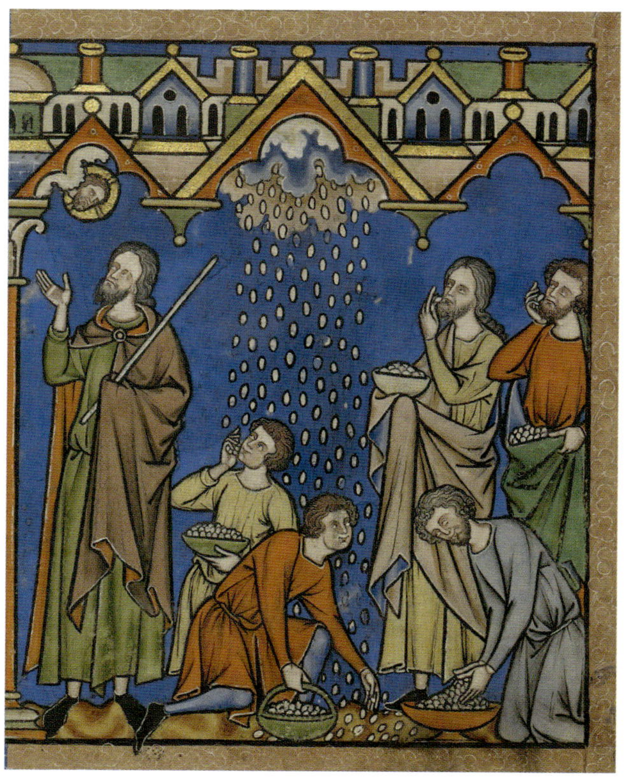

46. Picture Bible, Paris, c.1250. The quails are not illustrated, only the fall and gathering of manna is shown. New York, Pierpont Morgan Library, M638, fol. 9v.

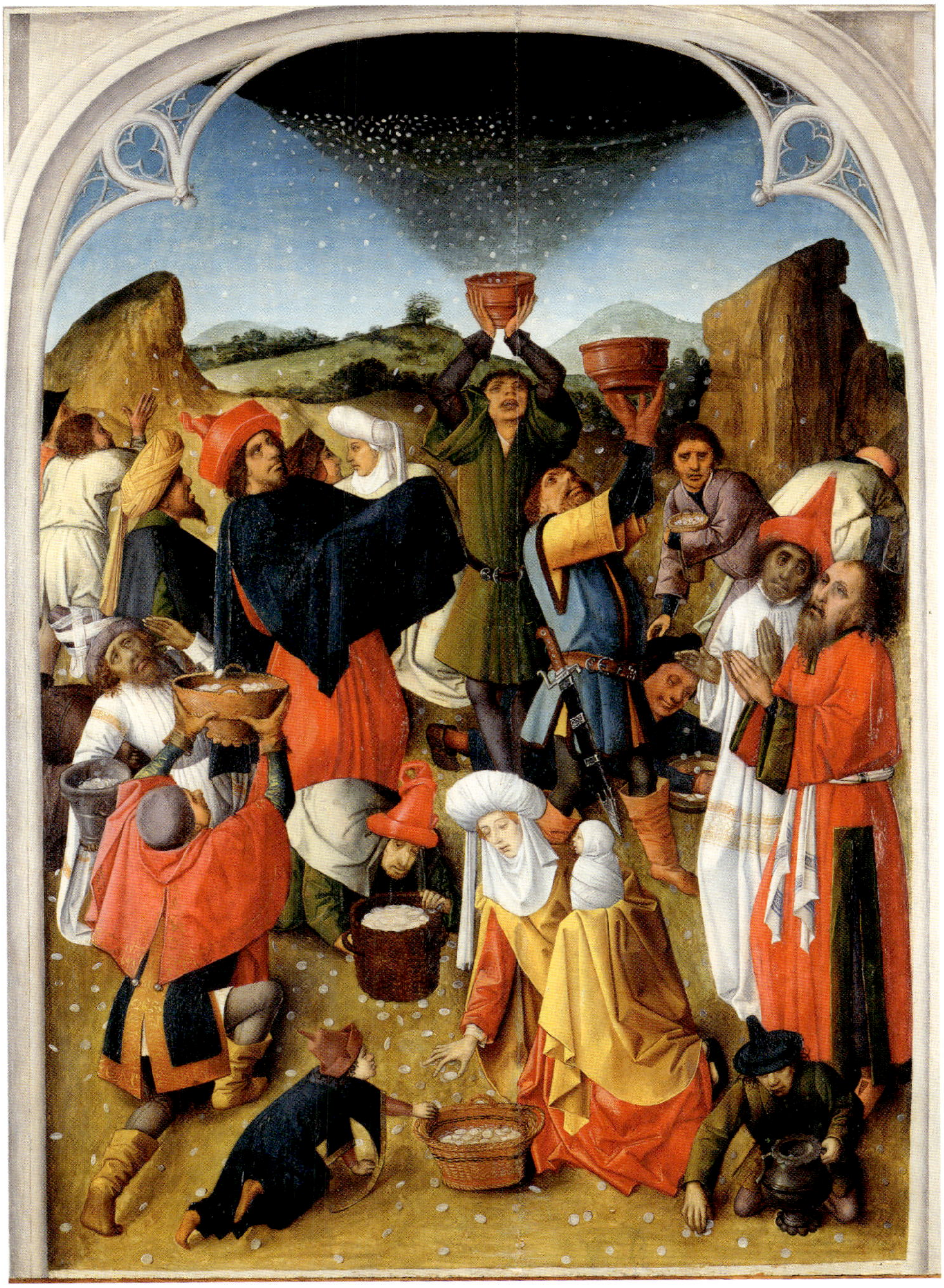

47. Master of the Manna Gathering, Dutch c.1470. The manna is in the form of wafers reminiscent of the unleavened bread of the Holy Communion. Formerly Douai Museum, destroyed in 1944.

rapid, almost feverish brushstrokes and strong contrasts of light and shade are typical of his later style, but it is the interpretation of the subject that is most revolutionary. Moses, seen from behind, points upwards where the Israelites have spread out a large curtain to protect themselves from the sun in the desert. This curtain, which dominates the composition, separates two worlds: God, from whom the manna descends, is hidden from man. It is also an altar cloth, emphasising this prefiguration of the Mass. The dead lambs in the foreground represent the sacrifices of the Old Testament that have been replaced by the redemptory sacrifice of Christ.

6
RUTH

Ruth is the Old Testament's epitome of loyalty and faithfulness and her book is a monument to religious tolerance. She was a Moabite (not a Jew); recently widowed, she insisted on accompanying her mother-in-law back to her native Judah. 'Where you go, I will go; where you lodge, I will lodge; your people shall be my people, and your God my God' (Ruth 1.16). They came to Bethlehem at the beginning of the barley harvest and Ruth began to glean in the field behind the reapers. It turned out that the field belonged to Boaz, a wealthy kinsman of her mother-in-law, who took her under his wing.

'At mealtime Boaz said to her, 'Come here, and eat some of this bread, and dip your morsel in the sour wine'. So she sat beside the reapers, and he heaped up for her some parched grain. She ate until she was satisfied, and she had some left over.' (Ruth 2.14)

The Latin Vulgate, followed by the King James Bible, has vinegar (*acetum*) for the drink in which the bread is dipped, somewhat different from the 'sour wine' of more recent translations. The original Hebrew word, *chomets*, denotes an acid beverage and can be translated as vinegar or sour wine. When mentioned in describing Ruth's meal or, in a different context, at Numbers 6.3, it is clearly considered a refreshing drink different from the wine offered to Jesus on the cross, which was mixed with gall (Matt. 27.34).[31]

The Book of Ruth was seldom illustrated in the early Middle Ages and, apart from two scenes in the Byzantine Octateuchs, it is only from the twelfth century that there are extensive picture cycles – those, for example, in the English psalter in Munich (Clm. 835, c.1200), the windows of the Sainte Chapelle in Paris, the numerous editions of the Bible moralisée and the fourteenth-century Italian Bible in Rovigo (MS 212).[32] They all show Ruth gleaning, but none of them include a picture of the reapers' meal.

However, this is shown in the mid-thirteenth-century Bible Picture Book in the Morgan Library (**48**). Ruth and three of the reapers are seated on the ground, a white cloth covering their clothes. Four men, also eating, stand behind them. In the middle there is a jug with a bowl on it containing the sour wine into which the reapers are dipping their bread.

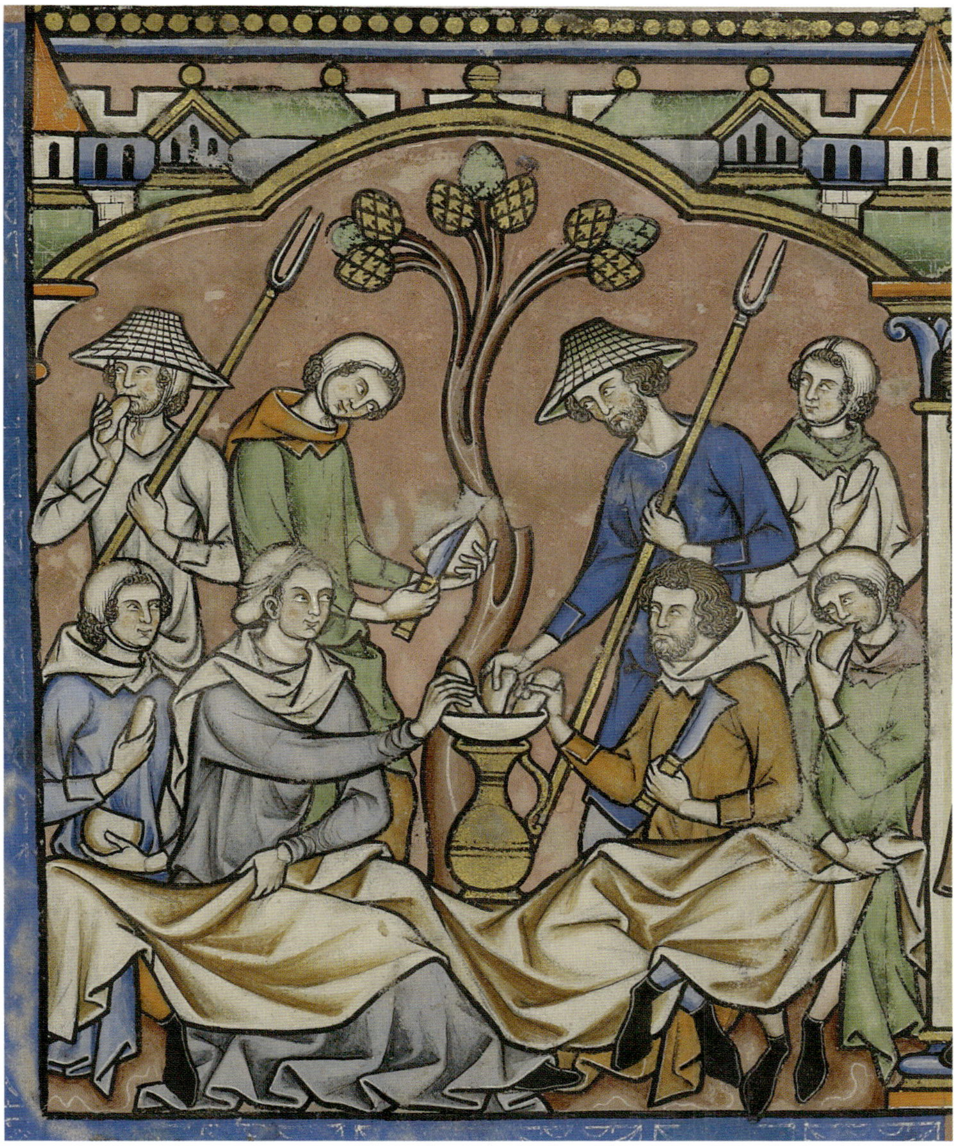

48. Picture Bible, Paris, c.1250. A rare example of peasants at a meal in Bible illustration. New York, Pierpont Morgan Library, M638, fol. 17v.

This is one of the very few illustrated biblical meals in which the peasants are seated on the ground, as opposed to the usual covered tables and benches or chairs. The meal shown here does not boast of formal table settings and utensils. Instead, some of the field workers still hold their tools while they eat to emphasise that this is a picture of eating to renew their strength before returning to work. Such scenes are equally rare in secular manuscripts. In Gaston Phoebus' *Book of the Chase* class distinctions are emphasised as the lord is seated at a table while the huntsmen sit on the grass beside a white cloth spread on the ground (e.g. Paris, BnF MS fr. 616). The story of Ruth ends happily. Ruth married Boaz and their son was Obed, father of Jesse and grandfather of David.

7
A SACRIFICIAL MEAL: ELKANAH, HANNAH AND PENNINAH

At the opening of the first Book of Samuel, we are told how Elkanah came every year to Shiloh with his two wives, Hannah and Penninah, to sacrifice. It was an important occasion, for the sanctuary at Shiloh rivalled Jerusalem at the time – it was later destroyed by the Philistines – and it is significant that Samuel was dedicated to God there.

'On the day when Elkanah sacrificed, he would give portions to his wife Penninah and to all her sons and daughters; but to Hannah he gave a double portion ('one portion' in the Latin Vulgate) because he loved her, though the Lord had closed her womb. Her rival used to provoke her severely, to irritate her, because the Lord had closed her womb. So it went on year after year; as often as she went up to the house of the Lord, she used to provoke her. Therefore Hannah wept and would not eat. Her husband Elkanah said to her 'Hannah, why do you weep? Why do you not eat? Why is your heart sad? Am I not more to you than ten sons?" (I Samuel 1.4–8)

As the text indicates, the sacrifice was followed by a sacrificial meal as laid down in Leviticus 7.11–18. 'And the flesh of your thanksgiving sacrifice of well-being shall be eaten on the day it is offered; you shall not leave any of it until morning' (Levit. 7.15). Clearly, the sacrifice is both a gift to God and an act of communal worship. The Passover meal is the most important sacrificial meal in the Old Testament, but Elkanah's offering is more typical of many such sacrifices in ancient Israel. Having offered the gift to God, the essence of the sacrificial meal lay in the social fellowship provided by the physical act of eating together.[33]

Pope Gregory the Great (c.540–604) identified Hannah with the Church and Penninah with Synagogue, and the rivalry between the two wives may be interpreted as an argument for monogamy. Yet the subject was never prominent for its symbolism and medieval depictions of it are found principally in manuscripts of the Bible, illustrating the opening of the first Book of Samuel. Most commonly, Elkanah is speaking to Hannah, while Penninah is accompanied by her children, without the meal being shown.

A fuller illustration, including the meal, appears in, for example, the great Bible from the abbey of Stavelot, near Liège, dated 1097. Four scenes are

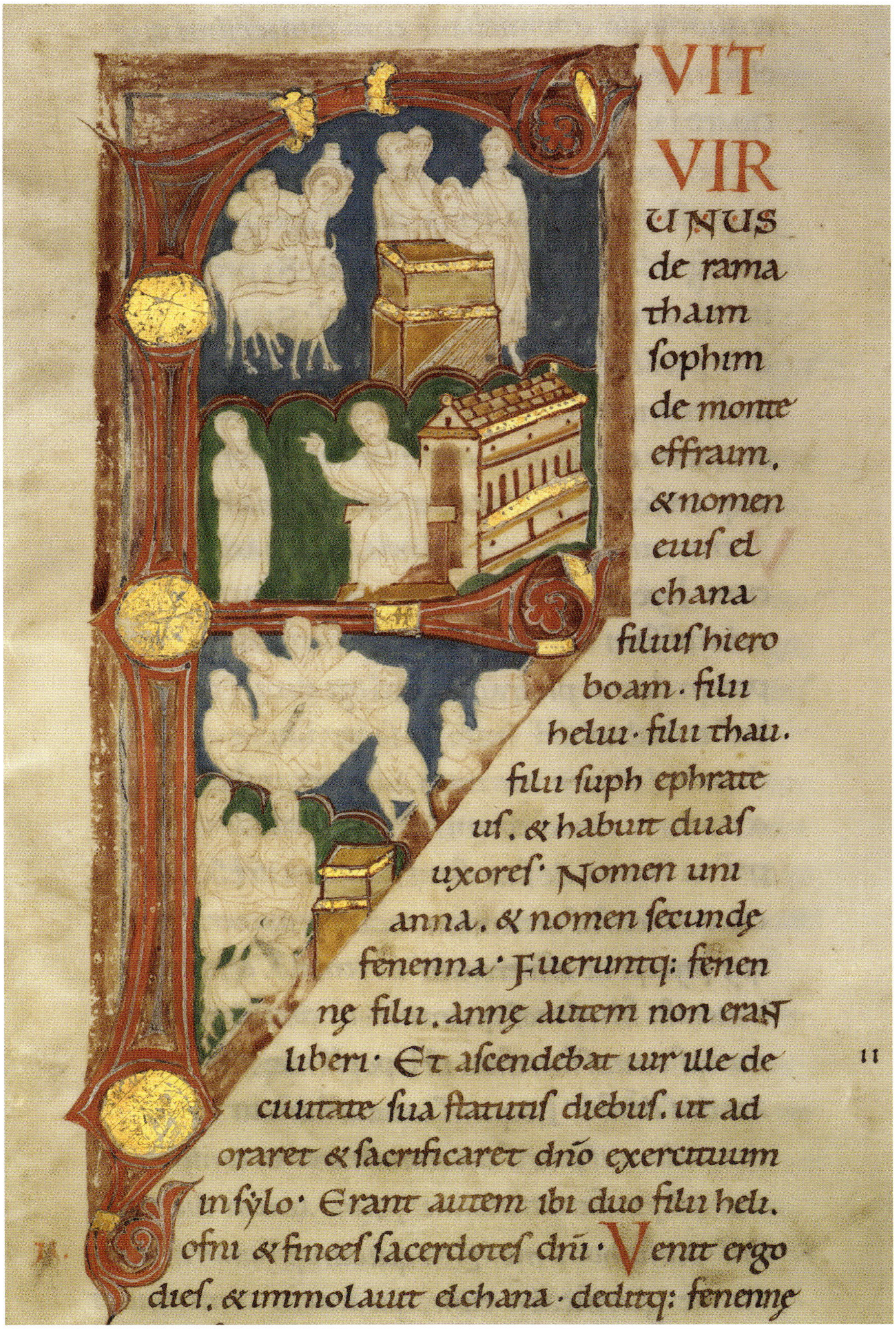

49. Bible from Stavelot Abbey, near Liège, 1097. The animal sacrifice and the meal with Elkanah, Hannah and Penninah are shown below. The story ends with the birth of Samuel. London, British Library, MS Add. 28106, fol. 97.

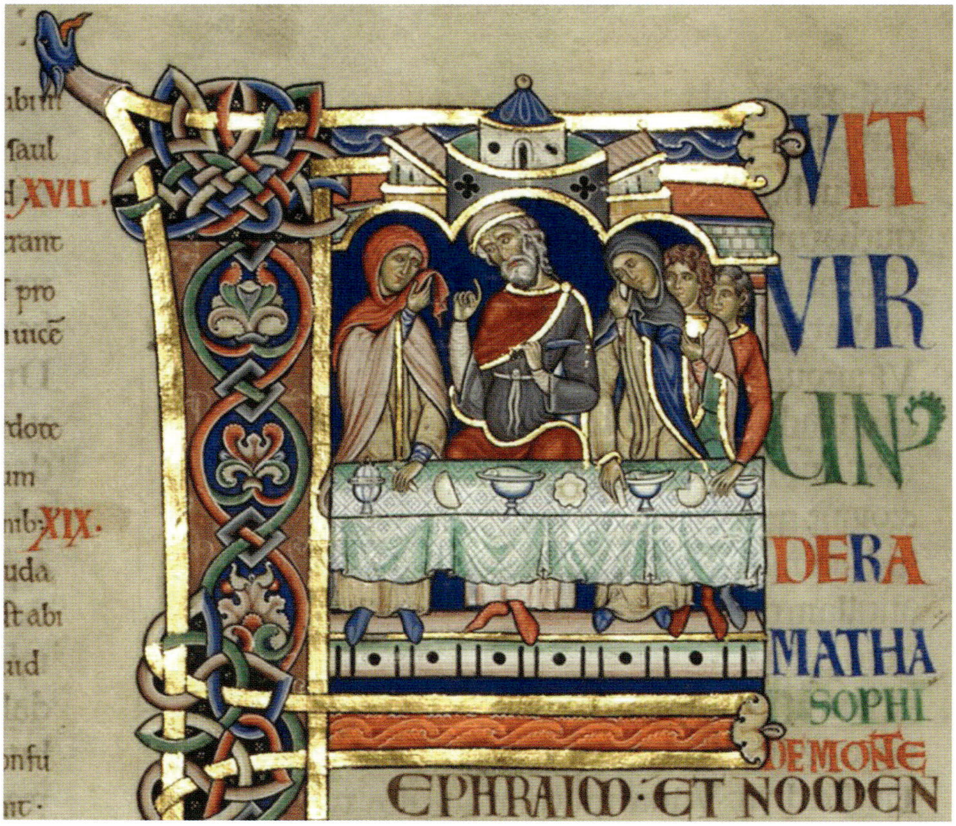

50. Winchester Bible, c.1170, fol. 88. At the meal, Elkanah talks to the weeping Hannah. Oddly, the dishes on the table contain fish, not the meat of the sacrificial animal. Winchester Cathedral Library.

neatly fitted into the initial F (**49**). Below is the animal sacrifice and the meal with Elkanah, Hannah and Penninah, with one son and a servant bringing the food. Above are the succeeding stages of the story: Hannah praying before the high priest Eli and, finally, Elkanah and Hannah with the infant Samuel before Eli. The meal itself figures more centrally in the Winchester Bible of c.1170, one of the masterpieces of English Romanesque illumination (**50**). At the table, Elkanah is talking to the weeping Hannah; on the other side we see Penninah with her two sons. Somewhat oddly, given the emphasis on 'flesh' for the sacrifice, the dishes on the table contain not meat but fish. Presumably the artist was used to depicting fish at biblical meals and was unaware of the Leviticus text in which meat is specified for the sacrificial meal. As we shall see, this is not the only example of an artist substituting fish for meat in the illustration (**98**).

8
THE BANQUET OF JOB'S SONS AND DAUGHTERS

Job was a man 'blameless and upright' and God insisted to Satan that he would retain his faith even if tragedy befell him.

'One day when the sons and daughters were eating and drinking wine in the eldest brother's house', three messengers came to Job in succession announcing the destruction of his flocks and property. 'Another came and said 'your sons and daughters were eating and drinking wine in their elder brother's house and suddenly a great wind came across the desert, struck the four corners of the house, and it fell on the young people, and they are dead; I alone have escaped to tell you." (Job 1.13–19)

Job, the personification of patient resilience in the face of adversity, was seen as a model of Christ and his Church, and the commentaries on the biblical Book of Job were extremely popular throughout the Middle Ages. In Byzantium, the *Catena* (commentary) on Job has survived in some fifteen lavishly illustrated copies dating from the ninth to the sixteenth centuries.[34] A late ninth-century copy in the Vatican Library shows the meal with the seven sons and three daughters reclining on a classical *stibadium*, their hands stretched out into two shared bowls of food on the table. Servants are bringing in cups and dishes, while more food and wine is being prepared below (**51**). Most of these manuscripts also contain a second scene with the building collapsing and masonry falling onto the diners. Like Belshazzar's feast, the splendid meal immediately precedes a shocking disaster.

In the West the commentary of Pope Gregory the Great, *Moralia in Job*, written in the years 579–95, was one of the most popular of all biblical commentaries and one of the very few to have been illustrated.[35] The meal is figured in two of the twelfth-century manuscripts, notably the one in Paris (BnF, MS lat.15675) produced at the abbey of Forest in Flanders in about 1160–70 (**52**). The oblong table contrasts with the semi-circular couch of the Byzantine composition but, again, the food, here clearly shown as fish, is grasped in the diners' hands. The emphasis is on the lively conversation among the brothers and sisters, which is echoed in the Latin inscription above: 'The siblings are joined together

51. Commentary on Job, Byzantine, late ninth century. Job's seven sons and three daughters reclining on a classical *stibadium*; the food is prepared below. Vatican Library, MS gr. 749, fol. 16v.

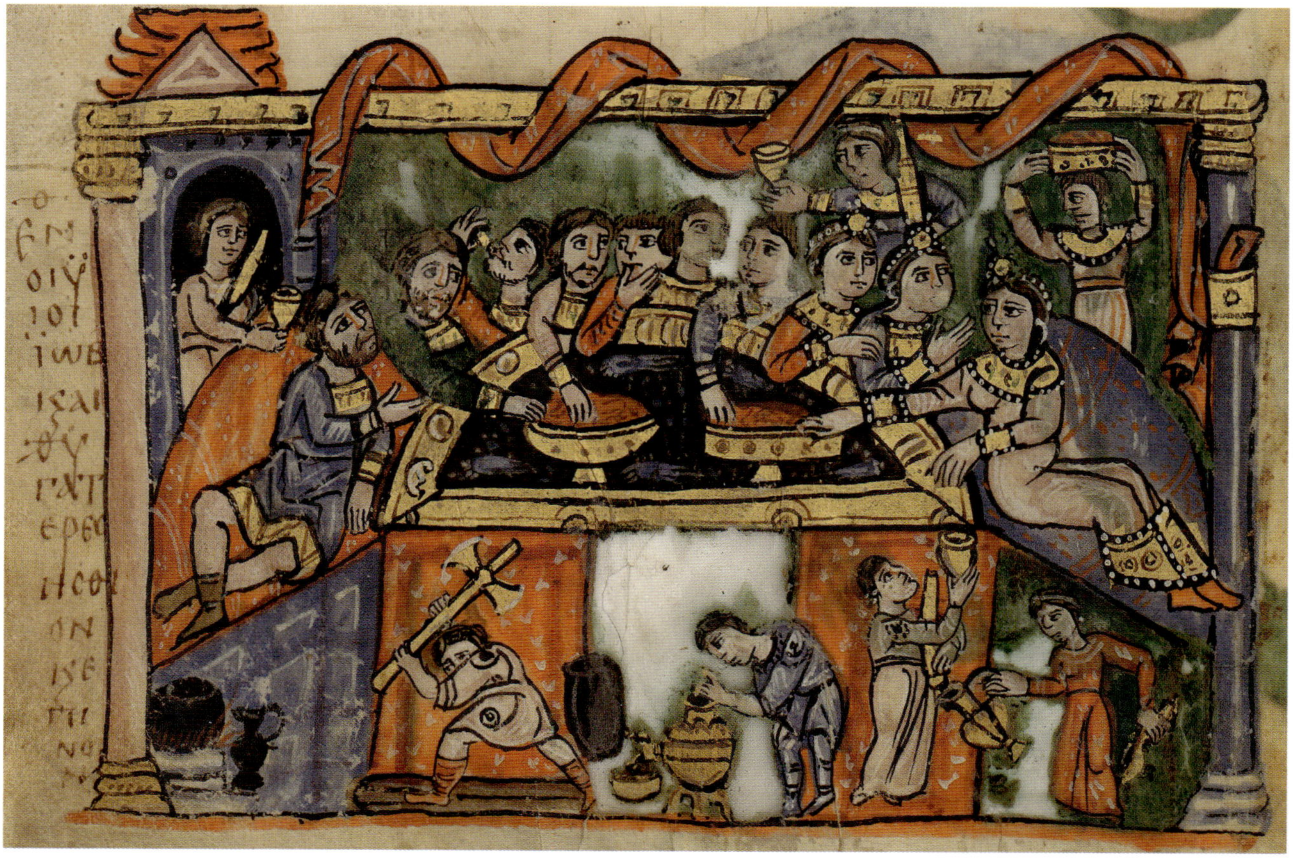

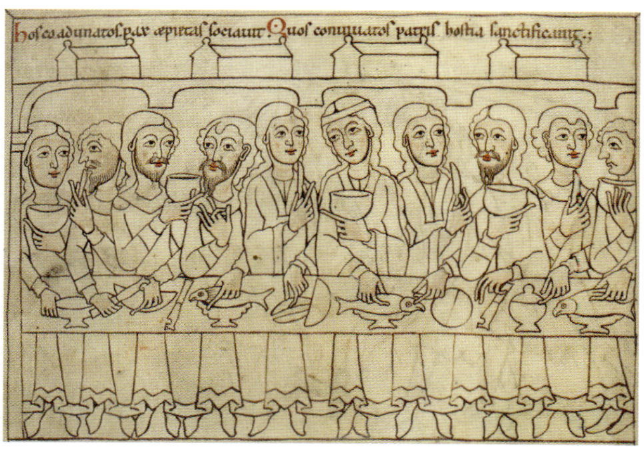

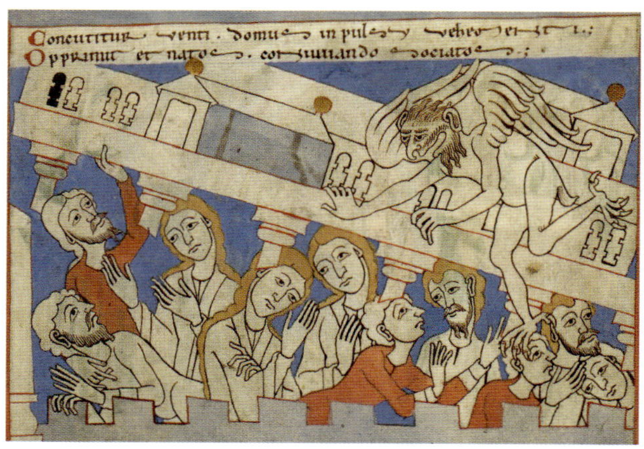

52, 53. Manuscript of the *Moralia in Job* by Pope Gregory the Great, abbey of Forest, Flanders, c.1160–70. Two scenes: the banquet, showing the lively conversation among the brothers and sisters, followed by the destruction of the house by the devil. Paris, Bibliothèque Nationale., MS lat. 15675, fols 3 and 5.

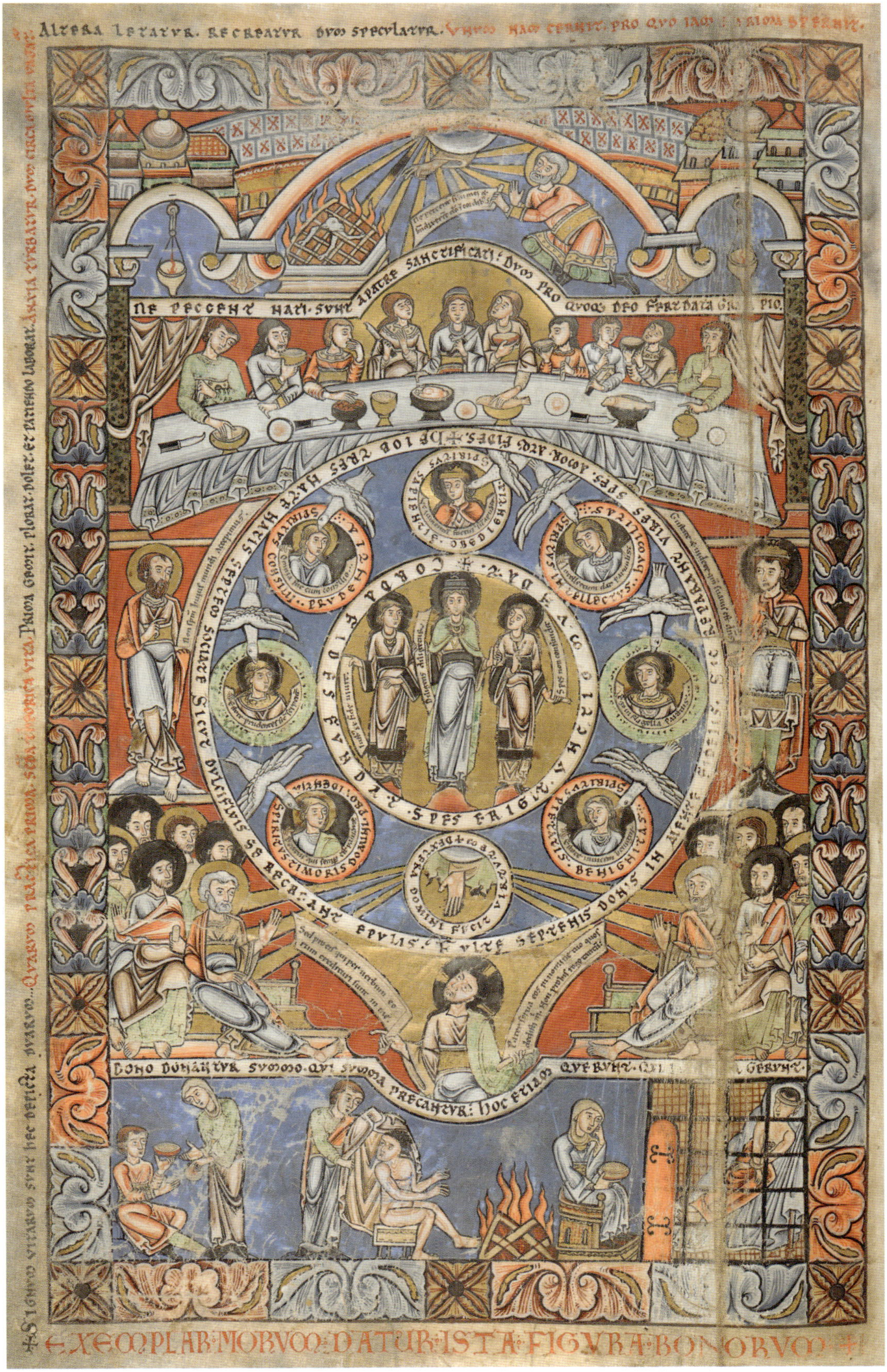

54. Bible from Floreffe Abbey, Flanders, c.1160. The meal heads a complex design illustrating the story of Job. London, British Library, MS Add. 17738, fol. 3v.

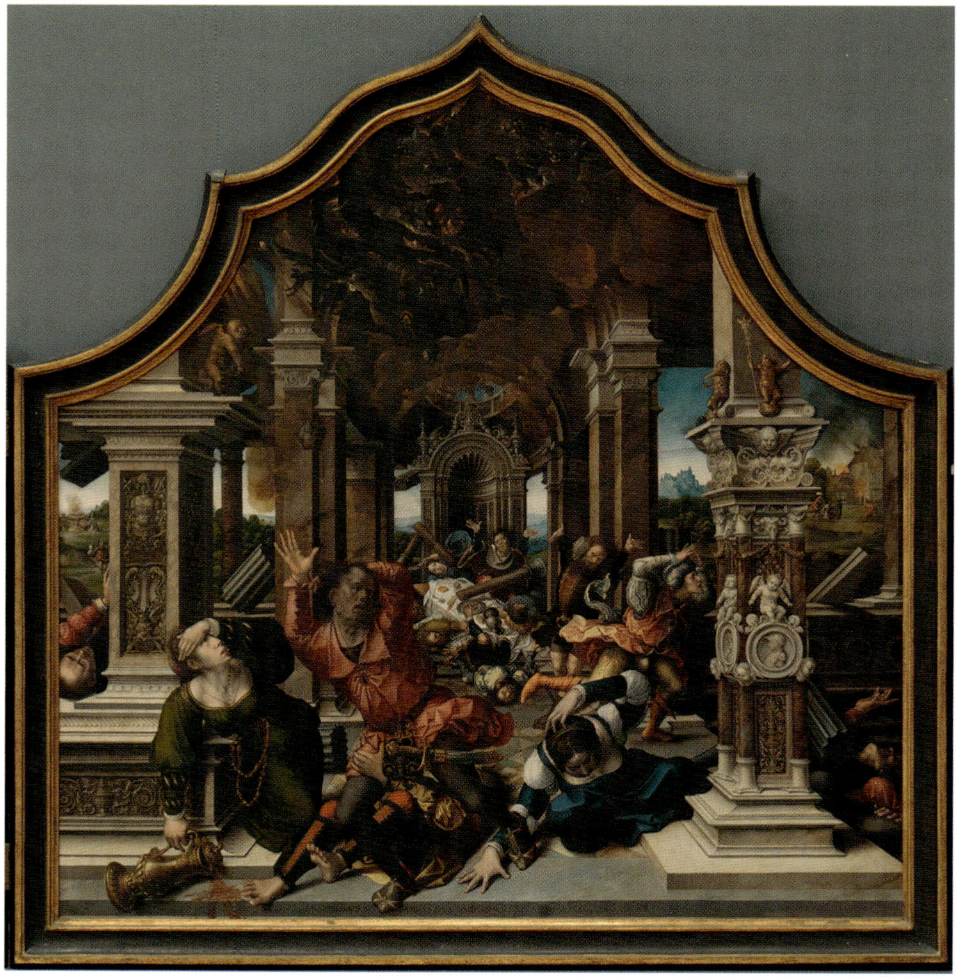

55. Bernart van Orley (c.1488–1541), Brussels, dated 1521. Central panel of an altarpiece devoted to Job, with the parable of Dives and Lazarus the beggar on the reverse of the wings. Brussels, Musées royaux des Beaux-Arts, no. 335.

in peace and piety; the convivial meal signifies the Host of the Father.' A second illustration shows the destruction of the house with the devil causing the collapse of the roof onto Job's children (**52**, **53**).

This meal is seldom depicted in medieval Bibles, as opposed to the Commentaries on Job. Most notable is the full-page miniature in the Bible of about 1160 from the abbey of Floreffe in Flanders (**54**). On the frontispiece to the second volume the meal heads a complex design illustrating the story of Job. The roundels below the meal refer to Gregory's commentary, which compared the seven sons with the seven Gifts of the Holy Spirit mentioned by Isaiah and the three daughters with the three theological virtues: Faith, Hope and Charity. The meal of Job's children is directly compared with the Last Supper, which is pictured on the opposite page.[36]

Outstanding among the later illustrations of the story is the central panel of an altarpiece dedicated to Job painted by Bernart van Orley in 1521 (**55**). The composition concentrates on the agonised panic of the sons and daughters as the building collapses. The altarpiece was commissioned by Margaret of Austria, daughter of the Emperor Maximilian and governor of the Netherlands from 1504. She was an important patron of the arts and it was presumably her idea to have scenes of the parable of Dives and Lazarus the beggar – discussed below, p. 110 – painted on the reverse of the wings to make a comparison between Job and Lazarus as personifications of patience.

9
BELSHAZZAR'S FEAST: THE WRITING ON THE WALL

At a great festival for a thousand of his lords, King Belshazzar of Babylon commanded that the vessels of gold and silver taken out of the Temple of Jerusalem by his father, Nebuchadnezzar, should be brought out and used.'Immediately the fingers of a human hand appeared and began writing on the plaster of the wall of the royal palace, next to the lamp stand' (Daniel 5.5). The wise men of Babylon failed to read what was written. So Belshazzar, at the queen's suggestion, sent for Daniel – an Israelite during the Babylonian captivity – who explained that the writing that was inscribed read: 'MENE, MENE, TEKEL, and PARSIN. This is the interpretation of the matter: MENE, God has numbered the days of your kingdom and brought it to an end; TEKEL, you have been weighed in the scales and found wanting; PERES (singular of parsin), your kingdom is divided and given to the Medes and the Persians' (Daniel 5.24–28). That very night Belshazzar was killed and Darius received the Chaldean kingdom.

It should be added that this biblical account, generally dated c.168–164 BCE, contains errors of fact. Nebuchadnezzar was not Belshazzar's father but a more distant ancestor, and the kingdom was taken over in 538 by Cyrus, not Darius.

As far as our topic of biblical food is concerned, it must be admitted that there is no mention here of food and yet this was one of the most dramatic and memorable of biblical feasts. 'The writing on the wall' remains a popular concept and the phrase 'weighed in the balance and found wanting' is also still in current use. Of the visual interpretations, Rembrandt's dramatic rendering in the National Gallery is doubtless the most widely known, but there were many others from the late sixteenth to the early nineteenth centuries. Its popularity during this period may be accounted for by the drama of its subject.

Yet its lack of typological symbolism meant that it does not appear at all in the surviving biblical illustrations of the Early Christian period and it remained relatively rare in the Middle Ages. Daniel in the Lions' Den, interpreted as a forerunner of the Triumph or Ascension of Christ, is depicted in Early Christian catacomb paintings, but no images

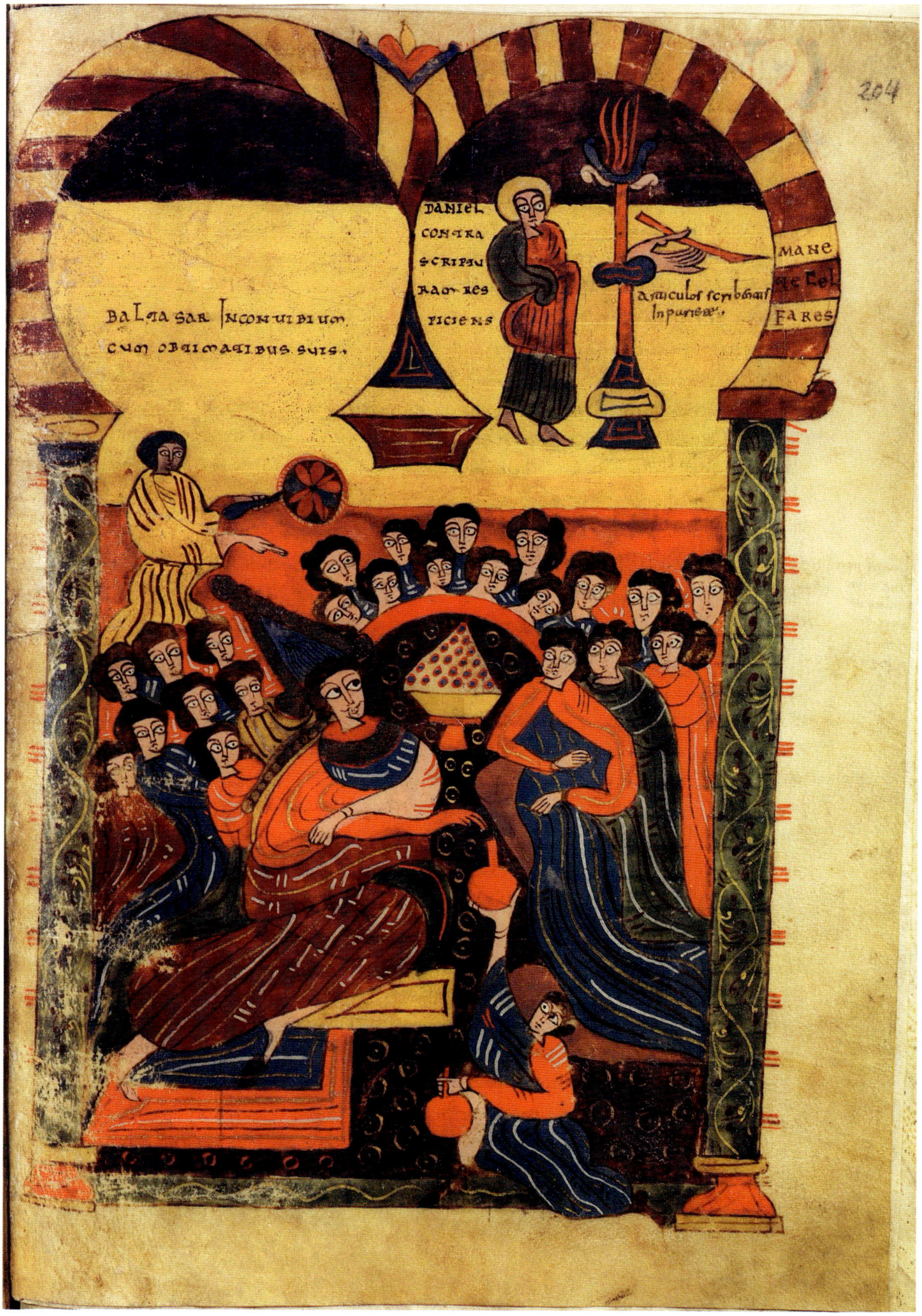

56. St Jerome's *Commentary on Daniel* (added to a manuscript of Beatus, *Commentary on the Apocalypse*), Northern Spain c.970. Valladolid, University Library, MS 433, fol. 204.

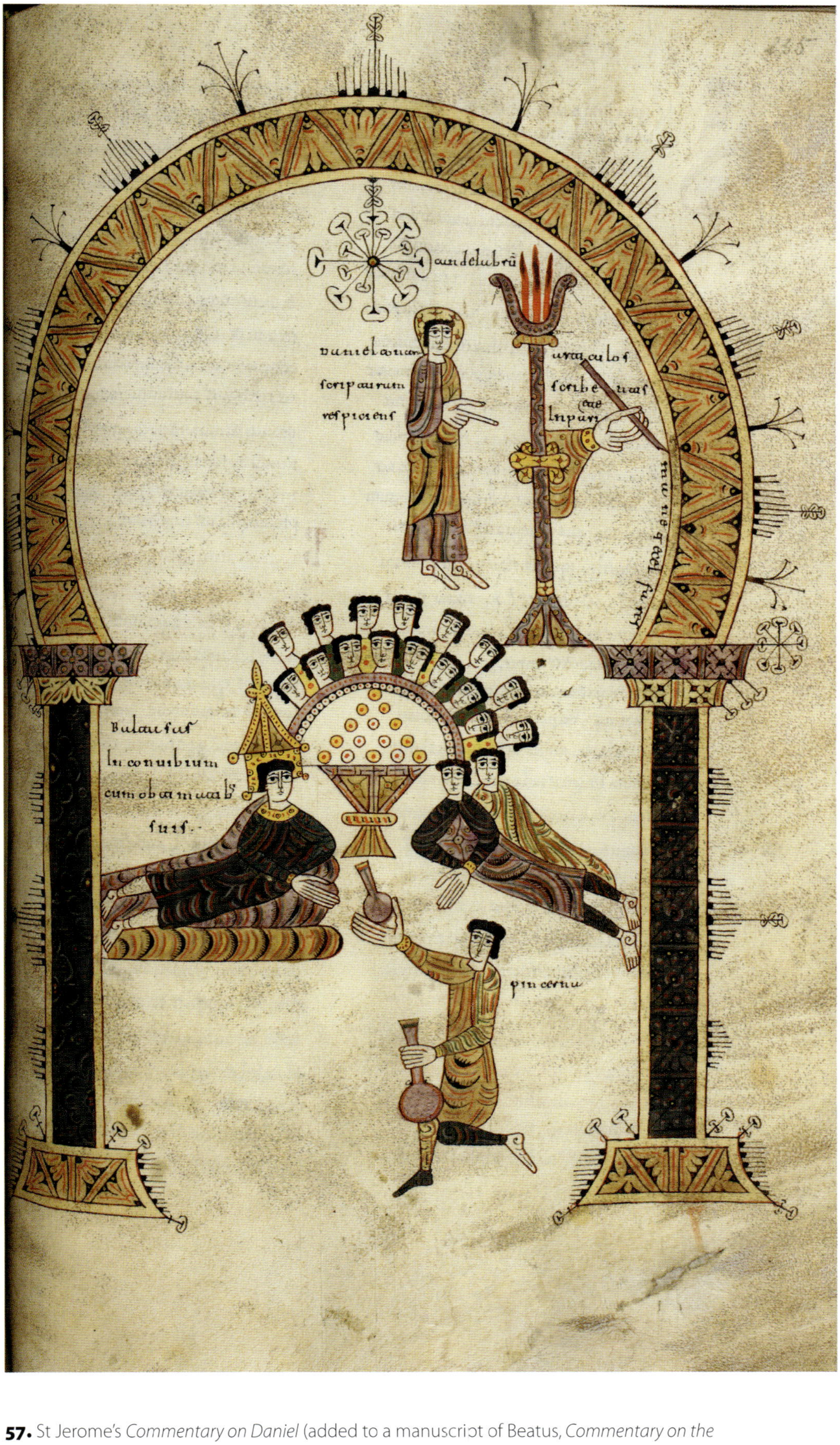

57. St Jerome's *Commentary on Daniel* (added to a manuscript of Beatus, *Commentary on the Apocalypse*) from S. Domingo de Silos, 1109. London, British Library, MS Add. 11695, fol. 235.

58. Scenes from the Book of Daniel, including Belshazzar's feast, in a Bible from the abbey of Sant Per de Roda, Catalonia, mid-twelfth century. The illustrations in this Catalan manuscript are closer to mainstream European art than to the distinctive Asturian style of the previous examples. Paris, Bibliothèque Nationale MS lat 6, vol. 3, fol. 66.

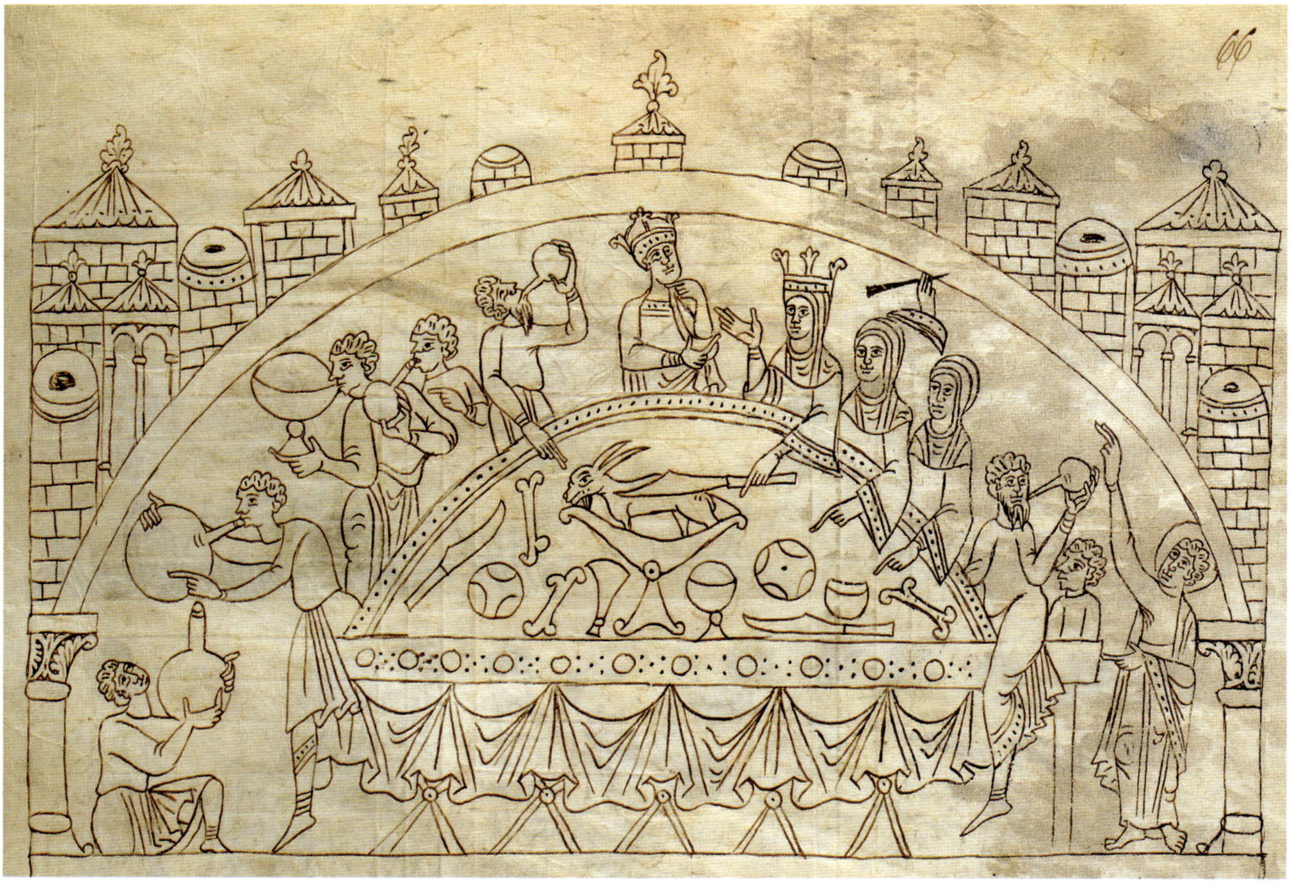

of Belshazzar's feast have survived from before the tenth century. Then it is to northern Spain that one must look to encounter a sudden blossoming of such depictions in the period c.950 to c.1100.

By 711 the Muslim invasion had left only a narrow strip of northern Spain in Christian hands. It was here that a well-known Commentary on the Apocalypse, attributed to Beatus of Liébana (d.798), was written. Its popularity is attested by the survival of two dozen copies, most of which retain all or some of their illustrations.[37] Eleven of these manuscripts also contain St Jerome's *Commentary on Daniel*, with its own series of illustrations. Adding this text to a commentary on the Apocalypse was a logical step, as the Book of Daniel, particularly the second half with its visions and predictions, was recognised as an early example of such apocalyptic texts.

Naturally enough, Belshazzar's feast was included among the Daniel illustrations added to the Beatus manuscripts. The composition, repeated with little alteration, shows Belshazzar reclining at a semi-circular table, around which the heads of the guests appear (**56**, **57**). A large bowl in the centre – filled with round objects, possibly bread rolls – and bottles or jugs brought by a servant represent the vessels stolen from the Temple in Jerusalem. Above, the figure of Daniel explains the writing on the wall, which is being inscribed by a hand adjoining the lamp stand. Although the story is compressed into one scene rather than showing Daniel's explanation separately, this remains a very literal illustration.

Belshazzar's reclining posture in the manner of ancient Rome and the semi-circular table suggest an ultimate derivation from a much earlier composition.

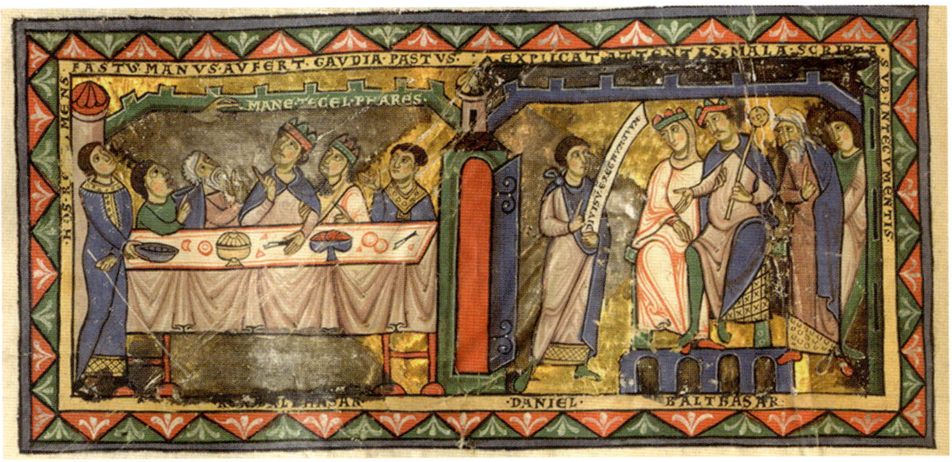

59. Illustration to Daniel, Gumbertus Bible, Regensburg c.1180. The banquet is on the left, Daniel's explanation on the right. Erlangen, University Library, MS Bibl.1, fol. 227v.

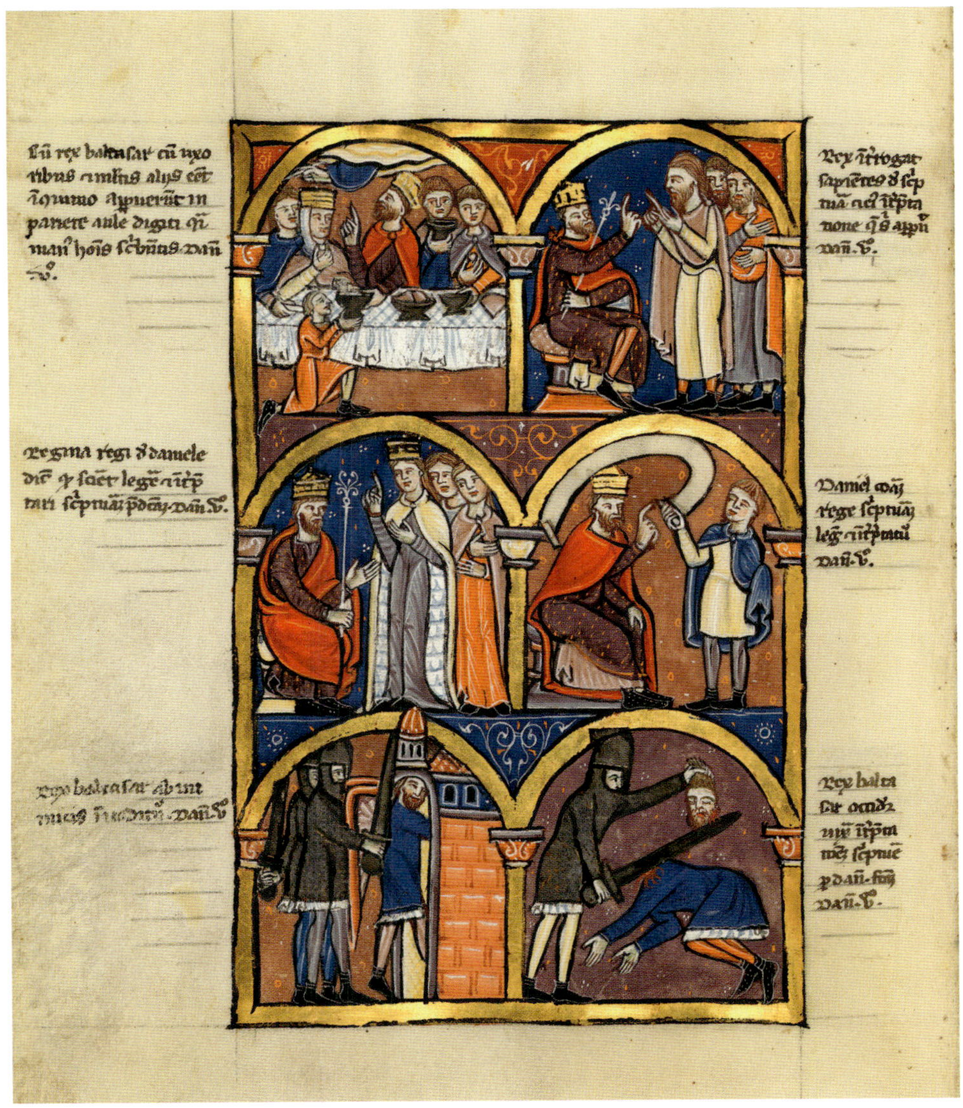

60. Illustration to Daniel in an Old Testament sequence in an English Psalter, c.1200–10. The sequence is expanded to include Belshazzar speaking to the wise men and the queen advising him to consult Daniel. Munich, Bayerische Stiftsbibliothek, Clm. 835, fol. 106v.

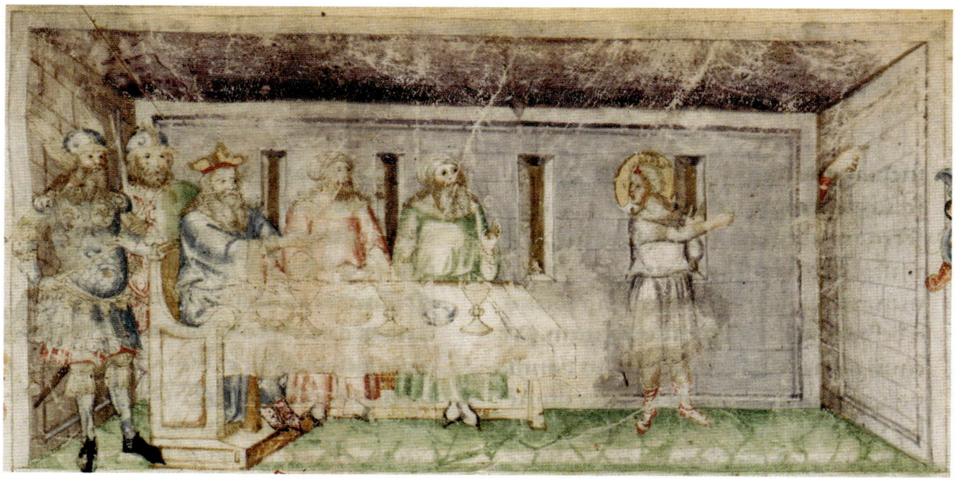

61. Illustration in a manuscript of Dante's *Divine Comedy*, c.1327–30, with the scene of Daniel's explanation. The hand writing on the wall is presumed to be Dante's in this context. Chantilly, Musée Condé, MS 597, fol. 31.

Yet the style is very different from anything to be found elsewhere in Western Europe. The figures, with their goggle eyes and linear treatment, are entirely two-dimensional, though this suppression of space is balanced by the dominance of strong colours. The style has been called 'Mozarabic', to indicate a derivation from Islamic art, and the term remains in general use, although close comparisons of the figure style have been difficult to find.

Daniel's popularity in Spain is also attested by the full illustrations to his book contained in two mid-eleventh-century Catalan Bibles: one from the abbey of Sant Per de Roda (**58**), the other from that of Santa Maria de Ripoll (Vatican Library, MS lat. 5729).[38] Catalonia belonged to the Mediterranean world and these illustrations are much closer to the mainstream of European art than to the distinctive style of the Asturian Beatus Apocalypse manuscripts. In the Roda Bible Belshazzar's feast still takes place at a semi-circular table, but the king is seated in the centre, surrounded by the queen and his concubines on the right and nobles busily drinking from bottles and cups on the left. A goat in a large bowl dominates the table setting. Of the diners, only Belshazzar, with his chin resting on his hand in a gesture of anxiety, is looking at the handwriting on the wall, which Daniel is busy explaining. The composition is much closer to the later examples of the scene in northern Europe than to the Beatus manuscripts.

Outside Spain, Belshazzar's feast is included only in the very fullest picture cycles. A giant Bible probably produced at Regensburg in about 1180, the so-called Gumbertus Bible, has over 150 scenes. Equally, the English psalter of c.1200–10 in Munich is exceptional in containing depictions of 176 scenes from the Old Testament. In both cases Daniel's explanation is shown separately from the feast itself (**59**, **60**). The whole story is told most fully in the English psalter: the feast itself, the wise men speaking to Belshazzar, the queen advising him to ask Daniel and, finally, Daniel's explanation. The Gumbertus Bible has a shorter narrative, consisting only of the feast and the explanation, but the drama of the occasion and the apprehension on the faces of the diners is most tellingly conveyed.

The dramatic content of Belshazzar's feast led to its being treated allegorically in non-biblical contexts. A miniature attributed to Buonamico Buffalmacco in a manuscript of Dante's *Inferno* (c.1327–30) shows Daniel's explanation to the king, who is seated at the table with two guests (**61**). The link between Daniel and Dante has been interpreted as suggesting that the ultimate source of the Divine Comedy is no less miraculous than that of the writing on the wall.[39]

Both the intense drama of the occasion and the oriental costumes made Belshazzar's feast a popular subject, particularly in seventeenth-century Netherlandish painting, but only Rembrandt's large picture of about 1636–38 has remained widely known (**62**). King and guest are open-mouthed, transfixed by the inscription being written on the wall amid a powerful blaze of light. As opposed to the earlier versions of the subject, where it is given in Latin, it is here, more correctly, in Hebrew, strangely to be read

62. Rembrandt van Rijn (1606–69), c.1636–38. For the first time, the writing on the wall is given in Hebrew. London, National Gallery.

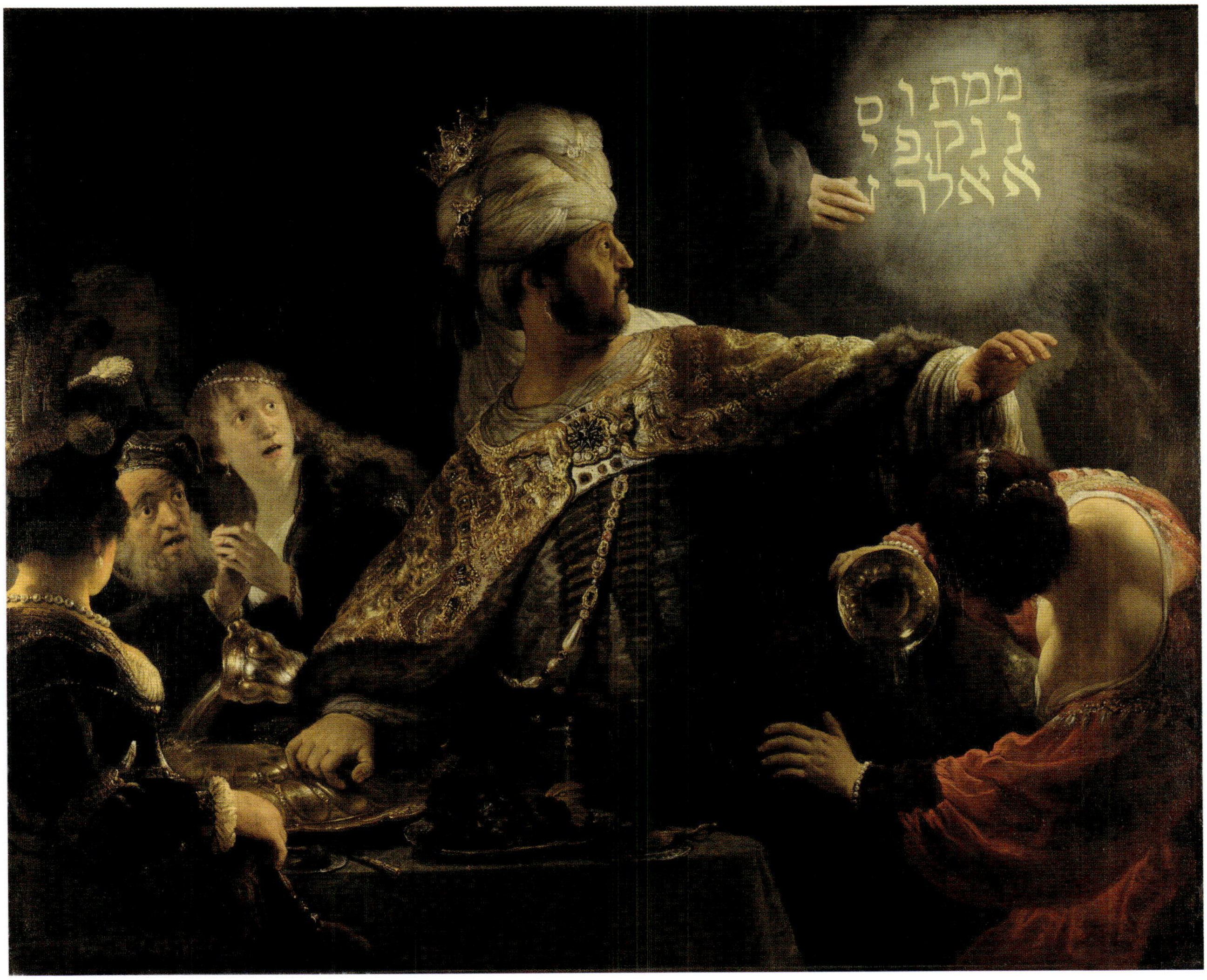

in vertical columns starting on the right: 'Mene mene tekel upharsin'. Rembrandt had learnt this form of the inscription from the Jewish theologian Manaseh ben Israel, of whom he had etched a portrait in 1636 and who moved into a house next to his three years later.

In the excitement of the moment wine is being spilt from two of the gold vessels that had been taken from the Temple of Jerusalem by Nebuchadnezzar. The dishes on the table are filled with fruit – grapes, figs and a pear – indicating that this is the dessert course of the banquet and also demonstrating the popularity of still life painting in the seventeenth-century Netherlands. A fork and a spoon are also shown on the table; both had come into widespread use by this time.

10
FORBIDDEN FOOD

'From among all the land animals, these are the creatures that you may eat. Any animal that has divided hoofs and is cloven footed and chews the cud but you shall not eat the camel … the rock badger … the hare … the pig, for even though it has divided hoofs and is cloven footed it does not chew the cud.'

'Anything in the seas or the streams that does not have fins and scales … they are detestable to you'. 'These you shall regard as detestable among the birds. They shall not be eaten … the eagle, the vulture, the osprey, the buzzard, the kite … raven … owl …'. (Leviticus 11.3–19)

'These are the animals you may eat, the ox, the sheep, the goat, the deer, the gazelle, the antelope … and the mountain sheep. Any animal that divides the hoof and has the hoof cloven in two and chews the cud … you may eat. Yet … you shall not eat the camel, the hare and the rock badger because they chew the cud but do not divide the hoof. And the pig, because it divides the hoof but does not chew the cud, is unclean for you.' (Deuteronomy 14.3–8).

(In addition, the list of seafood and birds as in Leviticus 11).

The Jewish dietary laws, based on these passages in Leviticus and Deuteronomy, were assembled in rabbinic pronouncements in about 200 CE and remained in force until the Reform movement gathered strength in the nineteenth century. At the Pittsburgh Conference in 1885, for example, the dietary laws were redefined as the product of particular historical circumstances and not necessarily of central importance to all followers of the religion.

Traditionally, these dietary regulations have been seen as resulting from a concern for public health. Pigs are clearly dirty and liable to pass on diseases, particularly in the hot Middle Eastern climate. Such explanations are still widely believed, but they have been increasingly questioned in recent decades. Pigs are not inherently dirtier than other animals and it has been pointed out that, of all animal-transmitted diseases, the most dangerous is probably anthrax,

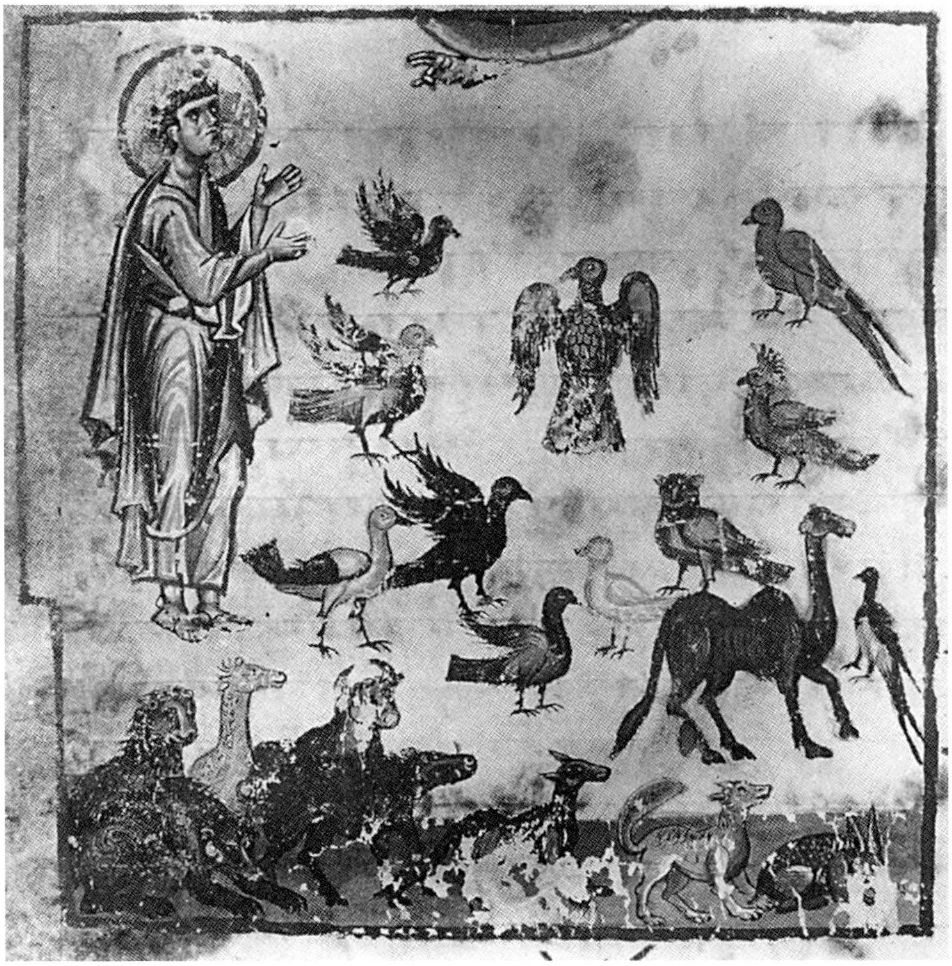

63. Byzantine Octateuch, c.1125–50. There are far more animals and birds than are mentioned in the Bible. Istanbul, Topkapi Serayi Museum, MS Gr. 8, fol. 282.

which is spread by sheep, goats and cows, but not by pigs. Indeed, it may be that pigs were singled out because they are so difficult to herd and hence not popular with nomadic pastoralists.[40] The emphasis on the cloven hoof and chewing the cud, which clearly excluded carnivores, indicates that the acceptable animals were herbivores, possibly following in the vegetarian tradition of Adam and Eve in Paradise. Whatever the origin of these rules, their key function was to enforce the observation of the laws of God. Dietary rules, furthermore, reinforce the table fellowship of any particular group observing them and are common to most religions worldwide.[41] At the time of Joseph, for instance, 'the Egyptians could not eat with the Hebrews, for that is an abomination to the Egyptians' (Gen. 43.32).

The rules laid out at length in Leviticus 11 and Deuteronomy 14 have remained of importance to the Jewish religion, but they were not taken over by the Christians and not deemed to be of symbolic significance for the events of the New Testament. Consequently, the scene of Moses expounding these laws was very rarely depicted in Christian book illustration. One of the few exceptions is the scene in the Byzantine Octateuch manuscripts where it illustrates the Leviticus text. The Octateuch in the Topkapi Serayi Museum in Istanbul of about 1125–50, for example, shows Moses receiving God's instructions and gesturing towards the birds and animals that fill the picture (**63**). There are no aquatic animals or reptiles, but far more animals and birds than are mentioned in the Bible. Apart from the four unclean animals listed – camel, badger, hare and pig – the artist has added a lion, bear and giraffe, as well as an ox, which is actually clean. The eleven birds of prey include a heraldic eagle in the centre, an owl, a parrot and a raven. The artist's enthusiasm in including so many animals and birds

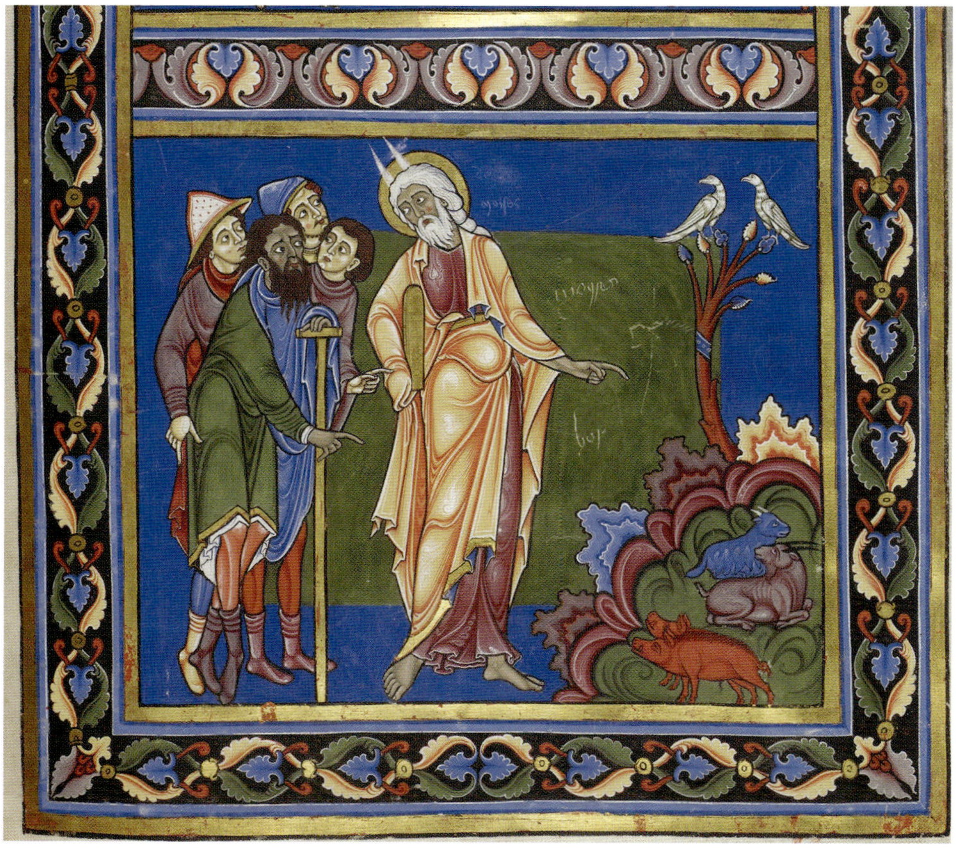

64. Bible from the abbey of Bury St Edmunds, c.1135, frontispiece to Deuteronomy. The horned Moses is pointing to sheep and goats, which are clean, and to two hogs and two birds of prey, which are unclean. Cambridge, Corpus Christi College, MS 2, fol. 94.

implies a knowledge of illustrated books of natural history.[42]

A more concise illustration appears in the great Romanesque Bible of about 1135 from the abbey of Bury St Edmunds, where it is placed in the frontispiece to Deuteronomy, immediately below a picture of Moses and Aaron expounding the law to the people of Israel (**64**). Moses is horned as a result of an earlier confusion over the Latin *cornutus* – meaning 'rayed' as well as 'horned' – the word used in the Bible to describe him as he descends from Mount Sinai. Here he looks back at a group of Israelites while pointing, with a marvellously extended index finger, to the animals. Sheep and goats are clean, the two hogs and two birds of prey are unclean. The Bury Bible provides a rare case in medieval manuscripts where we know the name of the artist. Master Hugo is recorded several times in the abbey's records and we might agree with the words of the chronicle, which describes it as 'incomparably painted'.[43]

THE NEW TESTAMENT

Nearly all the images discussed so far, under the Old Testament heading, were produced for Christians. Their religion had accepted the Hebrew Bible as the word of God, even though it had been surpassed by the story of salvation through Jesus Christ. Yet, although the Old Testament was interpreted as a forerunner of the Gospels, the civilisation it reflected was an ancient one and it is worth keeping in mind that the New Testament reflects the historical period of the Roman emperors, as opposed to the distant past of the Old Testament patriarchs. As we have seen in the examples of the Passover meal and the sacrificial meal of Elkanah and his wives, animal sacrifice was central to the Jewish religion. However, in the period of the destruction of Jerusalem in 70 CE, Jews no longer living in the Holy Land were considering ways in which it could be replaced. It was never adopted by the Christian religion. St Paul had ruled that there was no need for Christians to take up this practice, as Jesus had been sacrificed instead.

Another basic change was in the attitude to the biblical dietary laws. Moses had expounded the list of forbidden food to the Israelites (**63**, **64**) and the concept of unclean food survived in the New Testament.[1] Acts 10.14 describes Peter hearing a voice saying: 'Get up Peter, kill and eat.' But Peter said 'By no means Lord: I have never eaten anything that is profane or unclean.' Even so, Christians never adopted the Jewish rules of kosher foods. Abstinence and fasting have played a considerable part in the Christian religion and gluttony remains a cardinal sin, but there has never been a codified set of rules governing the imbibing of specific foods. For Christians a liberal position towards food is indicated by Matthew 15.11: 'It is not what enters the mouth that defiles man, but what proceeds out of the mouth.'

Yet the emphasis on the act of eating together remained as strong and fundamental as ever. The importance of the Passover meal was replaced by the centrality of the Last Supper to the Christian religion.[2] This is also reflected in the other meals at which Jesus was present and it gave the depiction of the meals a prominent part in New Testament illustration. Like the meals themselves, such imagery was used to strengthen and spread the faith.

11
JOSEPH COOKING FOOD AT THE NATIVITY

Many biblical illustrations have no basis in the text of the Bible, as we have seen in the case of Eve's apple. Most famously, the ox and ass at the Nativity, which appear in the earliest illustrations, are never mentioned in the Gospels. The scene of Joseph preparing the food at the Nativity is another such example. In general terms, it is part of the growth of everyday scenes added to images of the Nativity from the second half of the fourteenth century. This was in line with the growth of bourgeois culture in towns and with the increasing humanisation of religious imagery which enabled the lay community to identify with the stories portrayed.

The case of Joseph played a particular part in this development. In the Early Christian and early medieval periods his paternity was effaced as part of the emphasis on the divine origin of the Christ child. Yet, from the thirteenth century, the commentaries of Franciscan theologians in particular began to reconstruct his role as part of the growing emphasis on the humanity of Christ. As early as 1261 St Bonaventure emphasised Mary's role as virgin, wife and mother, while, half a century later, Nicholas of Lyra, another Franciscan, wrote of the Virgin's marriage to Joseph as necessary for the Child, for the mother and for the community of believers. The mid-fourteenth-century Italian manuscript of the *Meditations on the Life of Christ*, by a Franciscan theologian, contains an extensive and very human description of the Nativity, and its numerous illustrations give Joseph a prominent role. This tendency culminated in 1413–18 when Jean Gerson, in Paris, launched his campaign of writings and sermons to promote the sanctity of Joseph and the importance of his place as the legal father of the Christ child.[3]

The development of these theological interpretations profoundly affected the imagery of the Nativity and of Joseph's role in particular. In the course of the fourteenth century he is no longer shown merely seated or standing at the picture frame but increasingly taking part in the proceedings, such as helping the midwife in preparing the infant's bath. Most popular among such motifs and occurring particularly frequently in the period around 1400 is that of Joseph cooking food in a pot over a fire beside the Virgin's bed.

In an early example, Master Bertram's altarpiece of c.1380 from St Peter's Church, Hamburg, Joseph's role as husband and father is emphasised in showing him handing the child to his mother so that he can attend to the preparation of the meal which is cooking on the fire below (**65**). More typically, he is seated in the foreground, stirring the food in a pot placed on the fire. A variation on the theme shows him pumping up the fire either with bellows, as in a French Book of Hours of

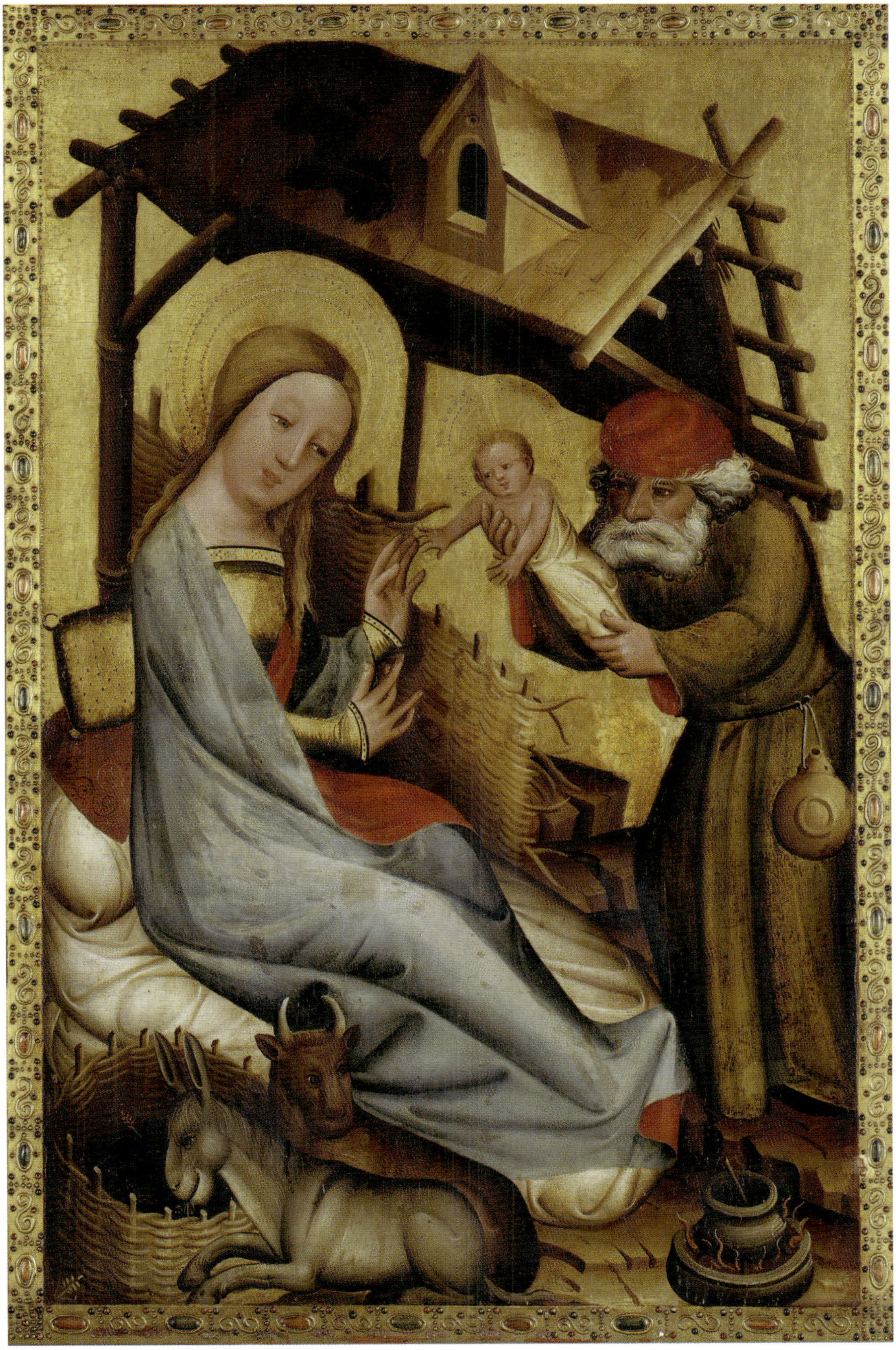

65. Master Bertram (c.1340–1415), panel from the altarpiece from St Peter's Church, Hamburg, c.1380. Joseph hands the child to Mary so that he can attend to the food cooking on the fire below. Hamburg, Kunsthalle.

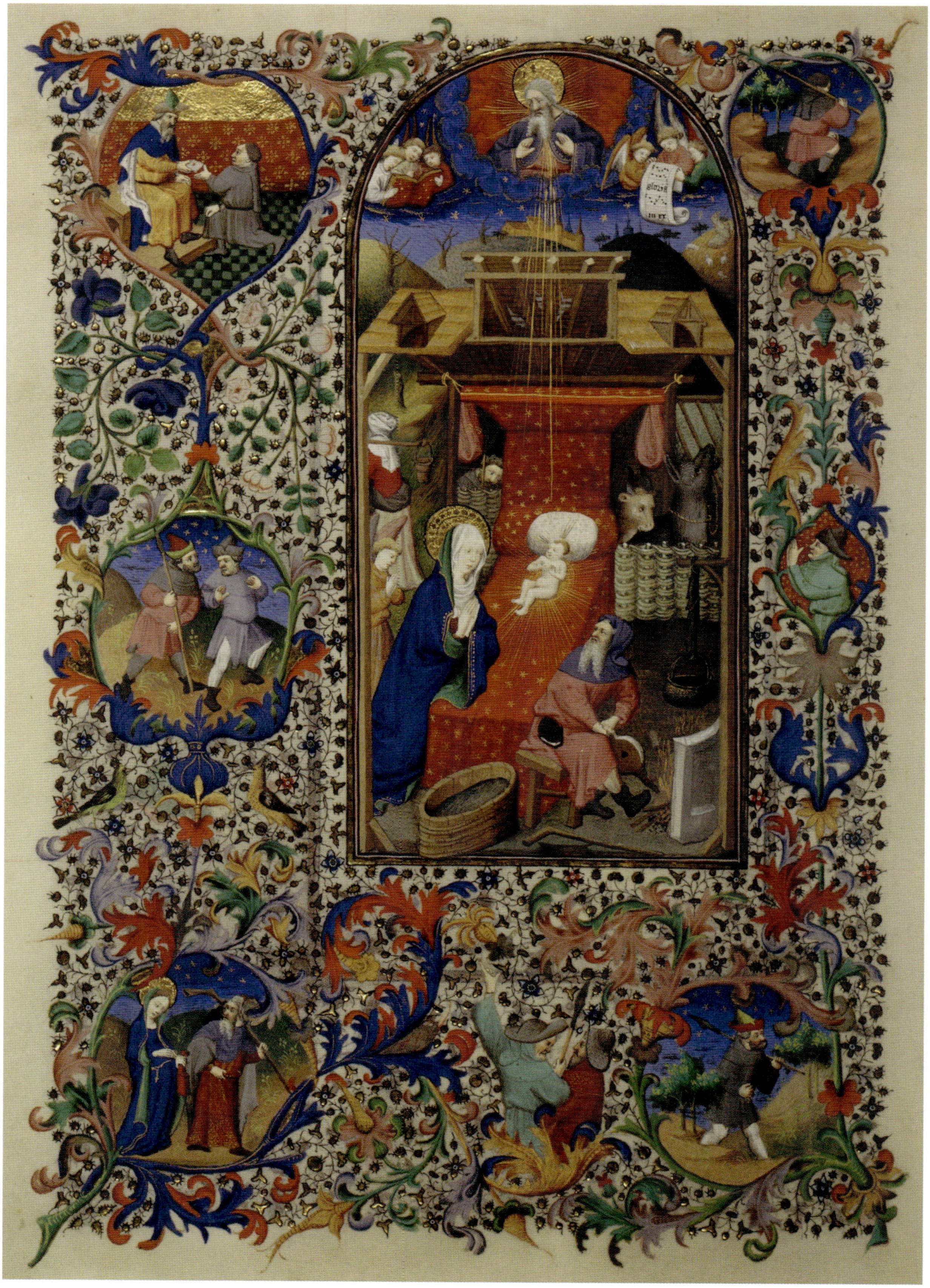

66. Book of hours illuminated by the Master of the Bedford Hours, French, c.1420. Joseph pumping up the fire with bellows. Vienna, Nationalbibliothek, MS 1855, fol. 59.

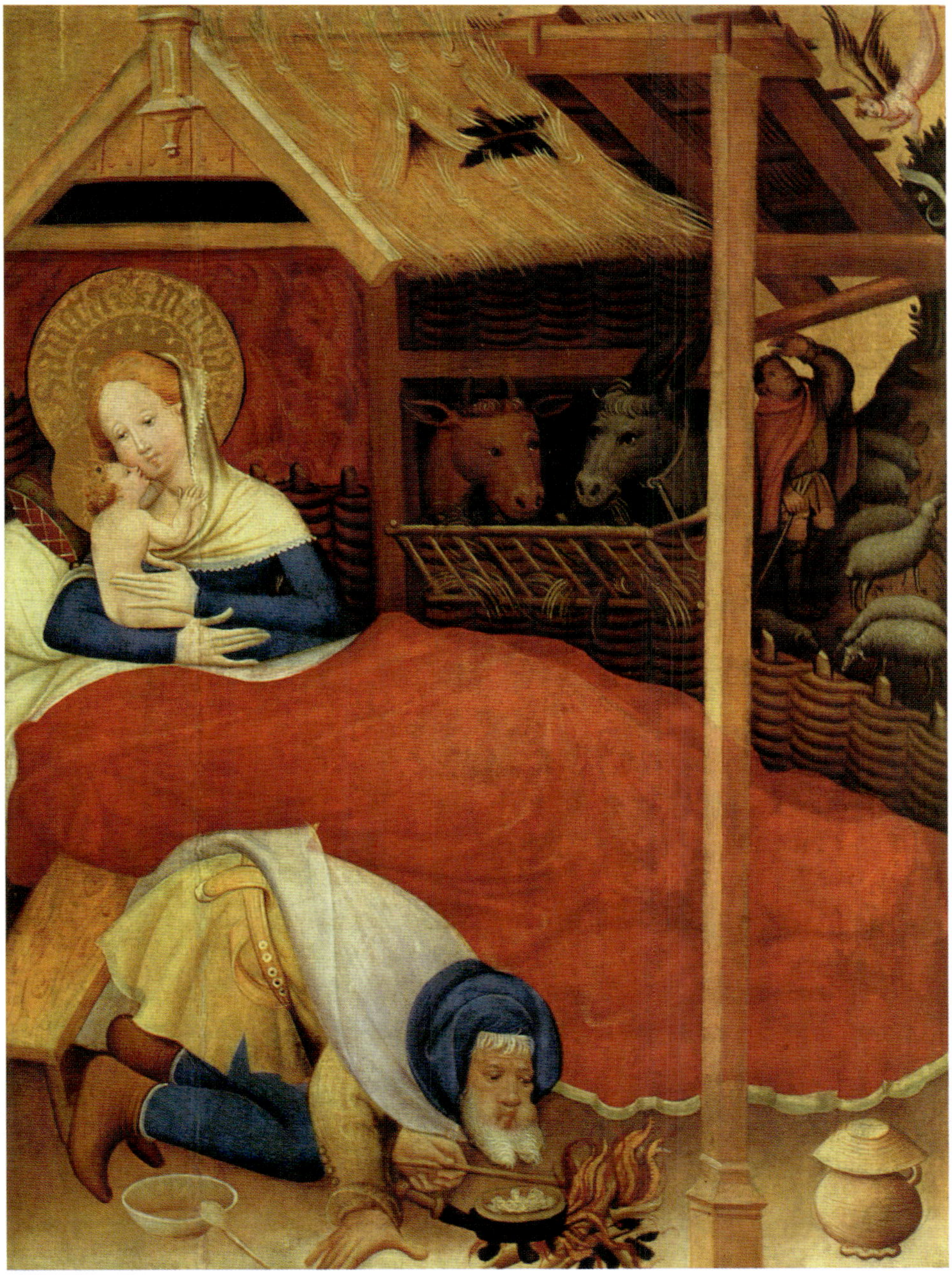

67. Conrad von Soest (c.1360–after 1422), panel from the altarpiece in the church at Bad Wildungen near Dortmund in Westphalia, dated 1403. Joseph blowing on the fire while cooking.

c.1420 (**66**), or by kneeling and blowing on it, as, for example, in the altarpiece of 1403 by Conrad von Soest in the church at Bad Wildungen near Dortmund in Westphalia (**67**). Precisely what is being cooked in these pots is not clear. The usual words of identification used, such as soup, broth or stew, seem more suitable for the mother than for a new-born infant, but that is hardly the point. What mattered was Joseph's newly proclaimed role as a caring and nurturing husband and father.

12
THE WEDDING AT CANA

On the third day there was a wedding in Cana of Galilee, and the mother of Jesus was there. Jesus and his disciples had also been invited to the wedding. When the wine gave out, the mother of Jesus said to him, 'They have no wine.' And Jesus said to her, 'Woman, what concern is that to you and to me? My hour has not yet come.' His mother said to the servants, 'Do whatever he tells you.' Now standing there were six stone water jars (Latin: hydriae) … Jesus said to them, 'Fill the jars with water.' And they filled them to the brim. He said to them, 'Now draw some out and take it to the chief steward.' So they took it. When the steward tasted the water that had become wine and did not know where it came from … the steward called the bridegroom and said to him, 'Everyone serves the good wine first and then the inferior wine after the guests have become drunk. But you have kept the good wine until now.' Jesus did this, the first of his signs, in Cana of Galilee, and revealed his glory: and his disciples believed in him. (John 2.1–11)

The story of Christ turning water into wine was very important as his first miracle, the opening episode of his public life. It was also a popular subject for illustration from Early Christian times, as it was seen as alluding to the Last Supper. This had been the interpretation of St Cyprian as early as the mid-third century (*Epistle* 63) and it became the standard view when it was expounded by St Ambrose (*De virginibus*, 3.1.1.)

This link with the Last Supper is emphasised in a fourth-century wall painting formerly in the catacomb of S. Pietro and Marcellino in Rome, where seven figures are seen reclining at a semi-circular table.[4] Jesus stands in the foreground tapping on six glass jars with his staff. Most of the Early Christian illustrations of the Wedding at Cana, however, omit the meal at the table and reduce the scene to its bare essentials, showing only Christ tapping the jars with his staff. The staff, which recurs in most of the early versions of the scene, is the thaumaturgical magic staff of classical art. In the early fourth-century Trinity sarcophagus in the Lateran Museum, for example, Jesus, who is shown beardless in these early depictions, is tapping one of the three jars placed

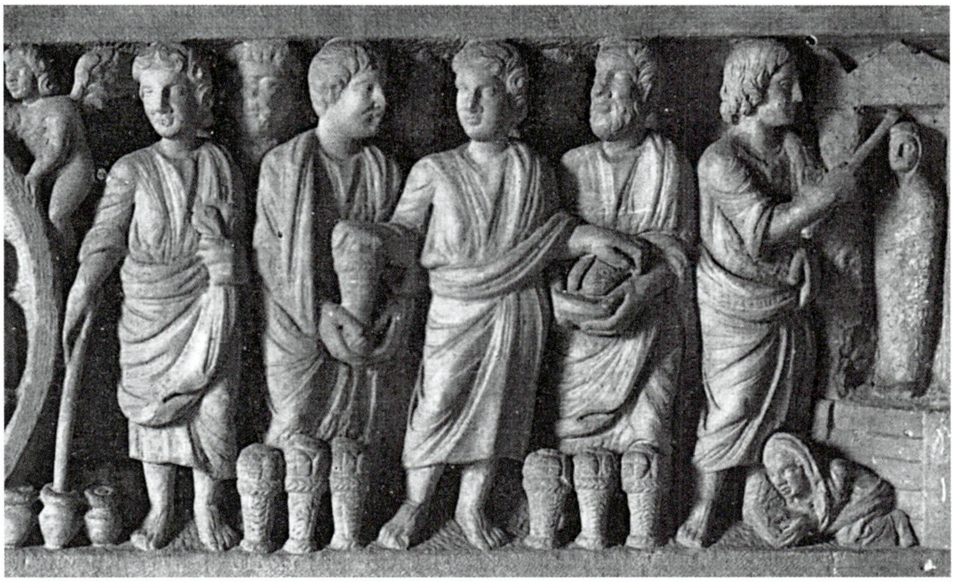

68. Stone relief, Rome, Trinity Sarcophagus, c.315. The Miracle of the Wine at the Wedding at Cana, with Jesus tapping the jar, is shown next to the Miracle of the Loaves and Fishes. Rome, Lateran Museum, no. 104.

at his feet (**68**). The scene is shown next to the Multiplication of Loaves and Fishes, with which it is often paired in the Early Christian period.[5]

Mary, who figures so centrally in the biblical text, is not shown in illustrations of the miracle at Cana until after 500. In an early ninth-century ivory in the Victoria & Albert Museum, which is probably based on an Early Christian composition, she is shown between the servant pouring the water from an amphora and Jesus holding his staff into the flow at the jars (**69**).[6] Increasingly, in both Byzantine and Western art, the meal at the table is illustrated in order to make the link with the Last Supper more explicit and vivid. The so-called Golden Gospels, produced at the abbey of Echternach, near Trier, in about 1031, depicts the couple at a table within a building, while outside Mary directs the servant pouring water into a barrel which Jesus is in the act of blessing (**70**).[7] More closely linked with the image of the Last Supper is the version in a manuscript from Salzburg, the Gospel lectionary of the abbey of St Erentrud of about 1140 (**71**).

The emphasis on the meal, so different from most of the Early Christian representations of the miracle, remains standard, but the later medieval versions are more concerned with the domestic nature of the wedding celebration. Giotto, in his fresco in the Arena Chapel in Padua (c.1305), shows the scene in an elegant interior with well-dressed guests (**72**). At the head of the table Jesus, his hand raised in blessing,

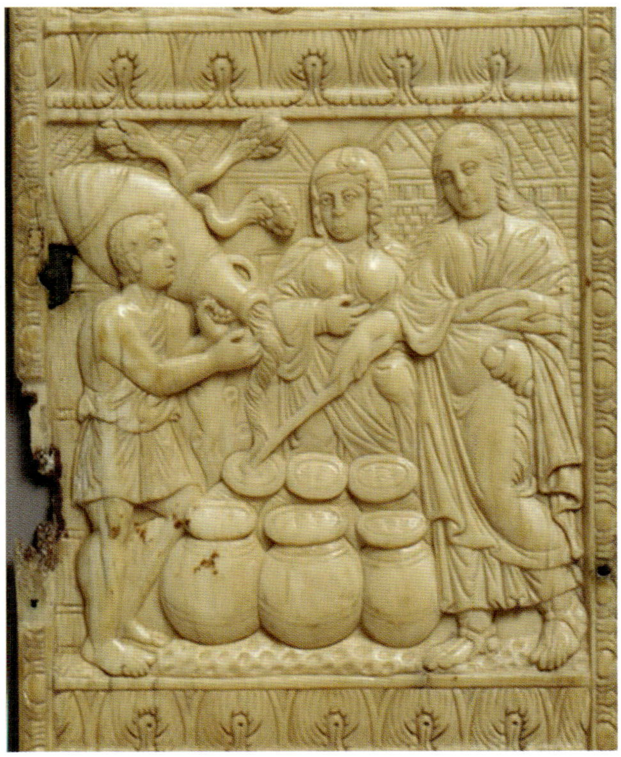

69. Panel from an ivory diptych carved with the Miracles of Christ, Carolingian, early ninth century. Jesus holds his staff into the water as it is turned into wine. Mary is shown in the centre. London, Victoria and Albert Museum, no. A.47a–1926.

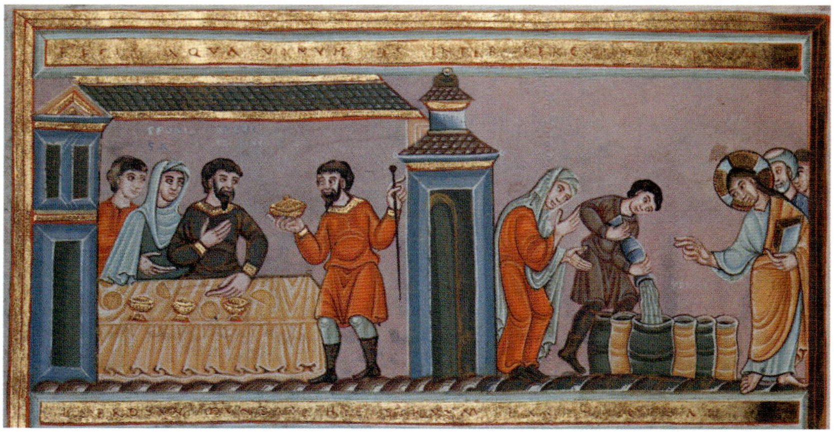

70. 'Golden Gospels' from the Abbey of Echternach, near Trier, c.1030. On the left, the couple is being served at the table, while Mary directs the servant and Jesus performs the miracle on the right. Nürnberg, Germanisches Nationalmuseum, MS 2 156 142, fol. 53v.

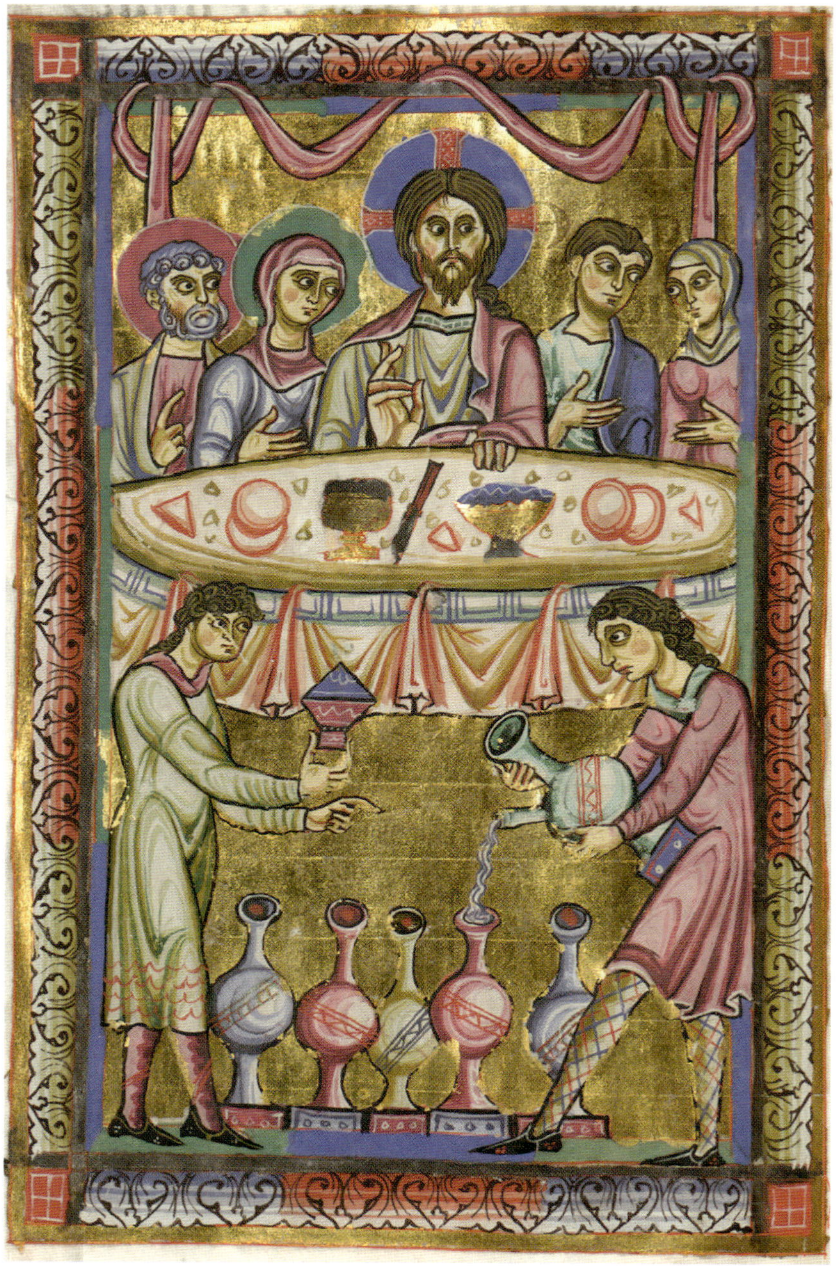

71. Gospel Lectionary of the abbey of St Erentrud, Salzburg, c.1140. Although the table is covered with fruit and dishes, both the gesture of Jesus and the symmetrical composition are closely linked with images of the Last Supper. Munich, Bayerische Staatsbibliothek, MS lat.15903, fol. 22v.

72. Giotto (c.1267–1337), wall painting in the Arena Chapel (Capella Scrovegni), Padua, c.1305. The bride sits next to Mary; the groom next to Jesus.

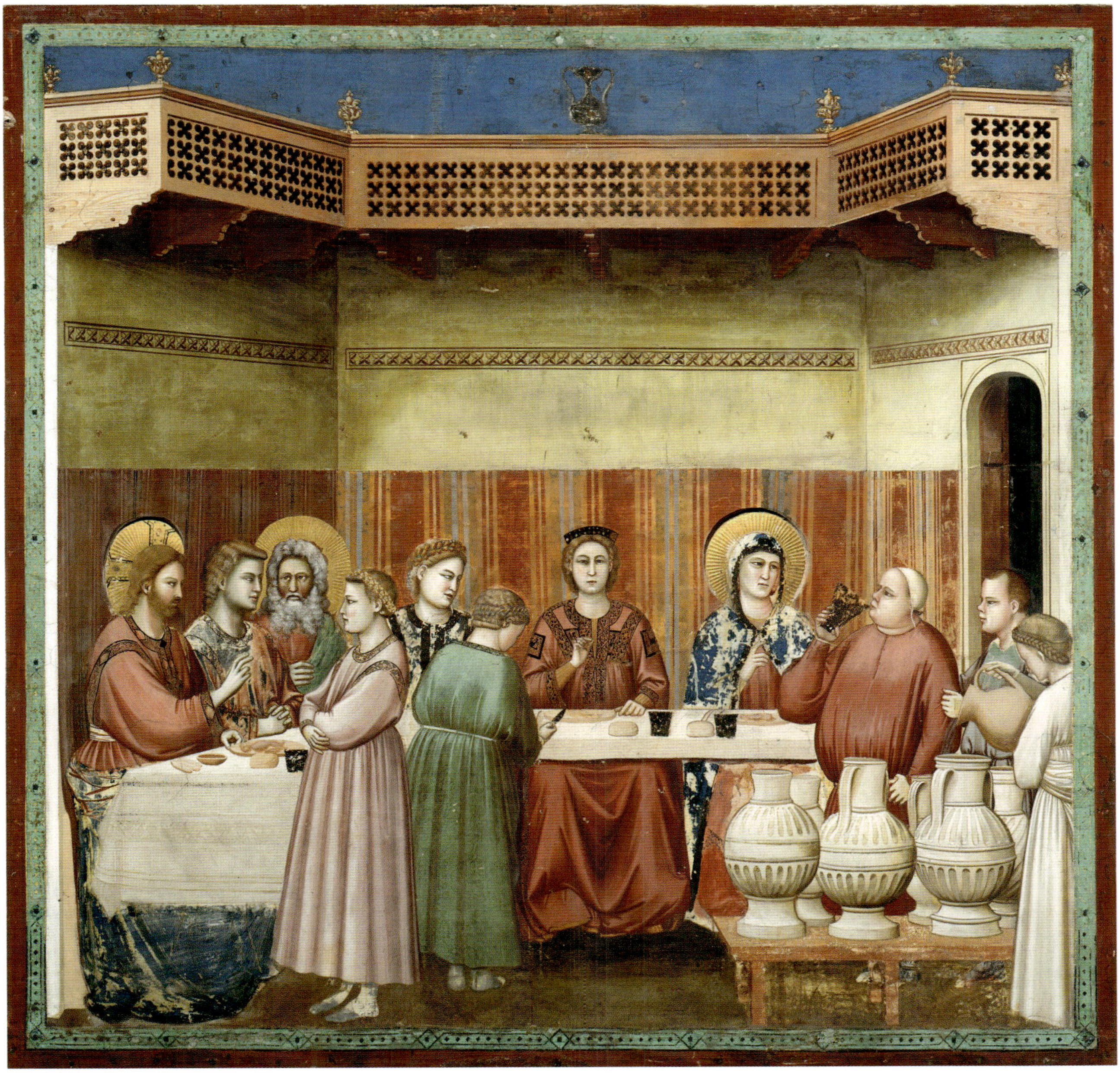

is speaking to a young woman, while another female servant is pouring water into one of the six jars set on a sideboard. The bride is seated at the centre of the table next to the Virgin. Her gesture of the index finger placed on the thumb has been interpreted as signifying her demand for only a small portion of food.[8] The groom sits between Jesus and an elderly bearded apostle, identified as St Andrew on account of his distinctive dress of red tunic and green mantle.

A near contemporary wall painting in the Upper Church of St Francis at Assisi is partially destroyed, but it does show a growing interest in the food served at the banquet, including fowl, fish and bread. Precise depiction of different tableware is to be seen in a fresco of about 1320–40, attributed to Pietro da Rimini, in the sanctuary of San Nicola at Tolentino, in the Italian Marches (**73**). This was part of the extensive decoration carried out for the Augustinian

73. Wall painting attributed to Pietro da Rimini, Sanctuary of San Nicola at Tolentino, the Italian Marches, c.1320–40, showing contemporary wooden, glass and pottery vessels on the tables. From this period the food itself is also more clearly depicted. The donors are kneeling below.

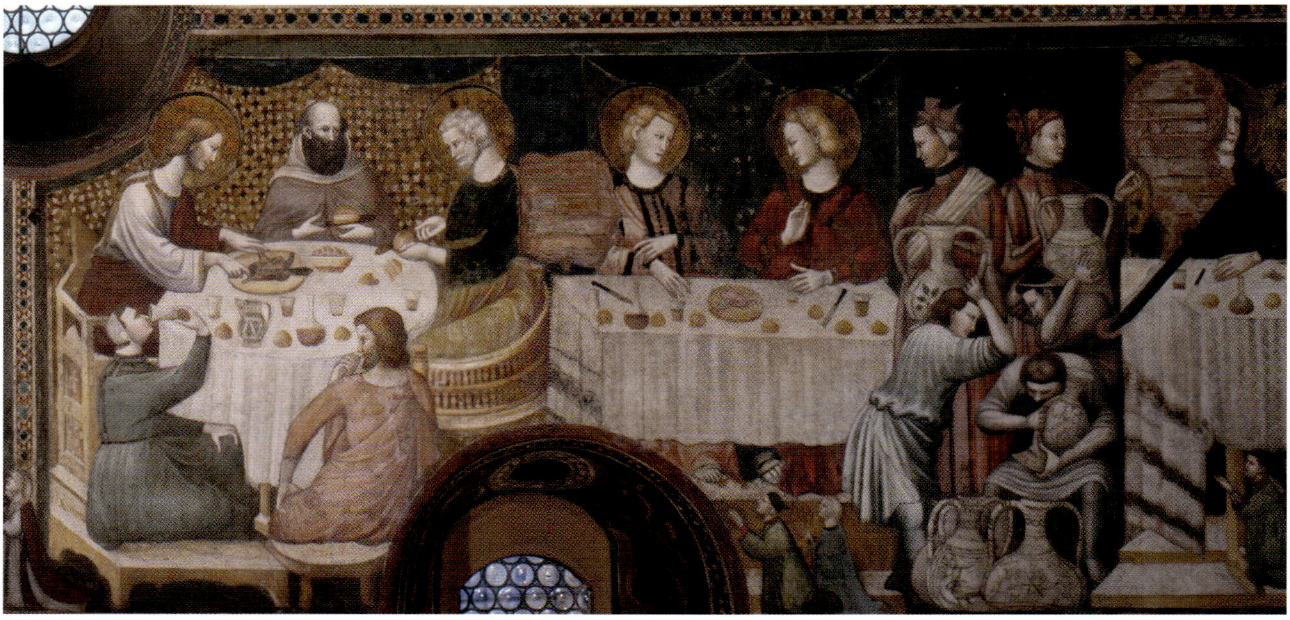

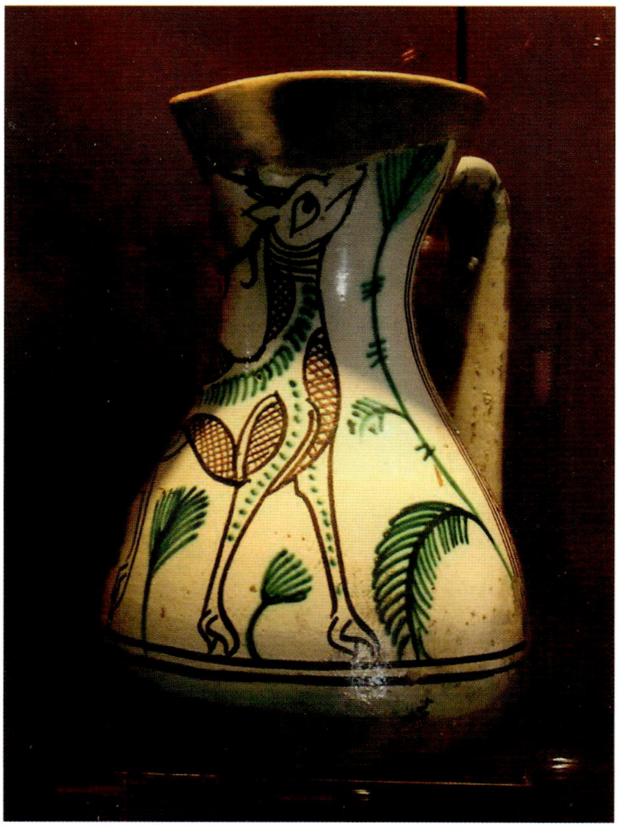

74. Maiolica jug, c.1300, to compare with the one on the round table at Tolentino. Bologna, Museo Medievale.

hermits, who were seeking the canonisation of Nicholas of Tolentino at the time.[9] The meal is shown taking place at three tables covered by patterned table cloths. On the round table at the left the fowl is being carved by a youthful apostle on a wooden trencher, the glass decanter is convincingly of the period and the ceramic jug has the shape and decorative design of early fourteenth-century tin glazed pottery. This is an early maiolica jug, characterised by its trefoil-shaped mouth and pedestal base with geometric and floral decoration, of a type made in Tuscany and Umbria as well as in the Marches (**74**).[10] The servants are attending to the elaborately dressed bride and bridegroom seated at the central table and also serving the table on the right, reserved for Jesus and Mary. The Wedding at Cana as depicted at Tolentino is unusual in taking place at three separate tables in a composition larger than any other of the life of Christ scenes in the chapel. It is also the only one to show two couples of kneeling donors, which raises the possibility that it is symbolically linked with actual weddings of the time.

The Wedding at Cana is less commonly illustrated in the course of the fourteenth and fifteenth centuries than in earlier times, but there is one surviving

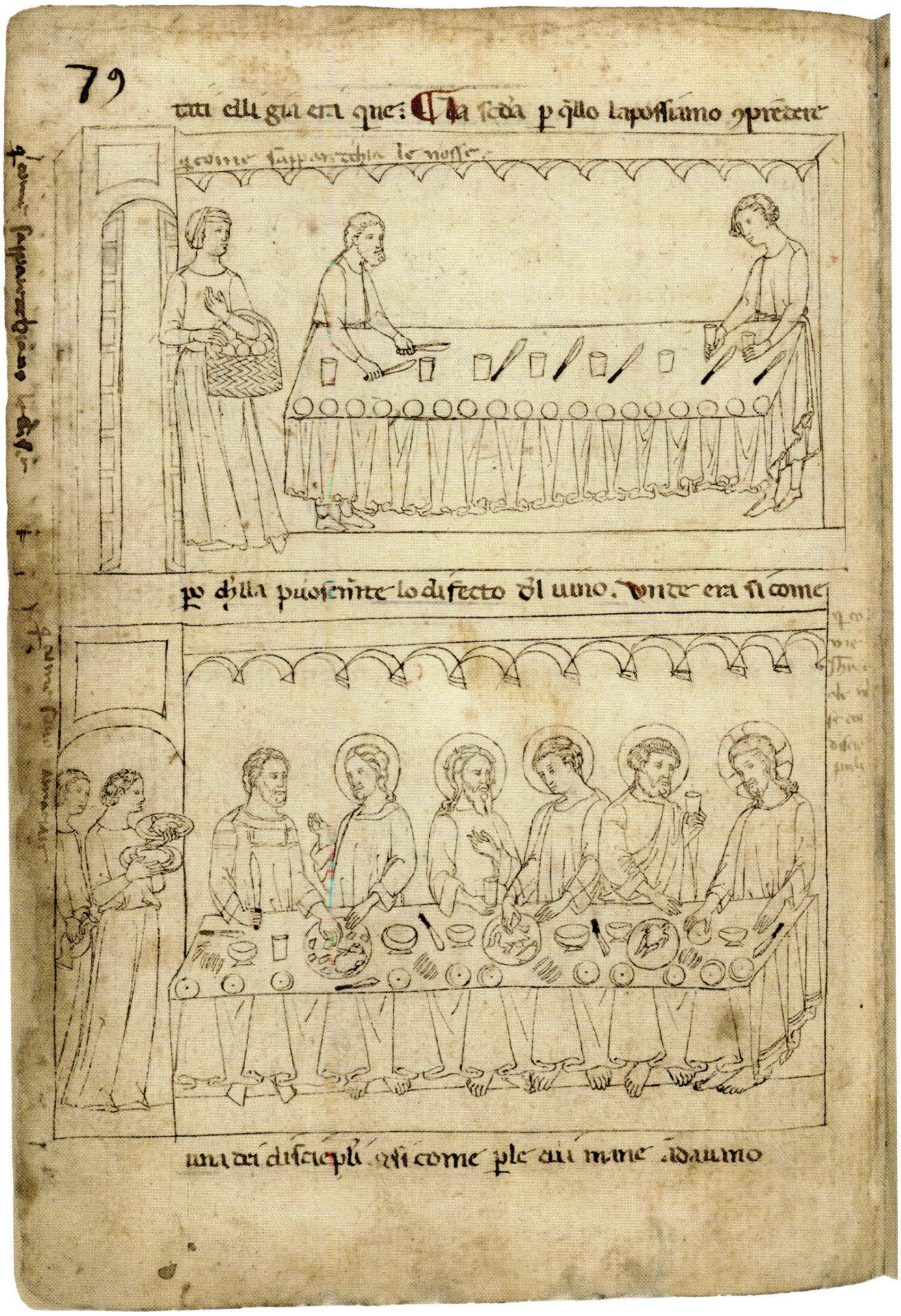

75. Outline drawing from the *Meditations on the Life of Christ*, Italian, mid-fourteenth century. A rare scene of the servants laying the table, followed by the meal itself. Paris, Bibliothèque Nationale. MS Ital. 115, fol. 79v.

manuscript in which the story is fully told in seven separate scenes. This mid-fourteenth-century manuscript is the most extensively illustrated of the *Meditations on the Life of Christ*, a Franciscan text that achieved great popularity throughout Western Europe.[11] It publicised the idea, taken from St Jerome, that the bridegroom could be identified with St John the Evangelist, and emphasised the role of the Virgin in noting the shortage of wine and taking pains to remedy the situation. She is the only woman, apart from the servants. To emphasise the merits of celibate life all the guests are men and even the bride is never seen. The two opening scenes show the servants, two men and a woman, laying the table with glasses, knives and bread rolls, an activity seldom separately illustrated (**75**). Then follows the first view of the

76. Gerard David (d.1523), oil painting on panel, Bruges, c.1500. The groom is carving the fowl and a boy is bringing in a pie to add to the fruit and dishes on the table. Paris, Musée du Louvre.

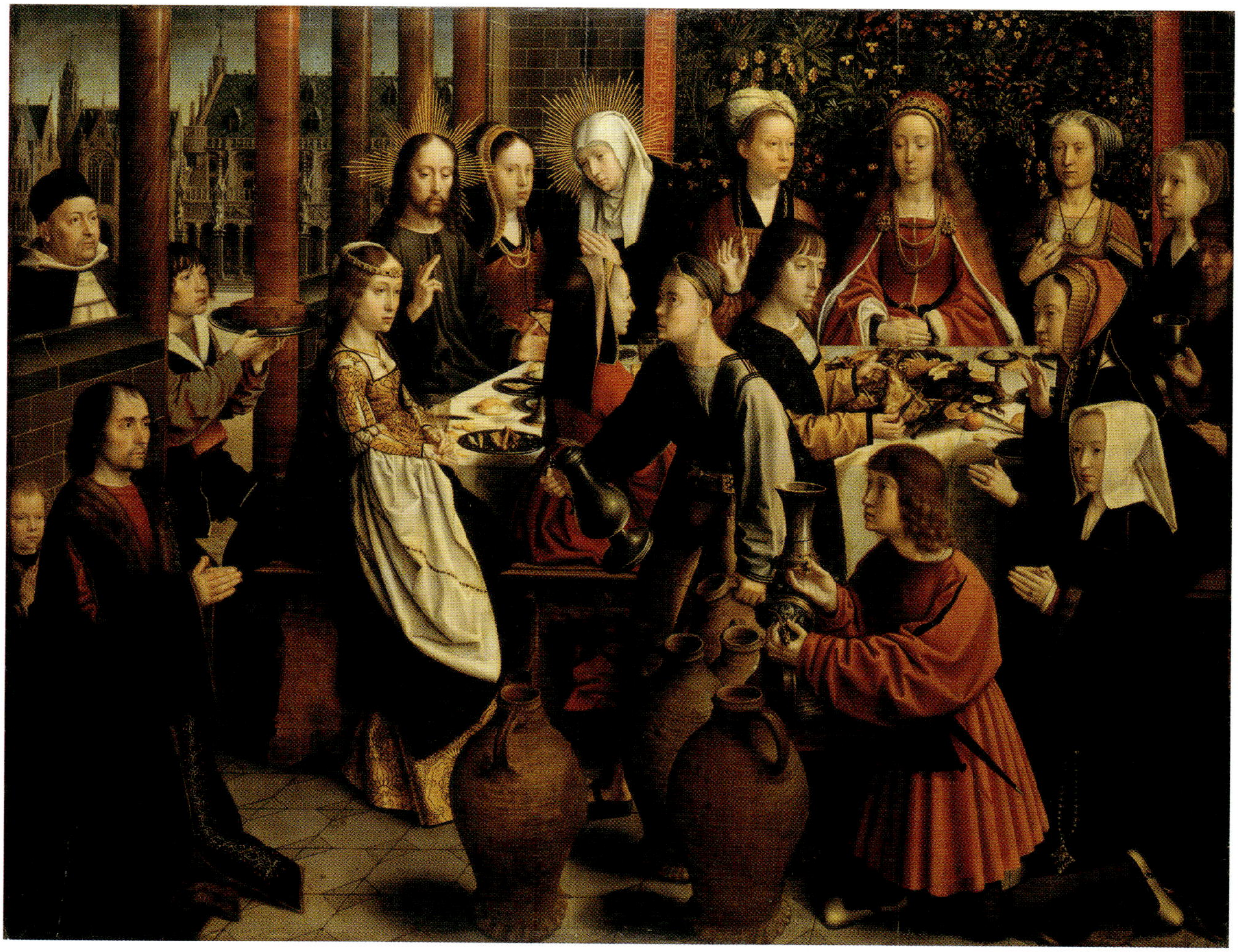

meal, with apostles helping themselves with their hands to the food placed in the dishes while Christ, modestly seated at the end of the table, reservedly fingers a piece of bread. The story unfolds in the following five scenes, but the food on the table remains the same.

By contrast, from about 1500 this biblical subject became one of the main vehicles for the depiction of festive and increasingly well-attended banquets. An early example of this trend is the oil painting by Gerard David (d.1523) formerly in the Confraternity of the Holy Blood in the upper church of St Basil at Bruges (**76**). The scene takes place in a room with a view through a colonnade onto the cathedral square. The elegantly dressed bride is seated in front of a floral tapestry, a symbol of fecundity; her groom stands opposite, carving the fowl. Jan de Sedano, the donor, kneels in the foreground, his wife facing him on the right. To add to the dishes and fruit on the table, a boy is coming in holding a pie on a plate. Meanwhile, two servants are pouring the water from earthenware jars into silver flagons while Jesus raises his right hand.

The most famous renderings of the subject in the later sixteenth century are the near contemporary ones of Tintoretto (1561) and Veronese (1562–63) (**77**, **78**). Both were commissioned to decorate monastic refectories in Venice: Tintoretto for the Frati Crociferi (subsequently moved to S. Maria della Salute), Veronese for the Benedictine abbey of San Giorgio Maggiore. Both are large paintings showing the exuberant aristocratic banquet crowded with a multitude of figures in grandiose settings – a dazzling display of wealth as it had developed by the mid-sixteenth century.[12] Both are also characterised by the Venetian emphasis on strong colour and elaborate costumes. Yet in all other aspects they are very different. Tintoretto's composition, set in a grand interior, is asymmetrical, with the table on the left extending to the far end of the room. The strong sunlight spreading from the windows illuminates the bride and the female guests sitting on the right of the table. Five dishes piled high with food are set in front of the guests, but it is impossible to identify their contents. The emphasis is on the servants with the jars in the foreground; a guest holds out her glass to receive the wine. Under the distant arcade, a servant wearing a turban is bringing in a basket of bread.

In contrast with Tintoretto's elegant interior and asymmetrical composition, Veronese has given the banquet an exterior setting, structured with the Palladian architecture of San Giorgio Maggiore, and a composition of spectacular symmetry. Such settings are typical of Veronese but they are also indicative of the fact that, as there was not yet a permanent single-purpose dining room, banquets in summer were often held outside in a garden or loggia. The calm figure of Christ is seated in the centre of the tumultuous crowd of guests, servants and musicians. The richly dressed princely guests, including the bride and bridegroom, are at the left table, opposite the clerics gathered on the right. Both the central position of Christ and the royal pomp of the occasion were emphasised by Pietro Aretino's Italian Commentary on the New Testament,

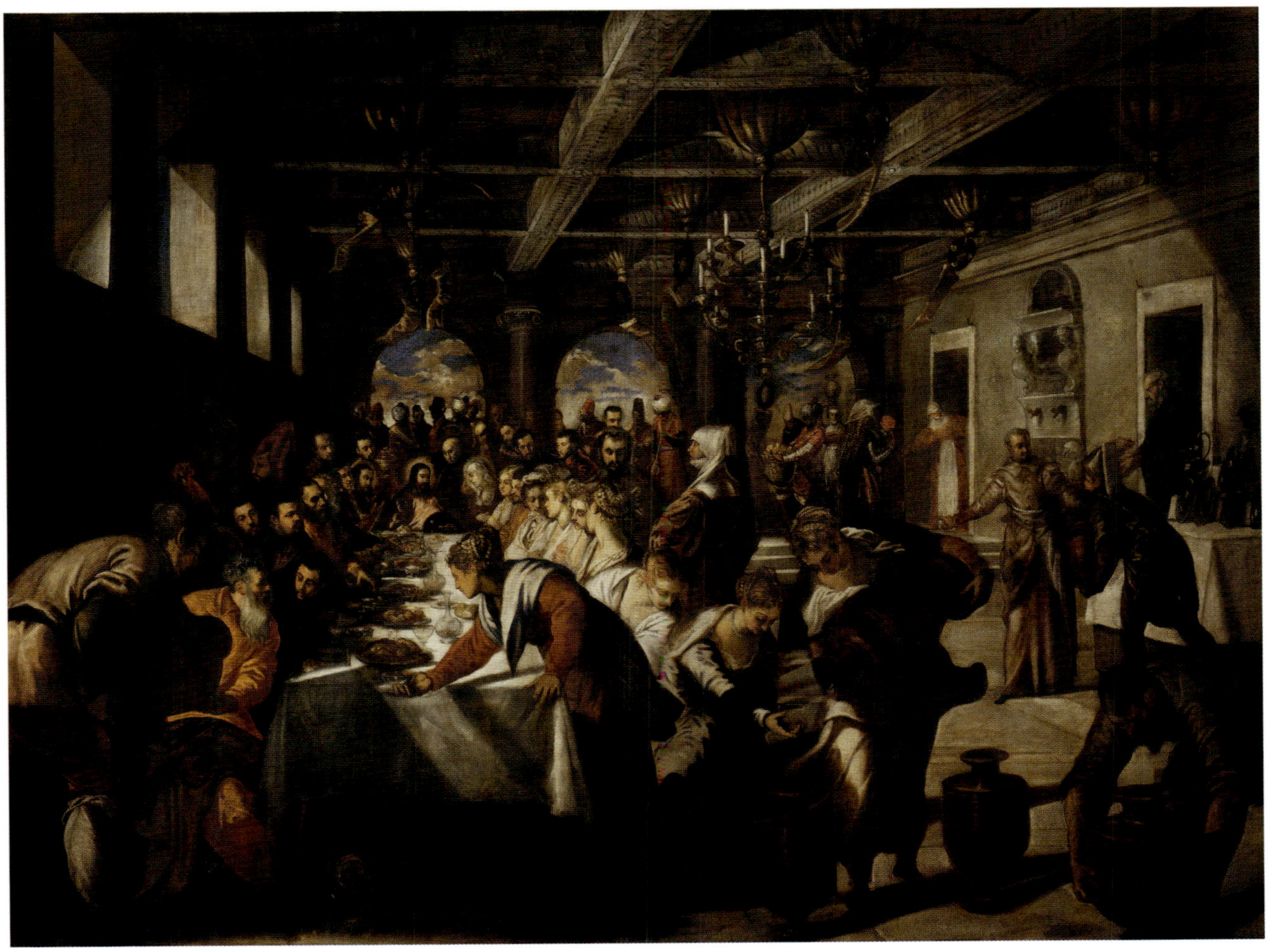

77. Tintoretto (1518–94), oil painting on canvas, 1561. Venice, S. Maria della Salute, sacristy. The setting of a grandiose aristocratic banquet becomes the norm in the sixteenth century.

78. Paolo Veronese (1528–88), oil painting on canvas, 1562–63. Paris, Musée du Louvre. The exterior setting is reinforced by the huge size of this painting (6.69 × 9.90m). The precision of the faces, hairstyles and costumes contrasts with the lack of detail when it comes to the food.

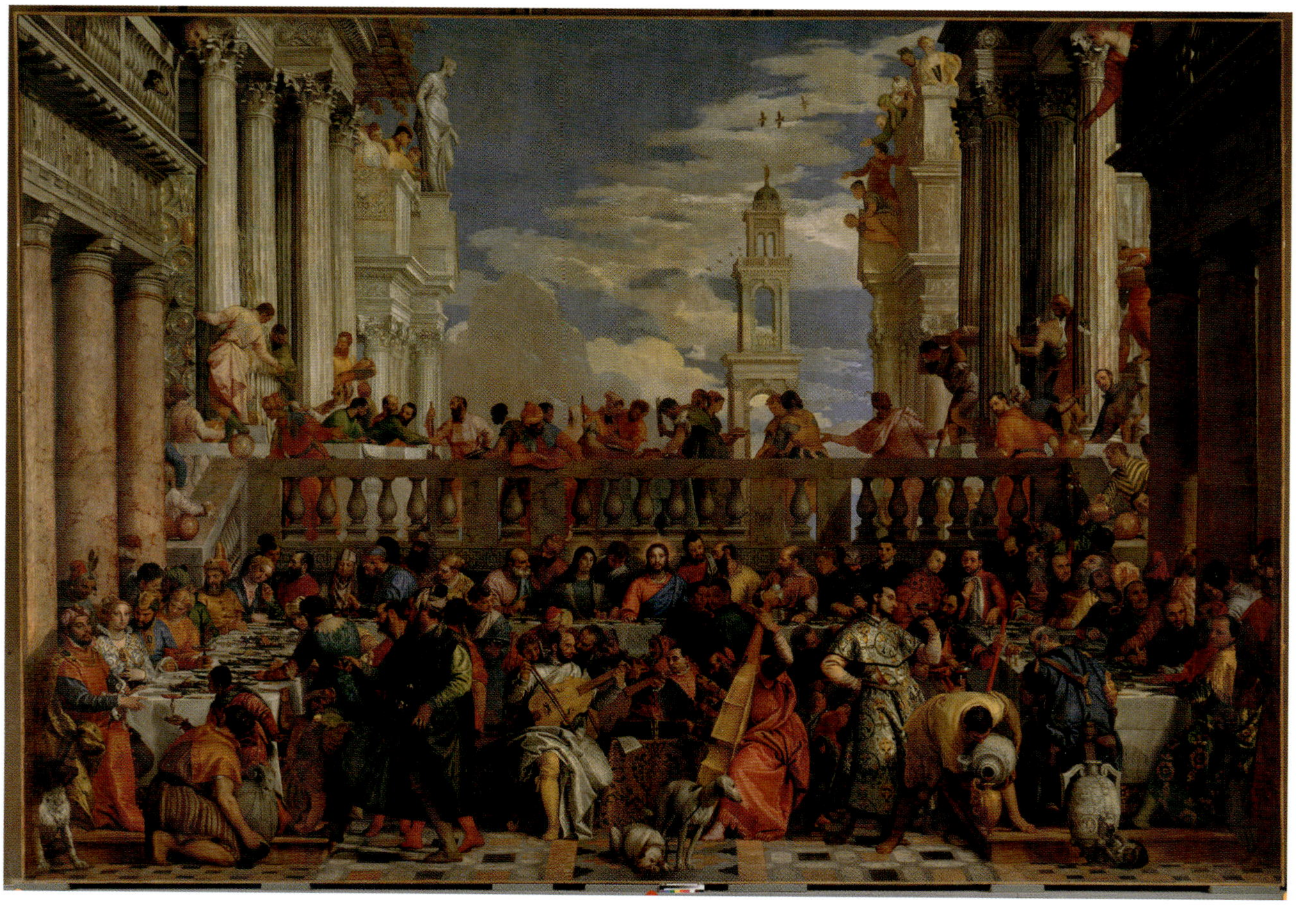

published in 1535, which contained a long paraphrase of the Wedding at Cana. Aretino lived in Venice and may well have been personally acquainted with Veronese.[13]

Each guest has a plate or trencher and a fork. The woman at the far end of the table on the left is using her fork to pick her teeth. Again, there is a large number of filled dishes on the tables, but most of the contents are difficult to identify. More so even than the earlier examples of this scene, there is a striking contrast between the extraordinary precision of the faces, hairstyles and costumes and the almost complete indecipherability of the food. On the left-hand table one can recognise a melon, while the small white balls have been identified as 'candy', a sugar dessert imported by Venetians from the Levant, evidence of the ever growing popularity of sugar in Europe at the time. A pie prominent on the right-hand table confirms that pies, stuffed with food of all kinds, savoury and sweet, had become one of the most prized items at such meals. In the biblical text describing the Wedding at Cana it is implied that the miraculous wine comes towards the end of the meal, when the original supply has run out, and here the guests are clearly on the dessert course, though it should be said that all the numerous preceding courses combined a mix of sweet and savoury items. This raises the question as to why the servants in the upper register are chopping meat and carrying fowl or lamb in dishes even when the guests below are already eating their dessert. It is likely that these preparations are for the secondary guests, but the central figure chopping lamb immediately above the seated Christ may well be meant to convey a Eucharistic meaning.

13
MIRACLE OF LOAVES AND FISHES

After this Jesus went to the other side of the Sea of Galilee also called the Sea of Tiberias … Jesus went up to the mountain and sat down there with his disciples. Now the Passover, the festival of the Jews was near. When he looked up and saw a large crowd coming towards him, Jesus said to Philip, 'Where are we going to buy bread for those people to eat?' … Andrew … said to him 'There is a boy here who has five barley loaves and two fish. But what are they among so many people?' Jesus said make the people sit down … So they sat down about five thousand in all. Then Jesus took the loaves and when he had given thanks, he distributed them to those who were seated; so also the fish as much as they wanted. When they were satisfied, he told his disciples, 'Gather up the fragments, so that nothing may be lost.' So they gathered them up, and from the fragments of the five barley loaves, left by those who had eaten, they filled twelve baskets. (John 6.1–14)

The story is told six times in the Gospels in two differing versions. In the first – Matt. 14.13–12; Mark 6.31–44; Luke 9.10–17; John 6.1–14 – there are five loaves and two fishes to feed five thousand. A second feeding in the same area is described in Matt. 15.32–39 and Mark 8.1–10. Here there are seven loaves and several fish and the remains fill only seven baskets. Mark (8.18–20) mentions both miracles as separate events.

The precise location where these events took place was identified by a little-known writer called Atheria, who made a pilgrimage there in the fifth century, as Tabgha, near Capernaum, on the Sea of Galilee. The church dedicated to the Multiplication of the Loaves and Fishes was probably destroyed during the Arab invasions in the seventh century and remained unknown until its excavation in the 1930s.[14] Among its decorations was a floor mosaic, probably sixth century, representing a basket surrounded by two fish (**79**). At the top of the basket four loaves, each marked with a cross, are clearly identified, despite the simplification of forms of this provincial version of the Byzantine mosaic style.

Christ's miracle of the feeding of the five thousand echoes the multiplication of food by Elijah and Elisha in the Old Testament. On one occasion, Elisha orders that twenty loaves be given to feed 100 men: 'Give it to the people and let them eat, for thus says the Lord "They shall eat and have some left"' (2 Kings 4.42–44). For Early Christian commentators, the Miracle of Loaves and Fishes, like the Wedding at Cana, was interpreted as symbolising the Eucharist. John's Gospel follows the feeding of the five thousand with a discussion of the bread from heaven which contains the key words of Christ: 'I am the bread of life. Whoever comes to me will never be hungry' (John 6.35). This link with the Last Supper, which was apparently not itself depicted at the time, explains the popularity of the feeding of the five thousand in Early Christian art, particularly in catacomb paintings and on sarcophagus reliefs. In the catacomb depictions, of which there are about a dozen surviving examples, mainly of the fourth century, the single figure of Christ is shown tapping the baskets with his staff. On sarcophagi Christ is seen blessing the loaves and fishes, which are handed to him respectively in a basket and on a dish by two apostles. The other baskets, their weave meticulously delineated, stand at the apostles' feet (**68**).

This three-figure composition remains the standard form even when the illustration was extended to include the feeding of the multitude. A sixth-century fragment of the Gospel of St Matthew, discovered at Sinope on the Black Sea but originating in Syria or Palestine, shows the traditional scene of Christ's blessing on the left accompanied by nine figures sitting on the ground and eating (**80**). In the centre the emphasis is on the seven full baskets specifically mentioned by Matthew as being left over when the crowds had eaten their fill. The text of Matthew 15.32ff. is written in huge Greek letters in gold on purple parchment. As in the other pages in this manuscript, the illustration is accompanied by prophetic figures holding scrolls referring to Old Testament forerunners of the scene depicted. On the right, Moses refers to the clean food of Deuteronomy 12.18: 'there you shall eat in the presence of the Lord'; while, on the left, David's scroll refers to Psalm 145.15: 'the eyes of all look to you and you give them this food in due season'.[15]

The Early Christian composition of Christ blessing the loaves and fishes held by two apostles was again taken up in the early ninth-century ivory diptych in the Victoria & Albert Museum (**81**), which also contains the Wedding at Cana (**69**). Yet in nearly all later renderings of the scene the feeding of the multitude is also included. The Gospels of the German emperor Otto III, produced at the abbey of

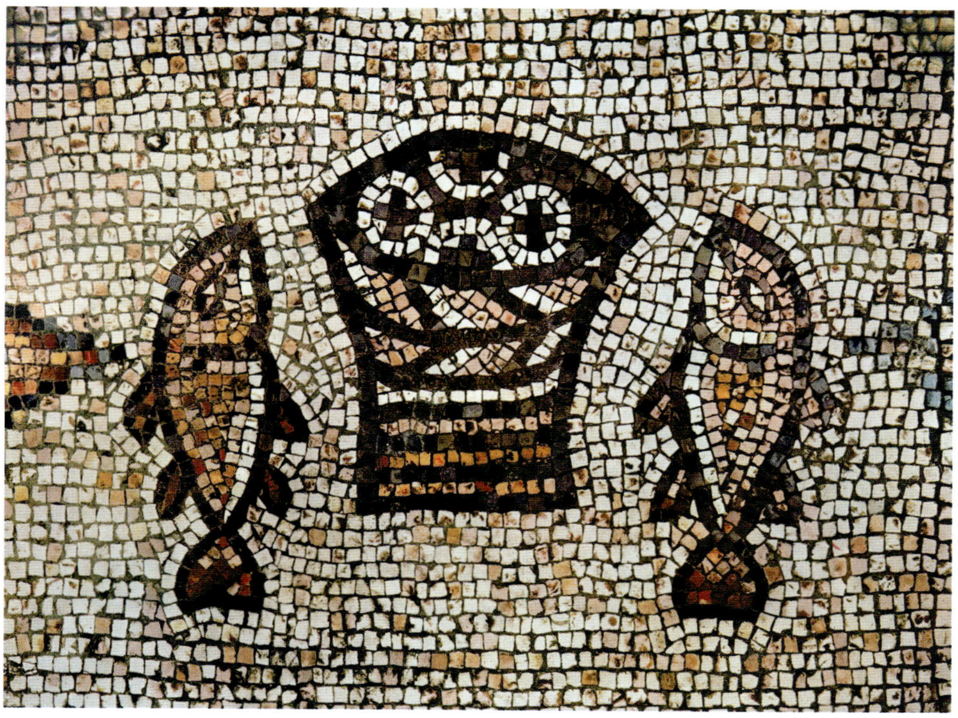

79. Floor mosaic, two fish and four loaves, sixth century. Tabgha, Israel, Church of the Multiplication of Loaves and Fishes.

80. Illustration from a manuscript of the Gospel of St Matthew (codex Sinopensis), Syrian or Palestinian, sixth century. Christ blessing the loaves and fishes, the multitude eating while the remaining seven baskets are shown in the centre. Paris, Bibliothèque Nationale. MS suppl. gr.1286, fol. 15.

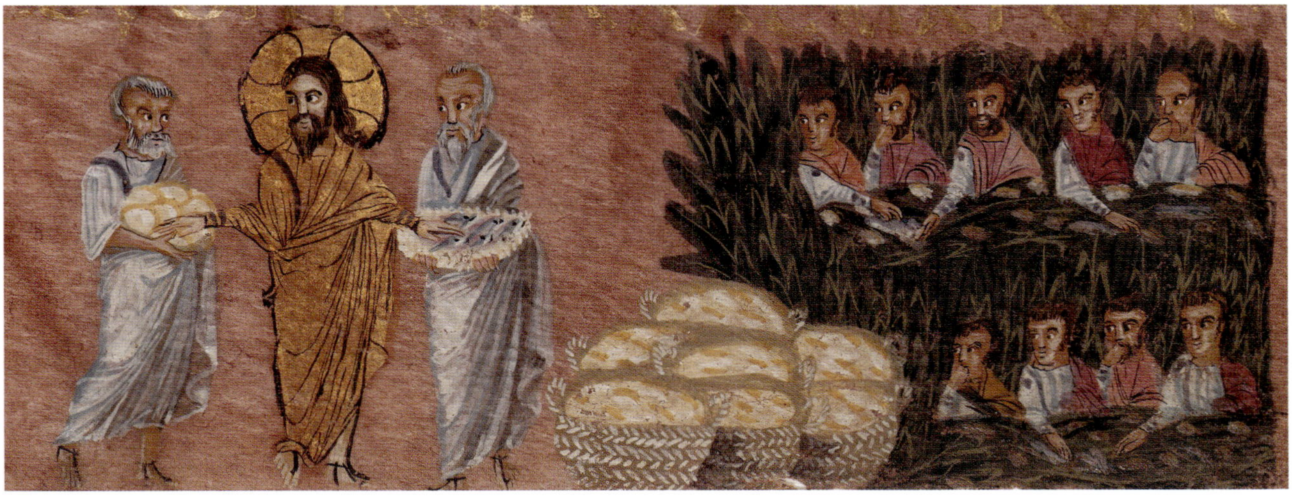

Reichenau in about 998–1001, has Christ's blessing in the upper register while, below, three groups of people are seated on the ground around the twelve baskets of loaves specifically mentioned in John 6.13 (**82**). This is one of the most expressive of the numerous early medieval versions of the story. The thoughtful other worldliness of Christ and the apostles is contrasted with the ravenous multitude, all looking up at the source of their salvation while eagerly eating.

Like the Wedding at Cana, the Multiplication of Loaves and Fishes is much less frequently illustrated in the twelfth to fourteenth centuries than in earlier periods. The emphasis in illustrated cycles is on the central subjects of Christ's Nativity and Passion rather than on the miracles. Among the exceptions to this generalisation is the Westminster Abbey altarpiece of c.1260. This is partially destroyed and the scene is no longer discernible in detail, but it clearly shows Christ himself handing out the bread to the seated multitude.[16] This interpretation of the event reappears in another English version, the Queen Mary Psalter – so-called because it was seized by a customs official and presented to the Tudor queen in 1553 (**83**). This is a richly illuminated East Anglian manuscript of about 1310–20, one of the most fully illustrated of all English psalters and clearly produced for an aristocratic patron.

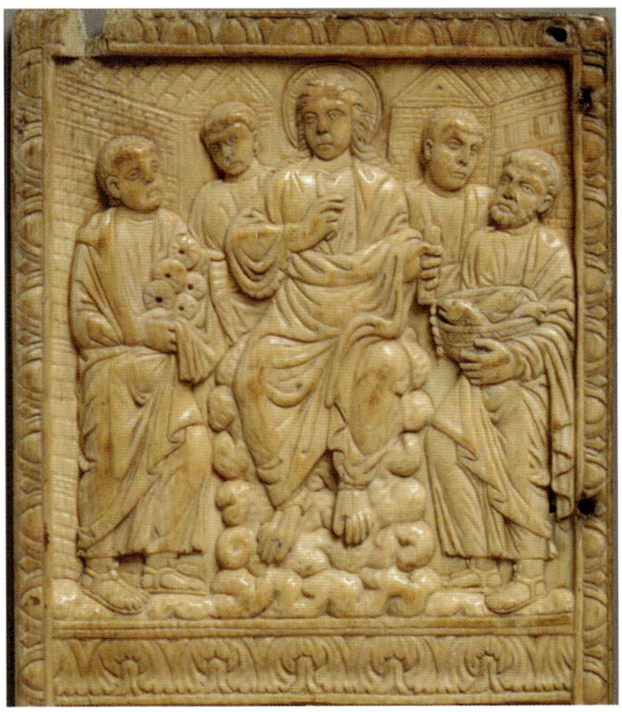

81. Panel from an ivory diptych carved with the Miracles of Christ ('Andrews diptych'), Carolingian, early ninth century. Christ is beardless, as in Early Christian depictions. London, Victoria and Albert Museum, A.47–1926.

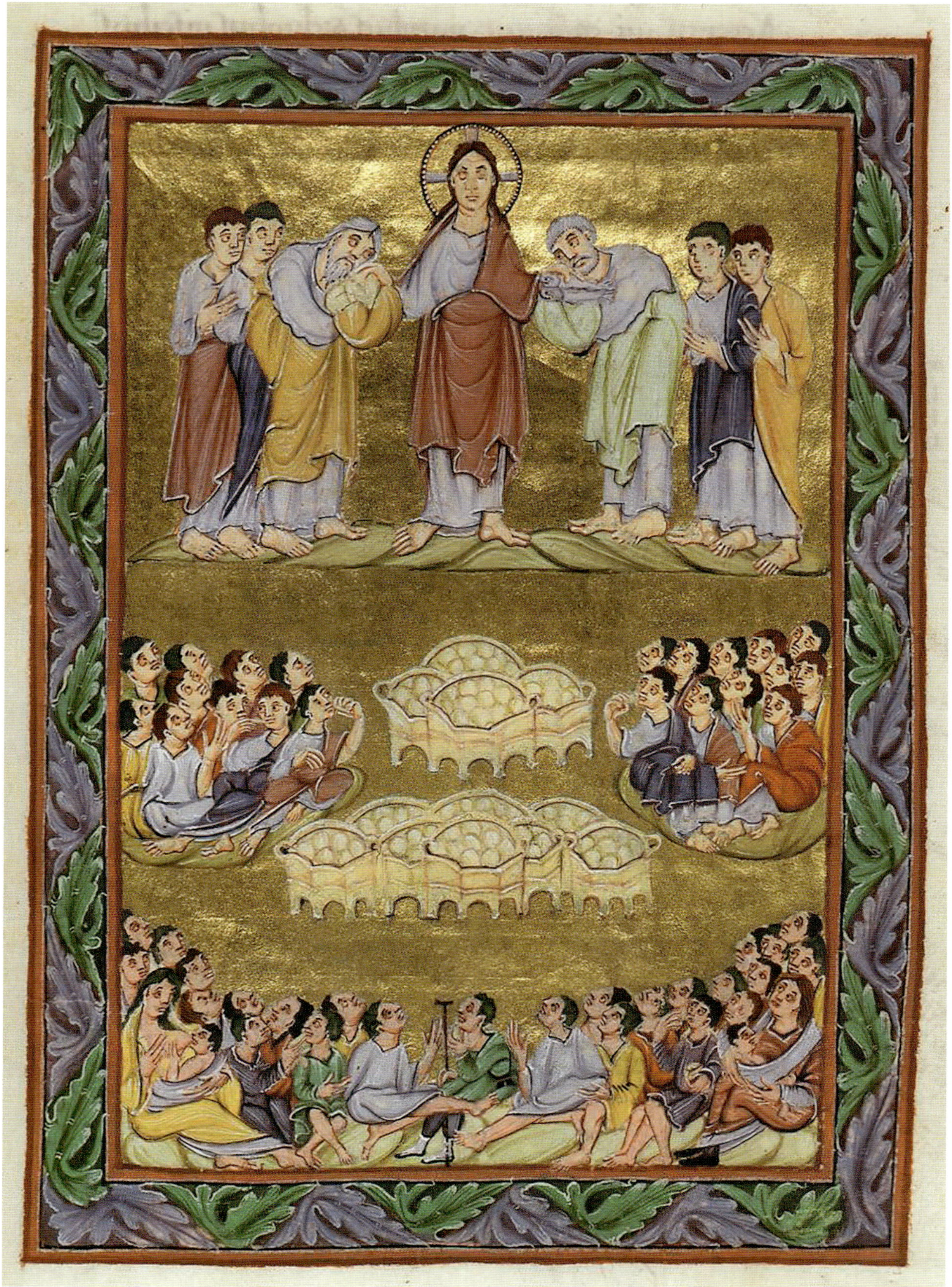

82. Gospels of Otto III, c.998–1001, from the abbey of Reichenau. Here twelve baskets are left over, following John's Gospel. Munich, Bayerische Staatsbibliothek, Clm. 4453, fol. 163.

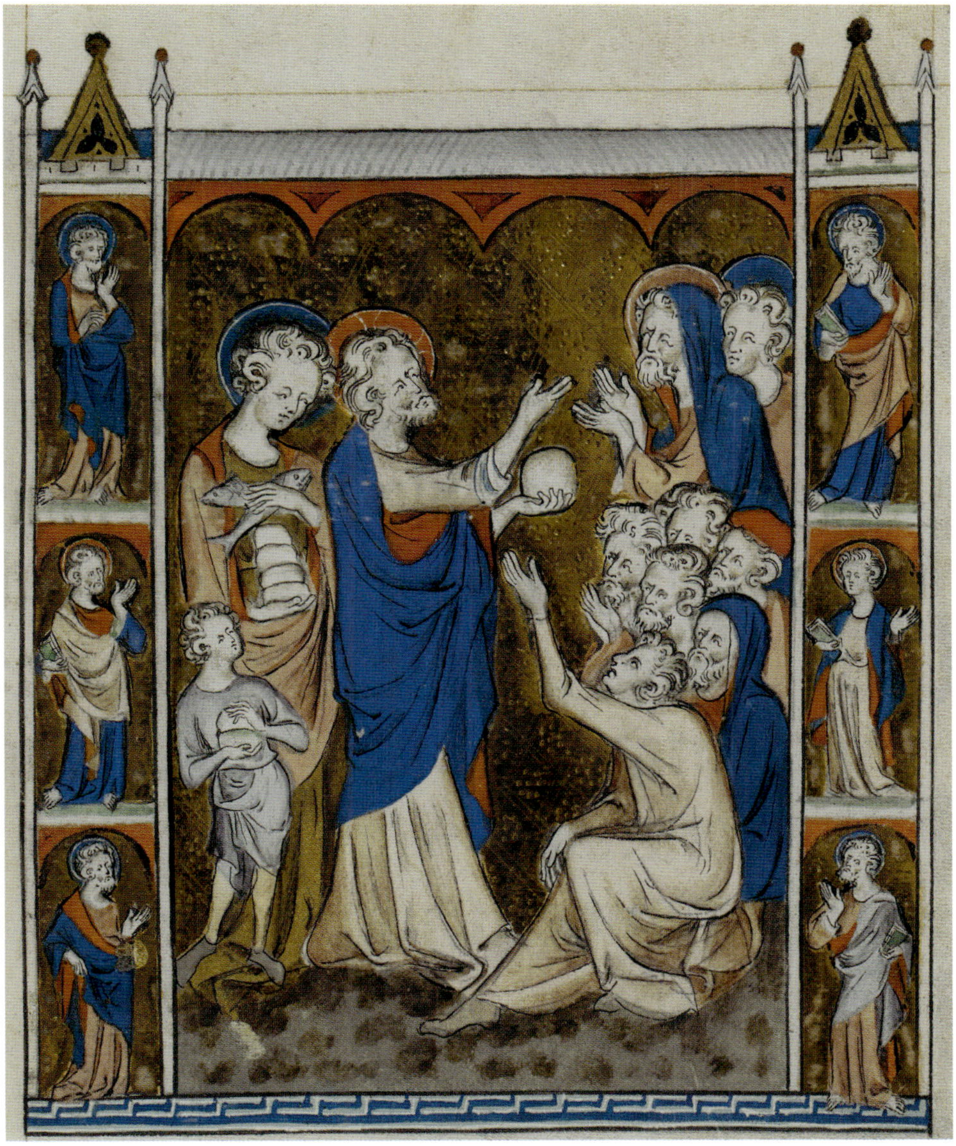

83. Queen Mary Psalter, East Anglia, c.1310–20. An apostle holds the loaves and fish, but this is also an early example of the boy holding loaves mentioned by John. British Library, MS Royal 2.B.VII, fol. 169.

There are two large miniatures at each of the eight liturgical divisions of the psalms. The Feeding of the Five Thousand appears together with the Wedding at Cana at the opening of Psalm 68 (69 in the current numeration), beginning with the words 'Save me O god, for the waters have come up to my neck.' This plea for deliverance is usually illustrated by a picture of Jonah and the whale, which more directly refers to the waters, but there are other examples of the Multiplication of the Loaves and Fishes depicted in psalters at Psalm 68. In the Queen Mary Psalter the loaves and two fishes are held by an apostle behind Jesus, but this is also an early example of the emphasis on the boy mentioned in John's Gospel as 'having five barley loaves and two fish', who is shown here holding two loaves.

He becomes a central feature in most of the subsequent compositions of the scene. For example, he is prominently holding a plate with two fish in a famous Book of Hours of c.1414–16, the *Très Riches Heures* of Jean duc de Berry, the younger brother of Charles V, king of France (**84**).[17] This is the masterpiece of the Limbourg brothers, who were notable for their naturalistic rendering of landscape, showing far greater depth than other artists of the time. The miracle illustrates one of the Lenten Masses, which appear only rarely in Books of Hours. Not surprisingly in a manuscript of such aristocratic patronage, the figures of the 'hungry multitude' are very grandly dressed in exotic oriental costumes, though the artist has followed the biblical text in showing them seated on the grass, as in Matthew 14. The figure of God the Father in the lobe at the top presides over the scene, as he does in other miniatures in this manuscript.

The tradition of having such well-dressed figures reappears at the end of the fifteenth century in, for example, the central panel of a Flemish triptych attributed to the Brussels artist known as the Master of the Catherine Legend and now in the National Gallery of Victoria at Melbourne (**85**).[18] Here the diners are mainly in contemporary costume of about 1490, apparently more in need of spiritual than physical food. The composition is unusual in placing Christ and the apostles in the distance, leaving the emphasis entirely on the individually portrayed

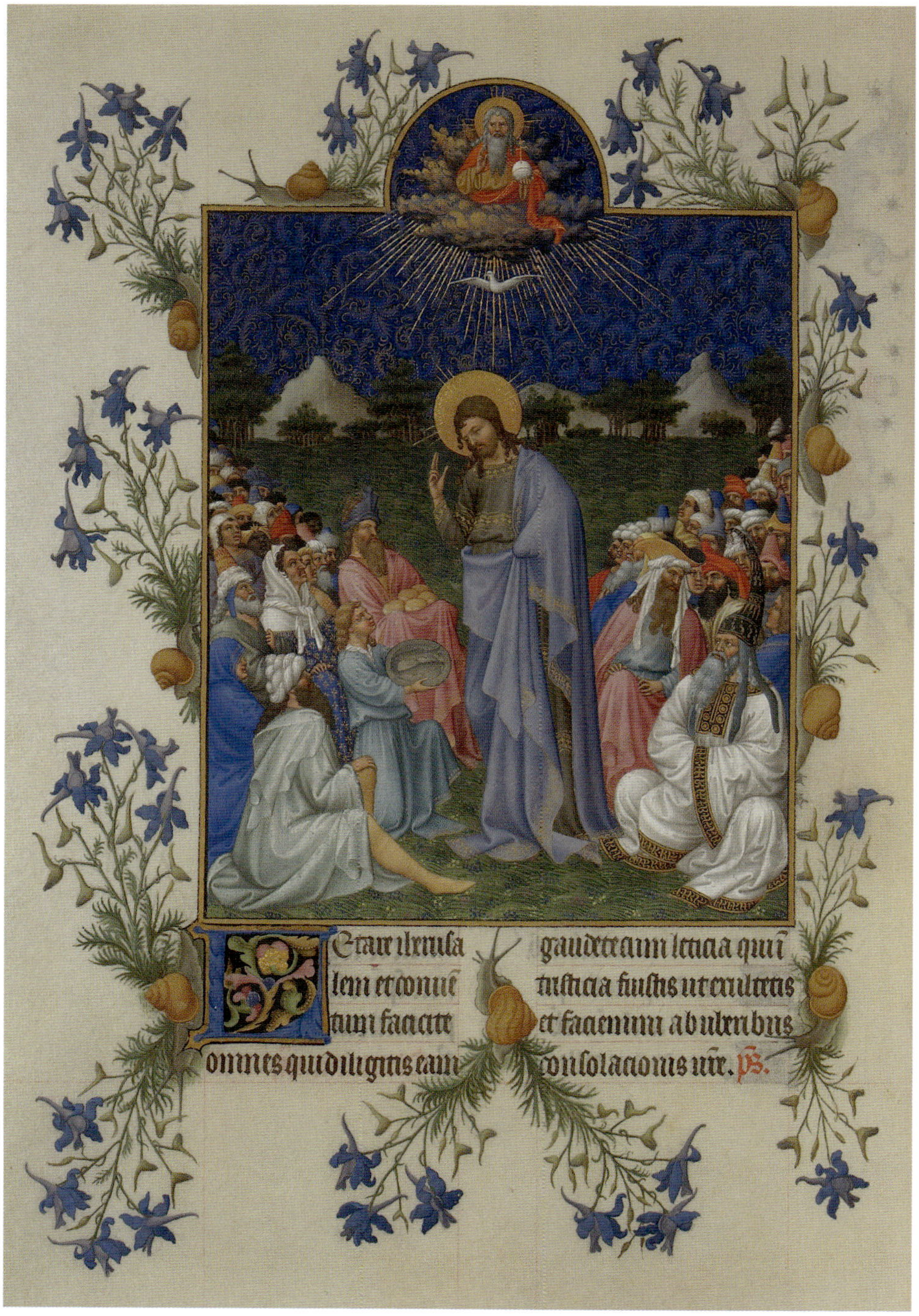

84. Book of Hours, the *Très Riches Heures* of the Duc de Berry, c.1414–16. The hungry multitude is very grandly dressed in exotic oriental costumes, while the boy holding two fishes stands before Christ. Chantilly, Musée Condé, MS 65, fol. 168v.

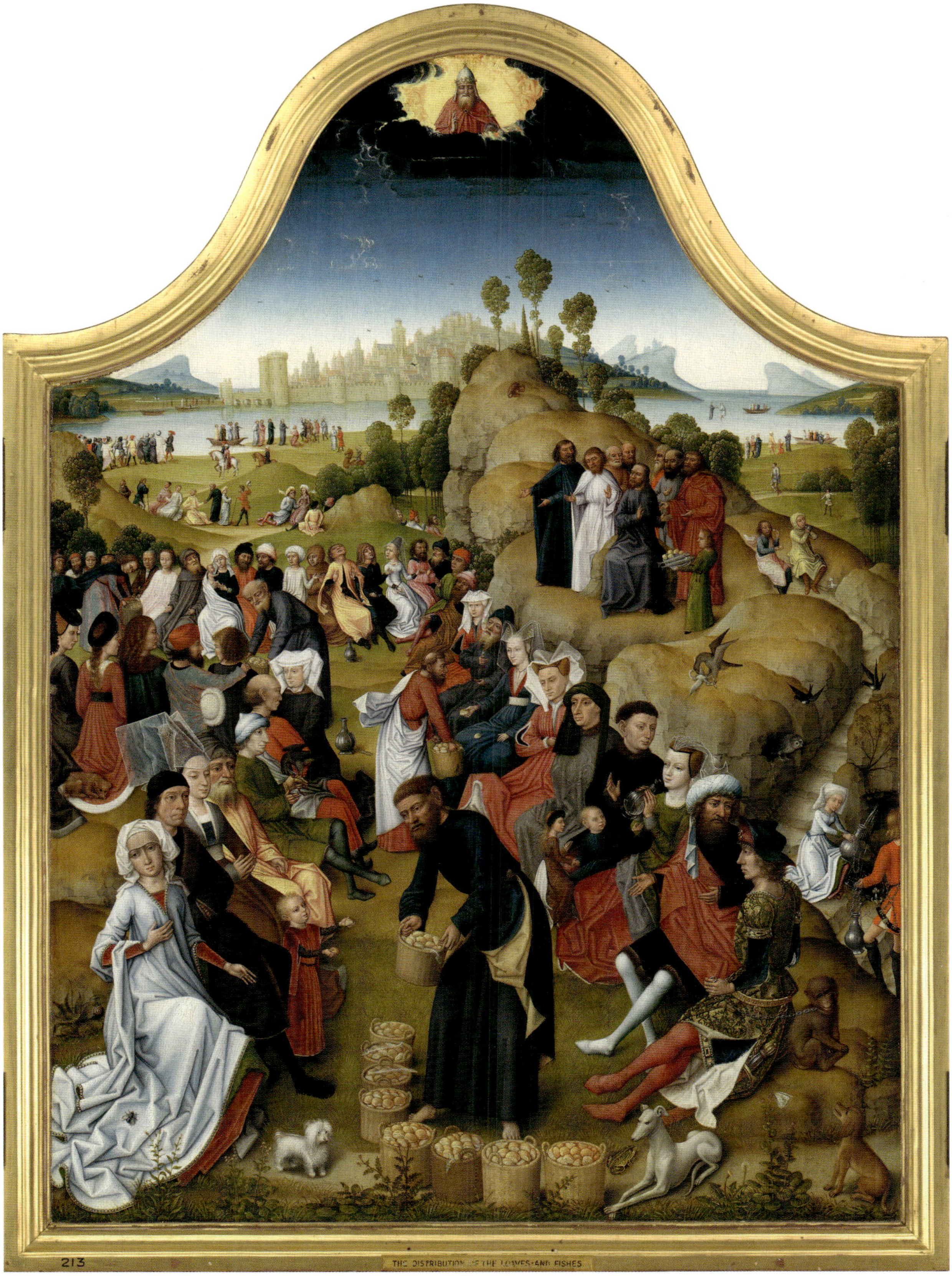

85. Master of the Catherine Legend, central part of a triptych, oil on panel, Brussels, c.1490–1500. The diners are in refined contemporary costume of the 1490s. The miracle has been moved to the middle ground. Melbourne, National Gallery of Victoria.

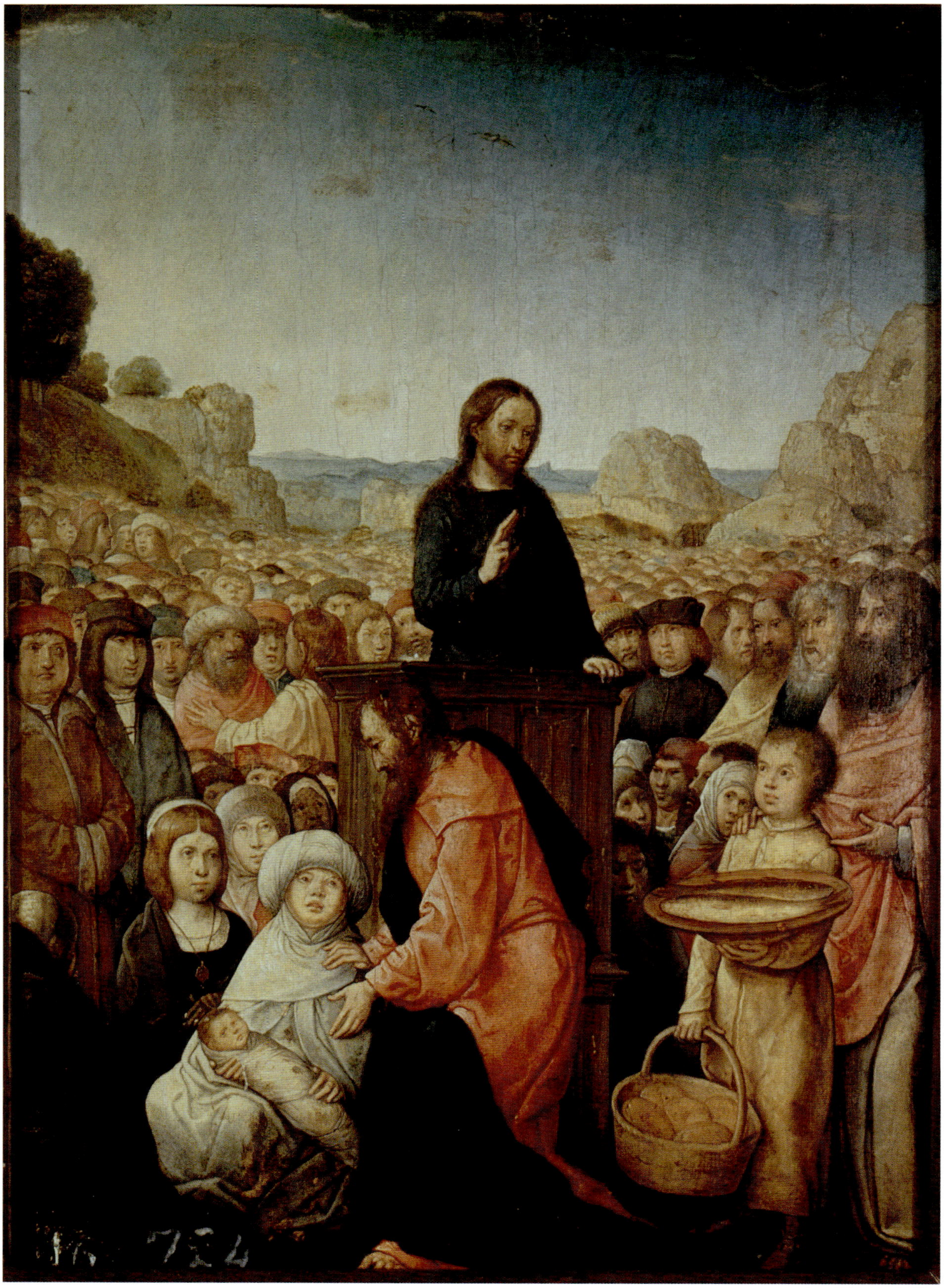

86. Juan de Flandes (c.1465–before 1519), a Flemish artist working in Spain. Oil on panel, c.1500. Queen Isabella, the artist's patron, is modestly seated on the ground next to the woman holding a baby. Madrid, Royal Palace.

87. Domenico Fetti (c.1589–1623), oil painting from the Church of S. Orsola in Mantua, 1618. The starving multitude is more realistically shown and emotionally charged than in the earlier examples. Mantua, Palazzo Ducale.

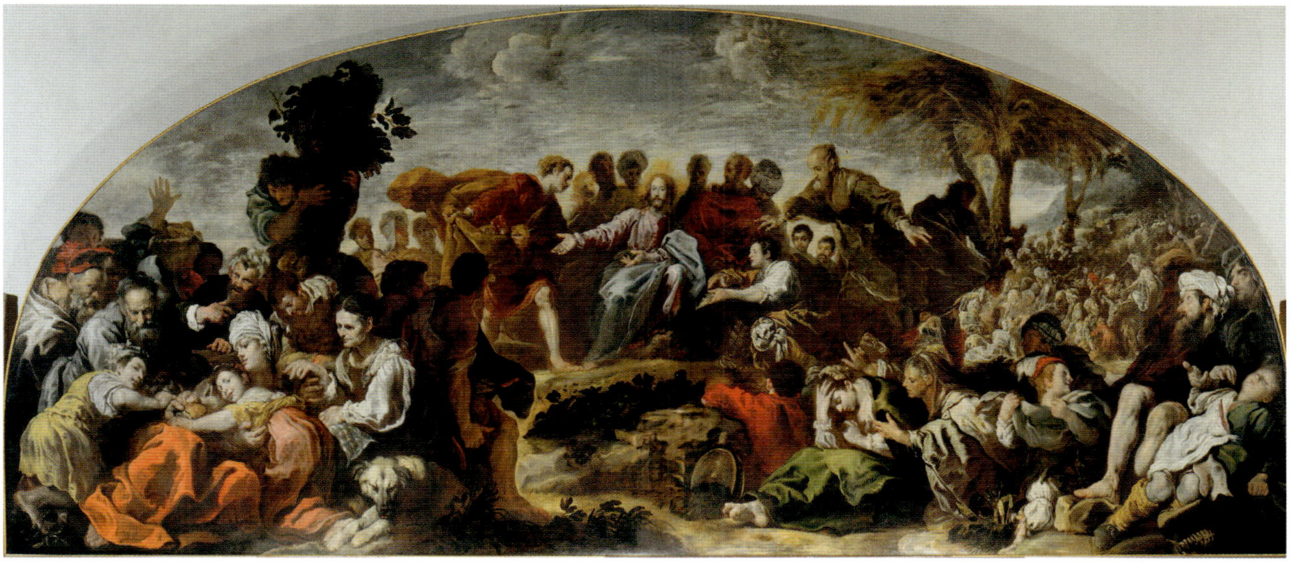

diners being served by the apostles in the foreground. The two dogs at the very front, a fox terrier and a greyhound, guarding the baskets of loaves, reappear several times in other paintings by this artist.

A rather different rendering of the miracle is to be seen in the composition by Juan de Flandes, one of the forty-seven such small panels painted in about 1500 for Queen Isabella of Castile (**86**).[19] Christ is on a late Gothic wooden pulpit, blessing the bread and the fish held in a basket and a large dish by the boy standing prominently at his side. The multitude stand in serried ranks behind Christ, crowded into the far distance, while the emphasis is on the group of figures in the foreground. An apostle comforts a woman holding a baby and behind her is Queen Isabella, the painter's patron. She is sitting on the ground in an exceptionally humble position for a queen. The man behind her on the left may possibly be her husband, King Ferdinand of Aragon, but the other identifications that have been suggested are more hypothetical. The man on the right of the pulpit has been variously interpreted as Christopher Columbus and a self-portrait of the artist, but the emphasis is on the centrality of Christ and the attendant boy holding five loaves and two fish, as the text demands.

A century later the huge canvas painted by Domenico Fetti (c.1589–1623), court painter to Ferdinand II Gonzaga, duke of Mantua, for the church of S. Orsola, provides a strong contrast to the traditional calm of many of the earlier compositions (**87**).[20] The theatricality is typical of the Counter-Reformation period, when such imagery was expected to convey the power of religious faith. Indeed, in many ways Fetti has followed the example of Tintoretto, who emphasised the miracle as personifying Christian charity in his version of the subject in the Scuola di S. Rocco in Venice (**150**). Yet it is Fetti who has more clearly expressed human sorrow, the despair caused by hunger, in a convincing manner seldom achieved by his predecessors. In particular, the group on the right, with the man in a turban looking despairingly up to Jesus while pointing to his hungry child, and the women comforting each other, have turned this traditional biblical subject into a call for social concern.

14
A SINFUL WOMAN IS FORGIVEN: SUPPER IN THE HOUSE OF SIMON THE PHARISEE

One of the Pharisees [a Jewish religious party] asked Jesus to eat with him, and he went into the Pharisee's house and took his place at the table. A woman in the city, who was a sinner, having learnt that he was eating at the Pharisee's house, brought an alabaster jar of ointment. She stood behind him at his feet, weeping, and began to bathe his feet with her tears and to dry them with her hair. Then she continued kissing his feet and anointing them with the ointment. Now when the Pharisee who had invited him saw it, he said to himself '… she is a sinner.' Jesus spoke up and said to him 'Simon, I have something to say to you' … Then turning towards the woman, he said to Simon, 'Do you see this woman? … I tell you her sins, which were many, have been forgiven' … Then he said to her, 'Your sins are forgiven.' (Luke 7.36–48)

A different version of the story is told by Matthew (26.6–13) and Mark (14.3–9), who place the event in the house of Simon the leper in Bethany and describe the woman's action as pouring the ointment on Christ's head, adding that this has prepared him for burial. John (12.1–8) identifies the sinner as Mary, sister of Martha and of Lazarus, and adds that Judas was present at the meal.

None of the Gospel passages identify the sinful woman and it was not until about 600, with Pope Gregory the Great's sermons on John, that she became firmly identified as Mary Magdalen. This was the woman first mentioned by name in Mark 15 as a witness at the Crucifixion and she was revered as one of the female followers of Christ. Indeed, she was the one who had seen him in the garden after the Resurrection (John 20). However, she is described as being 'cured of evil spirits' in Luke 8. Gregory's identification of her as the repentant sinner, and by implication a prostitute, in the house of Simon the Pharisee also takes up the negative view of this woman, who had been seen in the Early Christian centuries as a follower of Jesus at the Easter events.[21]

Unlike the Wedding at Cana and the Multiplication of the Loaves and Fishes, with their links with the Last Supper, this meal was rarely, if ever, depicted in the Early Christian period. The earliest surviving representation of Mary Magdalen

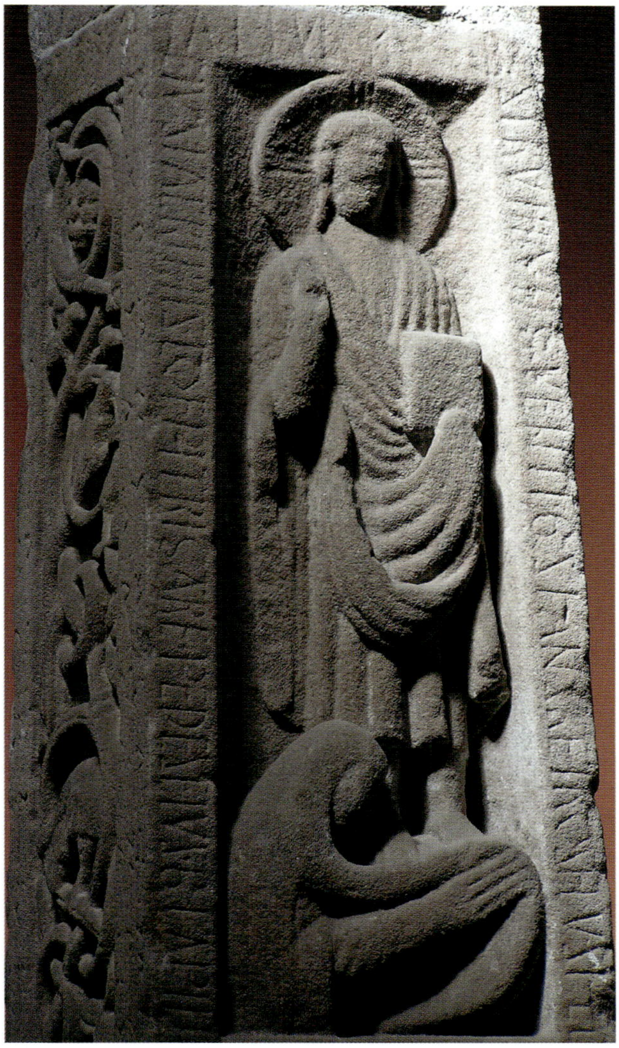

88. Stone cross, Ruthwell Church, Dumfriesshire, eighth century. Mary Magdalen drying Christ's feet with her hair.

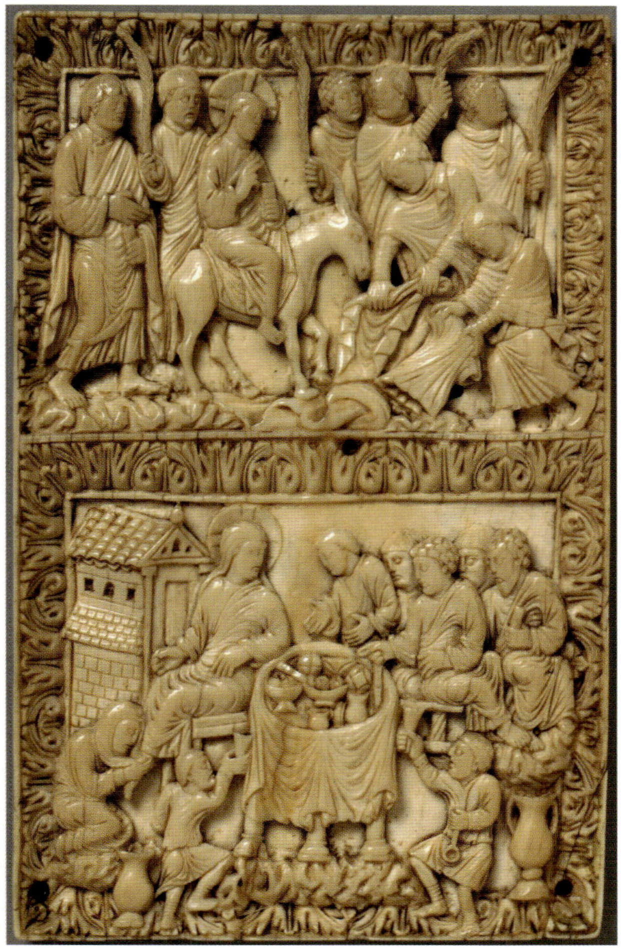

89. Ivory panel from Lorraine (Metz), c.870–80. No food is mentioned in the biblical text, but in this illustration the table is covered with bread rolls and dishes containing meat and other substances and jugs. London, Victoria and Albert Museum, no. 257-1867.

drying Christ's feet with her hair is on the large early eighth-century Anglo-Saxon stone cross in the church at Ruthwell, Dumfriesshire (**88**). This very classical-looking carving in one of the central panels of the cross shows the scene pared down to its essence. There is no meal, simply the standing figure of Christ with Mary Magdalen at his feet: the conversion of this woman from a state of sin to one of grace.[22]

The Gospel story is more fully illustrated in a Carolingian ivory from Lorraine (Metz) of about 870–80 in the Victoria & Albert Museum (**89**).[23] Mary Magdalen kneels before Christ, drying his feet with her hair, while Simon and the other Pharisees are in discussion with him. Two small figures at the front of the table offer cups of wine. The actual food is never mentioned in any of the Gospel texts, but is here shown in some detail according to the artist's invention or that of the model he may have used. Round bread rolls, a dish containing meat and various other dishes and jugs are fitted onto a small round table covered with a long cloth. Christ's reclining posture, the fact that he is beardless, as in earlier Western depictions, and the naturalistic draperies of the figures all suggest that there may have been a late classical model for this image.

Exactly the same scene but in a fully developed Romanesque form appears among the series of illustrations of the life of Christ in the famous psalter

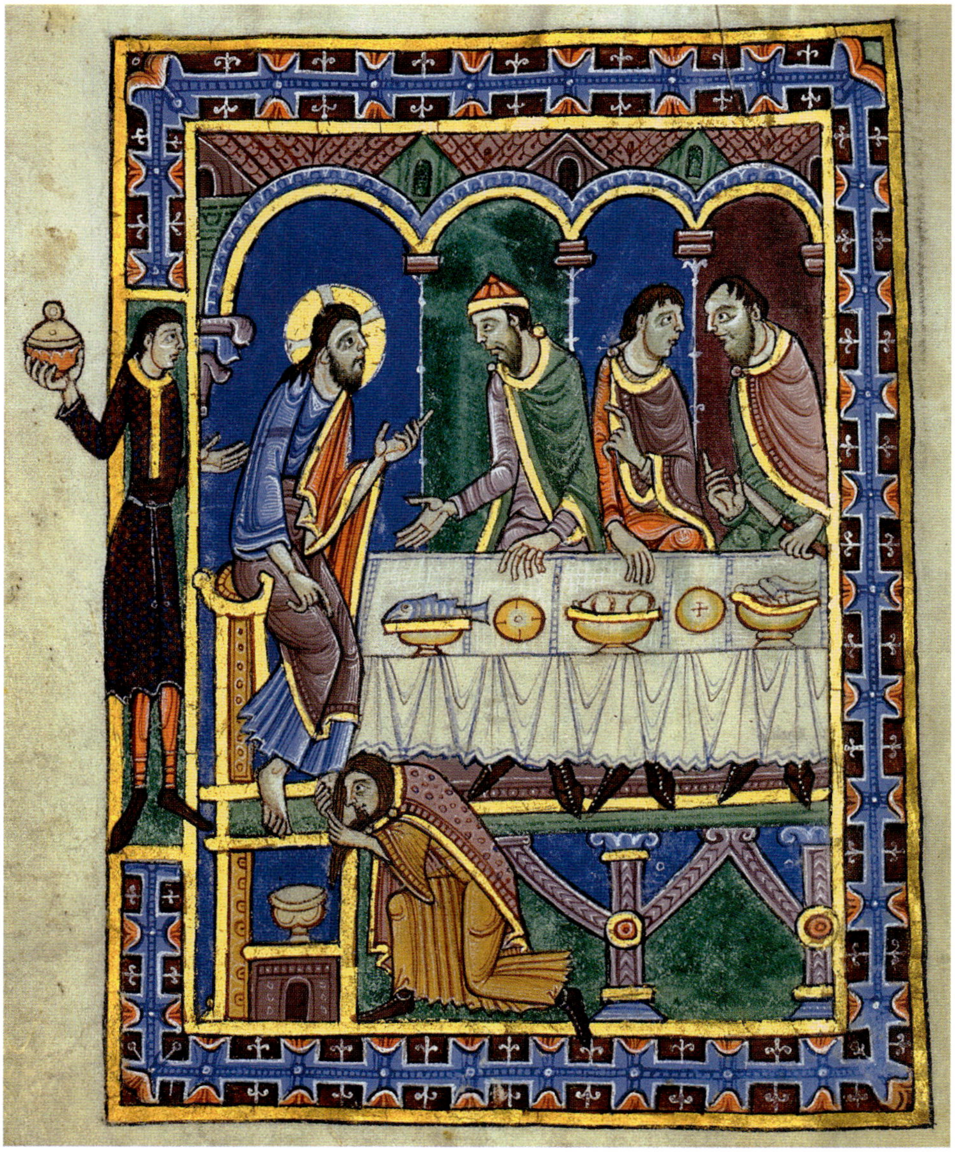

90. Psalter linked with St Albans Abbey, c.1120–30. The emphasis is on Christ disputing with the Pharisees, while blessing the forgiven sinner at his feet. Hildesheim Cathedral Treasury (p. 36).

of about 1120–30 linked with St Albans Abbey (**90**).[24] Fish, meat and bread are clearly laid out on the table and a servant, standing beyond the frame, is bringing in an ointment jar, but the emphasis is on the gestures that illustrate the central theme of the Gospel text. Christ is in direct dispute with the Pharisee while at the same time pointing to the figure of Mary Magdalen at his feet, the sinner who, he is insisting, should be forgiven. This confrontation and the accompanying gestures remain a constant feature in most of the future representations of the subject.

Meanwhile, other illustrations depict the alternative setting in the house of Mary, Martha and Lazarus in Bethany, as described by John, who identifies the sinner as Mary, the sister of Martha. An early image of this interpretation is in the Gospel lectionary of Egbert, archbishop of Trier (977–93), probably produced at the abbey of Reichenau (**91**). Martha is bringing in the food, while the inscription '*Maria*' clearly identifies the sinner as her sister. It was left to biblical commentators to decide whether she was identified with Mary Magdalen or whether this was a separate event. Again, in accordance with John's text, Judas is seated at the table among the apostles.

In one of the frescoes dated 1365–66 by Giovanni da Milano in the Rinuccini Chapel in the Church of S. Croce in Florence, we are back with the traditional composition (**92**).[25] Jesus again points to the Magdalen and to the diners, the central apostle taking up the argument more than Simon, who is busy raising the cloth on the trencher while discreetly glancing at the sinner below. One servant is placing a trencher with a calf on the table, another is bringing a fowl into the room. As the name indicates, Giovanni da Milano came from northern Italy, but he was working in Florence from 1346 and from his style he may be described as a follower of Giotto. He successfully applies the new methods of depicting interior space, but it is the facial expressions of the figures and the humanity they convey that are more resonant. Unusually, the older apostle on the right is shown actually eating a piece of bread held in his fingers. As the inscription on the frame below explains, the devils escaping from the roof are the seven demons driven out of Mary Magdalen by Jesus as described by Luke 8.2.

Just as Giovanni da Milano placed this scene in a central position in the tympanum above the other scenes related to Mary Magdalen, so did the German painter Lukas Moser in his altarpiece dedicated to her in the church at Tiefenbronn in Swabia (**93**). The altarpiece, which also contains three legendary scenes of the Magdalen, including her journey to Marseilles after the Crucifixion, is inscribed with the artist's name and the date 1432. This is the only documented work by Moser, seen as one of the leading German artists of the fifteenth century, and when, in 1969, a book appeared claiming that the signature was false and that no such painter existed, the outcry spread to the newspapers. However, a conference of specialists in art history, palaeography and conservation, held in Munich in 1971, concluded that the inscription was genuine and Moser's name should be reinstated. Only the new reading of the date as 1432, instead of 1431, was widely accepted.[26]

The scene is set in the open air with a floral trellis behind the diners, who sit at a trestle table. Moser has placed it at Bethany at the house of Mary and Martha, with Martha serving the food as she did in the Egbert Codex (**91**). One of the dishes she holds contains what appears to be a pie. As the altarpiece is dedicated to Mary Magdalen while Martha is bringing in the food, this is clearly a case where the identity of the two Maries has been conflated. At any rate, the sinner is in the traditional posture, only differing in that her hair is in plaits, which have to

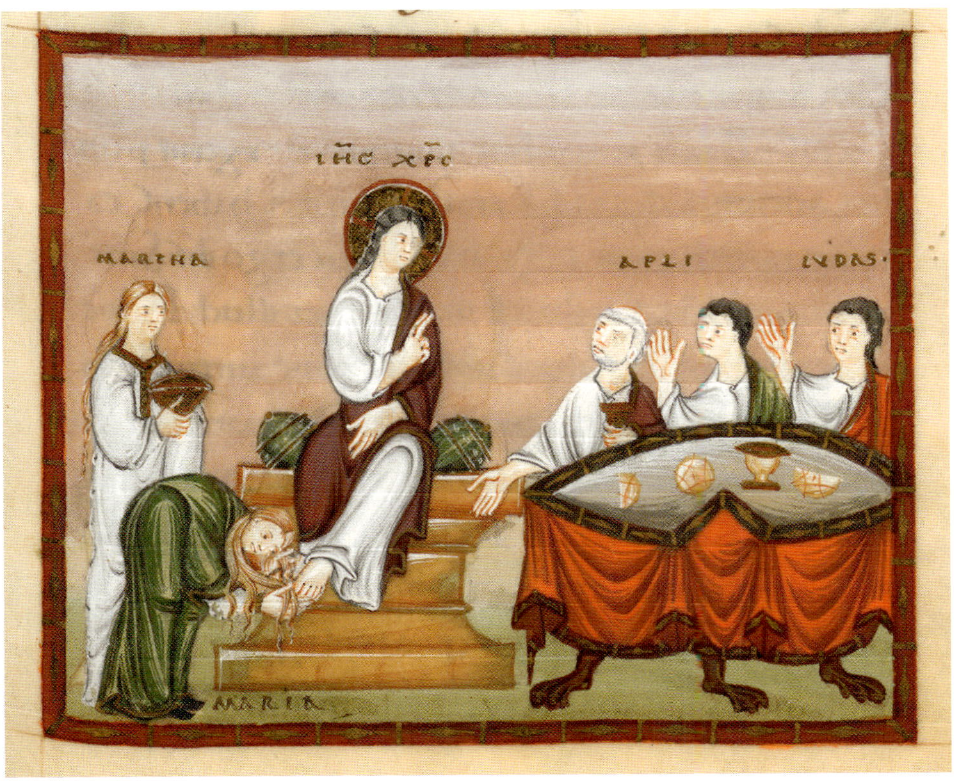

91. Gospel Lectionary of Egbert, archbishop of Trier, Reichenau, c.990. The setting is in the house of Mary and Martha, sisters of Lazarus, as described in John's Gospel. Trier, Stadtbibliothek, MS 24, fol. 65.

92. Wall painting by Govanni da Milano (active 1346–69), c.1365, in the Rinuccini Chapel in the Church of Santa Croce in Florence. Unusually, the apostle on the right is shown actually eating a piece of bread held in his fingers. The devils escaping from the roof are the seven demons driven out of Mary Magdalen by Jesus (Luke 8.2).

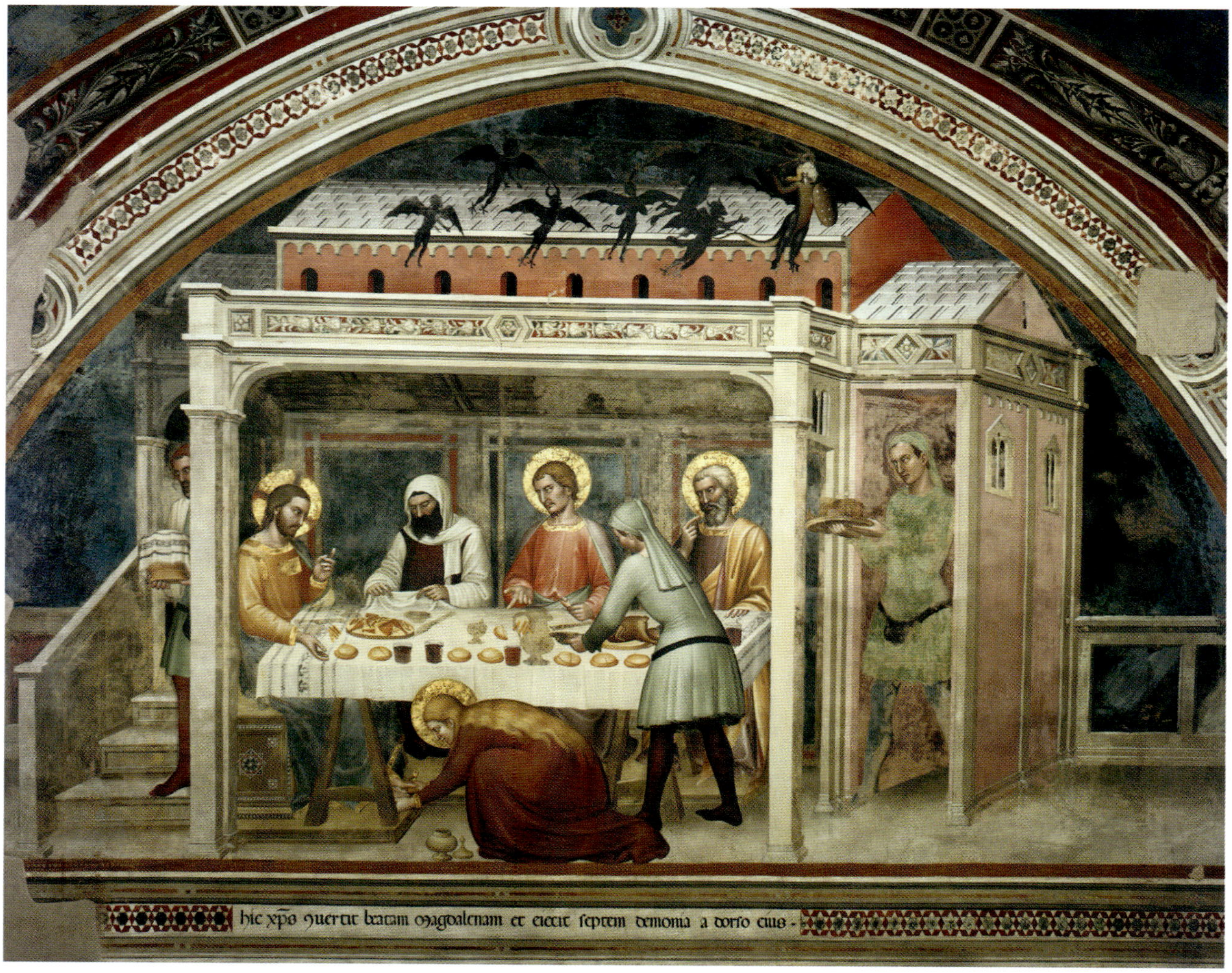

be loosened on one side to allow her to dry Christ's feet. The man whispering to St Peter, who has been identified as Lazarus, is more probably Judas, who is at the meal according to John 12.4.

The subject was increasingly popular in the fifteenth and sixteenth centuries and in the majority of cases the scene was set in the house of Simon the Pharisee. In the painting of about 1465 by Dieric Bouts of Louvain (**94**) the setting is in a modest interior and due attention is paid to the gesture of Jesus, to the finely dressed Pharisee and the patron, a Carthusian monk. Yet the main focus is on the table, seen somewhat from above, whose contents are painted in the meticulously realistic detail of an early still life. Two dishes contain fish, bread rolls are scattered on the table and jugs, glasses and knives are prominently displayed.

Whereas Veronese offered his viewers an insight into the splendour of an aristocratic banquet (Brera Gallery, Milan, c.1570), Nicolas Poussin (1594–1665), who lived much of his life in Rome, delved back into the civilisation of ancient Rome and showed the diners reclining on couches around a table (**95**). This was an archaeologically derived rendering of the *triclinium*, the predecessor of the *stibadium*, or semi-circular couch, which became the more

93. Lukas Moser, upper panel from the altarpiece dated 1432, dedicated to Mary Magdalen, in the Church at Tiefenbronn in Swabia. Martha is serving the food.

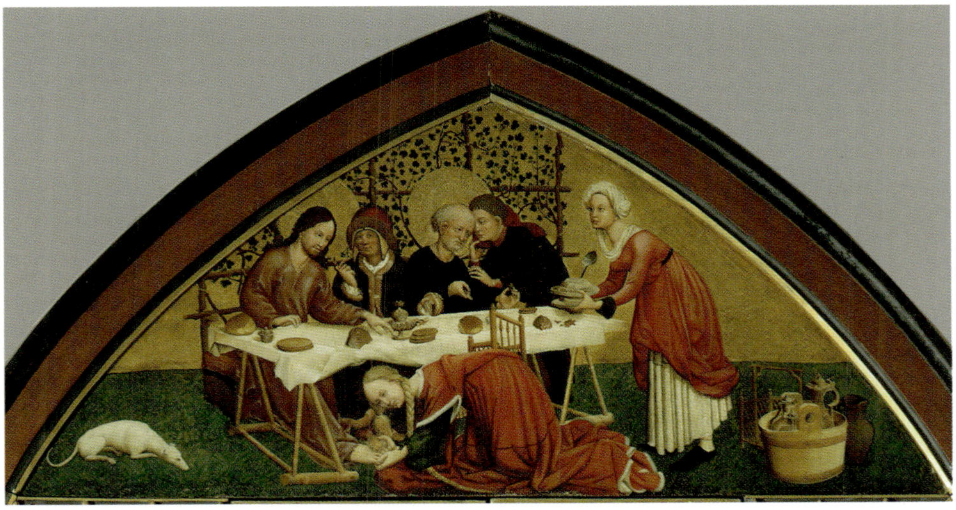

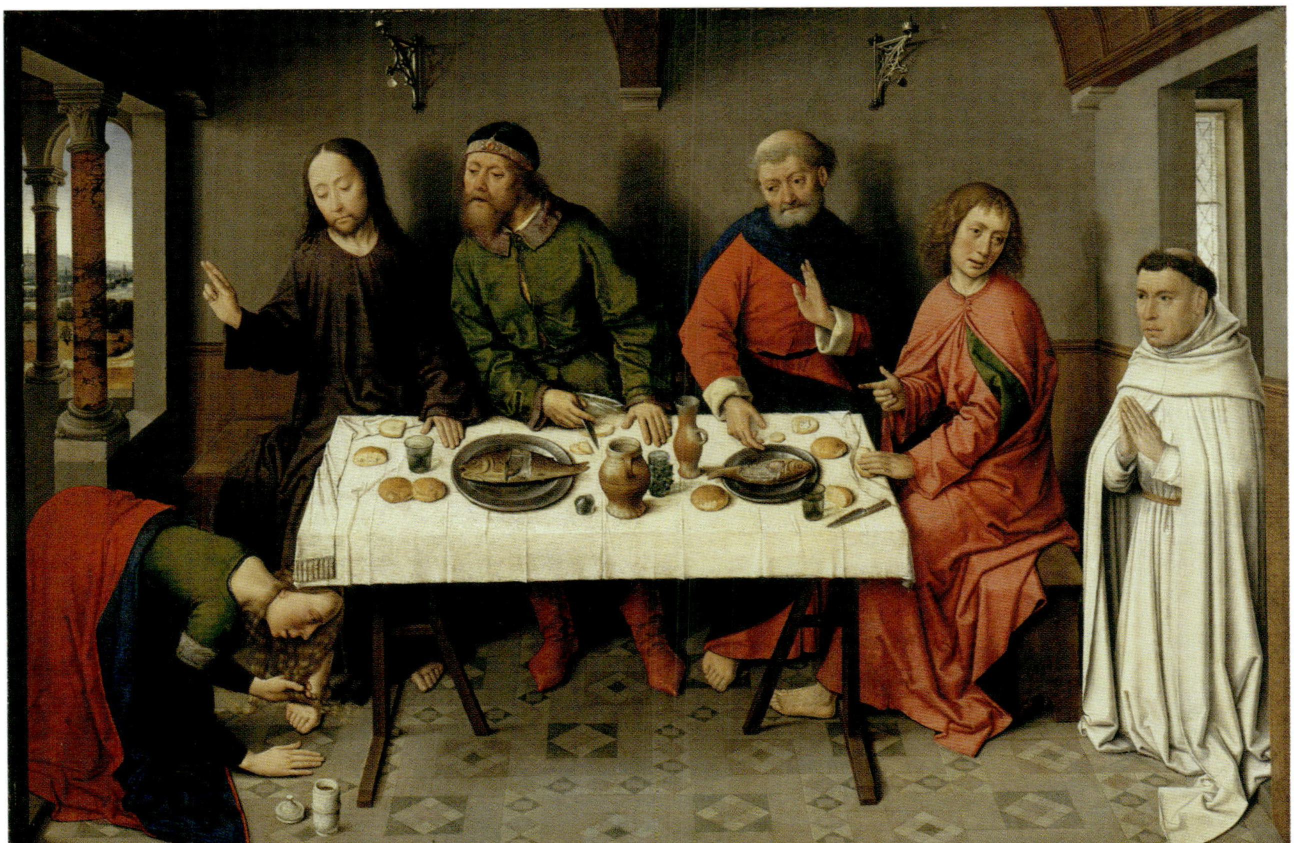

94. Dieric Bouts (c.1415–75), oil painting on panel, Louvain, c.1465. Most striking are the expressions of the Pharisee, the two apostles and the patron, a Carthusian monk, but the central focus is on the food and dishes on the table. Berlin, Gemäldegalerie.

95. Nicolas Poussin (1594–1665), oil painting of *Penance* from the series of the Seven Sacraments, 1647. An example of Poussin's interest in archaeological research, this is his version of the Roman *triclinium*, with the guests reclining on couches. The Duke of Sutherland Collection, on loan to the National Gallery of Scotland, Edinburgh.

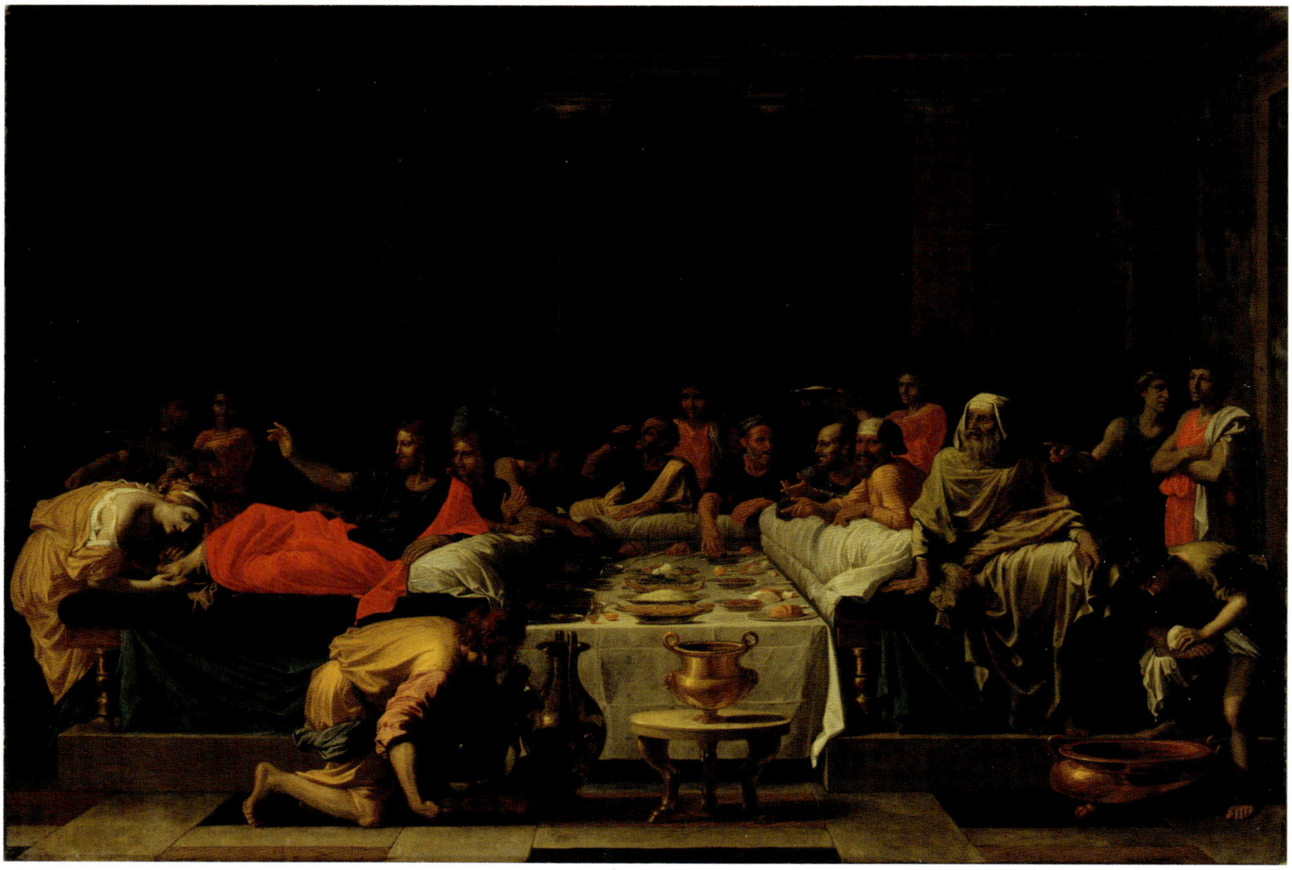

common form in the Early Christian period, as can be seen, for example, in several sixth-century illustrations of the Last Supper (**123**, **124**).

Among Poussin's best-known religious paintings are his two series of the *Seven Sacraments*, the first for the classical scholar Cassiano dal Pozzo, completed in 1642 (duke of Rutland, Belvoir Castle), the second for his friend Paul Fréart de Chantelou in 1644–48 (duke of Sutherland, on loan to the National Gallery of Scotland, Edinburgh).[27] To illustrate five of the seven sacraments he chose episodes from the Gospels, of which the sinful and penitent woman anointing Christ's feet was the subject representing Penance. This picture in the first series was destroyed in a fire at Belvoir Castle in 1816, but the one from the second series survives to demonstrate Poussin's close interest in the classical Roman setting for the meal. This had been a matter for archaeological research since the late sixteenth century, surfacing notably in the publication *De Triclinio* by Pedro Chacon in 1588. Poussin was keen to display his erudition in matters of classical archaeology and wrote to his patron specifically about his depiction of the triclinium in his composition of Penance.[28] Following classical models, the flat couch runs around three sides of the table; the guests lie at full length, with their feet away from the table. The host, sitting opposite Jesus, is wearing carefully researched rabbinical dress, including a Hebrew inscription on the band on his forehead. Of the food on the table, the bread, fish and fruit are traditional, whereas the pile of sugary sweets near the front, an indication of the increasing import of sugar into Europe from the sixteenth century, are more clearly contemporary.

15
CHRIST AT DINNER IN THE HOUSE OF LEVI

The Gospel of St Matthew (9.9) identifies the tax collector, named as Levi by Mark (2.14) and Luke (5.27), with the apostle Matthew. Luke contains the fullest description of the meal.

Then Levi gave a great banquet for him in his house and there was a large crowd of tax collectors and others sitting at the table with them. The Pharisees and their scribes were complaining to his disciples saying, 'Why do you eat and drink with tax collectors and sinners?' Jesus answered, 'Those who are well have no need of a physician, but those who are sick; I have come to call not the righteous but sinners to repentance.' (Luke 5.27–32)

The description of this meal and the moral proposed by Jesus is effectively the same as in the supper in the house of Simon the Pharisee, which may help to explain why it was so rarely illustrated. Among the half-dozen surviving depictions in medieval manuscripts, the earliest is in the lectionary of Egbert, archbishop of Trier, of about 990 (**96**). The Gospel passage (Mark 2.13–17) describing the meal was read on the Sunday of the sixth week of Epiphany, which accounts for its text and the illustration appearing in this manuscript. Three apostles are shown eating their meal sitting on a bench with a table cloth containing some bread spread on their laps. Neither Jesus, seated on the left, nor the Pharisees, standing on the right, are eating; the discussion is clearly more important than the meal.

Perhaps the only well-known depiction of this scene is the painting of 1572–73 by Paolo Veronese which, it turns out, had quite a different purpose (**97**). Veronese had been commissioned to execute a very large painting of the Last Supper to replace the one painted by Titian for the Convent of S. Giovanni e Paolo in Venice, which had been destroyed by fire in 1571. The central group is very like Titian's Last Supper, of which a copy survives, with Christ announcing that one of the company will betray him, but the crowd of guests and onlookers milling about on the left and right are very much Veronese's invention. The painting was completed on 20 April 1573 – the date is inscribed at the end of the staircase – but it raised objections from the Church authorities and Veronese was called for interrogation by the Tribunal of the Inquisition on 18 July.

Such interrogations were the result of the Council of Trent – the embodiment of the Counter-Reformation, the resolve of the Catholic Church to engage in battle with the Protestant Reformation. At the Council's session in 1563 strict rules were laid down to be followed in the supervision of religious imagery, in particular to ensure that due veneration was given to holy figures and the events in which they take part. There was no objection to the white-bearded apostle taking lamb from a dish with his hands – clearly still the normal way of eating – but the tribunal objected to particular figures, such as the servant with the bleeding nose and the man picking his teeth behind the column on the left. More generally, Veronese was asked: 'did anyone commission you to paint Germans, buffoons and similar things in that picture?' His defence was succinct: 'I received the commission to decorate the picture as I saw fit. It is large and, it seemed to me, it could hold many figures.'[29] He was given three months to fall into line, but as far as can be seen he made no changes to the composition. He did, however, give way over the subject of the Last Supper. The only addition was the inscription on the cornice of the end posts of the staircase, which newly identified the scene as 'the meal in the house of Levi according to Luke chapter 5'.

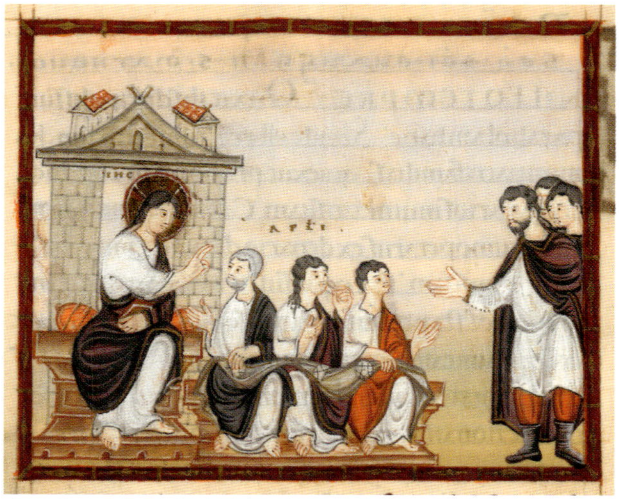

96. Gospel Lectionary of Egbert, archbishop of Trier, Reichenau c.990. A rare example of the apostles eating their meal sitting on a bench with a table cloth spread over their legs. Trier, Stadtbibliothek, MS 24, fol. 29.

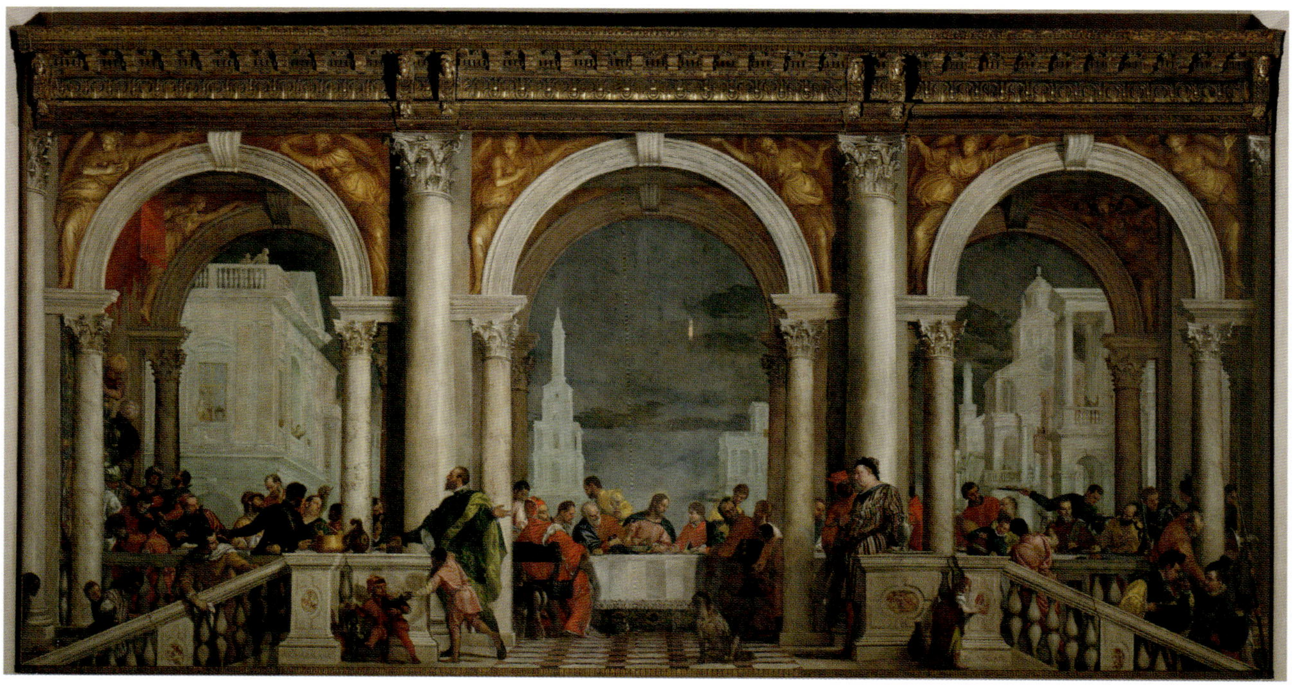

97. Paolo Veronese (1528–88), oil painting dated 1572, originally intended to illustrate the Last Supper but rejected as such by the Tribunal of the Inquisition. Venice, Accademia di Belle Arti.

16
PARABLES

The Parables spoken by Jesus and recorded in the Gospels principally by Luke (10–19) and also by Matthew (13–25) are clearly tales with a moral, but they are rarely explained in the biblical text. It was the earlier Church Fathers who provided moral and ethical commentaries for these often strange stories.[30] Unlike the Miracles, which played an important part in the evangelising success of the Early Christian Church and which were, as we have seen, frequently depicted at the time, the Parables appear only rarely in Early Christian and early medieval art. It is only from about 1000, both in Byzantium and in Ottonian Germany, that a larger number of illustrations survive. As far as food is concerned, of the roughly thirty Parables only four are centred on a meal, but these are among the most frequently illustrated.

THE KING'S SON'S WEDDING: THE GUEST WITHOUT A WEDDING GARMENT

Once more Jesus spoke to them in parables, saying: 'The Kingdom of Heaven may be compared to a king who gave a wedding banquet for his son. He sent his slaves to call those who had been invited to the wedding banquet but they would not come. Again he sent other slaves, saying 'tell those who have been invited: look I have prepared my dinner, my oxen and fat calves have been slaughtered and everything is ready … but they made light of it and went away … Go therefore in to the main streets and invite everyone you find to the wedding banquet.' Those slaves went out into the streets and gathered all whom they found, both good and bad, so the wedding hall was filled with guests.

But when the king came to see the guests, he noticed a man who was not wearing a wedding robe and he said to him, 'Friend, how did you get in here without a wedding robe?' And he was speechless. Then the king said to the attendants, 'Bind him hand and foot and throw him into the outer darkness where there will be weeping and gnashing of teeth. For many are called, but few are chosen.' (Matthew 22.1–14.)

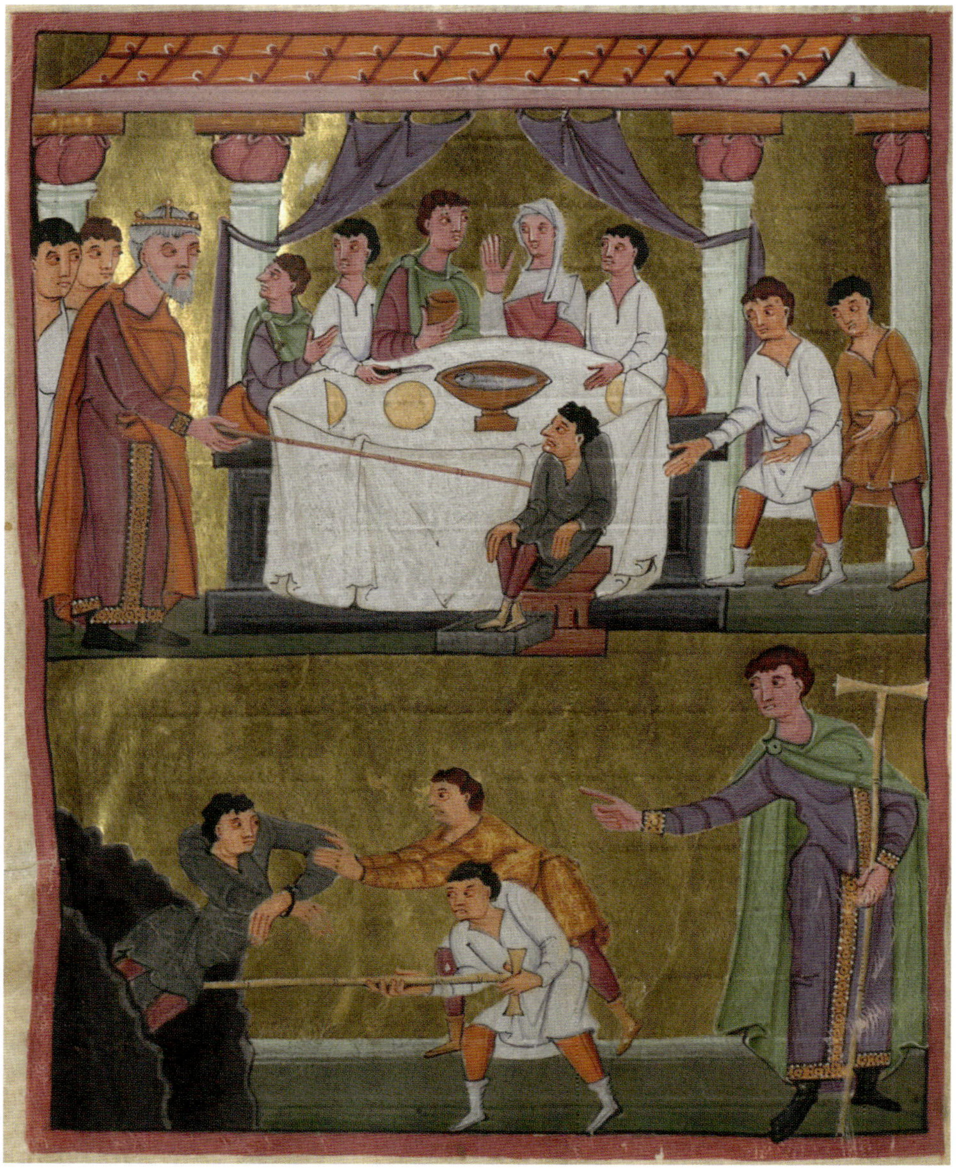

98. Gospel Lectionary, Reichenau c.1020. The biblical text mentions the 'oxen and fine calves' at this meal, but the artist has only pictured bread and fish. Below, the ill-dressed guest is thrown into the outer darkness. Munich, Bayerische Staatsbibliothek, MS lat. 23338, fol. 154v.

The first half of the parable – the invited guests refusing to come and being replaced by people from the street – is the same as the Great Supper in Luke 14 and the two were usually discussed together by commentators. The only difference is that Matthew's version has *prandium*, usually translated as dinner, associated with marriage, whereas Luke's is usually described as supper. The early commentators identified the kings as God the Father and the nuptials as the wedding of Christ and Church; it is the Jews who fail to attend, whereupon the Gentiles are called upon for the meal. The story of the inadequately dressed guest is unique to this parable. Appropriate garments are virtues; the dirty clothes imply an impure life and the wearer must be rejected by the Church.

As with most of the parables, there are no surviving illustrations from the Early Christian period. One of the earliest and most dramatic is the Gospel lectionary produced at Reichenau in about 1020 (**98**). The parable was read on the twentieth Sunday after Pentecost and the illustration was inserted at this point in the lectionary. The son, his bride and the guests are seated at a circular table facing the inadequately dressed guest, who sits on the opposite side in the manner of Judas at the Last Supper and who is being prodded with a stick by the king. His dress does not seem particularly inadequate when compared with

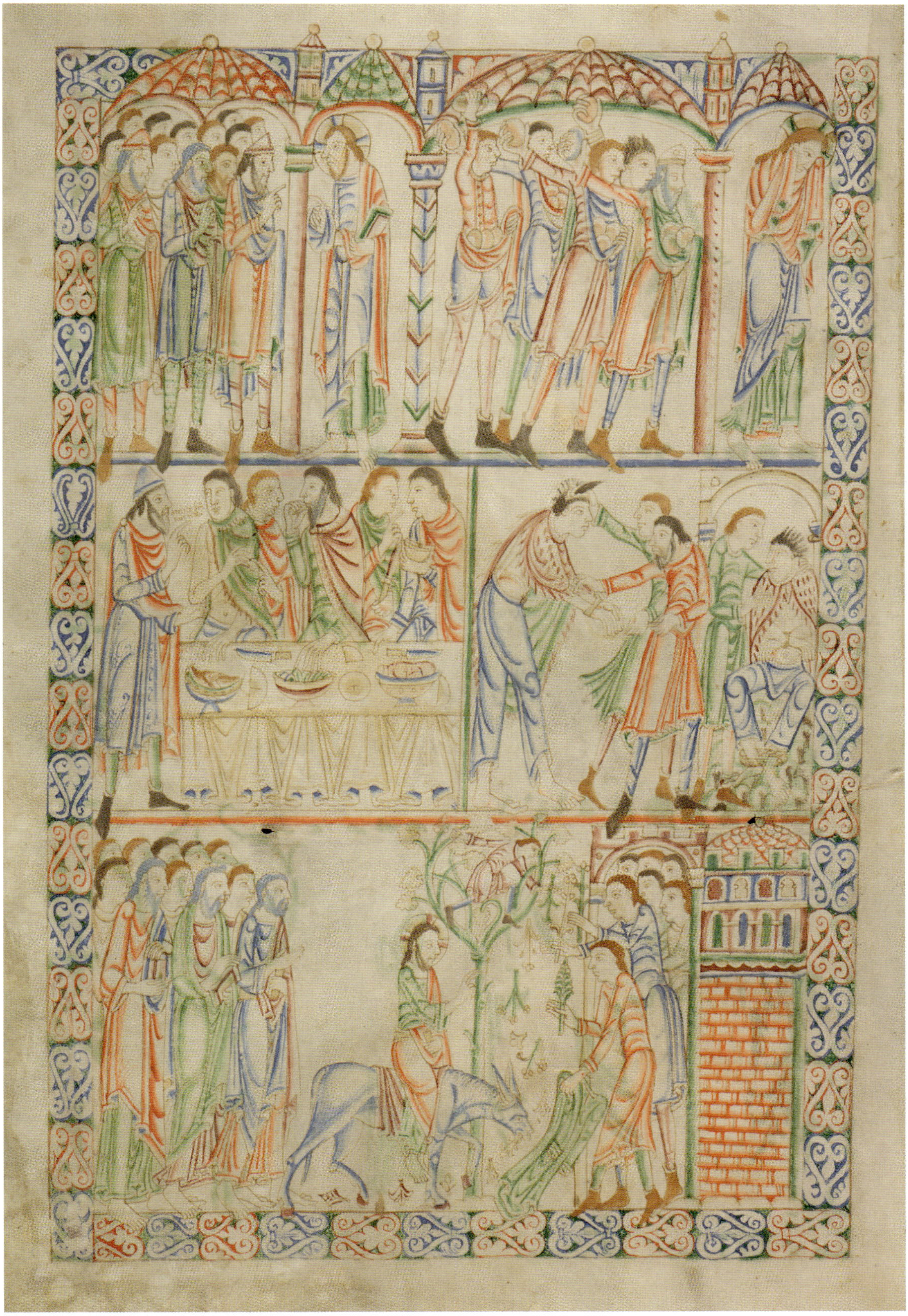

99. Drawings of the Life of Christ attached to a book of the Gospels, probably produced at the abbey of Bury St Edmunds, c.1130. The badly dressed guest is shown naked under his cloak; the food includes the calf mentioned in the text. Cambridge, Pembroke College, MS 120, fol. 2v.

that of the other guests; not surprisingly, perhaps, as they have all come in from the street. For once, the biblical text mentions specific items of food – 'my oxen and fat calves' – but on the table there is only fish and bread to be seen, demonstrating how little this mattered to the artist compared with the details of the narrative. This is continued in the lower register, where the guilty guest, his hands bound, is being thrown by two servants into the outer darkness, suitably represented by a dark cave. The servants and their master, possibly the king's son, hold two crosses, presumably to identify them as servants of the church.

An English illustration of the same sequence of events appears among the drawings of the Life of Christ attached to a manuscript of the Gospels probably produced at the abbey of Bury St Edmunds in about 1130 (**99**).[31] The host, wearing not a crown but a pointed hat, is addressing the guest, who is shown half-naked under his cloak. Most unusually, the words of the host, following Matthew's text, are written on the bare parchment between the two: 'Amice, quomodo huc intrasti …' (Friend, how did you get in here?). Contrary to the Reichenau manuscript, the food on the table includes the calf mentioned in the text. In a manner typical of the period, knives, but no forks or spoons, are shown on the table, and the central guest is shown helping himself with his hand in a dish. In the next scene the inadequately dressed guest's dress is confirmed by his bare feet. His hands are tied and he is being pulled by two servants, one of whom holds him by his hair. Finally he is shown in the 'outer darkness' under an isolated arcade, sitting on rocks. Following the text, he is now bound by his feet as well as his hands.

THE PARABLE OF THE GREAT SUPPER

Then Jesus said to him, 'Someone gave a great dinner and invited many. At the time of the dinner he sent his slave to say to those who had been invited, "Come; for everything is ready now." But they all alike began to make excuses. The first said to him, "I have bought a piece of land, and I must go out and see it; please accept my apologies." Another said, "I have bought five yoke of oxen and I am going to try them out; please accept my apologies." Another said, "I have just been married and therefore cannot come." So the slave returned and reported this to his master. Then the owner of the house became angry and said to his slave, "Go out at once into the streets and the lanes of the town and bring in the poor, the crippled, the blind and the lame." … "For I tell you, none of those who were invited will taste my dinner."' (Luke 14.16–24)

For 'the Great Supper' the Vulgate has *coena* (cena), usually translated as 'dinner', which was the Romans' principal meal, taken at noon. However, the early commentators agreed that this parable concerns the heavenly reward which Christ prepares as a great supper, the final meal of the day. The three unwilling guests were variously identified as heathens, Jews and Gentiles, and St Augustine added that the poor in the city were the humble who acknowledged their sinfulness.[32]

Again, the earliest surviving images are from Ottonian Germany. They appear among the illustrations to Luke in three manuscripts of the Gospels from the abbey of Echternach, near Trier. The earliest of these is the Golden Gospels, now in the museum at Nürnberg, dating from about 1030, in which the Great Supper faces the illustrations to the parable of Dives and Lazarus (**100**). Each of the three registers is headed by a title providing an abbreviated summary of the biblical text. To balance the meal of Dives and Lazarus opposite, the artist has placed the Supper at the top, while the two registers below contain the earlier sequence of events. The three excuses are clearly shown: the man who has bought the land, the

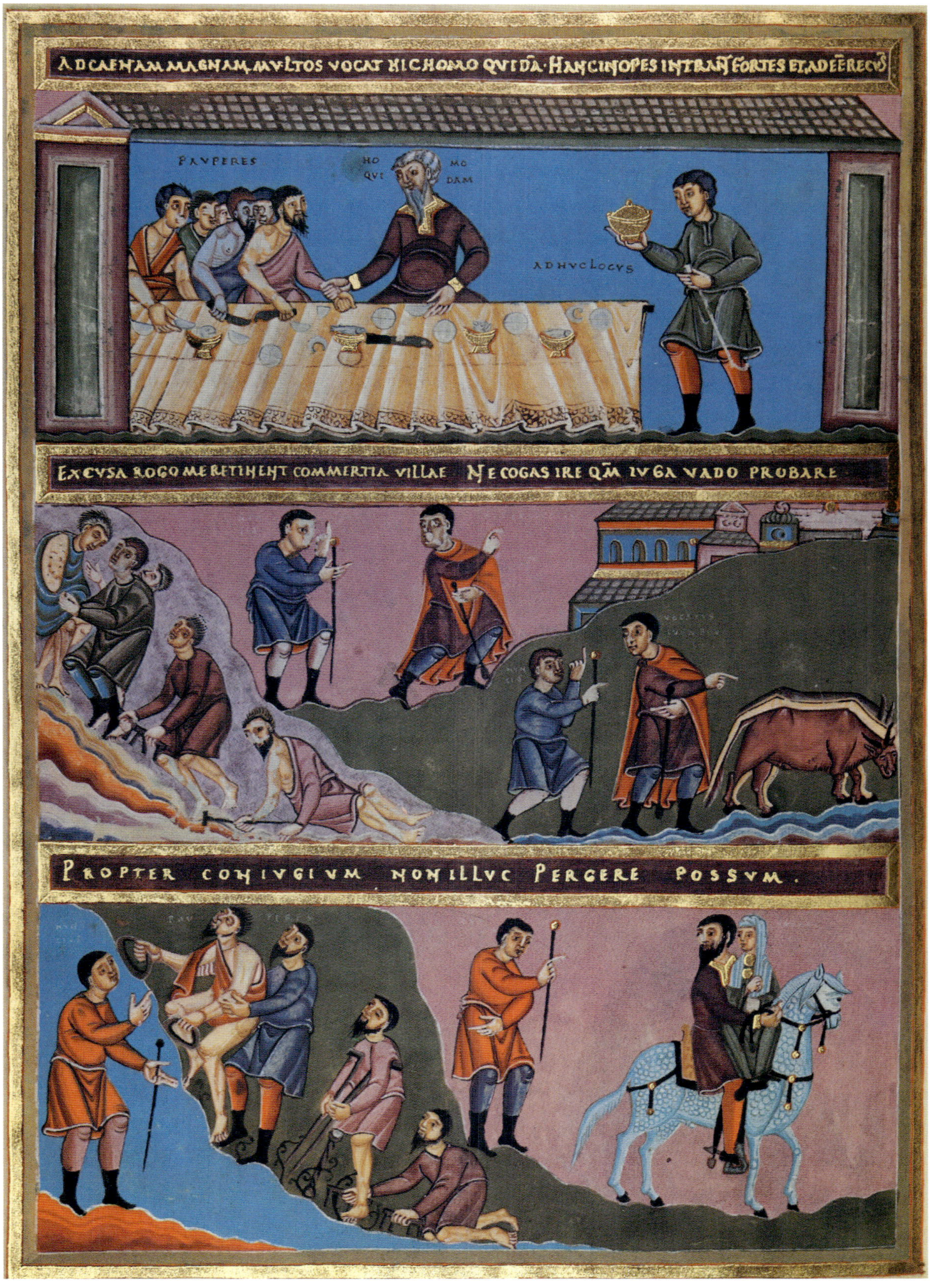

100. Golden Gospels from the abbey of Echternach, near Trier, c.1030. The meal is shown at the top, the guests' excuses in three scenes below, together with the poor, the crippled, the blind and the lame on the left. Nürnberg, Germanisches Nationalmuseum, MS Bibl.156 142, fol. 77v.

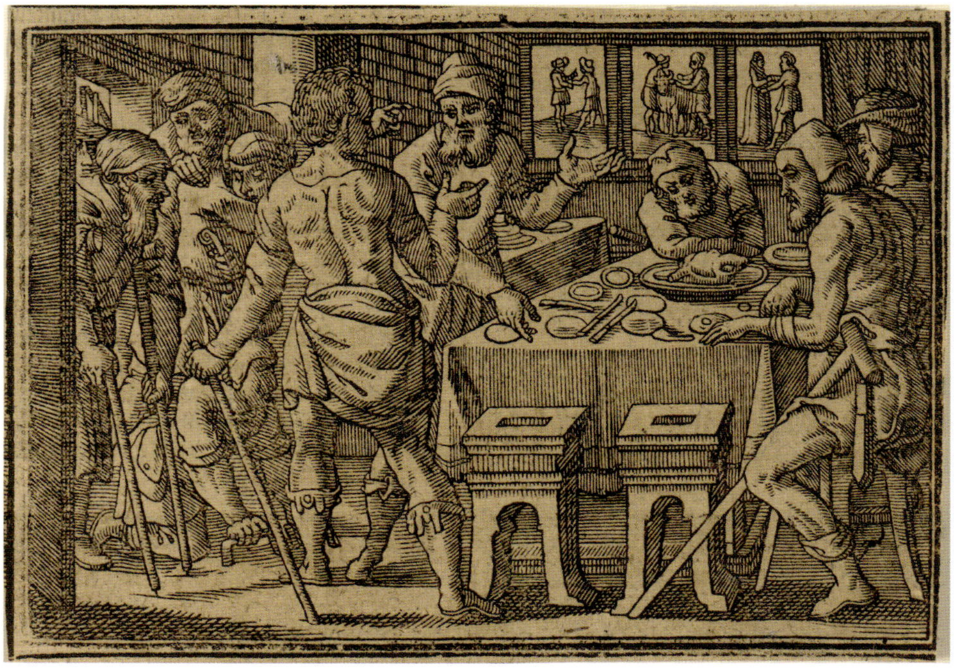

101. Woodcut by Paul Kreutzberger (died c.1660), published in Dilherr's German translation of the Bible in Nürnberg in 1670. The originally invited guests can be seen through the windows, each with the reason for their refusal to attend: buying land, buying oxen and getting married.

second with his oxen and, below, the third with his bride. On the left are the poor, the crippled, the blind and the lame, who reappear at the top seated at the table and welcomed by the landlord. There are only a few dishes on the table, but the servant is bringing in another and the importance of the occasion is underlined by the beautifully decorated table cloth.

The emphasis on the lame guests supported on sticks and crutches remains the standard feature of the illustrations. A vivid example is the woodcut of Paul Kreutzberger (d. about 1660) of Nürnberg (**101**).[33] It was published in Dilherr's German translation of the Bible in Nürnberg in 1670. There is a dish of meat on the table, but the emphasis is on the handicapped guests. At least one of them is pointing towards the window, beyond which one can see the three invited guests each appearing with the reason for their refusal to attend.

THE PARABLE OF THE PRODIGAL SON

Then Jesus said, 'There was a man who had two sons. The younger said to his father, "Father give me the share of the property that will belong to me." So he divided his property between them. A few days later the younger son gathered all he had and travelled to a distant country, and there he squandered his property in dissolute living. When he had spent everything, a severe famine took place throughout that country and he began to be in need …

… So he set off and went to his father. But while he was still far off, his father saw him and was filled with compassion; he ran and put his arms around him and kissed him. Then the son said to him, "Father I have sinned against heaven and before you; I am no longer to be worthy to be called your son." But the father said to his slave, "Quickly bring out a robe-the best one-and put it on him; put a ring on his finger and sandals on his feet.

And get the fatted calf and kill it, and let us eat and celebrate; for this son of mine was dead and is alive again; he was lost and is found!" And they began to celebrate.

Now his elder son … became angry and refused to go in. His father came out and began to plead with him. But he answered his father, "Listen! For all these years I have been working like a slave for you and I have never disobeyed your command, yet you have never given me even a young goat … But when this son of yours came back, who has devoured your property with prostitutes, you killed the fatted calf for him!" Then the father said to him, "Son, you are always with me, and all that is mine is yours. But we had to celebrate and rejoice, because this brother of yours was dead and has come to life; he was lost and has been found."' (Luke 15.11–32)

From the early Church Fathers to the twelfth-century *Glossa ordinaria*, the slaughtered fatted calf represents the sacrifice of Christ and the celebratory meal of the Eucharist. The older and younger sons may signify Jews and Gentiles, but an equally common interpretation had the younger son as the penitent sinner, returning to God the Father.

The earliest extant illustration of the parable is among the numerous biblical scenes contained within small compartments on four detached leaves formerly preceding the text of the Eadwine Psalter (so-called from the name of its scribe), produced at Canterbury in about 1150–60 (**102**).[34] The story unfolds in eight scenes, which follow the illustrations to the parable of Dives and Lazarus. Beginning with the Prodigal's departure, he is shown walking to the town and then at a meal with the prostitutes. No meal is mentioned at this stage in the biblical text. However, the elder son's complaint to his father that his brother had 'devoured his property with prostitutes' is usually illustrated in the form of a meal as a parallel and a contrast with the meal at the Prodigal's return. Herding pigs and the return home with the gift of the ring occupy the middle register, while the slaughter of the fatted calf, the celebratory meal and the father reproving the elder son appear below. These picture leaves have been shown to derive partially from Ottonian cycles and it is therefore at least possible that these illustrations of the Prodigal Son came from an earlier tradition, even though nothing survives.

The sudden popularity of the parable in the thirteenth century, particularly in French stained-glass windows, has been linked with its social content. The Prodigal's downfall is due to his 'dissolute living', succumbing to the temptations offered by the town, and the moral was relevant at the time of the rapid growth of towns in the thirteenth century.[35] Stained-glass windows in as many as seven cathedrals in the period 1200–70 tell the story in considerable detail, with due emphasis on the temptations of the city, including dice in a tavern and the meal with the prostitutes. In the north transept at Chartres (window 35) there are thirty scenes which can be read in registers from bottom to top (**103**). A register near

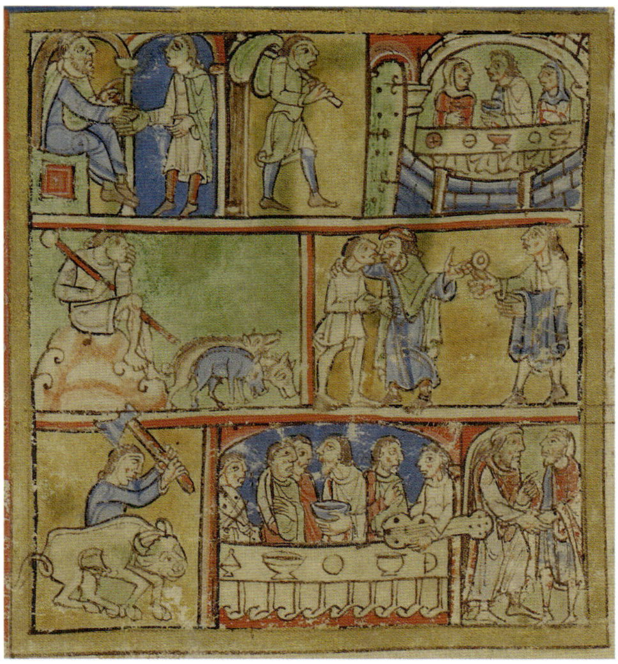

102. Detached leaf (detail) from a psalter, Canterbury c.1150–60. The story unfolds in eight scenes placed in the lower right-hand corner of the page. The Prodigal entertaining prostitutes at the top is contrasted with the celebratory meal on his return, shown in the lower register. New York, Pierpont Morgan Library, MS 521 recto.

the upper end contains the slaughter of the fatted calf, the cooking of the meal with a cauldron hanging over the fire and the elder son protesting to his father. Above, the celebratory meal is in the central roundel, accompanied at the sides by scenes of musicians playing and two servants bringing food in containers. Chartres has the largest number of scenes, but there are almost equally extensive cycles in the cathedrals of Bourges, Poitiers and Auxerre.

Confirming the subject's wide popularity, this is also the period when plays of the Prodigal Son begin to be performed and, indeed, it remained by far the most commonly dramatised of all the parables. There are versions in many languages, including French, Spanish, Dutch and German.[36] The meal with prostitutes in a tavern is usually included in such performances, whereas the meal of forgiveness at the end of the parable is seldom described in the surviving texts.

Outstanding among the rarer appearances of the Prodigal Son in illuminated manuscripts is that in the Gospels from the convent of Goslar in Saxony, dating from about 1230–40 (**104**).[37] Two scenes are contained within the letter F, which opens Luke's gospel (*Fuit in diebus Herodis regis* ...), even though the events depicted occur only in chapter 15. The lower compartment has the son's return to his father with the presentation of the ring, the robe and sandals. Above, the meal is shown with the slaughter and carving of the calf – though there are already three dishes of cooked fowl on the table – and two musicians playing a trumpet and a drum. At the table the father sits on a high-backed throne; in front of him the dish on the table is gold, in contrast with the other dishes of silver. He looks straight ahead in order not to favour either son, but it is the younger who sits on his right in the place of honour, with his hand almost touching his father's shoulder,

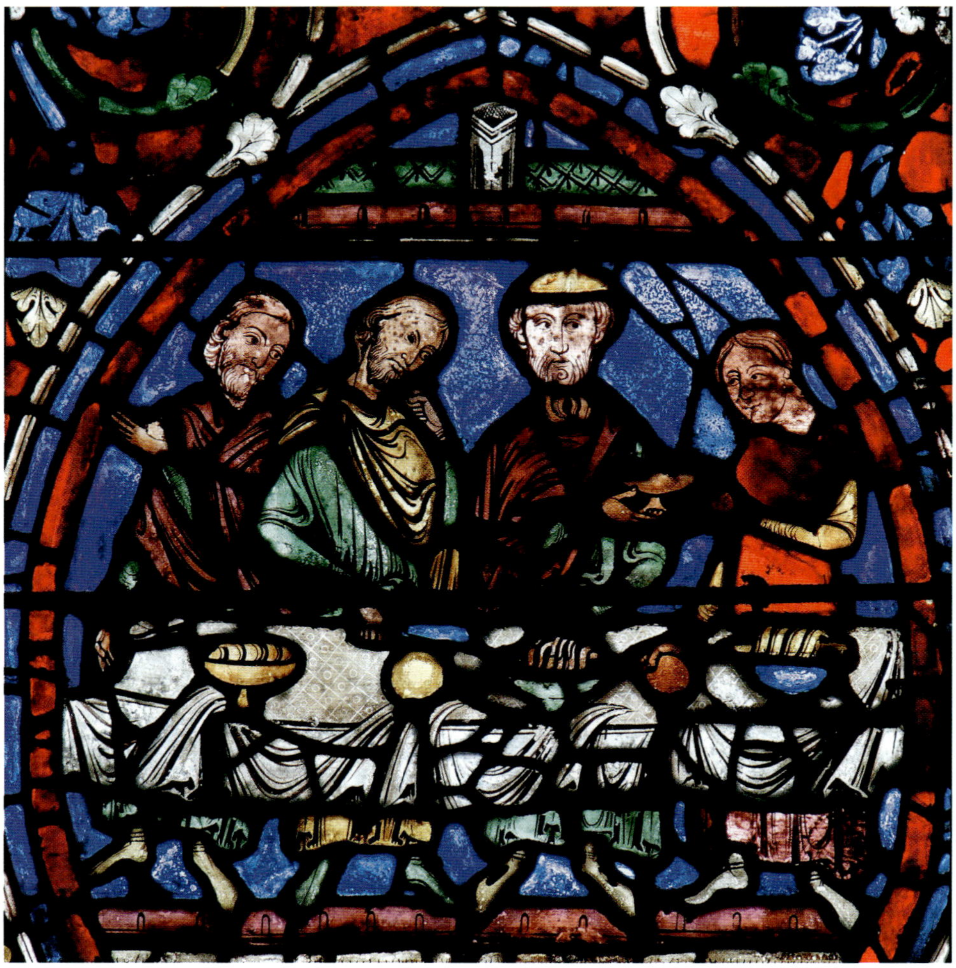

103. Chartres Cathedral, stained glass, north transept, Prodigal Son window, c.1200–10.This is the top of the window showing the celebratory meal.

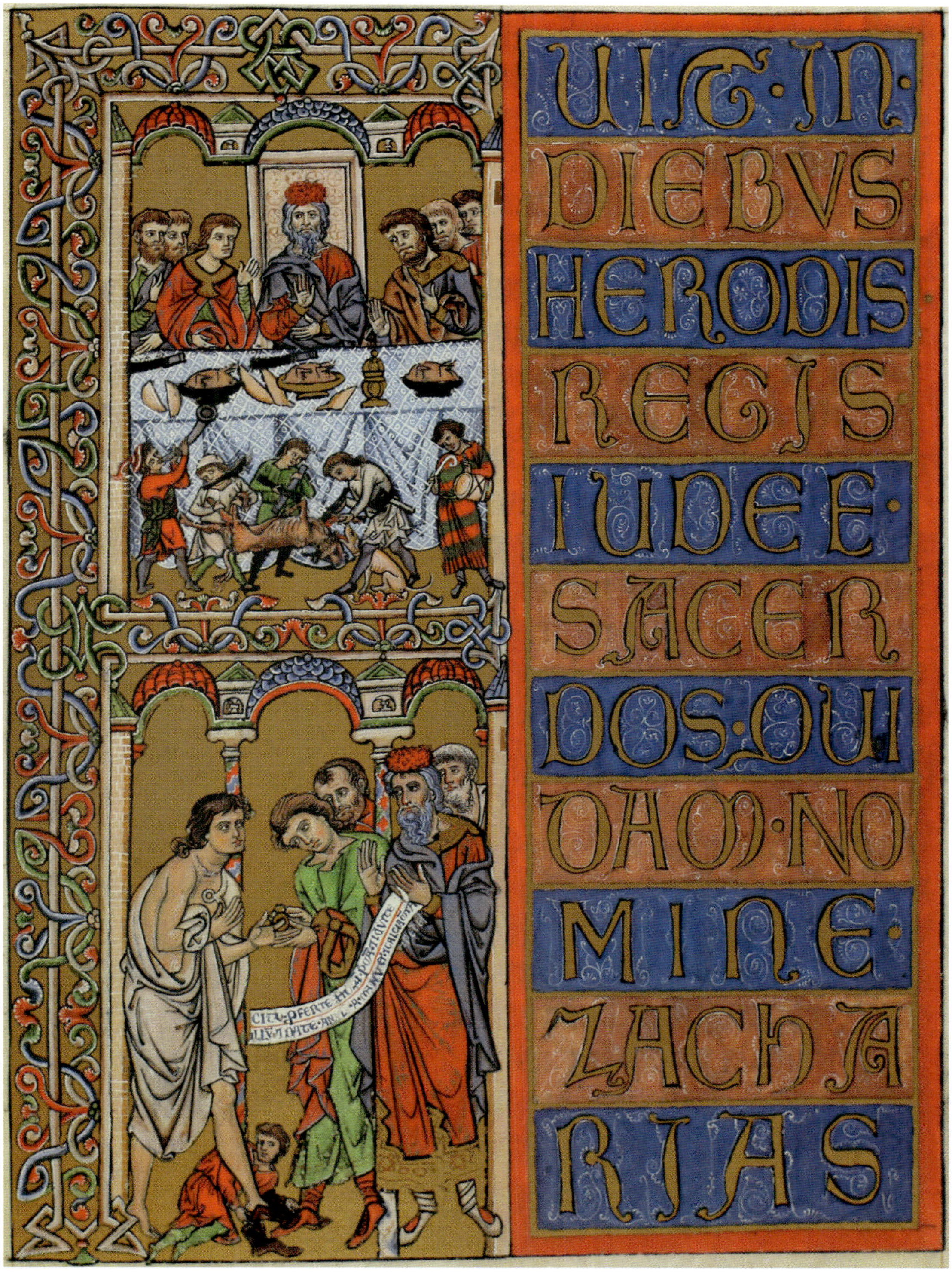

104. Gospels from the abbey of Goslar in Saxony, c.1230–40. Below: the Prodigal's return; he receives the gift of a ring from his father. Above: the slaughter of the fatted calf and the celebratory meal; the Prodigal sits on his father's right. Goslar, Stadtarchiv, MS B 4387, fol. 71.

while the elder is characterised by his furrowed brow. Like the scene of the return, below, the meal emphasises the moral of the penitent son and the merciful father.

Renaissance versions of the parable tended to concentrate on the slaughter of the fatted calf rather than the meal itself. For example, the large canvas by Leandro da Ponte, called Bassano (1557–1622), concentrates on the numerous activities of preparing the meal in the kitchen (**105**). Leandro was the son of Jacopo da Ponte but, unlike his father, he worked in Venice rather than in his native Bassano. The Prodigal's return, kneeling before his father, is shown at the doorway facing a Tintoretto-like landscape, but the bulk of the composition is concentrated on the activities of the kitchen staff. Apart from the calf, there are chickens hanging on the walls as well as being prepared, a basket containing fish in the foreground, vegetables and a cauldron being placed on the fire. The artist is demonstrating his skills as a painter of both genre and still life. The agitated figure gesticulating in the foreground is presumably the servant passing on the father's command to prepare the banquet. That the painting was held in high regard may be judged from the fact that it was subsequently presented by the duke of Medina to the Spanish king Philip IV (1605–65).

In Netherlandish painting the Prodigal's meal with prostitutes, which, as we have seen, featured in the medieval cycles, becomes a popular subject in its own right.[38] The version of Frans Pourbus the elder of Antwerp (1545–81) shows an elegant Prodigal recumbent in the foreground among well-dressed women, musicians and a jester (**106**). They are seated

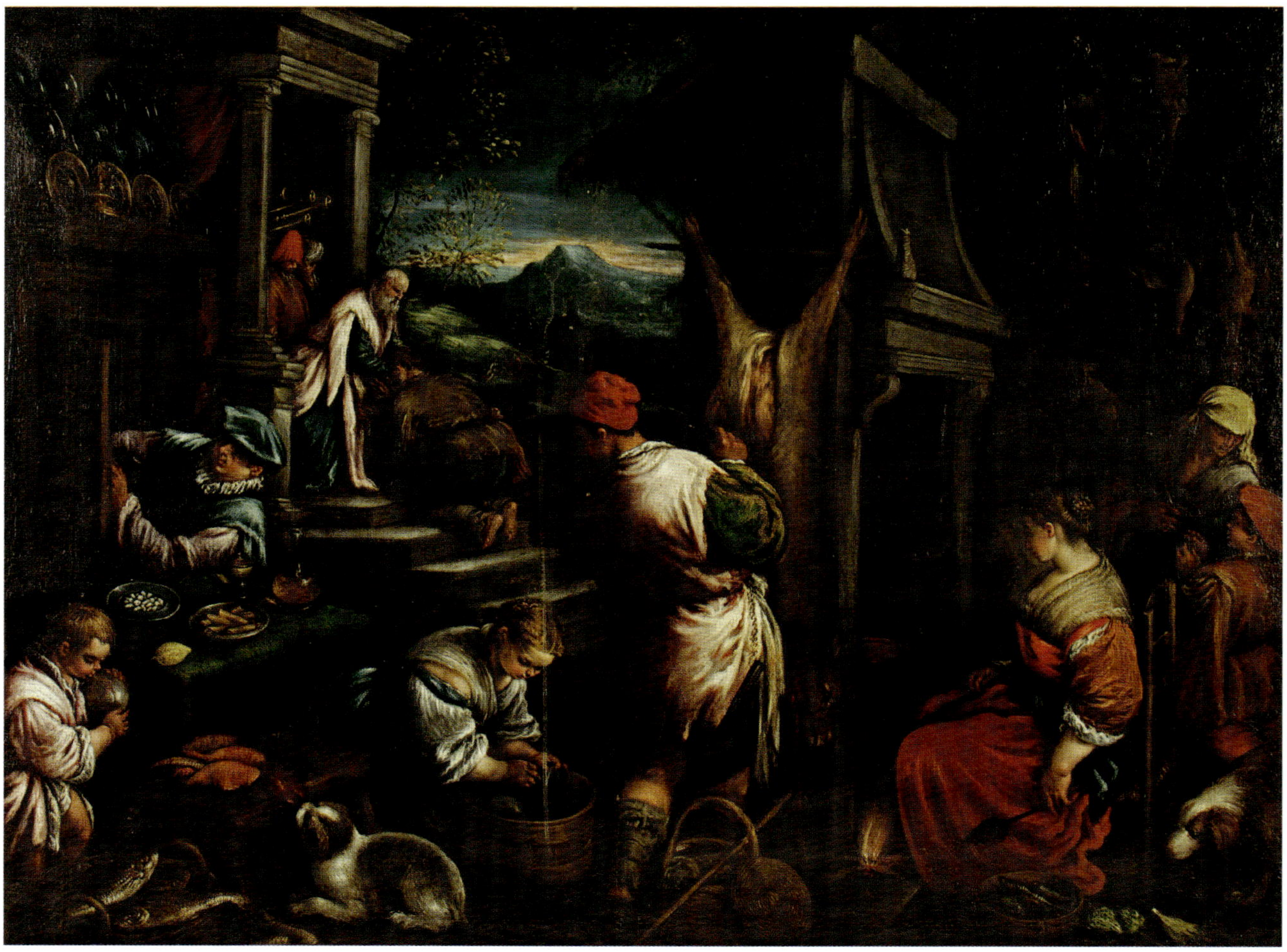

105. Leandro Bassano (Venice, 1557–1622), oil painting centred on the slaughter of the fatted calf. Bristol, City Art Gallery. This is a smaller version of the painting in the Prado, Madrid.

106. Frans Pourbus the elder (Antwerp, 1545–81), oil painting. The Prodigal Son's meal with prostitutes (detail). Fruit and sugar balls are shown in the dishes on the table. Antwerp, Museum Mayer van den Bergh.

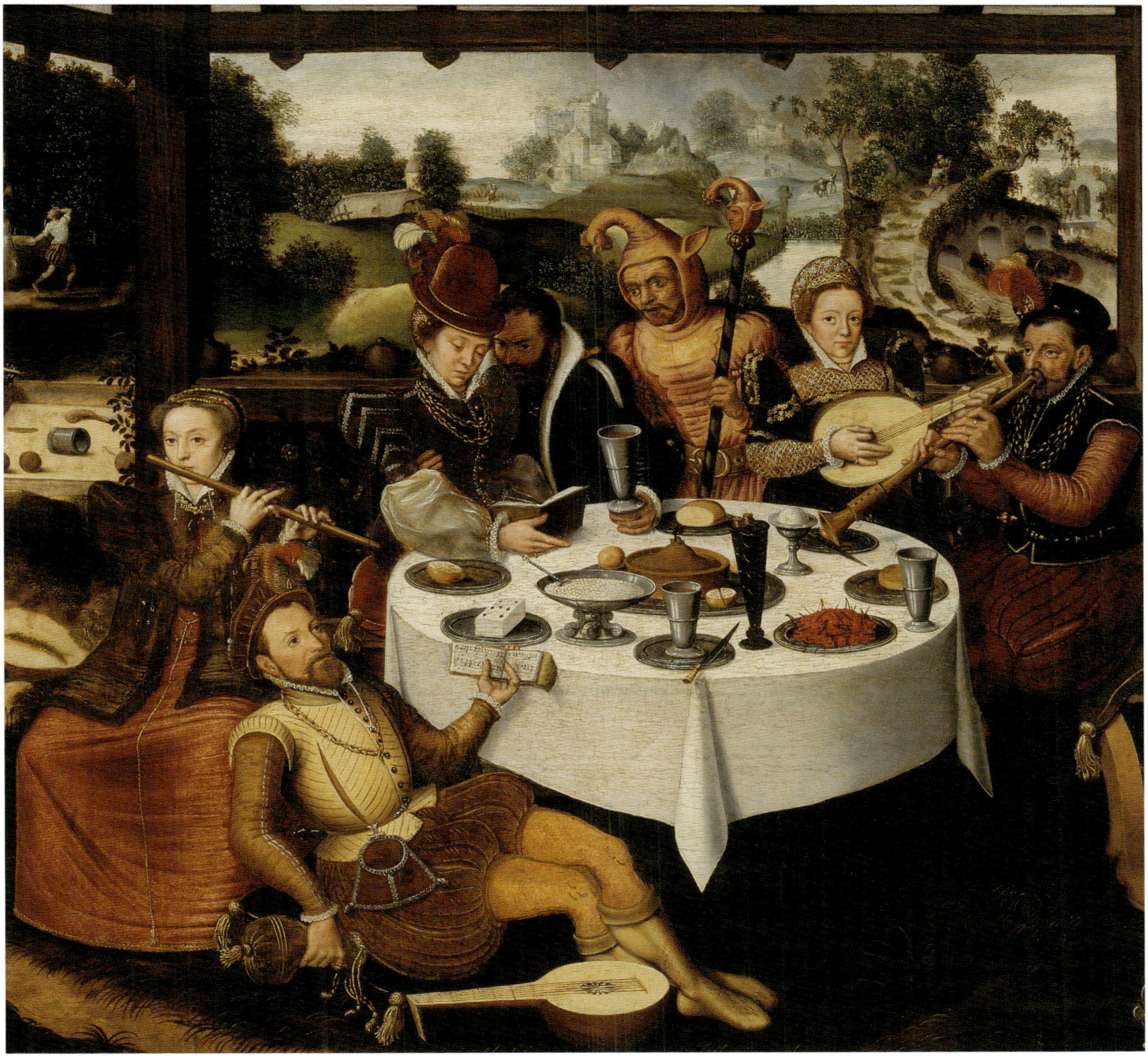

at a table richly covered with silver goblets and dishes of fruit and of sugar balls or 'candy', which we have seen in Veronese's Marriage at Cana. A servant is ratcheting up the cost on a board at the side. There are two further scenes in the background. On the left, the Prodigal is being beaten and stripped by a woman, not strictly in the biblical text but an epitome of his fall due to dissolute living which had been depicted since the time of the windows at Chartres. The return to his father can be discerned on the bridge on the right in the far distance – a reminder of the penitence and forgiveness that ends the story.

DIVES, THE RICH MAN, AND LAZARUS

There was a rich man who was dressed in purple and fine linen and who feasted sumptuously every day. And at his gate lay a poor man named Lazarus, covered with sores, who longed to satisfy his hunger with what fell from the rich man's table, even the dogs would come and lick his sores. The poor man died and was carried away by angels to be with Abraham. The rich man also died and was buried. In Hades, where he was being tormented, he looked up and saw Abraham far away with Lazarus by his side. (Luke 16.19–23)

The earliest Church Fathers, Irenaeus (second century), Tertullian (d. after 220) and Gregory of Nazianzus (d.390), took up the moral lesson of the parable. It is the beggar who goes to heaven while the selfish uncharitable rich man is duly tormented in hell. The story appears in compact form in one of the earliest extant illustrations, in the Gospels of Otto III produced at Reichenau in about 996 (Aachen Cathedral, **107**).[39] In the lower roundel the rich man is seated with his guests at a round table. He is

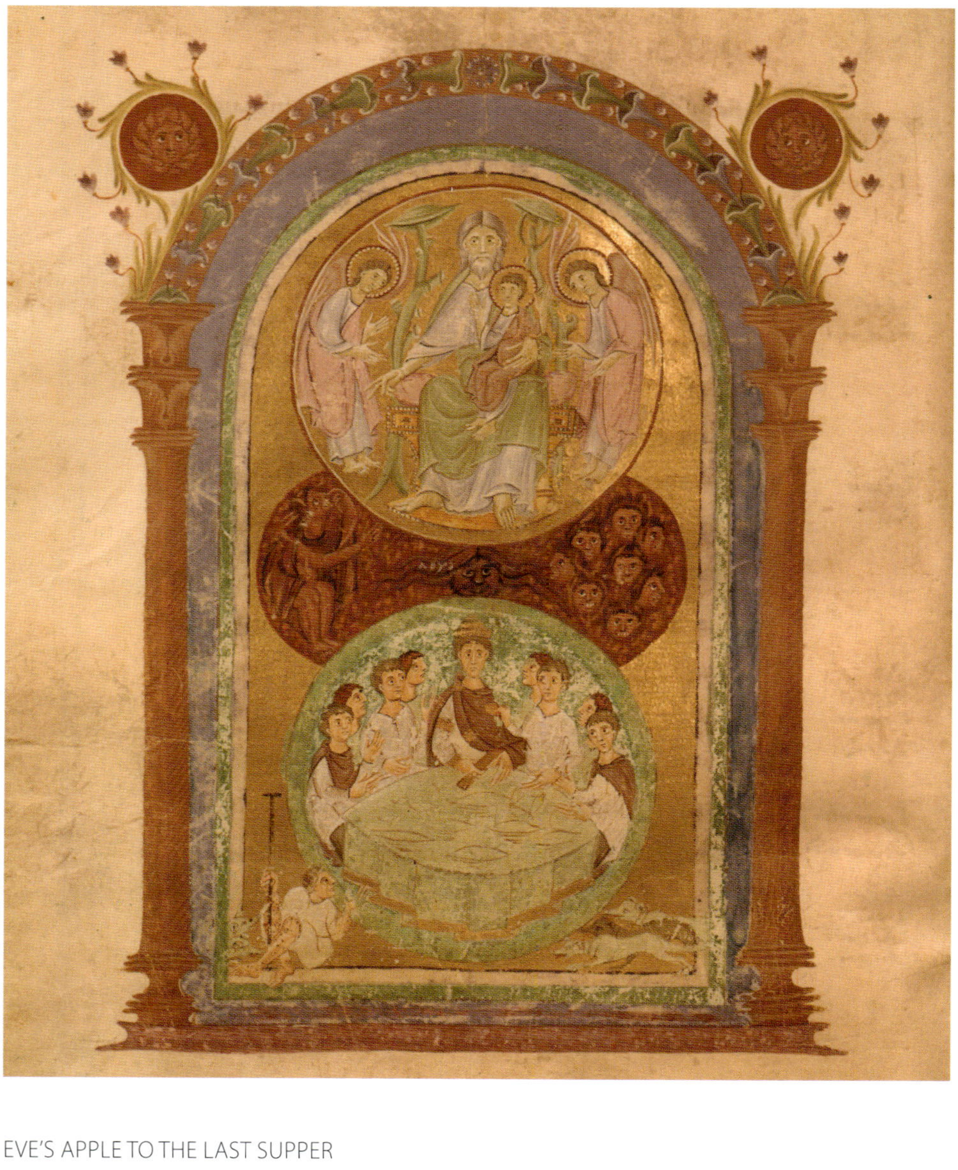

107. Gospels of Otto III from the abbey of Reichenau, c.996. Lazarus crouches below the rich man's table and is subsequently shown on Abraham's bosom while the rich man is in the darkness of hell. Aachen Cathedral Treasury.

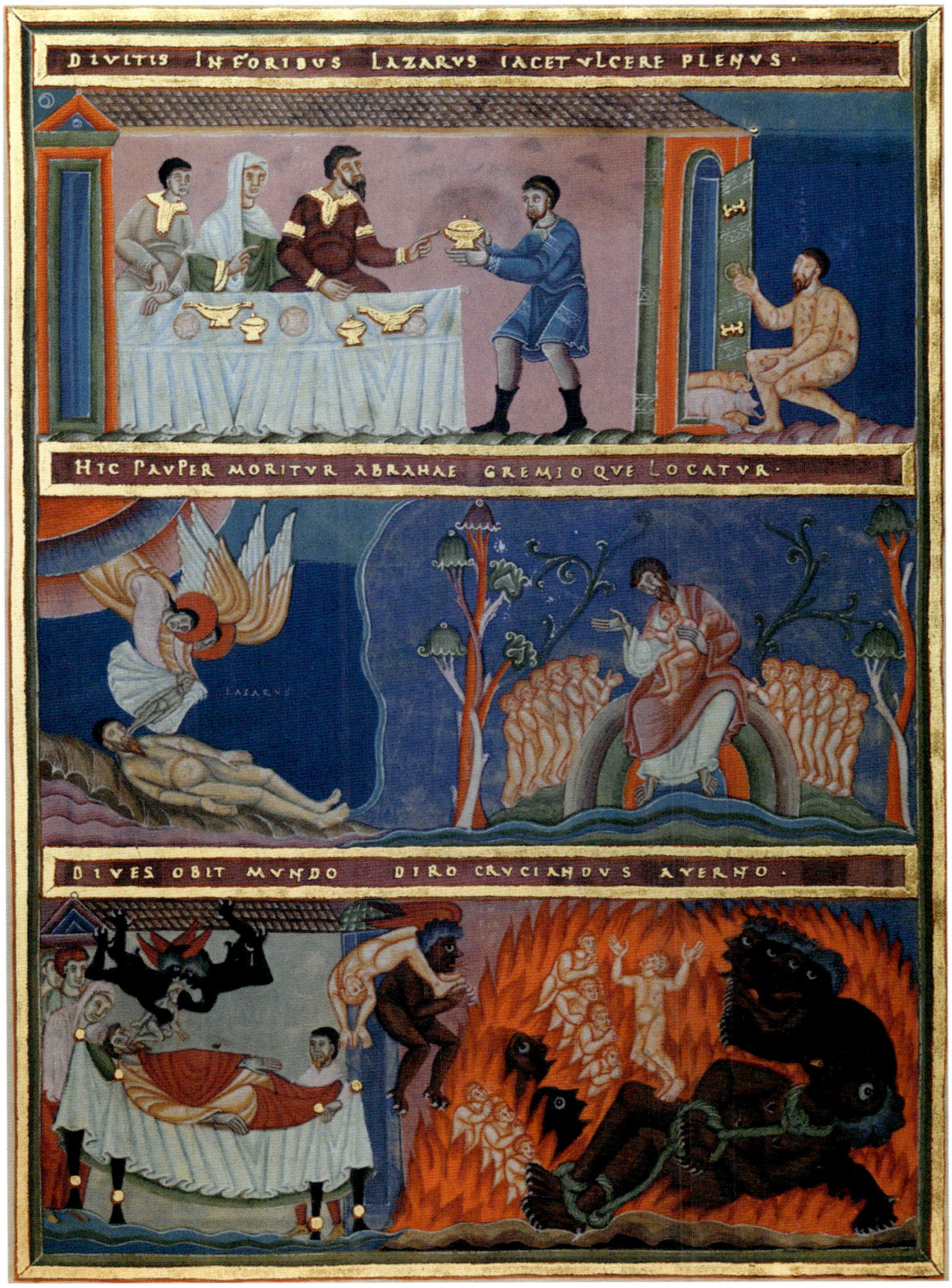

108. Golden Gospels from the abbey of Echternach, near Trier, c.1030. The meal is at the top, the respective fates of Lazarus and then Dives in the lower registers. Nürnberg, Germanisches Nationalmuseum, MS 156 142, fol. 78.

shown crowned, following Luke's description of his dress as 'purple and byssus' (the finest linen), which was taken from earlier commentaries to identify him as a king. Lazarus, tormented by dogs, squats below. There are numerous dishes and plates on the table, but none are shown containing any food. This scene is balanced by a roundel with Lazarus on Abraham's bosom at the top, while the rich man in the darkness of hell appears within a partially visible oval between the two.

A more extended narrative appears in two manuscripts of the Gospels from Echternach. The earlier of these is once again the Golden Gospels in Nürnberg, in which the parable takes its place among the illustrations to Luke (**108**). The meal is shown in the upper register, with Dives, his wife and a guest seated at the table, while Lazarus, covered in sores, is pleading at the gate. Dishes and goblets are clearly visible on the table and a servant is bringing in another bowl, but once again, no food is shown apart

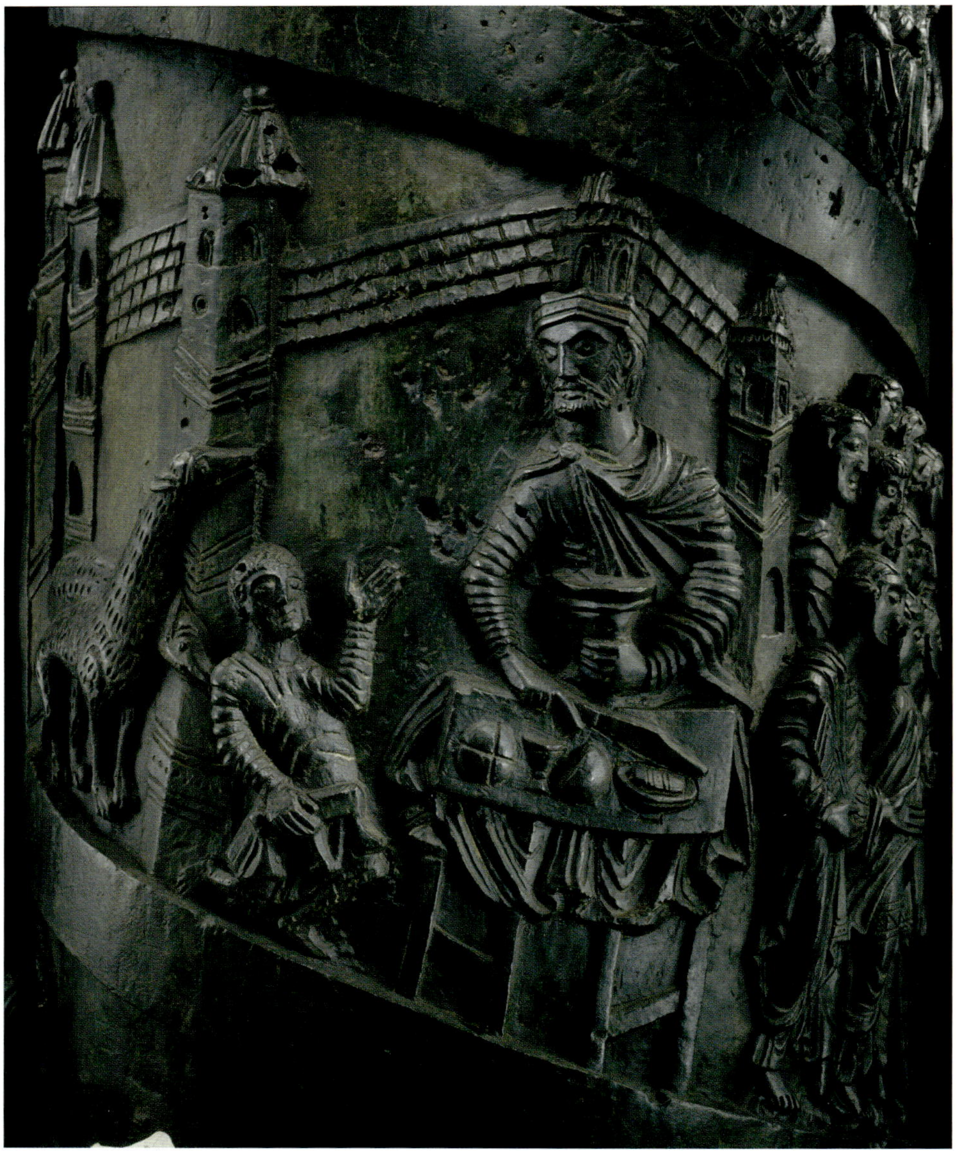

109. Triumphal column of Christ (detail), bronze, c.1020–30, Hildesheim Cathedral in Saxony. Dives holds a knife in his right hand; Lazarus is covered in boils and carries a clapper to warn of his approach.

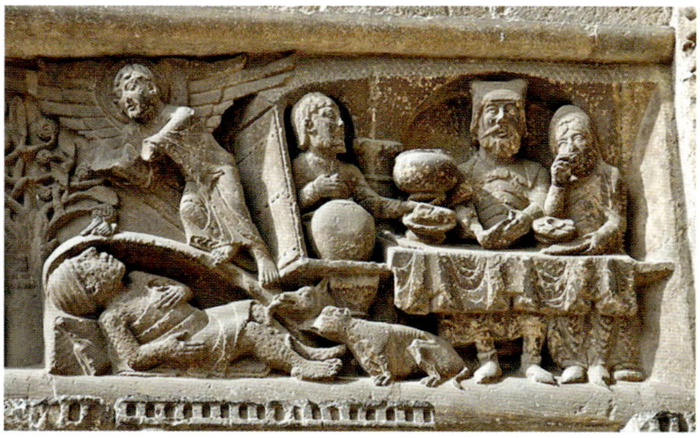

110. Abbey church of Moissac, stone carving in porch, c.1120–30.The meal, with Dives' wife eating from her hand, is on the right, Dives transported to Abraham's lap on the left.

from the loaves of bread. The narrative depends on the gestures of the two principal characters. Lazarus is pleading with upraised arm while Dives is signalling his negative response with a prominently extended index finger of his left hand. The respective fates of the two, with Lazarus on Abraham's bosom and Dives in hell, are figured in the middle and lower registers.

This way of recounting all the stages of the parable becomes standard. Another early example is on the triumphal column of Christ of about 1020–30 in Hildesheim Cathedral in Saxony (**109**). Under the inspiration of Bishop Bernward (993–1020), Hildesheim became a centre for artefacts of metalwork and this column was one of several outstanding monuments in bronze produced there at the time. Originally made for St Michael's Church in Hildesheim, it was intended as a triumphal column of Christ based on the Emperor Trajan's triumphal column in Rome. Twenty-four scenes of the life of Christ, from the Baptism to the Entry into Jerusalem,

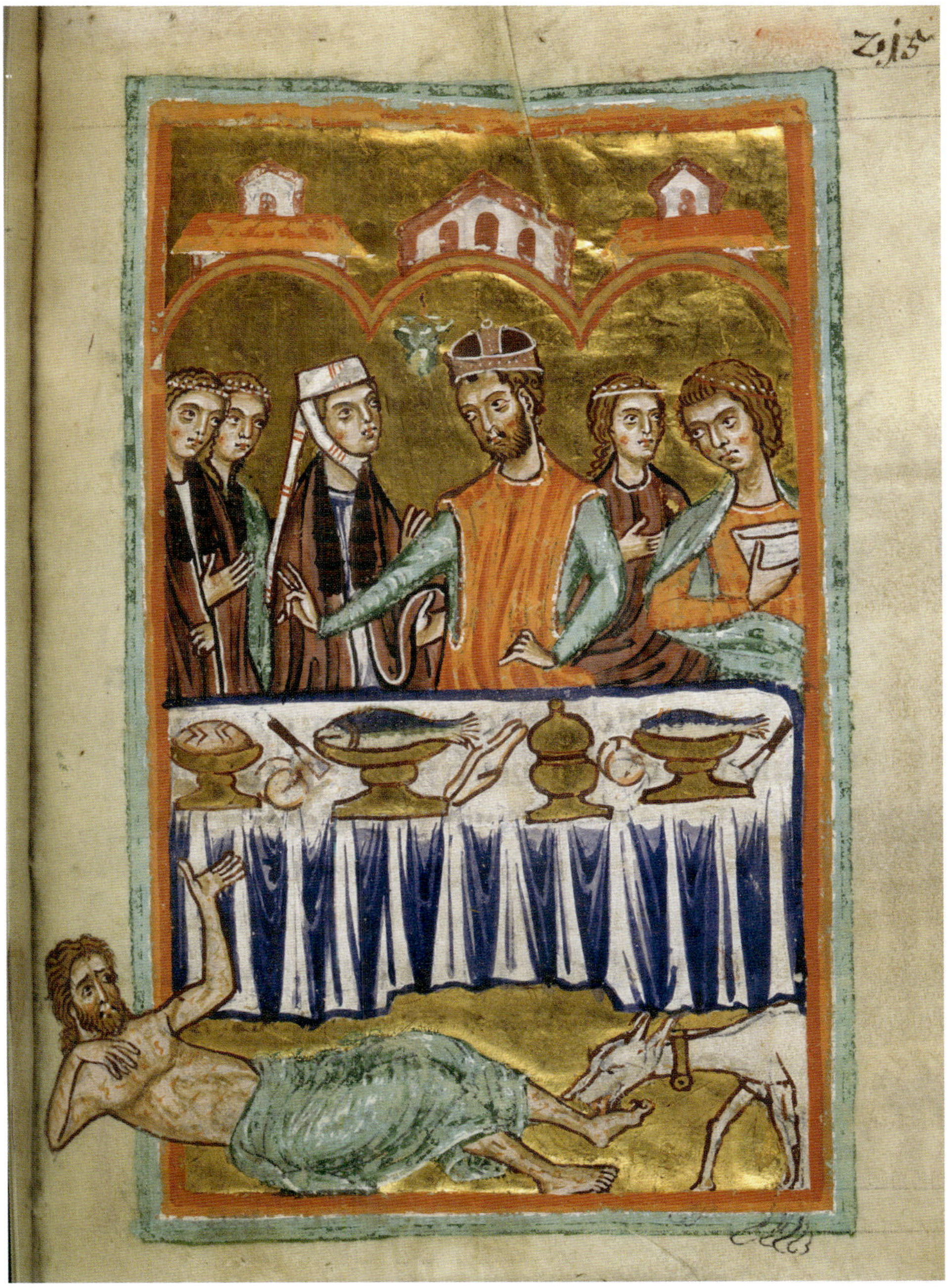

111. Gospel lectionary from the abbey of St Martin, Cologne, c.1220–30. Fish and knives are prominent on the table. Brussels, Bibliothèque Royale, MS 9222, fol. 108.

unfold in a spiral narrative. Dives is seated alone at the table, while Lazarus, covered in pock marks and dwarfed by two huge dogs, kneels below. The rich man holds a goblet in one hand and a knife in the other; his severe glance is contrasted with the pitiful expression of the beggar. The small table is covered in bread and dishes. Dives in hell and Lazarus on Abraham's bosom are shown in the following scene.

The increasing popularity of the subject in Romanesque sculpture, particularly in France, has been connected with the scourge of leprosy accompanying the growth of populations in towns. From the twelfth century hospitals were dedicated to St Lazare. This was Lazarus, the friend of Jesus whom he raised from the dead, but there was room for confusion with Lazarus, the beggar of the parable who was covered in sores. The cathedral at Autun was dedicated to St Lazare, but it was Lazarus the beggar who was depicted on a doorway capital in the north transept.[40]

Best-known of such sculptural representations is that on the west wall of the porch of the abbey church at Moissac, dating from about 1120–30 (**110**). The top register, carved in deep relief, shows the rich man with his wife at the table and a recumbent Lazarus about to be transported by an angel to Abraham, who is enthroned on the left. Under the arcades below, in a more damaged condition, we see the fate of Dives and, in the bottom register, to underline the moral of the story, figures of Avarice and Luxury accompanied by devils. The meal at the table is centred on the monumental figure of the rich man. At his side, his wife is shown bringing food to her lips in her right hand, while a servant standing in the doorway is bringing a jug and a dish with meat. The contrast between the imperious Dives and the recumbent Lazarus in his death throes could hardly be more explicit.

In the medieval liturgy the Parable of Dives and Lazarus was read out on Thursday after the second Sunday in Lent and illustrations of it are quite often included in Lectionaries, which cover the Gospel texts read through the liturgical year. An example is the lectionary of about 1220–30 from the Benedictine abbey of St Martin, Cologne (**111**). Only the meal is shown. Dives crowned as king, seated at the table, points towards Lazarus, who is lying below, with his head and shoulders beyond the picture frame. Prominent on the table are two dishes containing large fish, bread rolls and also two knives. The queen is shown in discussion with her husband, rather than pointing at Lazarus, as in some of the earlier illustrations.

Two centuries later an engraving by Heinrich Aldegrever, dated 1554, demonstrates the extent of the continuity of pictorial traditions (**112**). Costumes are brought up to date and the architecture of the interior is more realistically portrayed, but the composition has remained standard. Aldegrever was active 1502–55 as a goldsmith and engraver in Soest in Westphalia

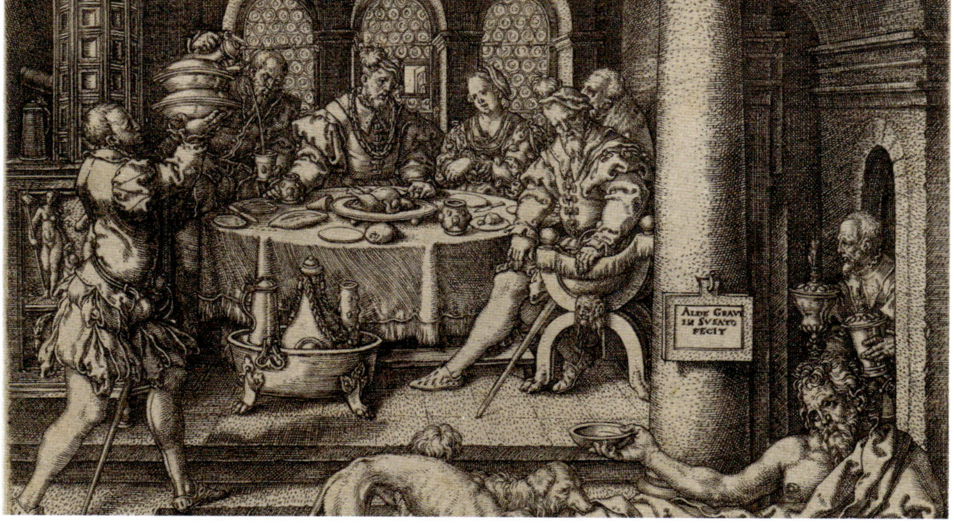

112. Engraving by Heinrich Aldegrever (active 1502–55, Soest, Westphalia), dated 1554. The costumes have been brought up to date, but the composition closely follows the pictorial tradition. British Museum, no. 1923–0417.27.

113. Frans Francken the elder (Antwerp, 1542–1616), oil painting, dated (?) 1605. The detailed portrayal of the food on the table is in the tradition of Netherlandish still life painting. Museum der Brotkultur, Ulm.

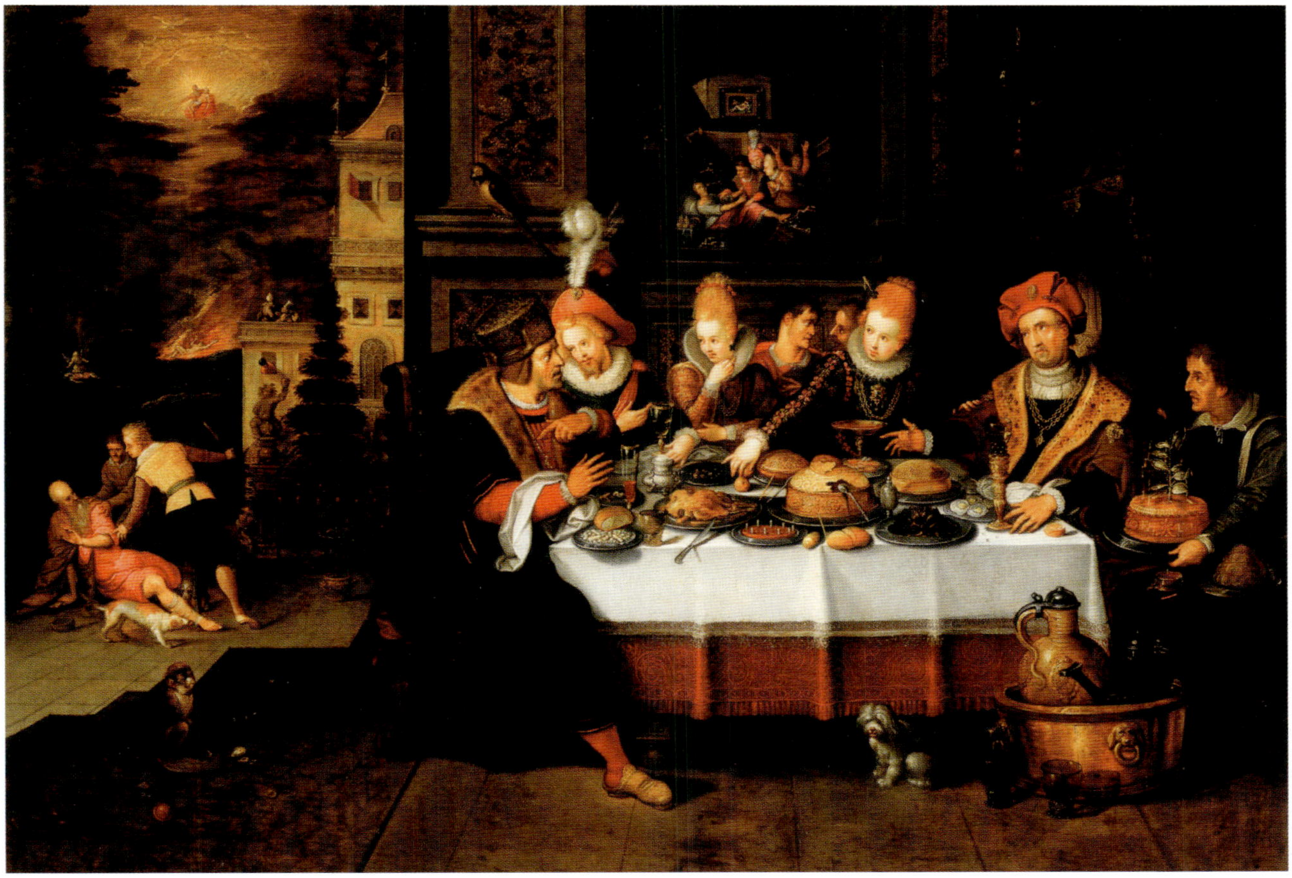

and, like many others, under the influence of Dürer. He belongs to a group called '*Kleinmeister*' – literally 'small masters' – so-called not to belittle their work but because they adhered to a small format. This is the second of Aldegrever's five engravings illustrating the Parable of Dives and Lazarus. Due emphasis is placed on the expensive clothes of the family and guests and on the contemporary German silver vessels, including a wine cooler on the floor. A fowl on a dish is prominent at the centre of the table. Lazarus's suffering and sorrow are likewise graphically portrayed. All the *Kleinmeister* were early Protestants, dubious about religious imagery, but free to illustrate the Parables as moral tales to be followed or warned against.

The emphasis on the diners' upper-class costumes remains a central feature in the small cabinet painting by Frans Francken the elder of Antwerp (1542–1616) (**113**). This is the age of the still life in Netherlandish painting and the richly laid table is weighed down by piles of food on bowls and plates, including a fowl, large pies, bread and fruit. Outside, a servant threatens Lazarus with a stick, but a brightly lit sky indicates his future in heaven, whereas the less happy deathbed scene of Dives is shown in a picture on the arcade behind the diners.

17
HEROD'S FEAST: THE DEATH OF JOHN THE BAPTIST

For John had been telling Herod, 'It is not lawful for you to have your brother's wife' and Herodias had a grudge against him, and wanted to kill him. But she could not … But an opportunity came when Herod on his birthday gave a banquet for his courtiers and officers and for the leaders of Galilee. When the daughter of Herodias came in and danced, she pleased Herod and his guests; and the king said to the girl, 'Ask me for whatever you wish, and I will give it.' … She went out and said to her mother, 'What should I ask for?' She replied, 'The head of John the baptiser.' Immediately she rushed back to the king and requested, 'I want you to give me at once the head of John the Baptist on a platter.' The king was deeply grieved; yet out of regard for his oaths … he did not want to refuse her. Immediately the king sent a soldier of the guard with orders to bring John's head. He went and beheaded him in prison, brought his head on a platter and gave it to the girl. Then the girl gave it to her mother. (Mark 6.18–28.)

(Matthew 14.1–11 has a shorter version without mention of a banquet.)

The Herod responsible for the death of John the Baptist was Herod Antipas, son of Herod the Great, the ruler who interviewed the three Magi at the time of Christ's birth and who was responsible for the Massacre of the Innocents. Herod Antipas, ruler of Palestine, was married to Herodias, granddaughter of Herod the Great, but from a different branch of his family. She married Herod Philip, whom she divorced in order to marry his half-brother Herod Antipas. It was owing to this offence against the rules of consanguineous unions that the Baptist had criticised her second marriage, which led to the events that cost him his life.

In many of the depictions Herodias is shown seated at the banquet, though the biblical text makes it clear that she was not there. Her daughter is described as going out to speak with the mother and then rushing back to Herod at the banquet. Neither Matthew nor Mark mention the daughter's name, but it is given as Salomé by Flavius Josephus' *Jewish Antiquities* (Bk. 18, ch. 5) written in the first century CE, not very long after the events it describes. Josephus does not deal with

114. Gospel of St Matthew (Codex Sinopensis), sixth century, Syria or Palestine. The diners recline on a semi-circular couch running round three sides of the table, while a servant brings the head of the Baptist to Herodias. Paris, Bibliothèque Nationale. MS Suppl. grec 1286, fol. 10v.

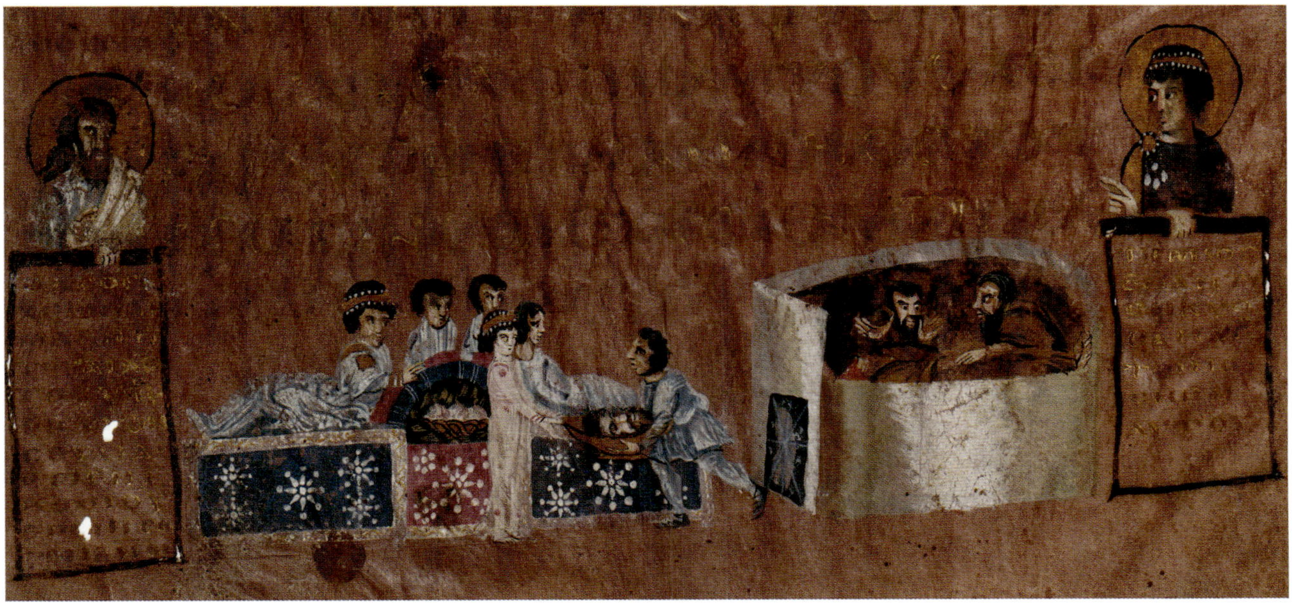

the banquet, but provides details of Herod the Great's genealogy, showing that Salomé was the daughter of Herodias and Herod Philip. From the time of the early commentators it was accepted that Salomé's dance was the centre of the story. St Ambrose condemned the erotic nature of dancing, which had such a forceful effect on Herod's decision: 'John, precursor of Christ, was beheaded at the wish of a dancing woman.'[41]

The seductive appeal of Salomé's dance doubtless added to the enormous popularity of the story and its depictions, but its importance in the Gospels is due to the historical and theological status of John the Baptist as the forerunner and herald of Jesus Christ. The son of Mary's kinswoman Elizabeth and her husband Zacharias, priest of Jerusalem, he became an itinerant preacher who washed in the Jordan those who confessed, ultimately baptising Jesus himself. Soon afterwards he was imprisoned for being openly critical of Herod for marrying his brother's wife. There is no mention in the Gospels of John's head being brought to Herod at the banquet, as is often seen in the illustrations. The image of the saint's head isolated on a charger is dramatic enough, but actually placing it in on the dinner table provided a truly horrendous and unforgettable climax.

The earliest depiction is in the sixth-century codex Sinopensis, which contains part of St Matthew's Gospel (**114**).[42] As we have seen in discussing the Miracle of the Loaves and Fishes, its illustrations are placed at the foot of the page and each scene is flanked by two Old Testament figures holding scrolls containing the prophecies relevant to the gospel text. The banquet is of central importance to the story and is included in the illustration even though it is not mentioned in Matthew's Gospel. Here, Herod, crowned, and his guests are reclining on a semi-circular couch (*stibadium*) running round three sides of a table, a form which replaced the oblong tables of the Roman *triclinium* in the fourth century.[43] The woman reclining opposite him may be Herodias, though she is not crowned. A servant is bringing the head of the Baptist to Salomé, who is standing in front of the table, which contains a basket filled with pomegranates. On the right there is the prison where two disciples gesticulate with horror over the Baptist's decapitated and bleeding body. Like the form of the table, the modelling of the faces and draperies is still in the tradition of classical naturalism insofar as it had survived in the sixth century. The two Old Testament figures with their prophetic scrolls are Moses, quoting

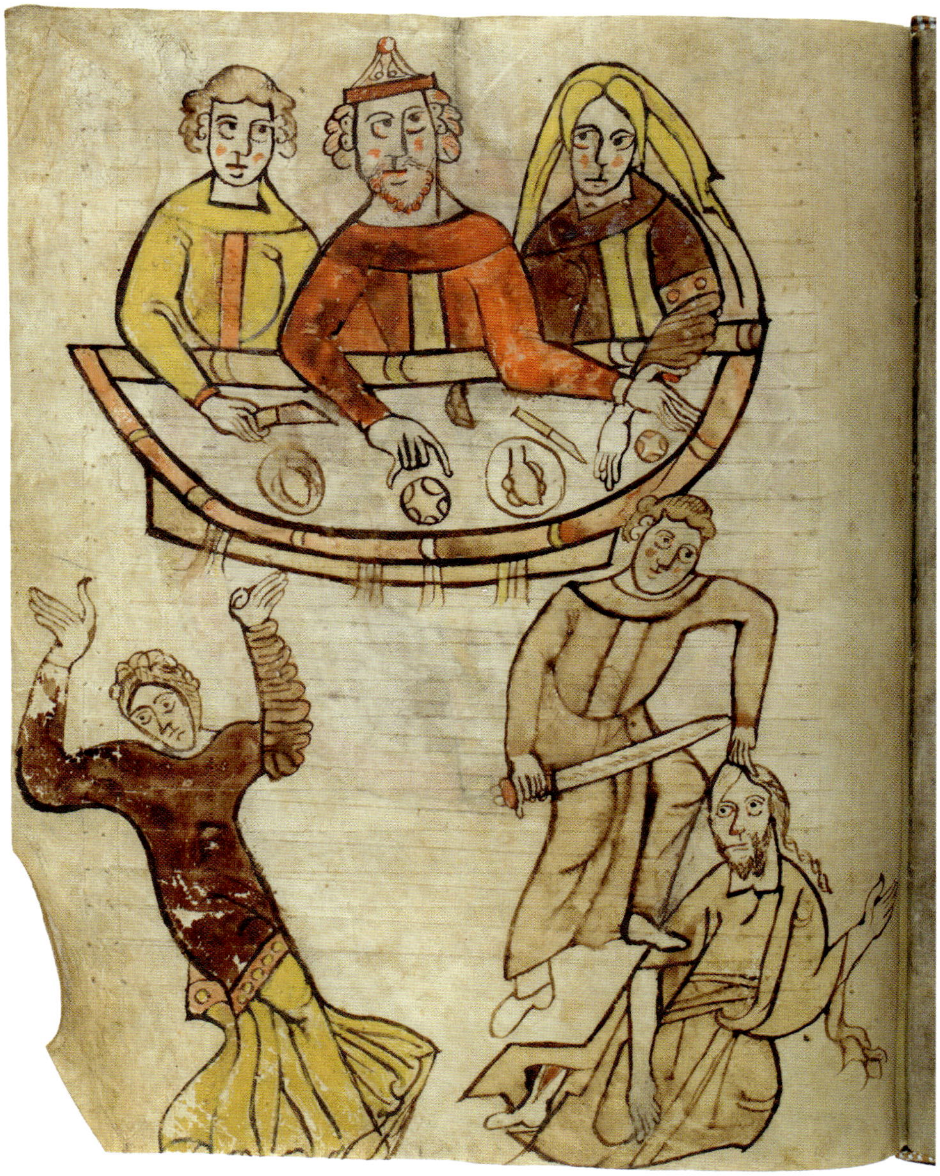

115. Gospels from Chartres, second half of the ninth century. The diners are now seated at a semi-circular table and Salomé is shown dancing. Paris, Bibliothèque Nationale. MS lat. 9386, fol. 146v.

Genesis 9.6, on the left, and David, with Psalm 116.15, on the right, concerning, respectively, the punishment for the shedding of human blood and the Lord considering the death of his faithful ones.

The earliest Western example, a Latin book of the Gospels from Chartres dating from the second half of the ninth century (**115**), has two somewhat crude drawings devoted to the martyrdom of the Baptist.[44] The meal, no longer at a Roman *stibadium*, is now shown at a semi-circular table at which both Herod, gesturing his promise, and Herodias are seated. Below it, Salomé's dance is next to the beheading, making it appear as though the martyrdom took place at the banquet. Salomé dances with her arms emphatically raised, while the body is slightly twisted, her left leg in front of the right. This became one of the most common of her dance postures, of which a great variety have been depicted. Indeed, there are about a dozen different dance postures in which she is shown – from the acrobatic to the sword dance – in the vast number of surviving images.

A century later the narrative more clearly unfolds. The Gospels of the Emperor Otto III, produced at Reichenau in about 996 (Aachen Cathedral, **116**) shows a similar sequence of events as the Sinope gospel fragment, but the changes in the composition are also notable. All the illuminations in the manuscript are full page and elaborately framed, and the narrative is developed from the top downwards. Here the meal is followed by the beheading in the prison and the scene of Salomé bringing the head to Herodias, a key event omitted in both the Sinope and Chartres Gospels. Above, Herod and his guests – all male – seated at a round table, are all looking towards the dancing Salomé, who is shown in the twisting cross-legged posture, more realistically portrayed than in the Chartres Gospels. The details of the story conveyed in these three scenes contrasts with the total emptiness of the table top. The diners are presumably waiting for the food to arrive while they enjoy the sight of the dancing girl.

Of the increasing number of illustrations of the scene in the twelfth century, perhaps the best known is the capital of c.1125–50 from the former cloister of the Cathedral of St Etienne in Toulouse (**117**, **118**). On one of the narrow faces of the capital Herod admires the dancing Salomé, a scene of erotic content unusual in the twelfth century. The beheading is shown on the narrow side, while the principal face of the capital depicts the executioner handing the Baptist's head on a charger to Salomé. Her figure is repeated as she passes the dish to her mother, who is seated next to Herod. There are several dishes of bread and meat on the table, but it is the Baptist's head that forms the focal point of the composition.

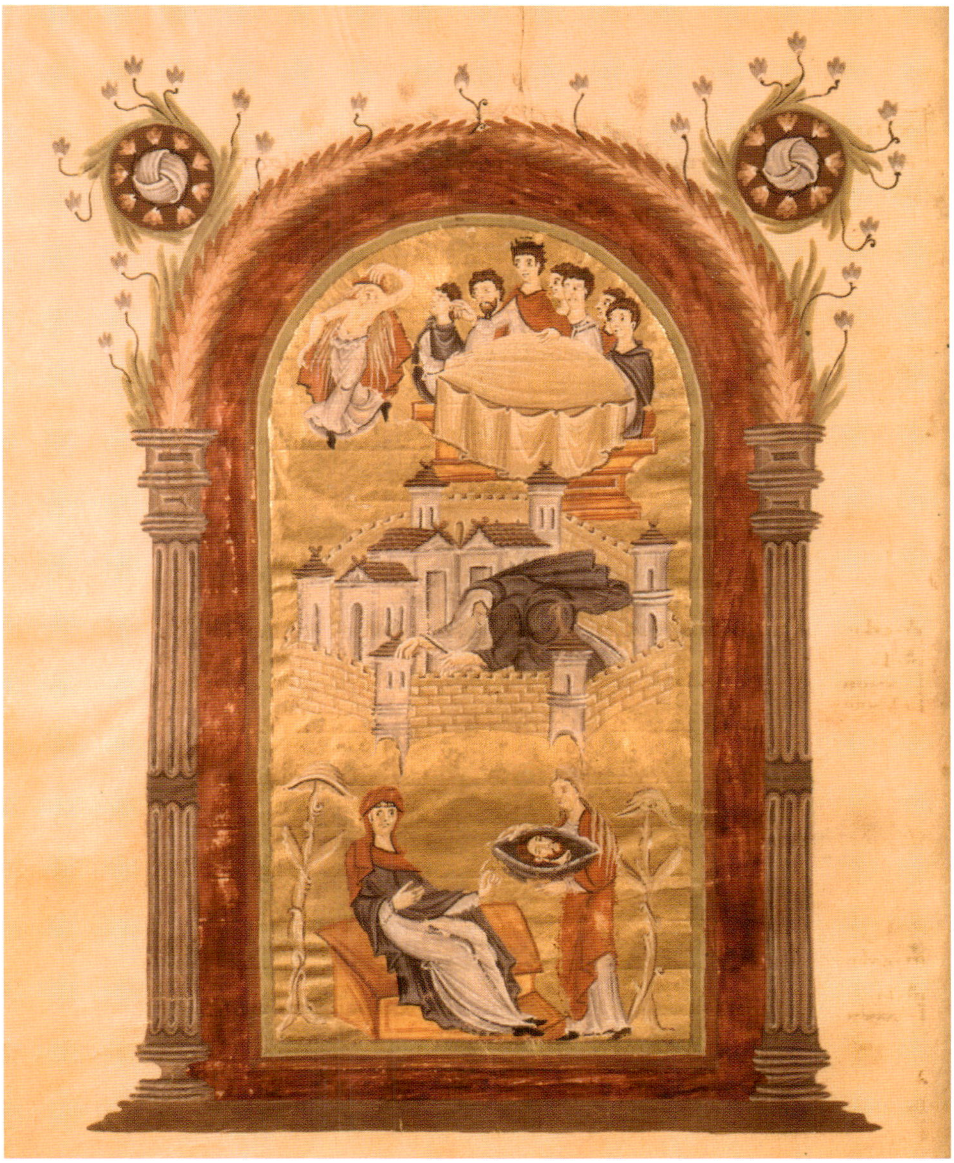

116. Gospels of Otto III from the abbey of Reichenau, c.996. The meal is at the top though there is no food on the table. Below, John is beheaded and then Salomé brings the head to Herodias. Aachen, Cathedral Treasury.

117, 118. Carved capital from the Cathedral of St Etienne in Toulouse, c.1125–50. Herod admires the dancing Salomé; the Baptist's head passed to Salomé and Herod's Feast. Toulouse, Musée des Augustins.

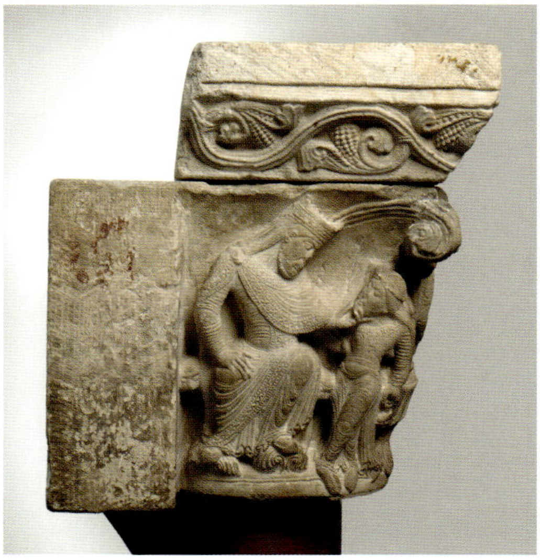

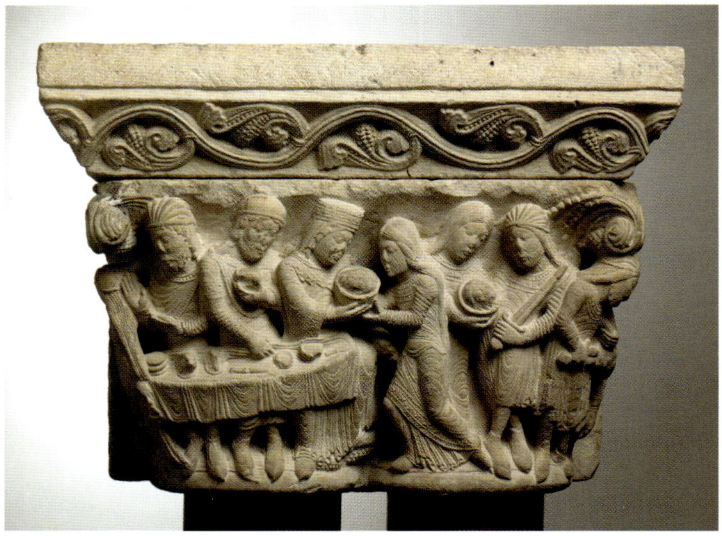

The growing popularity of the subject remains linked to the importance of John the Baptist, but it has also been suggested that its more frequent appearance on church sculpture in both France and Italy was at least partly due to the subject of Herod's marriage to his brother's wife. The issue of consanguineous unions of the kind that John had condemned had taken on contemporary relevance when it was raised at the first and second Lateran Councils in 1123 and 1139.[45]

Herod's feast also remains quite a common subject in cycles of the Life of Christ in illuminated manuscripts. One of the fullest is in an English psalter of about 1200–10, probably from Oxford (**119**).[46] Most of the Old Testament pictures precede the psalter text; those of the New Testament are in groups following four of the Psalms. The full-page miniature has the meal at the top, the beheading with Herodias awaiting the Baptist's head below. Herod and his male guests are at the table. Herodias is seated in the same space but not at the meal, while Salomé appears twice. On the left she is extracting Herod's promise and, in the centre, dancing with her back bent double and her arms outstretched. Her acrobatic posture has been described as that of a tumbler, but this implies walking on her hands, while the proposed link with Saracen women dancing also lacks precise evidence.[47] At the table, which is covered with knives, loaves and breadsticks, Herod and two of the guests are holding their cups; another takes a fish in his hand from a plate in front of him.

Among the numerous versions of the scene on wall paintings in Italian churches of the fourteenth and fifteenth centuries, the most famous is probably Giotto's fresco of about 1320 in the Peruzzi Chapel in the Church of Santa Croce in Florence. Unfortunately its rubbed and restored condition makes it difficult to appreciate. Equally well known is the gilt bronze relief on the hexagonal font in the Baptistery of Siena, the work of Donatello, dated 1423–25 (**120**).[48] Both the converging lines of the tiled pavement and the view of receding arches into the background render this relief a pioneer of geometric perspective. The story starts in the third room in the distance, where the executioner is holding up the Baptist's head and handing it to Salomé and her companions. In the background the guests gather at the table while Salomé dances and a soldier presents the head on a charger directly to Herod. This is contrary to the biblical text, but it had been shown in this form already by Giotto a century earlier. Most dramatic and individually striking are the gestures and facial expressions – Herod reclining in horror and the guest in the middle covering his agonised face with his right hand. The woman seated next to

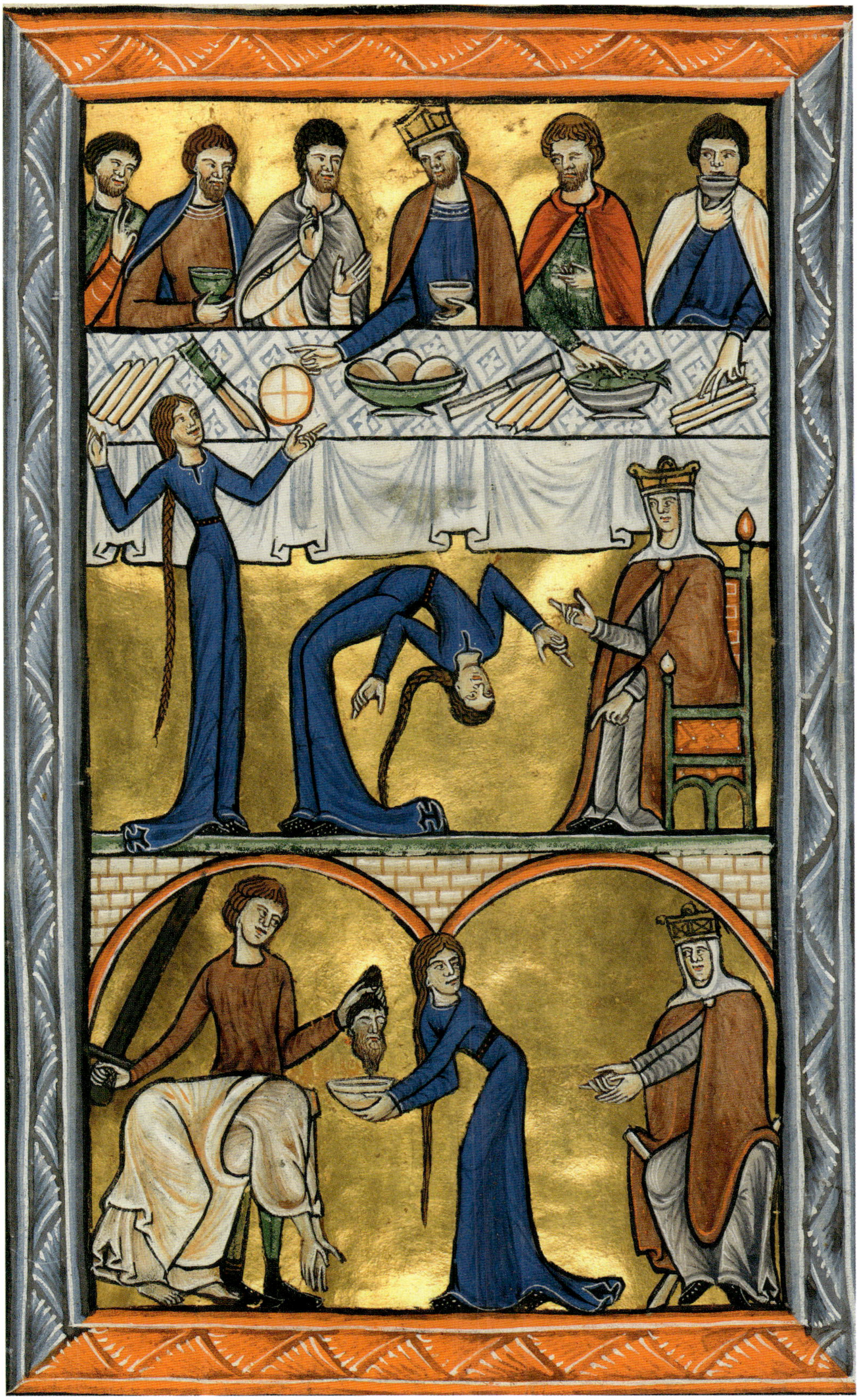

119. Psalter, probably from Oxford, c.1200–10. The guests are watching Salomé perform a dance; one of them picks up a fish in his hand. The beheading of St John is shown below. Munich, Bayerische Staatsbibliothek, MS lat.835, fol. 66.

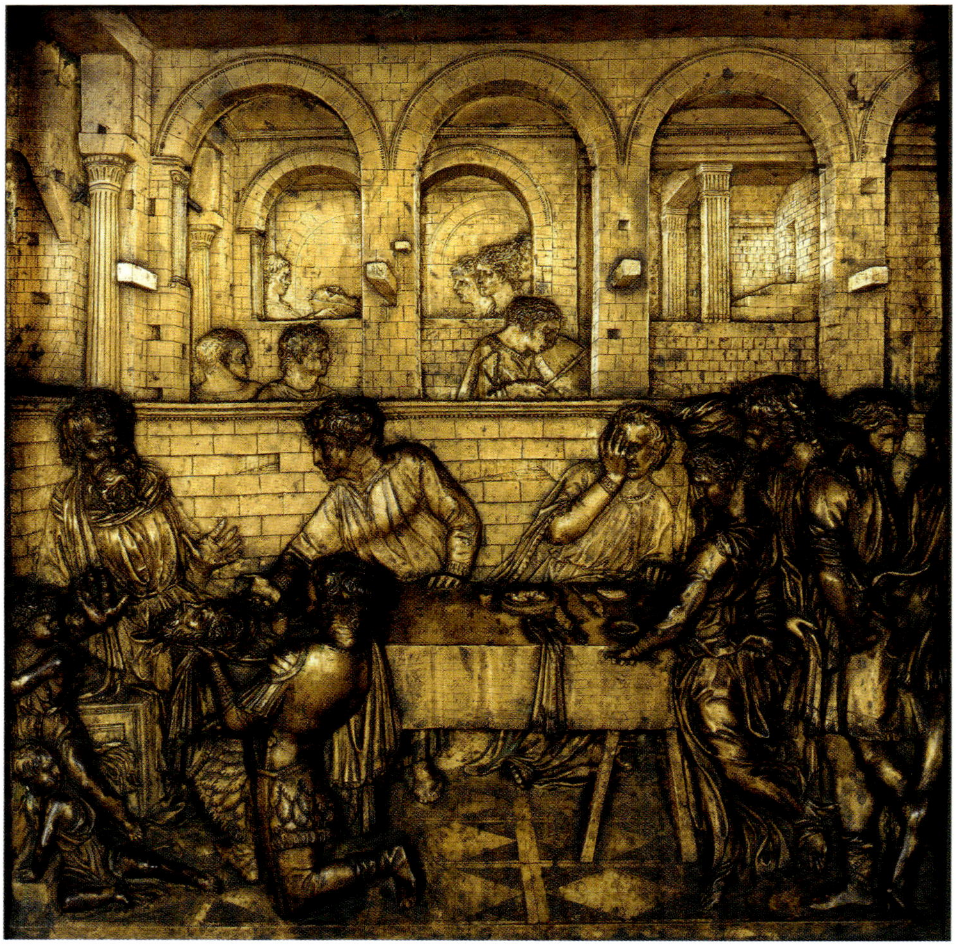

120. Donatello (Florence, 1386?–1466), gilt bronze relief on the font in the Baptistery of Siena, 1423–25. The story begins in the third room in the distance, but the emphasis is on the horror expressed by the guests as John's head is presented to Herod at the table.

Herod – probably Herodias – is calmer, as befits her role. The table is apparently set on both sides, with a napkin and a knife facing the viewer, together with a dish with a fowl. This is notable as a more naturalistic setting than anything earlier, but it is the expressions of the diners that are most memorable.

St John the Baptist was the patron saint of Florence and picture cycles of his life are common in the churches of the city and its surroundings throughout the fifteenth century. Of these, Herod's banquet is most fully depicted in Filippo Lippi's series of frescoes dating from 1452–64 in the choir of the Cathedral at Prato.[49] Domenico Ghirlandaio has a very similar composition, with three tables and Salomé dancing in the foreground, in his fresco in the Capella Maggiore of Santa Maria Novella in Florence (**121**).[50] This was commissioned by the banker Giovanni Tornabuoni in 1485 and the contract specified that the scene was to depict two episodes: the feast of Herod and the beheading. However, the martyrdom was not included; Ghirlandaio preferring to pare the story down to two incidents, Salomé dancing and the presentation of the head. Once again, it seems to be presented to Herod; at any rate, Herodias is sitting on the far side of the table. What differentiates this composition from its predecessors is the setting in the huge hall and the large numbers of guests, which makes it a clear forerunner of the biblical banqueting scenes of Veronese almost a century later (**97**). Again, meticulous attention has been paid to the guests' costume, particularly that of the women seated on the left, while the food, mainly fruit, is more summarily shown.

Herod's feast is more rarely depicted after about 1500 and in the later sixteenth and seventeenth centuries the subject of St John's martyrdom is mainly shown in the form of a close-up devotional image of Salomé holding up the head on a charger. An outstanding exception to this rule is Rubens' large canvas of Herod's feast dating from about 1635

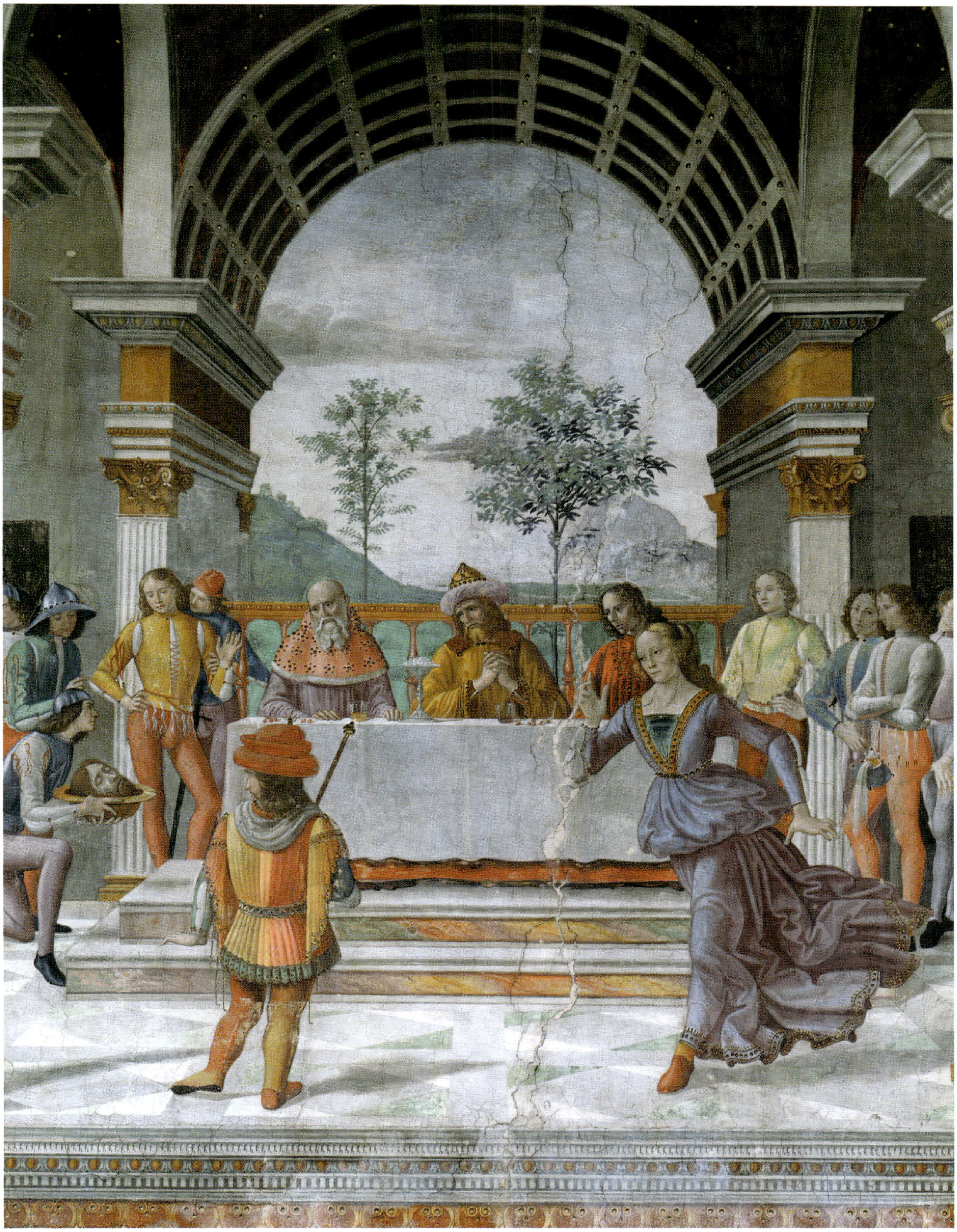

121. Domenic Ghirlandaio (1449–94), wall painting in the capella maggiore in the Church of Santa Maria Novella in Florence, 1485. An early example of the setting as an aristocratic banquet.

122. Rubens (1577–1640), oil painting, c.1631. Herodias is prodding the tongue of St John the Baptist. Edinburgh, National Gallery of Scotland.

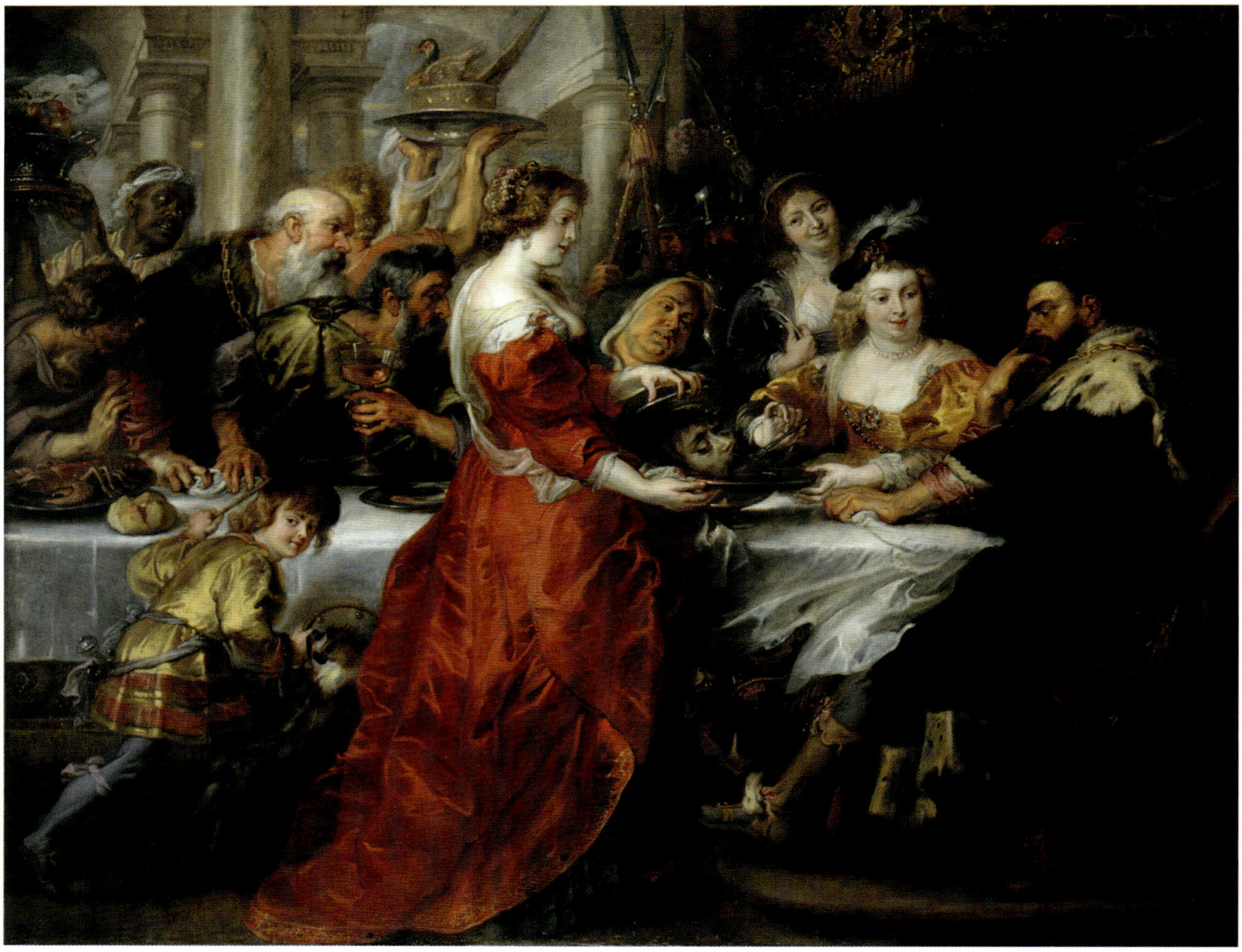

(National Gallery of Scotland, **122**).[51] The dramatic subject suited Rubens and he is recorded as painting it three times, but this is the only original to survive. Salomé, in a luxurious low-cut red dress, hands the charger to Herodias, who sits next to Herod at the head of the table. A fowl is being brought to the table and a dish on the left appears to contain a crab – hardly kosher, but then Jewish dietary laws were not relevant to the Romans. Most striking, and providing the focal point of the composition, is the action of Herodias, with a fork raised in her right hand, violating the sacred head of St John the Baptist. The fork is about to be prodded at his tongue in punishment for his attack on Herodias for marrying her brother-in-law. This is not Rubens' invention. The textual source for this scene is St Jerome's *Apologia against Rufinus* (Bk. 3.42), where he likens Rufinus to Herodias. Neither of them could understand the truth they were told and so 'they pierced with a hairpin the tongue which had told the truth'. The scene is depicted several times from about 1500 to the mid-seventeenth century. Whereas Rubens had turned Jerome's hairpin into a fork, most artists show the instrument of the attack as a knife, as, for example, in the altarpiece of 1511 by Quentin Massys in the Museum of Antwerp.

As a postscript, it might be added that the figure of Salomé reached another peak of popularity as an erotic icon in the later nineteenth century. Best known are Aubrey Beardsley's illustrations to Oscar Wilde's *Salomé* of 1894, which was put to music by Richard Strauss.

18
THE LAST SUPPER

The Passover with the disciples

On the first day of the Unleavened Bread the disciples came to Jesus, saying, 'Where do you want us to make the preparations for you to eat Passover?' … So the disciples did as Jesus directed them and they prepared the Passover meal. When it was evening he took his place with the twelve; and while they were eating, he said, 'Truly I tell you, one of you will betray me.' And they became greatly distressed and began to say to him one after another, 'Surely not I, Lord?' He answered, 'The one who has dipped his hand into the bowl with me will betray me.' … Judas, who betrayed him, said, 'Surely not I, Rabbi?' He replied, 'You have said so.' (Matthew 26.17–25)

The institution of the lord's supper

While they were eating, Jesus took a loaf of bread, and after blessing it he broke it, gave it to the disciples and said, 'Take, eat; this is my body.' Then he took a cup, and after giving thanks he gave it to them, saying, 'Drink from it all of you; for this is my blood of the covenant, which is poured out for many for the forgiveness of sins. I tell you, I will never again drink of this fruit of the vine until that day when I drink it new with you in my Father's kingdom.' (Matthew 26.26–29.)

Similar texts in Mark 14.12–25 and Luke 22.7–23. Both also mention the Passover lamb. John's text differs:

Jesus foretells his betrayal

After saying this Jesus was troubled in spirit, and declared, 'Very truly I tell you one of you will betray me.' The disciples looked at one another, uncertain of whom he was speaking. One of his disciples, the one whom Jesus loved, was reclining next to him (Vulgate: John 13.25 'recubuisset ille supra pectus Jesu'. Revised version: 'He leaning back, as he was, on Jesus' breast'). Simon Peter therefore motioned to him to ask Jesus of whom he was speaking … Jesus answered 'It is the one to whom I give this piece of bread when I have dipped it in the dish.' So when he had dipped the piece of bread and gave it to Judas … 'Do quickly what you are going to do.' (John 13.12–30)

The Last Supper differs radically from all the other biblical meals so far discussed in the huge number of images devoted to it. To cite one published statistic covering Italy in the period 1250–1497, the Last Supper accounted for 72 per cent of the images of biblical meals, followed at a far distance by the Wedding at Cana, with 7.9 per cent, the feast in the house of Simon, with 7.6 per cent, and the Multiplication of the Loaves and Fishes, with a mere 1.3 per cent.[52] It hardly needs saying that we are now dealing with an event of central importance in the Christian faith, both for its place in the narrative at the beginning of the Passion of Christ and for the theological content of the institution of the Eucharist. The words of Jesus, 'Take, eat this is my body' and 'drink from it all of you for this is my blood of the covenant' remain at the core of every Mass.

Church Fathers' commentaries date back to the fourth century, with St Ambrose introducing the transformationist view of the Eucharistic presence, emphasising the change in the nature of elements. This was clarified and expanded by Gregory the Great, who defined the words of consecration at the Eucharist as effecting a cosmic transformation that brings the body and blood of Christ into the mouths of the faithful.[53] Discussions of the different degrees of reality of Christ's body at the Eucharist came to the fore again in the ninth century and in the twelfth. This was when the concept of transubstantiation to define the reality of the transformation came into common use, to be defined as Church dogma at the fourth Lateran Council in 1215. Subsequently the newly discovered philosophy of Aristotle on physical matter was applied to the discussion, most notably by St Thomas Aquinas. Meanwhile, the Eucharist came to be seen as the most special of the seven sacraments and its links with eating became closer with the regulations concerning the bread and wine. The bread had to be wheaten grain, according to Christ's words, and the host white and thin, as opposed to the leavened bread of the Eastern Church.

Such conciliar ruling and general stipulations were part of the Church's attempts to undertake the

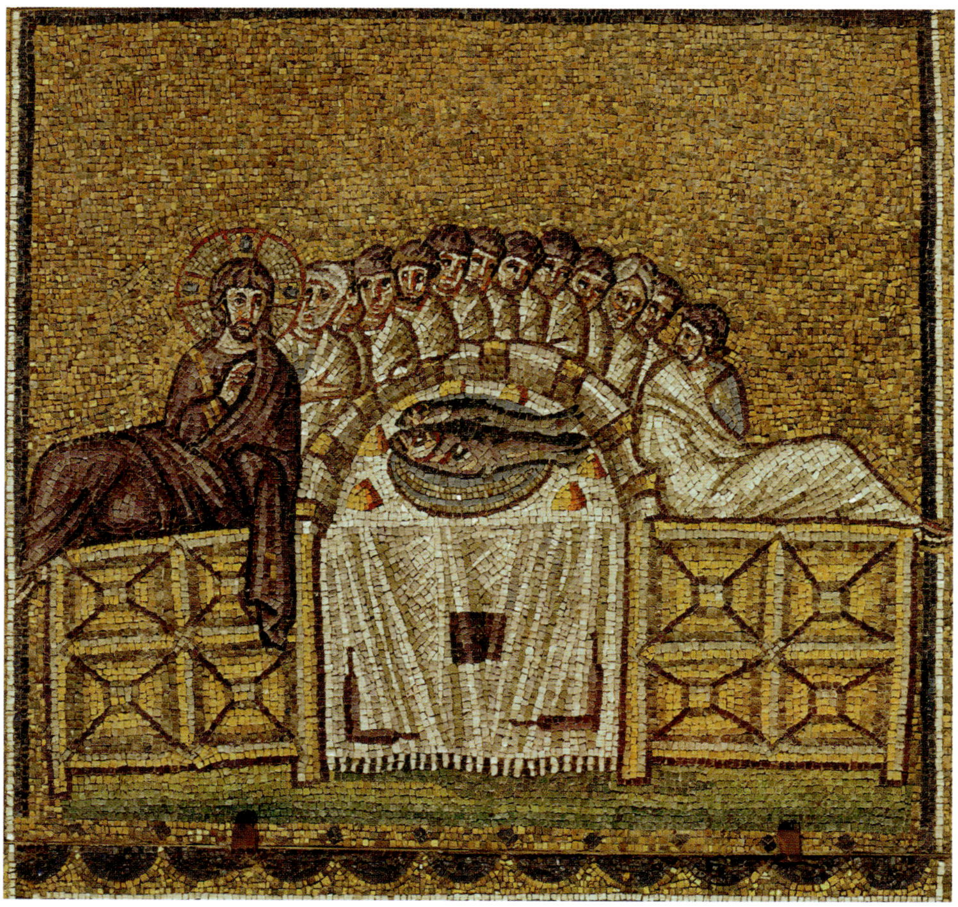

123. Ravenna, Sant Apollinare Nuovo, mosaic, 520–26. The style is Byzantine and the composition follows the eastern tradition of showing the diners reclining on a couch at a semi-circular table. The narrative is centred on Jesus foretelling his betrayal, while Judas reclines on the opposite side.

124. Greek Gospels (?) Constantinople, third quarter of the sixth century. The composition is the same as at Ravenna except that Judas, in the centre, is shown with his hand in the bowl. Rossano, southern Italy, Museo, MS 50, fol. 3 ('Codex Rossanensis').

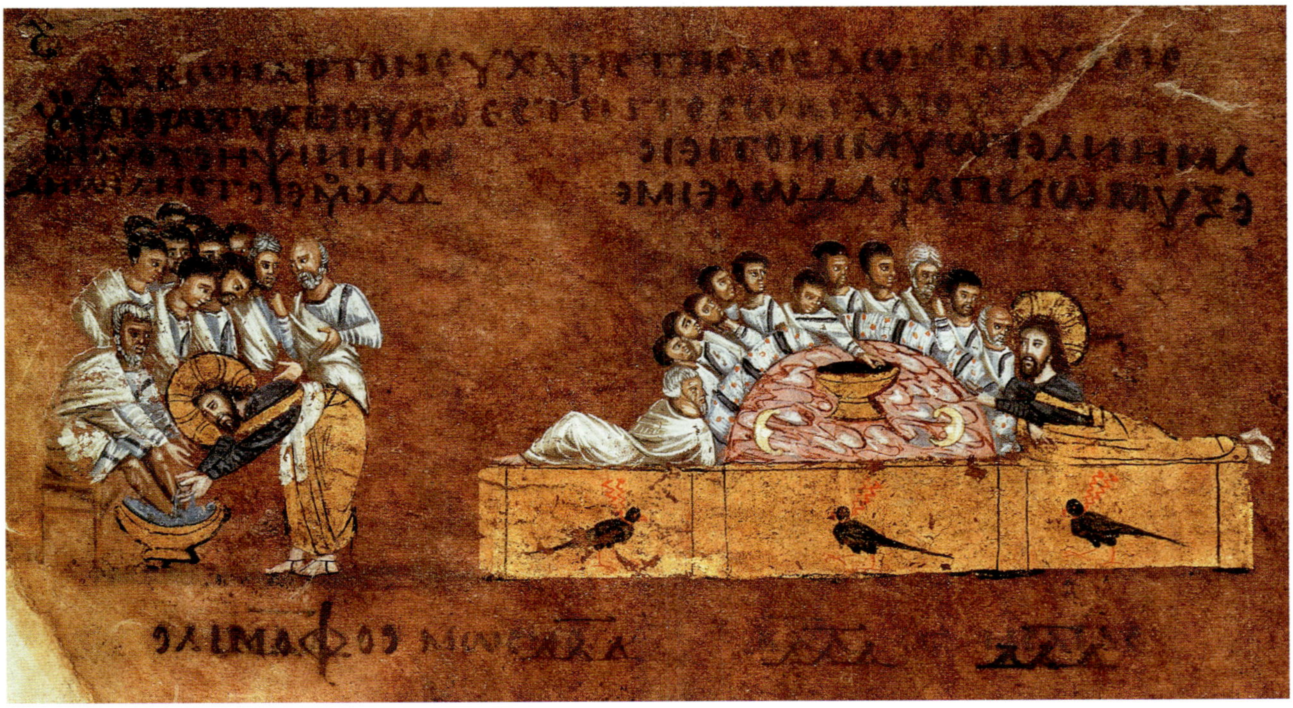

teaching of the laity at a time of growing populations in towns. It was with the support of the Dominicans that the *beguines*, or holy women, in Liège began to campaign for a new Eucharistic feast. This led to the institution of the feast of Corpus Christi, sanctioned by Pope Urban IV in 1264, and its spread in the fourteenth century, particularly in Italy, was a major factor in the rapidly increasing number of depictions of the Last Supper.[54]

As to the images of the Last Supper, it is striking that there appear to be none that survive before the fifth century. This contrasts with the other meals we have discussed, particularly the Wedding at Cana and the Multiplication of the Loaves and Fishes, which were depicted on sarcophagi and in catacombs two centuries earlier. It is likely that the Last Supper was considered too holy an event to be directly portrayed and therefore the other meals stood in for it, just as the Good Shepherd represented Christ on the walls of the Roman catacombs.

One of the earliest surviving depictions of the Last Supper begins the narrative of the Passion in the mosaics of Sant' Apollinare Nuovo in Ravenna (**123**).[55] Ravenna had become the imperial residence and the capital of what was left of the Western Empire after the Visigothic invasion of Italy in 402. The last Roman emperor was deposed in 476 and in 493 Theodoric, leader of the Ostrogoths, defeated the Visigoths to become king of Italy. It was he who had Sant' Apollinare Nuovo built and who continued the employment of artists trained in the Byzantine tradition to carry out a complex programme of mosaic decoration in c.520–26. At the Last Supper Christ and the apostles are in the Roman dress of tunic and cloak, reclining on a *stibadium*, a couch set round a semi-circular table. The moment depicted is clearly that of Christ announcing the betrayal: Judas is reclining opposite and is subject to the staring eyes of the other apostles. There is nothing on the table but five pyramid-shaped loaves of bread and the bowl containing two large fish.

The same setting appears in the later sixth-century Greek gospels from Rossano in southern Italy (**124**), only it is now Peter who is opposite Christ, while

125. Wall painting in the Benedictine abbey of Sant Angelo in Formis, near Capua, c.1080–90, closely following the composition of the sixth-century Rossano Gospels.

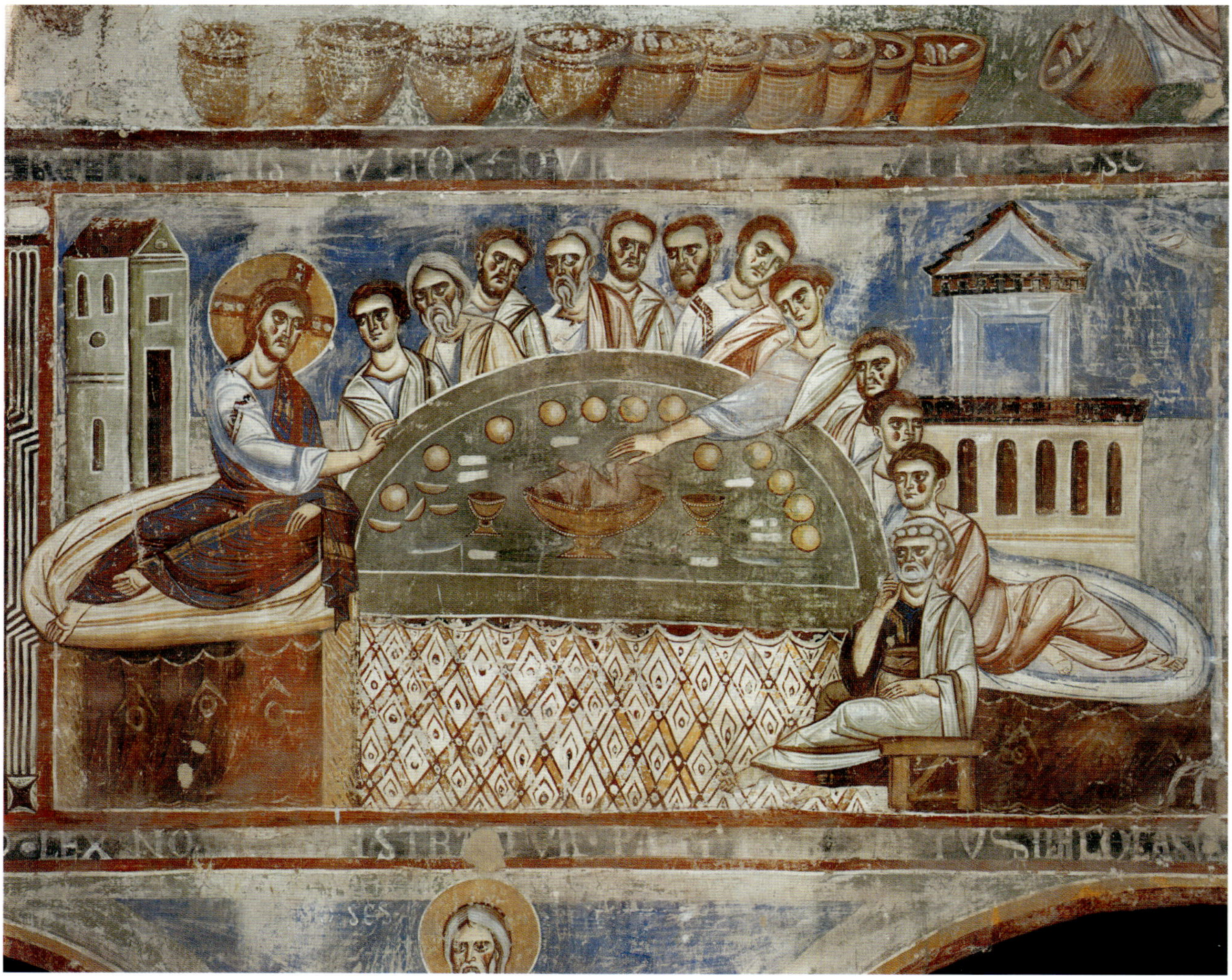

Judas has his hand in the bowl as Christ announces the betrayal. The communion of the apostles, with Christ handing out the bread and the wine to the standing apostles, is shown in two following scenes. The Rossano composition of the Supper remained standard in Byzantine art, still appearing in the wall of painting of about 1080–90 in the church of Sant Angelo in Formis near Capua (**125**), which is believed to reflect the lost paintings in nearby Monte Cassino.

In these early examples and, indeed, in the majority of the images of the Last Supper, the emphasis is on Christ's announcement of the betrayal. More occasionally, it is on the institution of the Eucharist, with Christ blessing the prominently displayed bread and chalice of wine. This is the subject of the earliest surviving Western depiction, the so-called Gospels of St Augustine, an Italian manuscript traditionally thought to have been sent by Pope Gregory the Great to Augustine, the future archbishop of Canterbury, with his mission to England in 597 (**126**).[56] The Roman *stibadium* has been discarded in favour of a round table at which the diners are seated. This specific image of the institution of the Eucharist, while relatively rare in the Middle Ages, comes to the fore in the later fifteenth to seventeenth centuries in, for example, the paintings of Dieric Bouts (1464–68), Tintoretto in S. Maria Maggiore in Venice (c.1543–44), Rubens (c.1632) and Poussin (1647) (**127**, **134–6**). The Bouts Last Supper triptych, which has been discussed in connection with the Passover meal, was an altarpiece commissioned by the Confraternity of the Holy Sacrament at St Peter's Church, Louvain (Leuven).[57] Unusually, the details of the patronage and the contract are fully recorded. The painting was commissioned in 1464 to mark the 200th anniversary of the official introduction of the feast of Corpus Christi in 1264 and the artist was instructed to take the advice of two theologians at the University of Leuven, Jan Varenacker and Egidius Bailluwel, who also suggested the four typological subjects for the wings. This painting is perhaps the earliest altarpiece of the Last Supper and this view of the institution of the Eucharist implies the presence of the priest conducting mass at the altar exactly facing Christ blessing the bread and wine in the picture.

The fact that the emphasis on the designation of the traitor was the more common subject has led to lengthy discussions of these two aspects of the representation of the meal. Leonardo's version alone (**128**) has engendered strongly held views on this point, not least those of Goethe in 1817, who ignored the Eucharistic importance of the occasion. Yet it should be remembered that the Last Supper stands for both the institution of the Eucharist and the drama of the betrayal. Often, indeed, it is difficult to say whether Christ's gesture indicated benediction or blame.[58]

Among hundreds of images there are endless differences of detail, but certain motifs are recurrent. Judas with his hands in the dish, literally illustrating the biblical text 'the one who has dipped his hand into the bowl' (Matt. 26.23), which we have seen in the Early Christian depictions, reappears, for example, in the choir screen carving in the Cathedral of Naumburg[59] and in Giotto's fresco in Padua (**131**, **132**), but is otherwise rare. In the Western liturgy the text of John became more influential and it is the illustration of John 13.8 – 'He who ate my bread has lifted his heel against me' – which became standard from the ninth century. Judas given the dipped bread in his mouth, or more rarely in his hand, may be seen

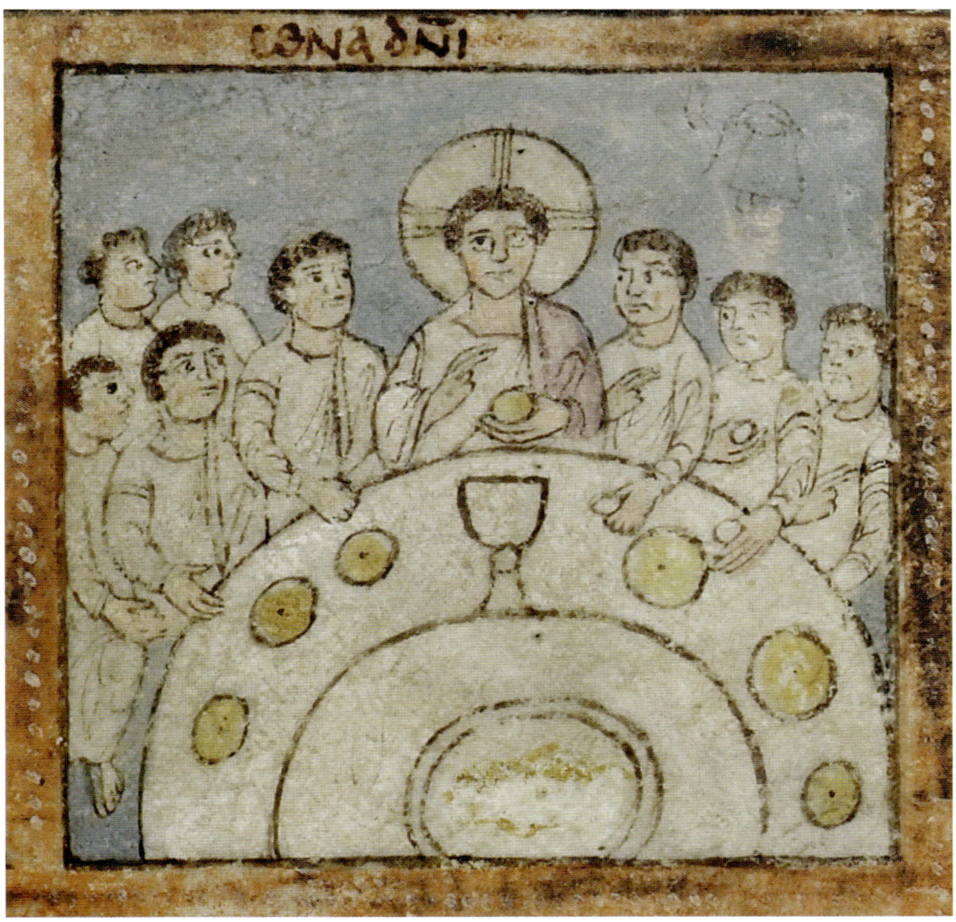

126. 'Gospels of St Augustine', Italian, second half of the sixth century. The institution of the Eucharist with Jesus blessing the bread and wine. Cambridge, Corpus Christi College, MS 286, fol. 125, detail.

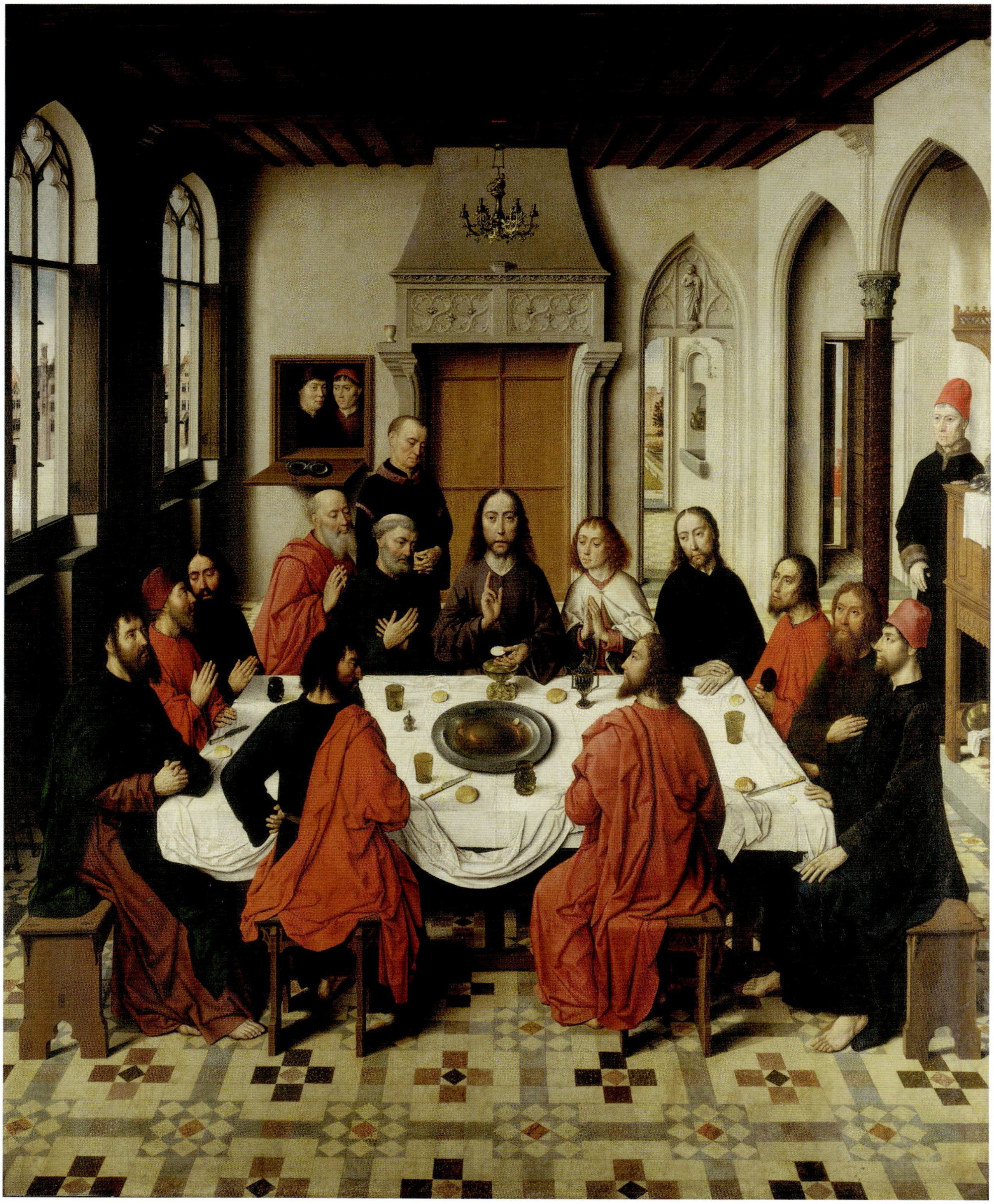

127. Dieric Bouts (d.1475), the institution of the Eucharist, central panel of the Last Supper altarpiece in St Peter's Church, Louvain, 1464–68. The priest conducting mass at the altar would face the picture of Christ blessing the bread and wine. The man standing to the right of the table is Bouts himself.

128. Leonardo da Vinci (1452–1519), wall painting in the refectory of the Dominican church of Santa Maria delle Grazie in Milan, 1495–98 (considerably restored). There are rolls and apples on the table and chicken pieces in some of the dishes, but most of them are empty.

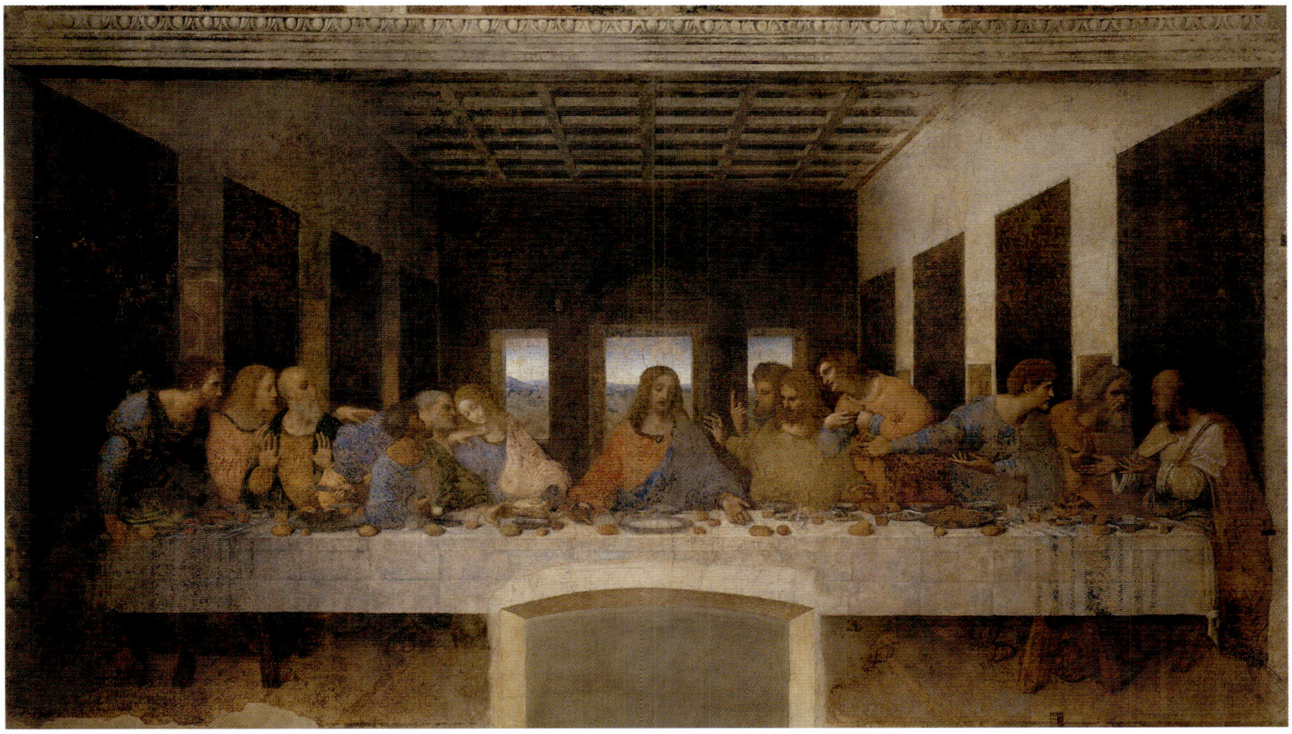

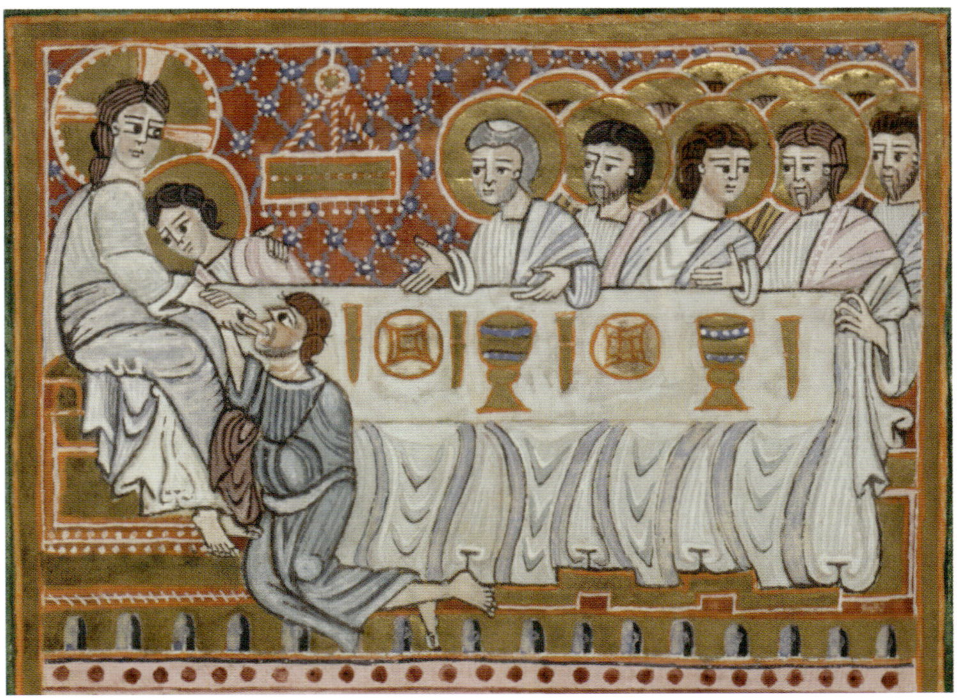

129. Gospels of Bishop Bernward of Hildesheim, c.1015.An early example showing St John lying on Christ's bosom, while Judas receives the sop in his mouth. Hildesheim Cathedral Treasury, MS 18.

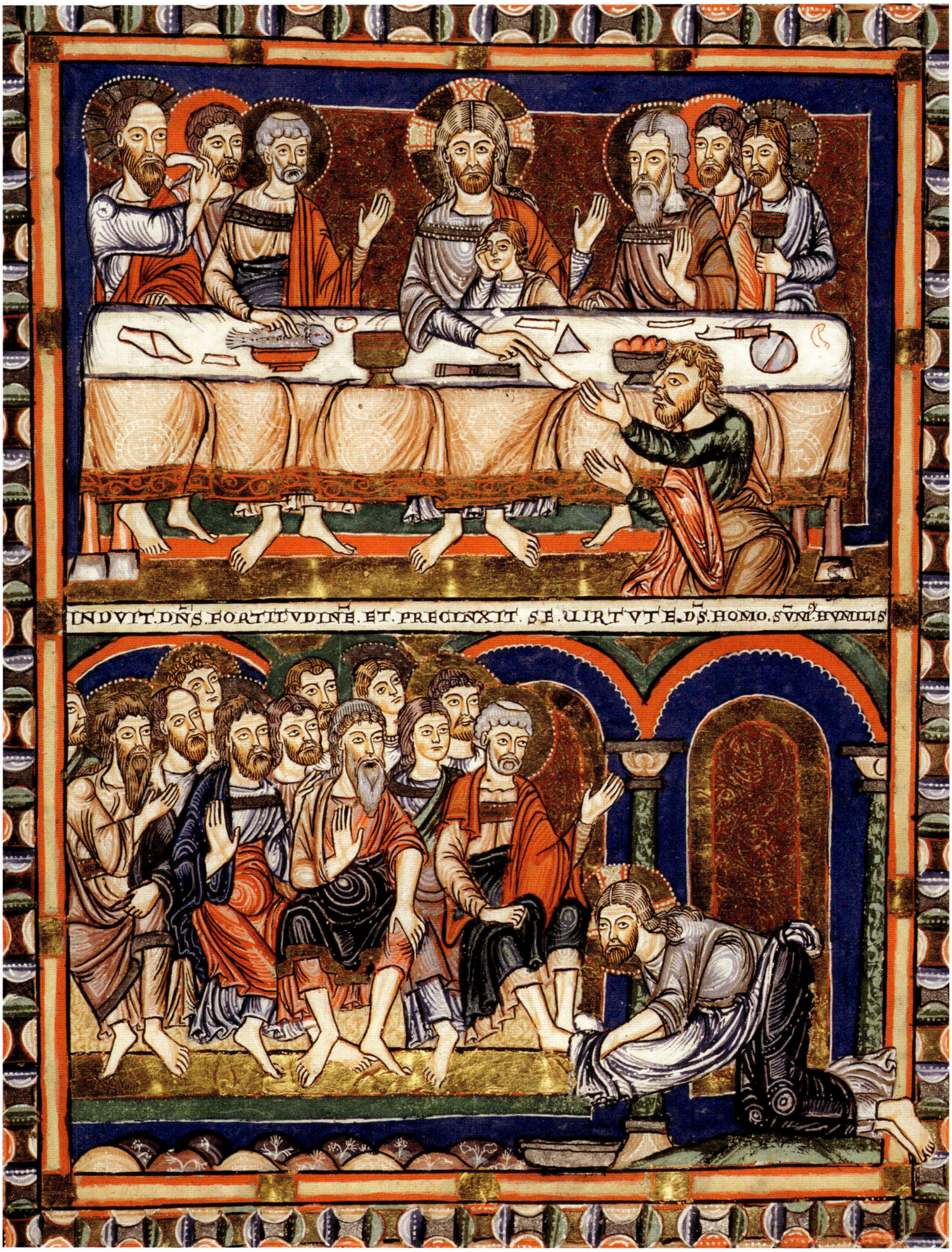

130. Gospels of Henry the Lion, duke of Saxony, from the abbey of Helmarshausen, c.1188. Another example of St John lying at Christ's bosom. Wolfenbüttel, Herzog August Bibliothek. Cod. Guelf. 105 Noviss 2º, fol. 170.

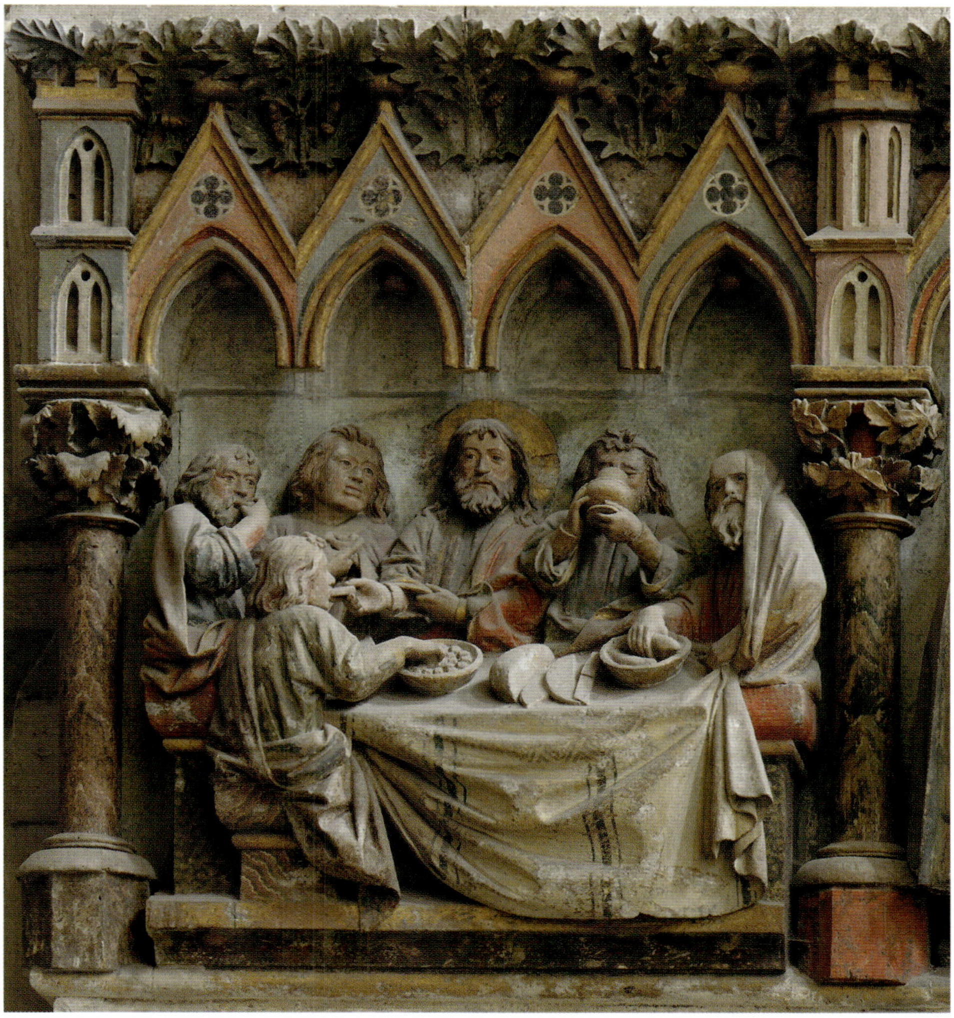

131. Stone carving, Naumburg Cathedral, choir screen, c.1250–70, notable for its unusually strong emphasis on the act of eating.

in seven of the illustrations reproduced here from the Hildesheim Gospels of c.1000 to the wall paintings of Giotto, Pietro Lorenzetti and Ghirlandaio (**129**, **132**, **133**, **138**). In most of these, and also in the Dieric Bouts altarpiece in Louvain (**127**), Judas is shown more or less isolated, sitting on the opposite side of what was now generally an oblong table.

A feature increasingly common from the ninth century is that of John lying on Christ's bosom, a posture based on the text of John 13.23: 'One of his disciples – the one whom Jesus loved – was reclining next to him.' This is less specific than the Latin Vulgate, which clearly states that 'he was leaning back on Jesus' breast'. This disciple was traditionally identified as John, and his proximity to Christ at the supper became a common motif, as we can see from the examples reproduced here (**129**, **130**, **132**, **138**). As far as Jesus' own place at the table is concerned, his position at its head in the earlier representations is usually replaced by a seat in the centre, but there are numerous exceptions, not least Giotto's in the Scrovegni Chapel in Padua (**132**). Yet the discussion of such compositional differences should not be allowed to obscure the principal content of all these images: the expression of the human emotions aroused at such a momentous occasion. From Ravenna to Rubens it is the expressed shock and concern of the diners, particularly at the surprise announcement that one of their company is a betrayer, that provides an indication of the artist's calibre.

The majority of the medieval illustrations of the Last Supper are in manuscripts, particularly of the Gospels. With the increase in the number of depictions from the time of the institution and spread of the feast of Corpus Christi in the thirteenth century the subject became widespread

132. Giotto (c.1267–1337) wall painting in the Scrovegni Chapel, Padua, c.1306. Giotto follows his predecessors in showing John on Christ's lap and Judas with his hand in the dish, but breaks from tradition in having apostles seated on both sides of the table.

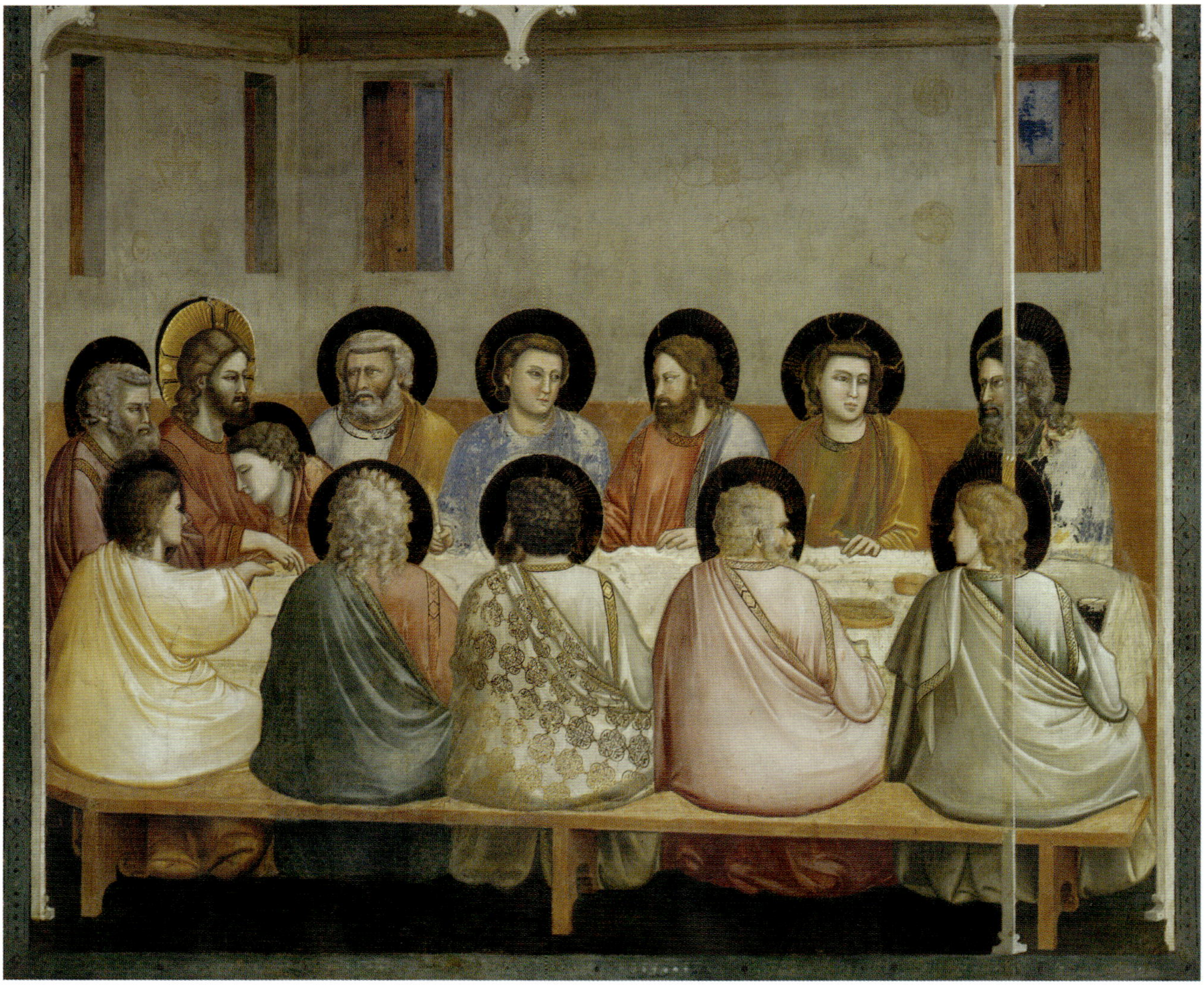

in other media, now including cathedral sculpture and wall paintings, and occasionally they emphasise the domestic aspect of the meal. The carving at Naumburg Cathedral focuses on the apostles in the act of eating (**131**). Even more unusually, Pietro Lorenzetti's painting in the New Testament cycle in the lower church of San Francesco in Assisi (c.1320–30) provides an amusing glance into the kitchen, where servants are washing the dishes and a dog eats up the remains from a plate (**133**). Such domesticity is seldom seen in depictions of the Last Supper, at least until Tintoretto's painting in Santa Maria Maggiore in Venice (**134**).

In the later fourteenth and fifteenth centuries the Last Supper, the most important meal of all, was quite often figured on the walls of monastic refectories, a tradition culminating in Leonardo's composition painted for the refectory of Santa Maria delle Grazie in Milan (**128**). The later versions stand somewhat outside this traditional composition. Tintoretto's painting in S. Maria Maggiore in Venice, one of the seven times he tackled the subject, shows the institution of the Eucharist as Christ passes the bread and wine to an apostle amid an outburst of heavenly light and floating angels in an otherwise dark setting (**134**). Rubens also concentrates on Christ blessing the bread and wine, while the most memorable expression is the horror of Judas as he considers his guilt (**135**).

Poussin likewise concentrates on the horror expressed by the apostles as they hear of the betrayal, while Judas is leaving the room (**136**). This provides the drama, yet the scene shows the institution of the Eucharist as an illustration of the sacrament. This is one of his second series of the seven Sacraments painted for his friend Paul Fréart de Chantelou in 1644–48. Here again, Poussin follows his archaeological interest in introducing the Roman *triclinium*, as he had done in a more convincing manner for the sacrament of the Penance in the same series (**95**).[60]

When it comes to the actual food set on the table, it is not surprising that for much of its history the depiction of the holiest of meals should have been more austere than in comparable compositions. As we have seen in the East Anglian psalter of Sir Geoffrey Luttrell, c.1330–45, there is a striking comparison between two similar pictures of meals. The one of the family feasting shows the table covered in bowls and dishes, with more food being brought in by the servants, in contrast to the Last Supper, which has only bread and fish (**137**).[61] Fish was the food for Jews on the Sabbath eve and we have seen that it became the symbol of Christ as well as the accepted holy food from the Early Christian period. Not surprisingly, it forms the staple food on the table of the Last Supper from the Ravenna mosaic to the fourteenth century (**123**, **130**, **131**, **137**).

The only other food sometimes depicted is the lamb, which is grasped by Judas in the wall painting at Sant' Angelo in Formis (**125**). This is logical insofar as the Last Supper took place at the Passover and both Mark (14.12) and Luke (22.7) specifically mention

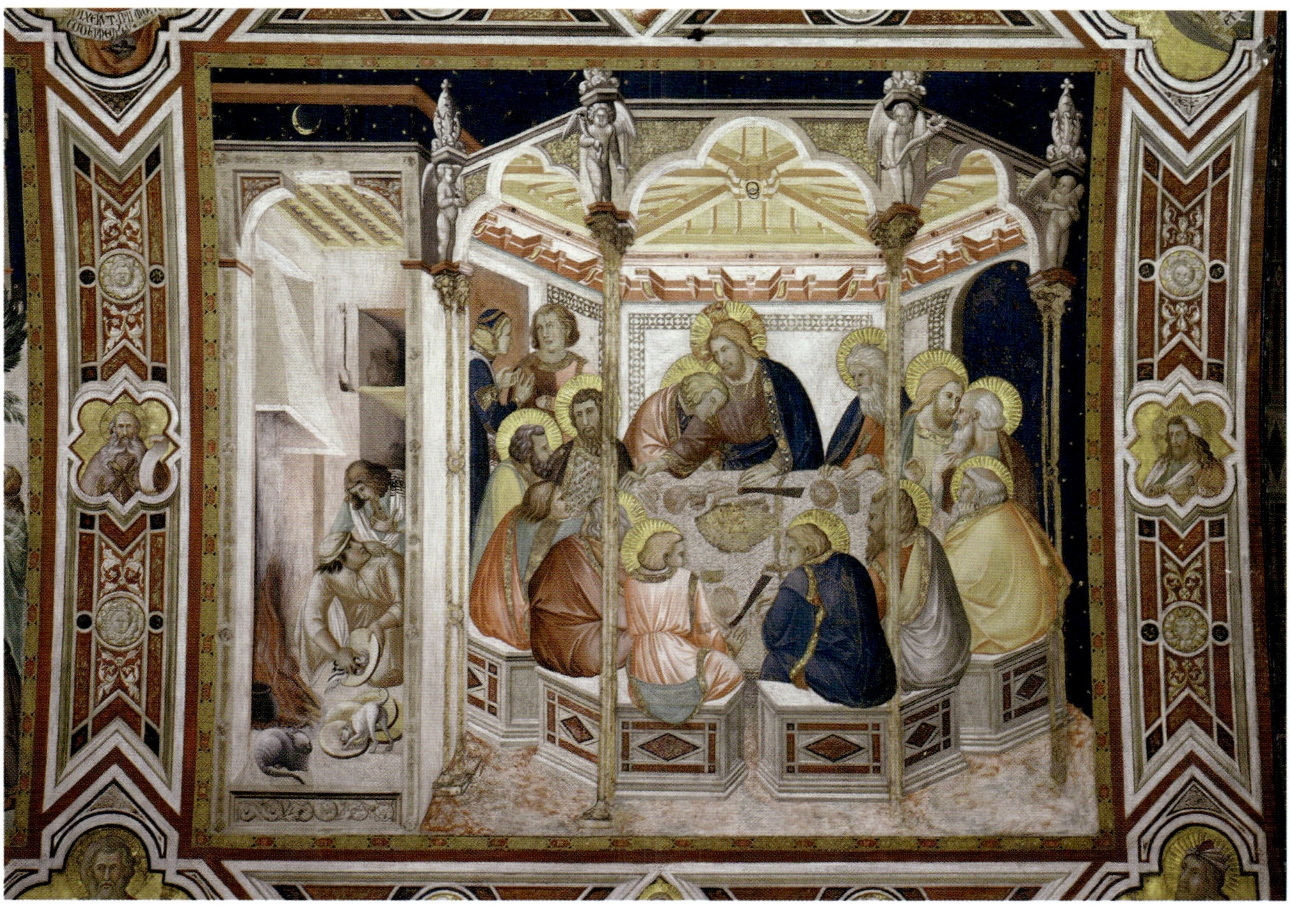

133. Pietro Lorenzetti (active c.1320–48), wall painting in the lower Church of San Francesco, Assisi, c.1330. The amusing kitchen scene is an unusual addition.

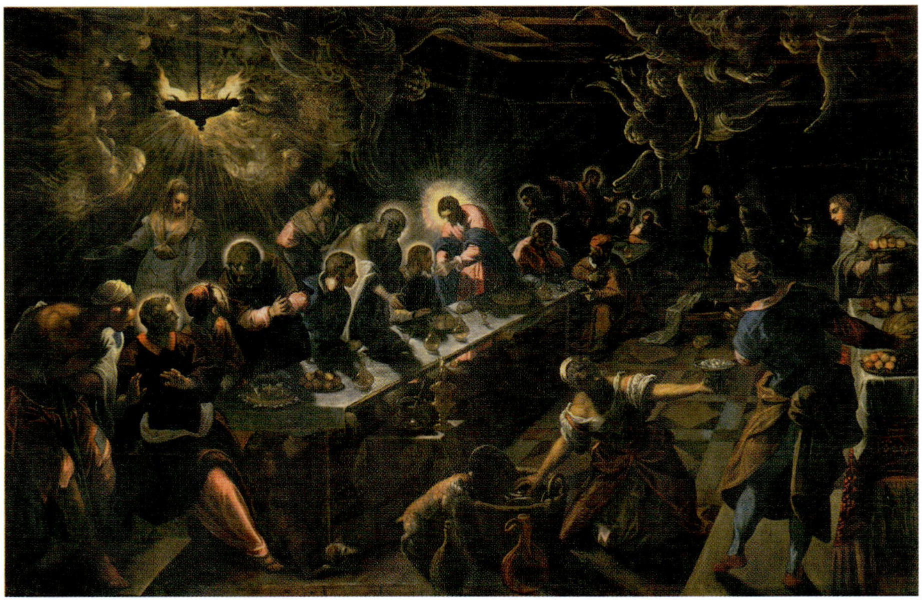

134. Tintoretto (1518–94), oil painting, c.1593–94, in the choir of the church of Santa Maria Maggiore, Venice. A revolutionary composition of the institution of the Eucharist.

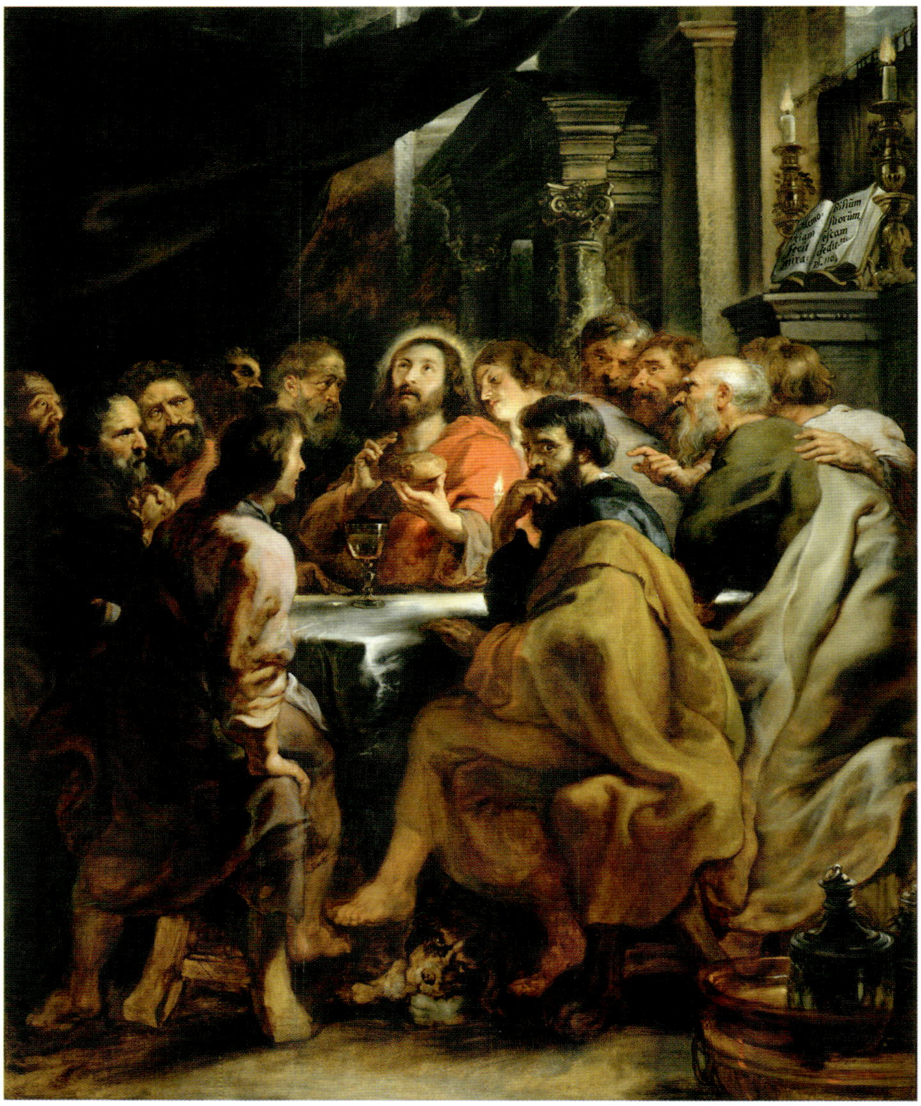

135. Peter Paul Rubens (1577–1640), oil painting on panel, c.1620, from the church of St Rambaud, Malines, emphasising both the institution of the Eucharist and the expression of Judas' guilt. Milan, Pinacoteca di Brera.

136. Nicolas Poussin (1594–1665), oil painting, 1647, of the Last Supper, illustrating the Sacrament of the Eucharist, one of a series of the Seven Sacraments, in a very Roman guise. Collection of the Duke of Sutherland on loan to the National Gallery of Scotland, Edinburgh.

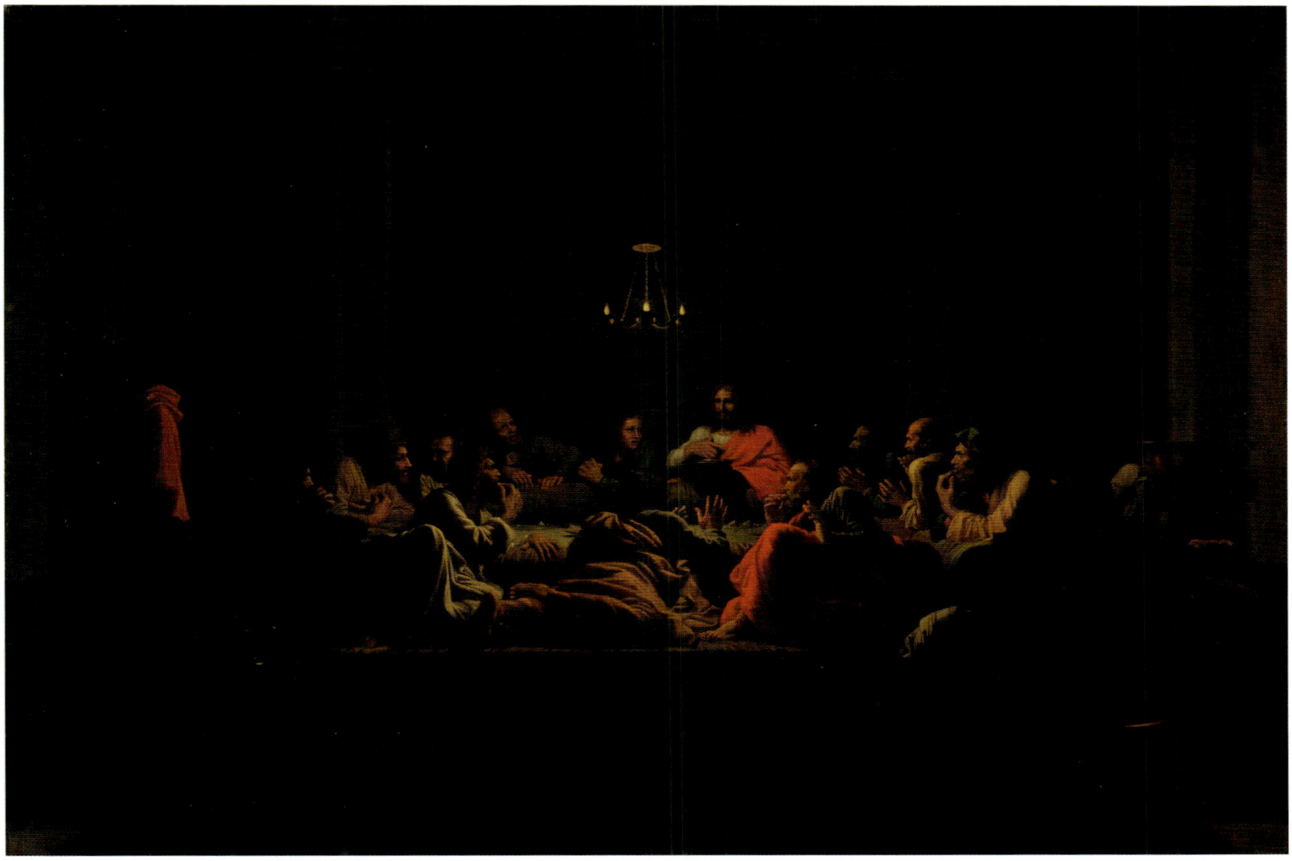

the sacrifice of the paschal lamb. However, John's description (13.1) was taken to imply that the meal took place during the preparation for Passover rather than at the precise time of the Jewish festival, which probably accounts for the relatively rare appearance of the lamb in the illustrations.[62]

On the whole, the austere table setting persists throughout the Middle Ages, though in the fifteenth century tables are more liberally covered. Domenico Ghirlandaio's fresco in the refectory of the Ognissanti in Florence has a variety of fruit on the table, which may well have been intended to contain symbolic meaning (**138**).[63] There are quite a lot of cherries, and, on account of its red colour and juice, the cherry has suggested the blood of Christ and is often represented with a Eucharistic connotation. Indeed, in Ghirlandaio's other version of the Last Supper in S. Maria Novella cherries are sprinkled over the whole table. An apricot, which appears here on the left, stood for the female sex organ from Roman times and became a symbol of sin to Christians. Here it is next to a piece of lettuce, one of the five bitter herbs ordered to be eaten by the Jews at Passover, which was interpreted in the Middle Ages as a symbol of the bitterness of penitence. The orange, shown on the right end of the table, was a symbol of redemption as well as of chastity. In this way, sin, visualised by the apricot, is balanced both by penitence, symbolised by the lettuce, and by redemption. This is not to claim that such symbolic content may be identified in every still life or bowl of fruit, yet Ghirlandaio's careful placing of these items and their regular appearance in this context in Renaissance paintings provide strong support for this particular interpretation.

Nevertheless, the setting remains austere in comparison with other biblical meals of the period.

137. Psalter of Sir Geoffrey Luttrell, East Anglian, c.1330–45. The meal, consisting only of bread, wine and fish, is much simpler than the illustration of the Luttrell family dinner in the same manuscript. British Library, MS Add. 42130, fol. 90v.

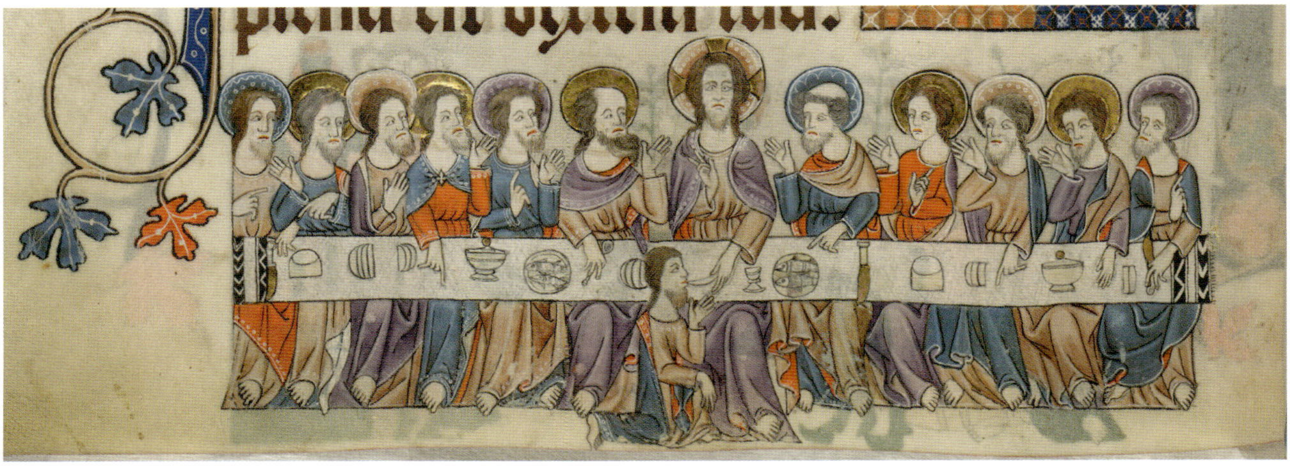

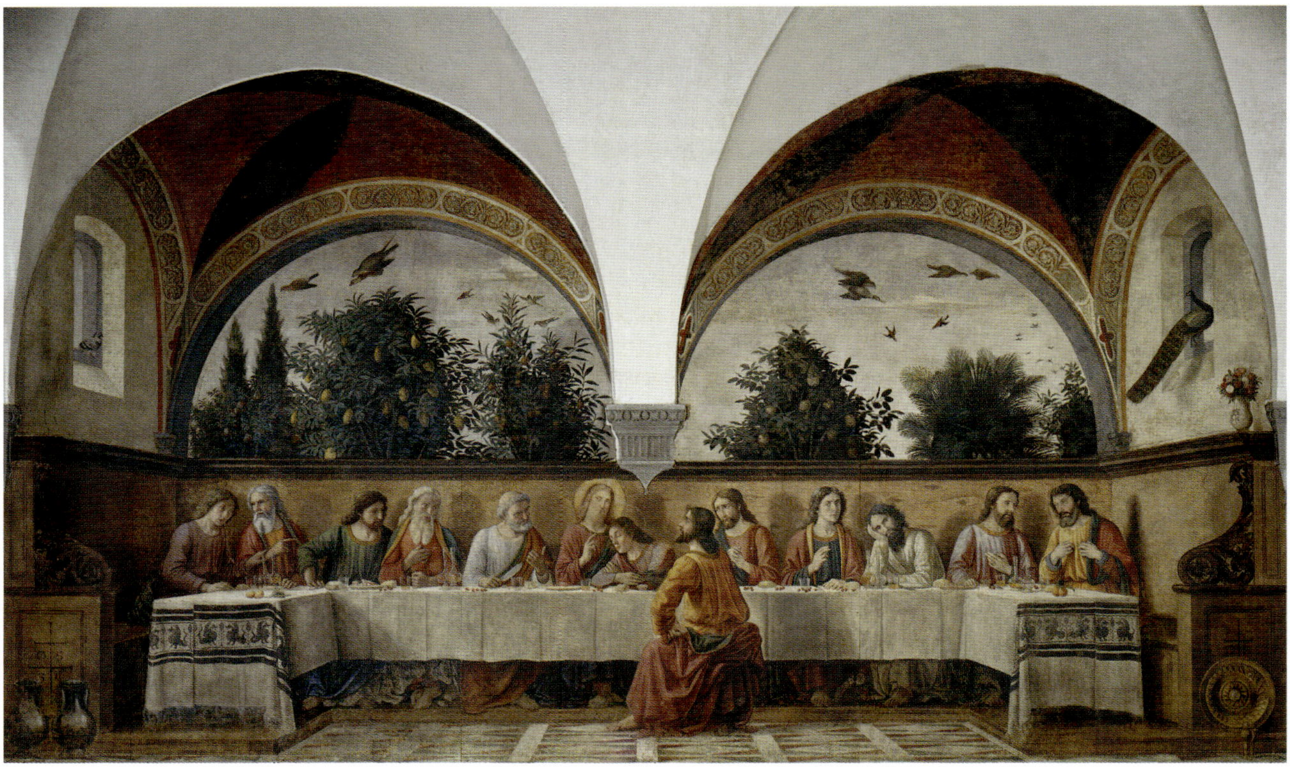

138. Domenico Ghirlandaio (1449–94), wall painting in the refectory of the Ognissanti monastery in Florence, c.1480. The different kinds of fruit on the table are discussed for their symbolic significance.

139. Antonio Baschenis (active 1450–90), wall painting in the church of San Stefano at Carisolo. Typical of such paintings of the Last Supper in the alpine region north of Venice, there are lots of crayfish on the table.

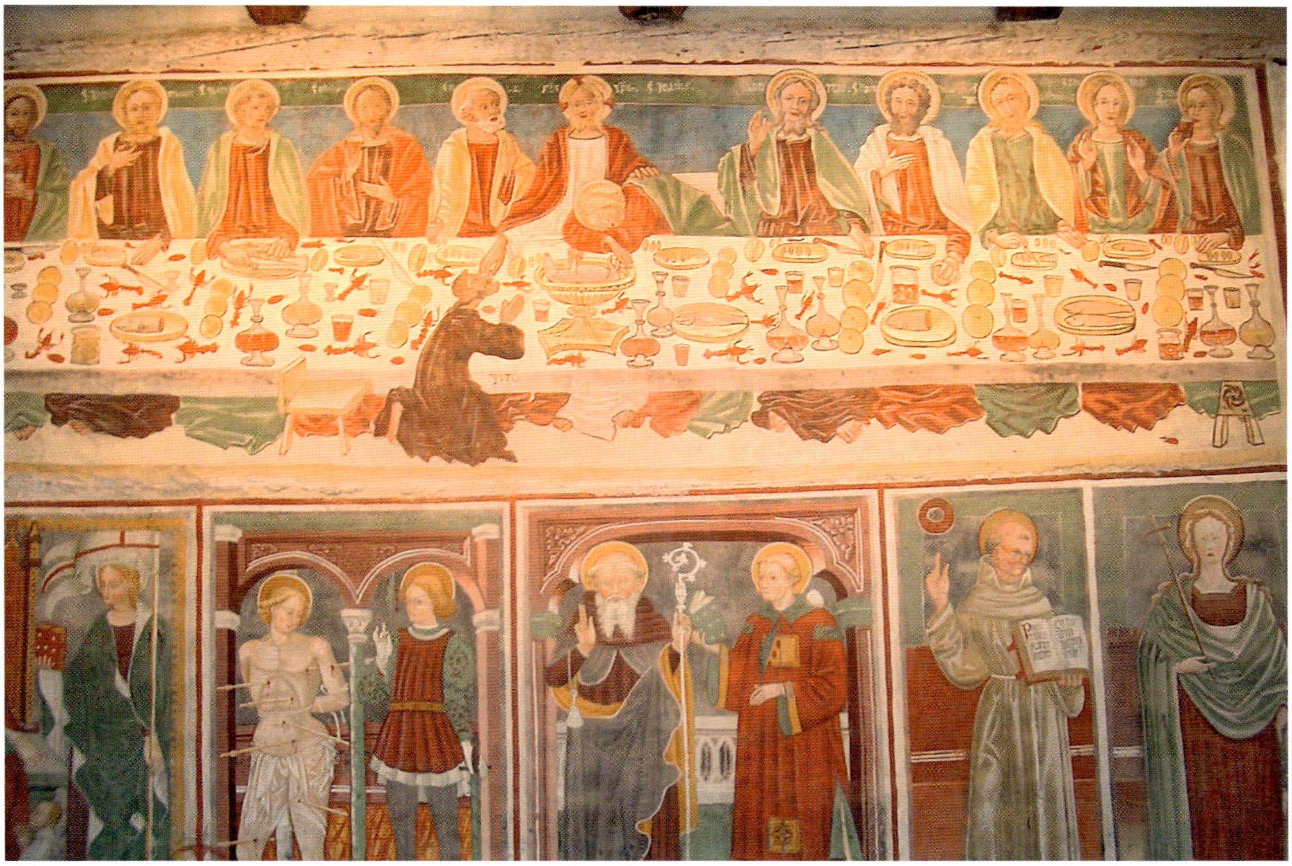

The same may be said of Leonardo's famous painting of 1498 in Milan, though its much damaged and restored condition prevents any firm conclusions (**128**). Even so, the copy made in about 1520 by Giovanni Pietro Rizzoli, called Gianpietrino (Royal Academy) is considered to be quite accurate and it provided evidence that helped the restoration of 1978–98. It includes the salt cellar spilt by Judas, which is lost in the original. Apart from the rolls, apples and lemons lying on the table, there are some chicken pieces on some of the dishes, but most of them are empty.

Only occasionally have stranger additions been detected on the table of the Last Supper. Byzantine paintings sometimes contain white radishes, as these had been served as a side dish at the Jewish Passover.[64] Occasionally, also, the table contains popular local foods. In the Alpine region north of Venice and Verona crayfish appear in the wall paintings of numerous churches from the fourteenth to sixteenth centuries (**139**). The fact that these were far from kosher was overridden by local custom and, in any case, as we have seen, the Christian Church had never adopted Jewish dietary laws. Crayfish were abundant in the mountainous streams and, when spread among the fish and fruit of the Last Supper table, they render the meal a more festive occasion than was fitting for the subject in monastic refectories.[65] Suggestions as to their possible symbolic meaning referring to sin and betrayal as linked with the seasons through the zodiac sign of cancer are harder to sustain. In any case, such intrusions are very rare among the mass of images in which the bread, wine and fish remain predominant.

19
SUPPER AT EMMAUS

After the Resurrection Jesus met two disciples on their journey to the village called Emmaus, about seven miles from Jerusalem but they failed to recognise him. (Luke 24.13–27)

As they came near the village to which they were going, he walked ahead of them as if he were going on. But they urged him strongly, saying, 'Stay with us because it is almost evening and the day is now nearly over.' When he was at the table with them, he took bread, blessed and broke it, and gave it to them. Then their eyes were opened, and they recognised him; and he vanished from their sight. (Luke 24.28–31)

Given the importance of the events described, it may seem surprising that the location of Emmaus remains a mystery and that even the distance from Jerusalem is unclear. The Latin sixty *stadia*, variously translated as sixty furlongs or seven miles, is contradicted in some early sources, which have 160 *stadia*. However, this lack of precise knowledge has not affected the biblical commentaries or illustrations. Following the text, the story of the Supper at Emmaus is illustrated in two parts: the meeting with the disciples on the journey and the meal itself. The two could be depicted together or separately and Christ's disappearance was sometimes added as a separate phase. Only scenes of the journey have survived from the Early Christian period, in, for example, the mosaics at S. Apollinare Nuovo in Ravenna (c.520), but both scenes were popular in the West from the ninth century. The subject was important for its place in the Easter liturgy and had attracted commentaries from the earliest Church Fathers. Cyril of Alexandria saw the Emmaus episode as the central act of demonstrating faith in the resurrection of Christ. It was a gradually discovered faith when the bread was blessed and broken which opened their eyes to his presence. In the text of the Latin Vulgate one of the disciples refers to the stranger they meet as a pilgrim (*peregrinus*) and Augustine (*Sermo* 234) described the road from Jerusalem to Emmaus as a symbol of the itinerary to be taken by all Christians in the company of Jesus. The journey was therefore interpreted as a pilgrimage.[66] This subsequently led to its dramatisations in the *Peregrinus* plays, which flourished from the twelfth century and remained an important factor in the popularity of its depictions.

An early illustration of two scenes is in the lectionary of Egbert, archbishop of Trier, probably produced at Reichenau in about 980–90 (**140**). At the meeting the two disciples are respectively inscribed *Cleopas*, whose name appears in the biblical text (Luke 24.18) but who is otherwise unrecorded, and *Lucas*. The second disciple remained unidentified, but this inscription reflected the tradition that it was Luke himself. Below, the meal itself takes place in a walled castle inscribed *Castel(lum) Emmaus*, again following the Vulgate, whereas it is simply described as a village in the English translation. As in most of the medieval examples, Jesus hands out the bread, but only rarely does he do so, as here, to only one disciple.

Outstanding among the numerous twelfth-century versions of the Supper at Emmaus are the scenes in the psalter linked with St Albans Abbey of about 1120–30 (Hildesheim Cathedral, **141**, **142**, **143**). This is one of the most famous of all English Romanesque manuscripts, opening with a sequence of some forty

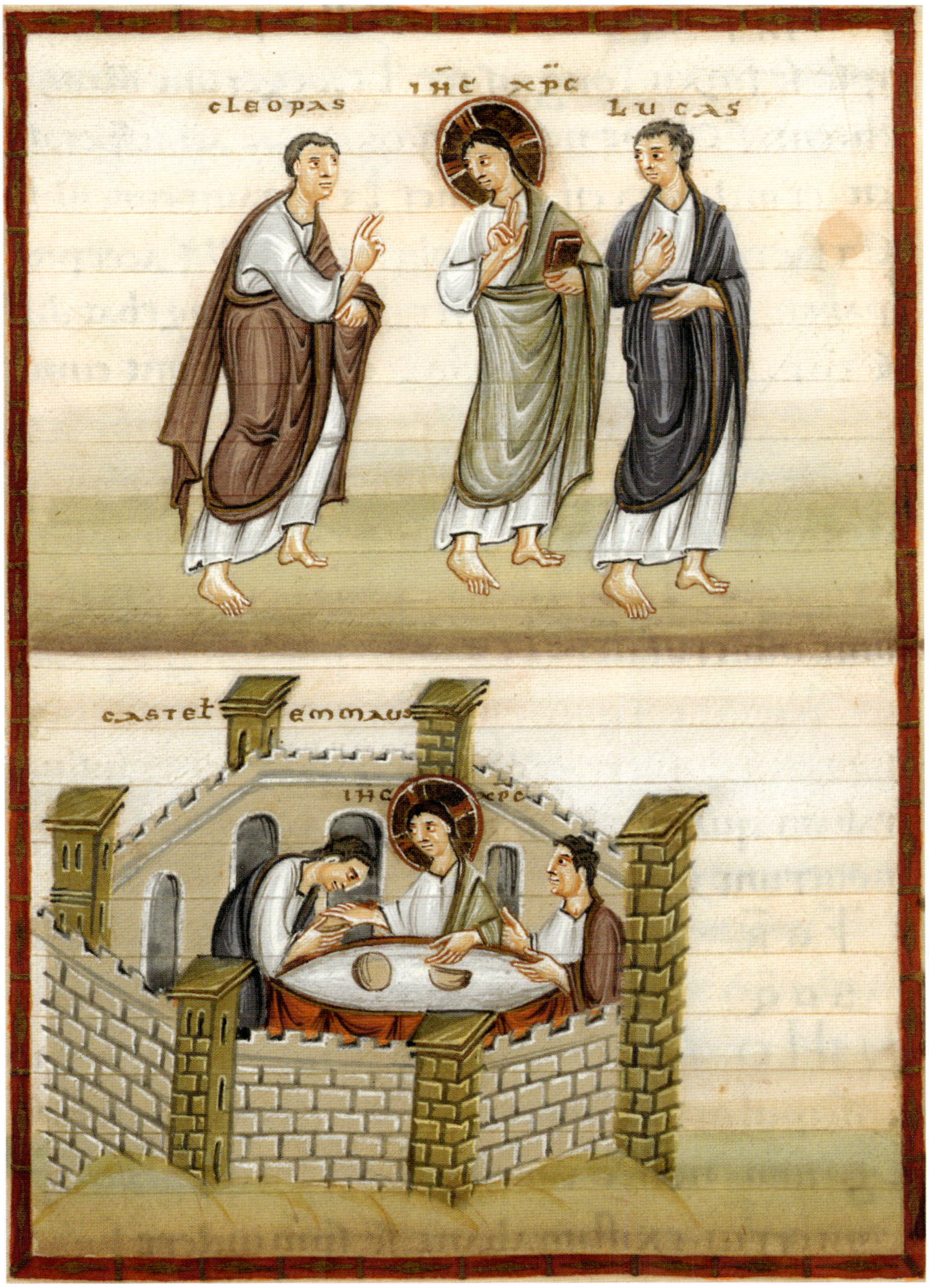

140. Gospel lectionary of Egbert, archbishop of Trier, Reichenau, c.980–90. The meeting with the two disciples on the road to Emmaus is shown above the meal itself. Trier, Stadtbibliothek, MS 24, fol. 88.

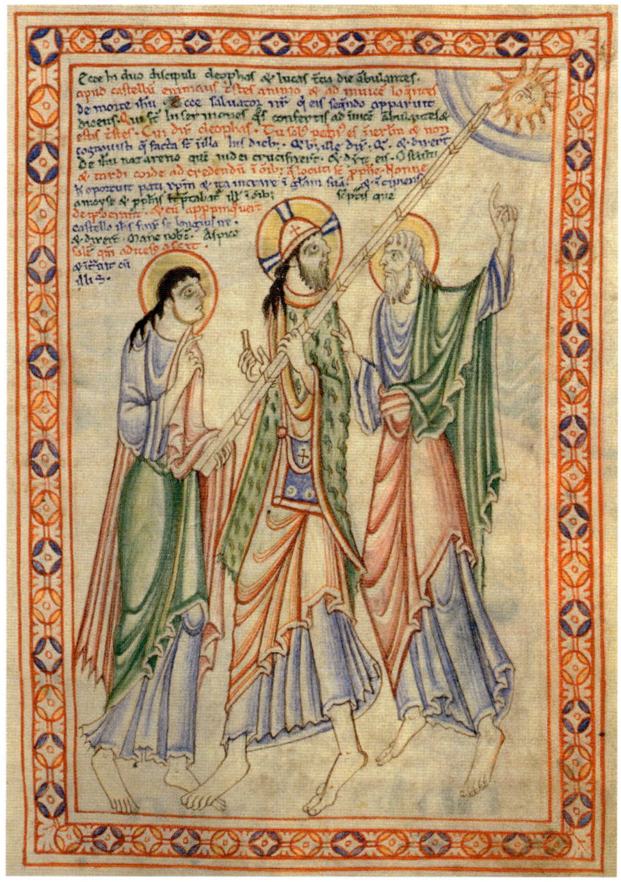

141

141, 142, 143. Psalter linked with St Albans Abbey, c.1120–30. The journey to Emmaus, the supper with the two disciples and the disappearing Christ are shown on three separate pages. Hildesheim, Cathedral Treasury (pp. 69–71).

miniatures of the life of Christ. The Emmaus scenes differ in that they are tinted drawings rather than painted miniatures and they are separated from the Christological cycle by fifteen pages, clearly being intended to stand as a sequence on their own. The first scene is of the meeting on the road and shows Christ dressed as a pilgrim, wearing a pointed cap, a furry cloak and a wallet marked with a cross, and holding a double staff. This corresponds with the stage directions of the *Peregrinus* plays, which also mention the appearance of the sun, and the text of which is quoted in the lengthy inscription.[67]

The meal itself again takes place in a *castellum*, with Christ handing out the bread to both disciples as they sit at a table sparsely provided with bread and fish. After this a third episode has been added to illustrate Christ's disappearance at the meal. Only his legs and feet are visible as he ascends to heaven, leaving the disciples with gestures of surprise. This is the earliest example of this scene and it was probably adapted from the composition of the disappearing Christ at the Ascension, an Anglo-Saxon invention of the eleventh century. It recurs occasionally in thirteenth-century versions of the scene[68] and a variant appears in the transept mosaics of the cathedral at Monreale executed for the Sicilian king William II in 1183–89.[69] Here, Christ, having blessed the bread in one scene, has completely disappeared in the next, leaving the two disciples with sorrowful expressions alone at the table.

In the twelfth century the Supper at Emmaus was also frequently figured on church capitals, at, for example, Chartres, Toulouse, Vézelay and Lincoln. Chartres Cathedral has a frieze of capitals running between the three doors on the west facade, the portal royal, dating from about 1145–55. The two Emmaus scenes are at the far right of the door, near the end of the Christological cycle (**144**).[70] Following the meeting on the journey the meal shows Christ with open arms offering the two pieces of bread to his companions, who are seated closely beside him.

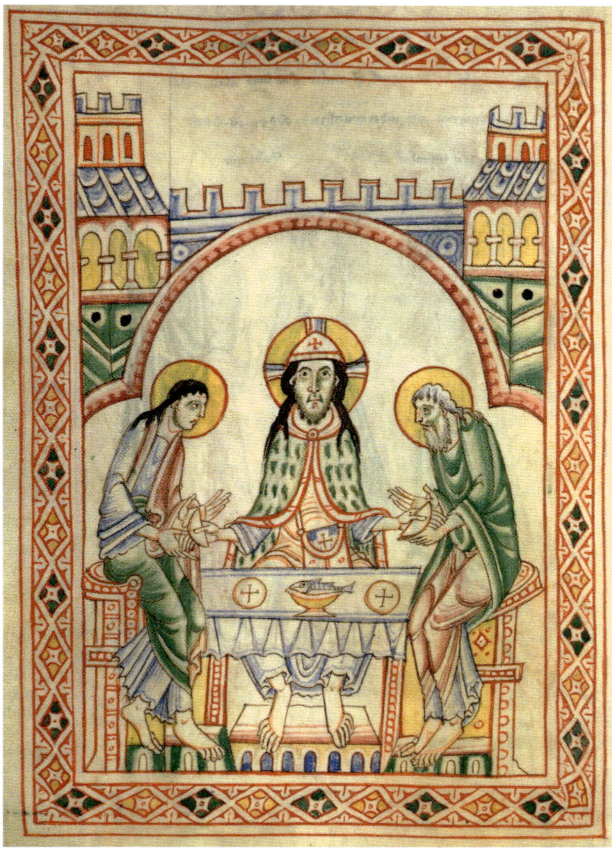

142

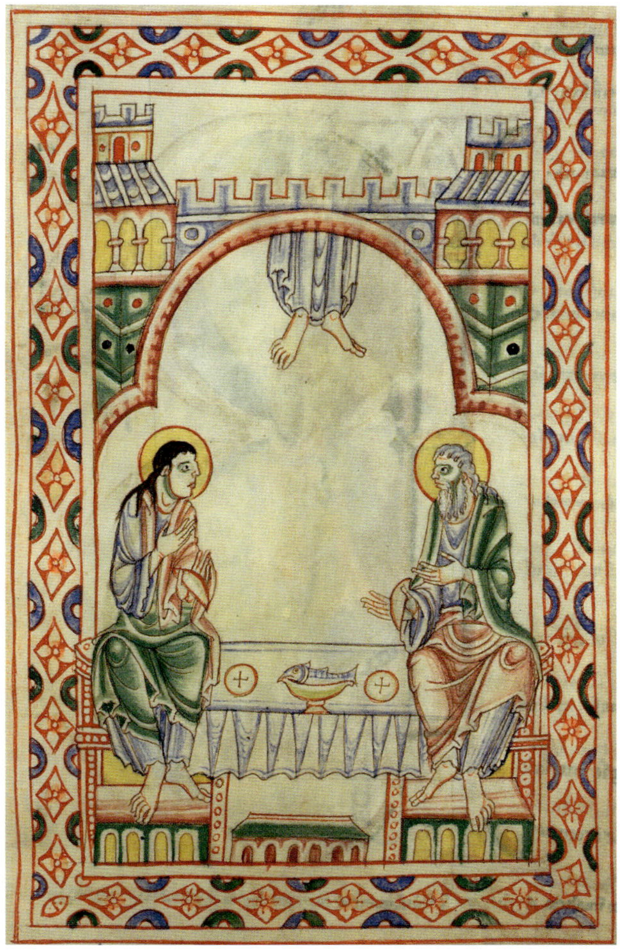

143

Pictures of the Supper at Emmaus are relatively rare in the later Middle Ages, whereas the Journey continues to be a popular subject. It is only with the sixteenth century that the meal again becomes frequently depicted. Indeed, the standard iconographical dictionary for the period lists 262 examples covering the sixteenth to eighteenth centuries, including renowned works by Dürer, Titian, Tintoretto and Rubens.[71] The Eucharistic celebration, the drama of the occasion and the emphatic gestures of surprise as Jesus is recognised by the two disciples all fitted well with the Counter-Reformation emphasis on the importance of visual art in fostering religious feeling. The fact that the meal took place in the evening allowed the painters of the generations from Caravaggio to Rembrandt to pursue their interest in the chiaroscuro effect.

One of the most famous versions is Caravaggio's large painting of about 1600 in the National Gallery (**145**). It breaks with tradition in many ways. Christ is shown young and beardless and the two disciples are realistically depicted as rough-looking workers in torn clothes. They differ from the classically portrayed figures traditionally shown, but so, to some extent, had the disciples in Veronese's version of about 1555 in the Louvre. Christ is blessing the bread with his left hand while the right is raised in a ritual gesture of Eucharistic celebration. Most striking is the dramatic gesture of surprise expressed by the older disciple, usually identified as Cleopas, as he recognises Jesus. He wears the shell, symbol of St James, to indicate his role as a pilgrim. The antiquarian Giovanni Bellori (1615–96) reported that Caravaggio was criticised for a lack of decorum in his depiction of faces and costume. In particular, the rustic nature of the two disciples and the servant wearing a hat were singled out for criticism.[72] Of the basket of fruit, Bellori was clear that the grapes, figs and pomegranates were out of season at an Easter event. Only the apples escaped this criticism. Caravaggio broke with tradition to

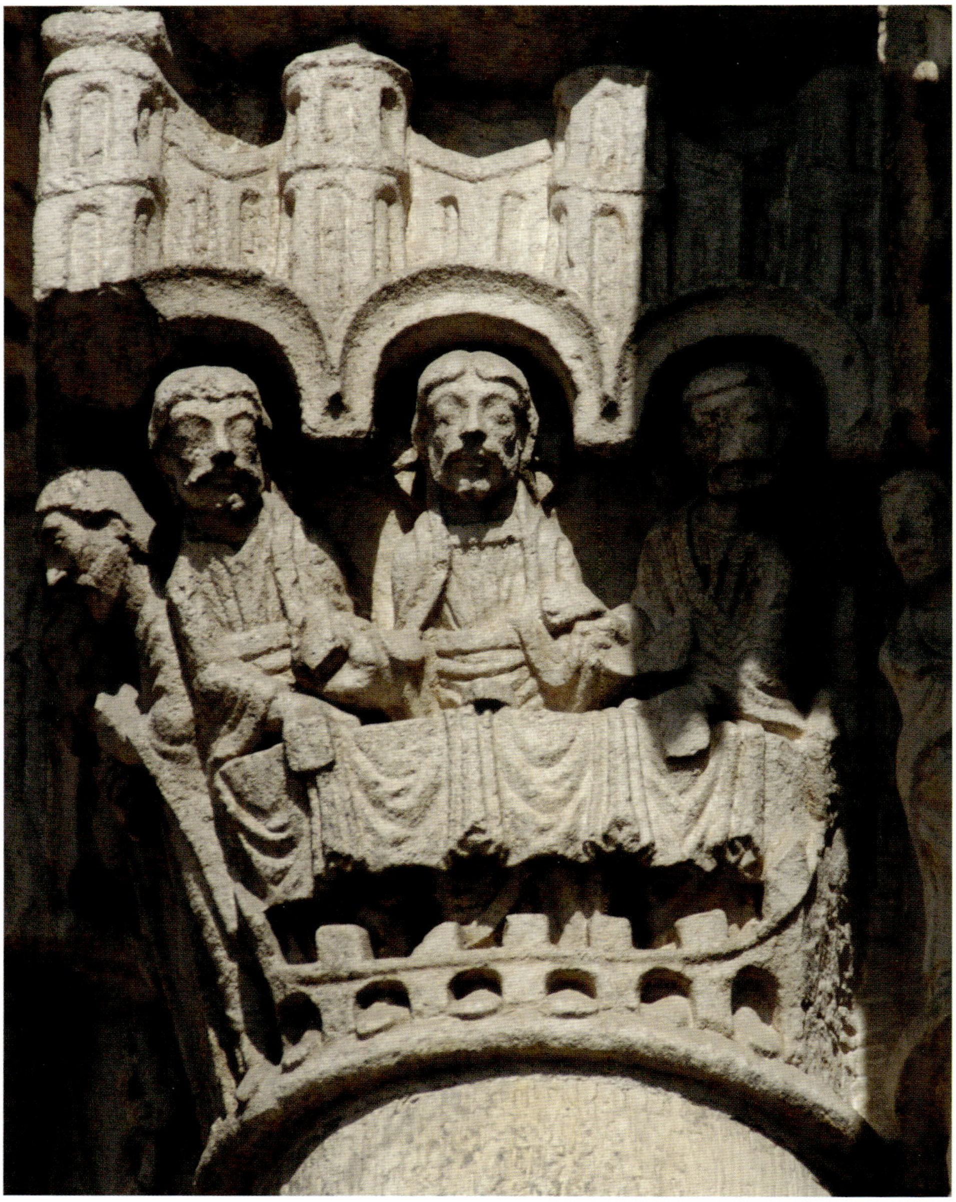

144. Chartres Cathedral, carved capital on the facade, c.1150. The meeting on the left is followed by the meal with Jesus handing out the two pieces of bread.

emphasise the message of Christian salvation to the poor, but he could not resist the lovingly painted still life of fowl and fruit.

Diego Velázquez, working in his native Seville in his early years (1618–23) conveys the same message as Caravaggio through a rather different form. In his *Kitchen Maid with the Supper at Emmaus* (National Gallery of Ireland, Dublin, **146**)[73] the religious subject is seen through a hatch in the background, just as the *Kitchen Scene* in the National Gallery (dated 1618) contains *Christ in the House of Mary and Martha*. Such compositions were not a new invention. There are several examples of religious events seen at a distance in domestic scenes in sixteenth-century Netherlandish paintings, notably by Pieter Aertsen (1508–75), whose work was widely known through engravings.

Unfortunately, Velázquez' painting has been cut down on both sides and the disciple on the left is no longer visible. Indeed, the whole scene in the hatch was painted over and uncovered during cleaning only in 1933. All the beautifully executed vessels, the mortar and pestle and jugs and plates appear in Velázquez' other paintings of domestic subjects, the so-called *bodegas*, of his Seville period. This one differs in that the kitchen maid is ethnically part

145. Caravaggio (1571–1610), oil painting, c.1600. Caravaggio was criticised both for the rough appearance of the apostles and for the still life showing summer fruit not available at Easter time. London, National Gallery.

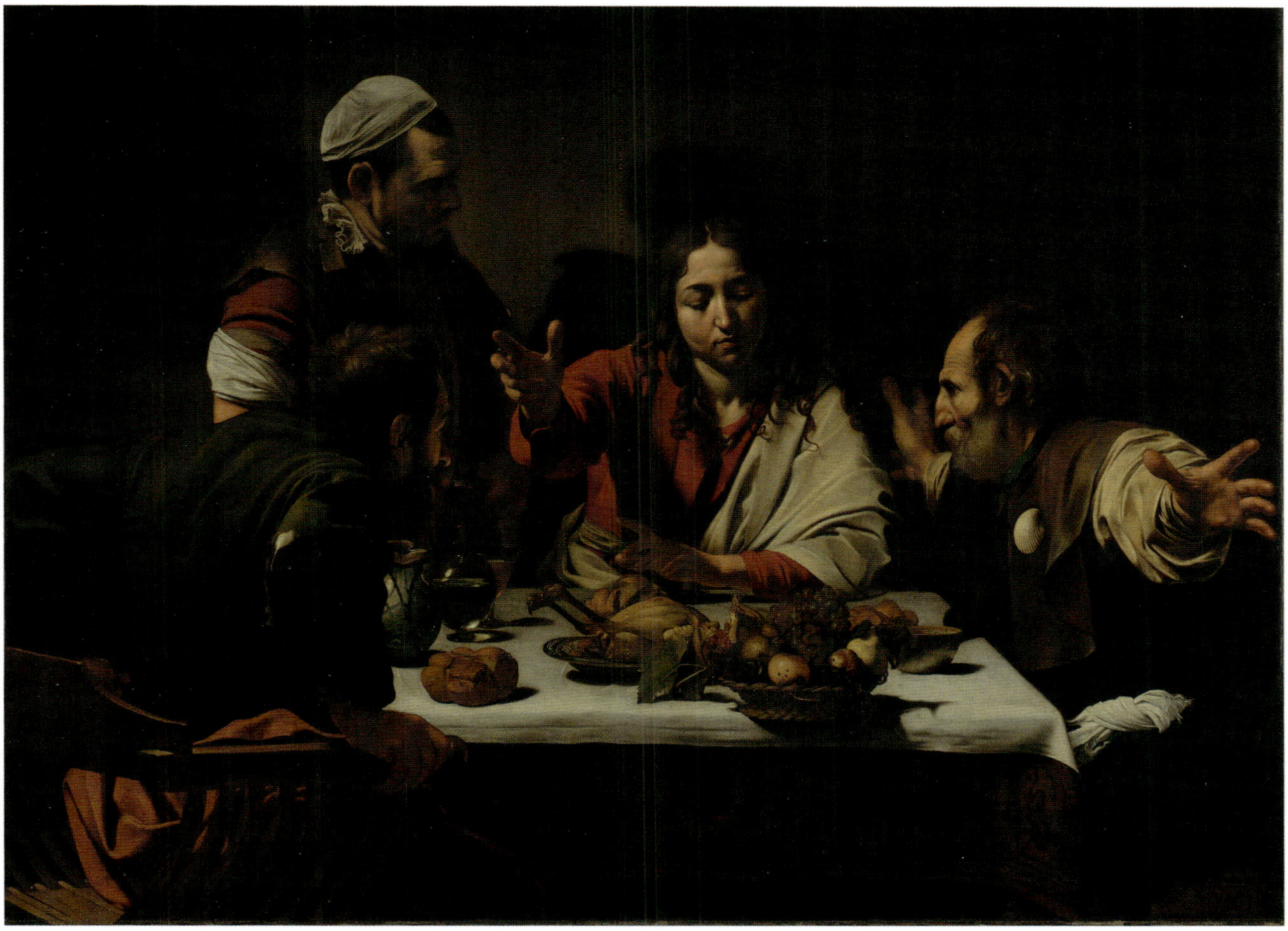

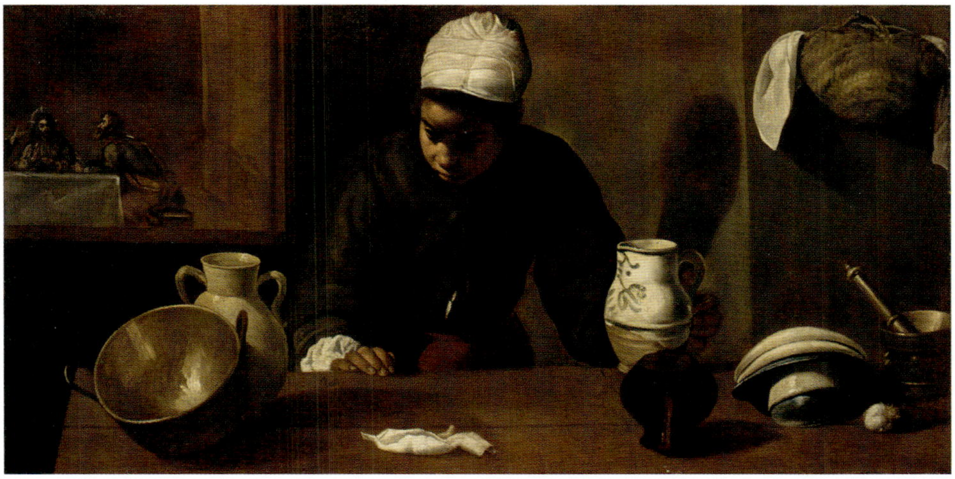

146. Diego Velázquez (1599–1660), painting of the Kitchen Maid with the Supper at Emmaus seen through a hatch on the left, c.1618. Dublin, National Gallery of Ireland.

147. Rembrandt (1606–69), panel painting, 1648. The asymmetrical composition and the chiaroscuro effect are close to Caravaggio, but the mood is infinitely calmer. The emphasis is on the spiritual nature of the occasion. Paris, Musée du Louvre.

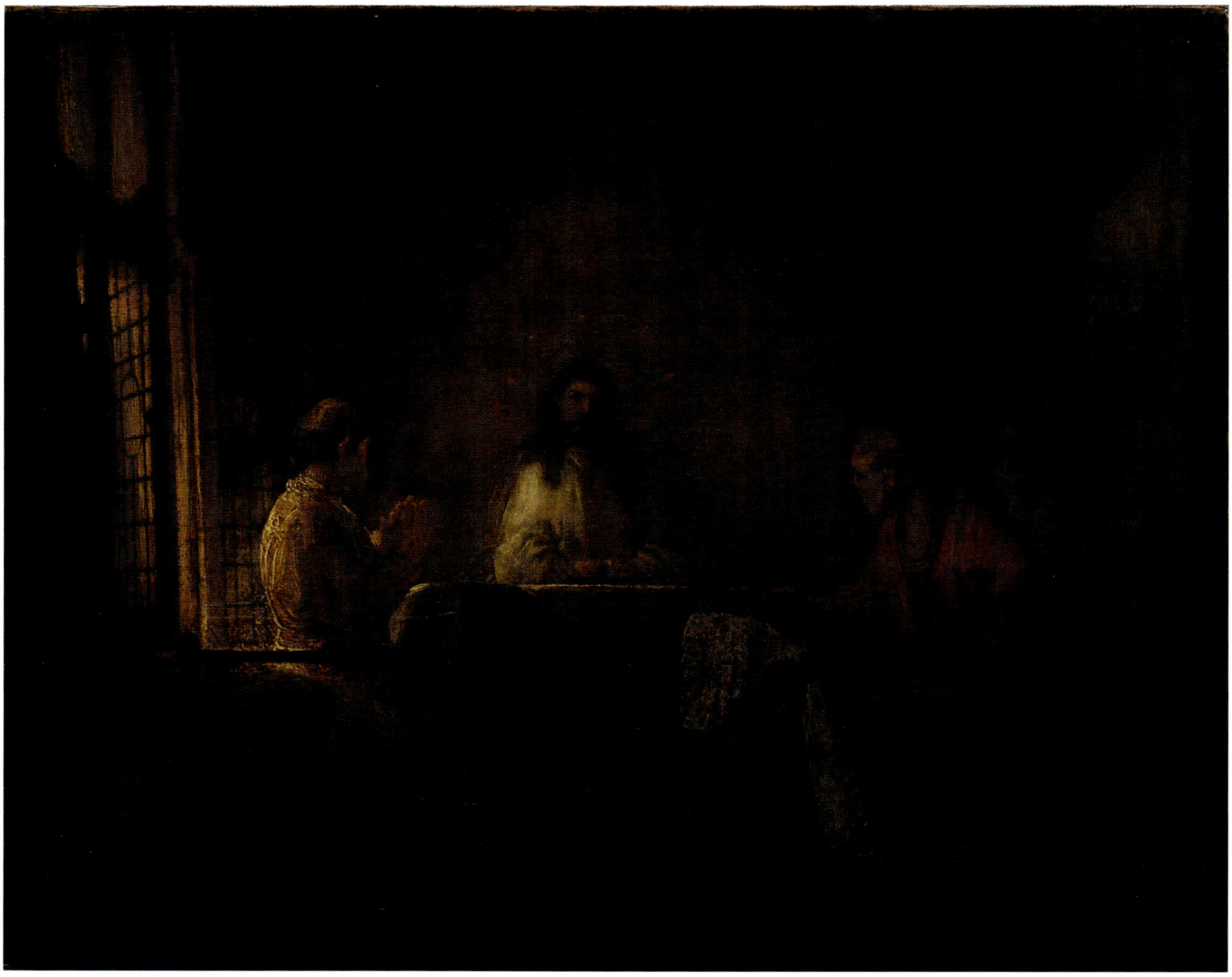

African, usually described as mulatto, and probably one of the many slaves in seventeenth-century Seville. She does not see the event taking place beyond the hatch and it is not clear whether her thoughtful expression reflects some understanding of the miraculous happening depicted. Yet there can be no doubt of the underlying meaning that salvation is possible for all Christians, irrespective of their social status or ethnic origin. In our context it should also be noted that it is usually biblical meals or events associated with them that provide the religious element in such secular scenes of cooking and meal preparation.

Rembrandt never attempted a Last Supper but instead painted the Emmaus scene several times. Best known is the panel in the Louvre, dated 1648 (**147**). Like Caravaggio, he emphasises the humble setting as well as the chiaroscuro effect. The painting is defined by the strong light coming from the left. In other ways this work is in strong contrast with Caravaggio's. The mood is much calmer and the disciples' surprise more internalised. Some meat on a dish is being brought in, but the table is practically empty, leaving the emphasis on the spiritual nature of the occasion, centred on the figure of Christ, light emanating from his halo, as he is breaking the bread.

CONTEXTS AND CONCLUSIONS

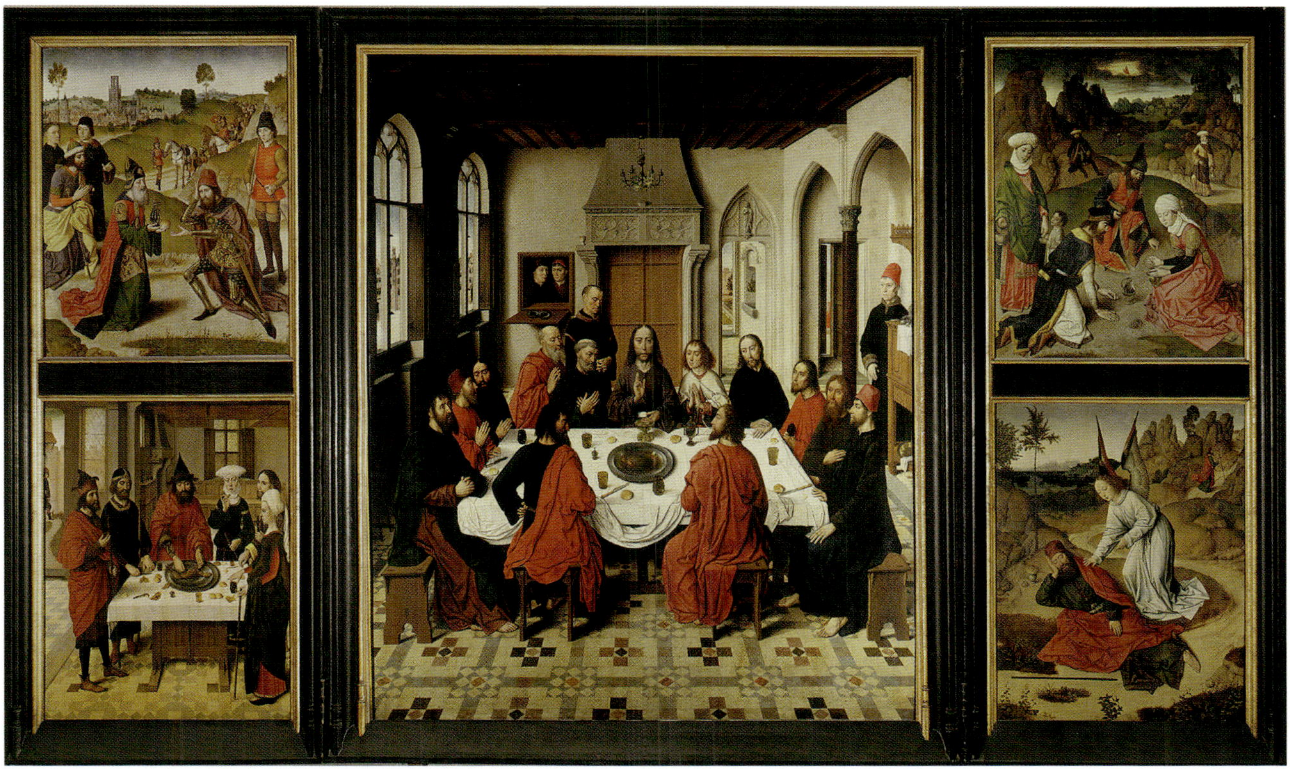

148. Dieric Bouts (d.1475), altarpiece in the church of St Peter, Louvain, 1464–67. The Last Supper in the central panel with four typologically related Old Testament scenes. Left panels: Abraham and Melchizedek; the Passover Meal. Right panels: Gathering Manna; Elijah fed by the Angel in the desert.

MEALS MOST FREQUENTLY ILLUSTRATED: TYPOLOGY AND SYMBOLISM

Having discussed some two dozen meals because they were the most frequently illustrated, the question arises: why just these out of the hundreds mentioned in the Bible? Some were events of obviously central importance: Adam and Eve and the Fall, the Last Supper, God's miracles providing food for mankind, in particular the Fall of Manna and the Multiplication of the Loaves and Fishes. Yet the most consistent factor underlying the popularity of all these scenes is their typological significance as Old Testament prefigurations of events in the Gospels and New Testament forerunners of the Last Supper. Indeed, the fundamental centrality of the Eucharist to the Christian faith lies at the heart of our subject.

We have come across typological symbolism, as expounded by the Church Fathers, from Early Christian sarcophagus reliefs and catacomb paintings and, from the twelfth century, these scenes were expanded into full narrative cycles common in all media, most spectacularly in the stained-glass windows of Gothic cathedrals. In the later Middle Ages these were further expanded in manuscripts of the *Biblia Pauperum* and, above all, of the *Speculum*

Tintoretto (Jacopo Robusti) (1518–94), typological canvases linked with the Last Supper in the upper church of the Scuola di San Rocco in Venice, 1576–81.

On the walls:

149. The Last Supper with Christ administering the host to St Peter.

150. The Multiplication of the Loaves and Fishes.

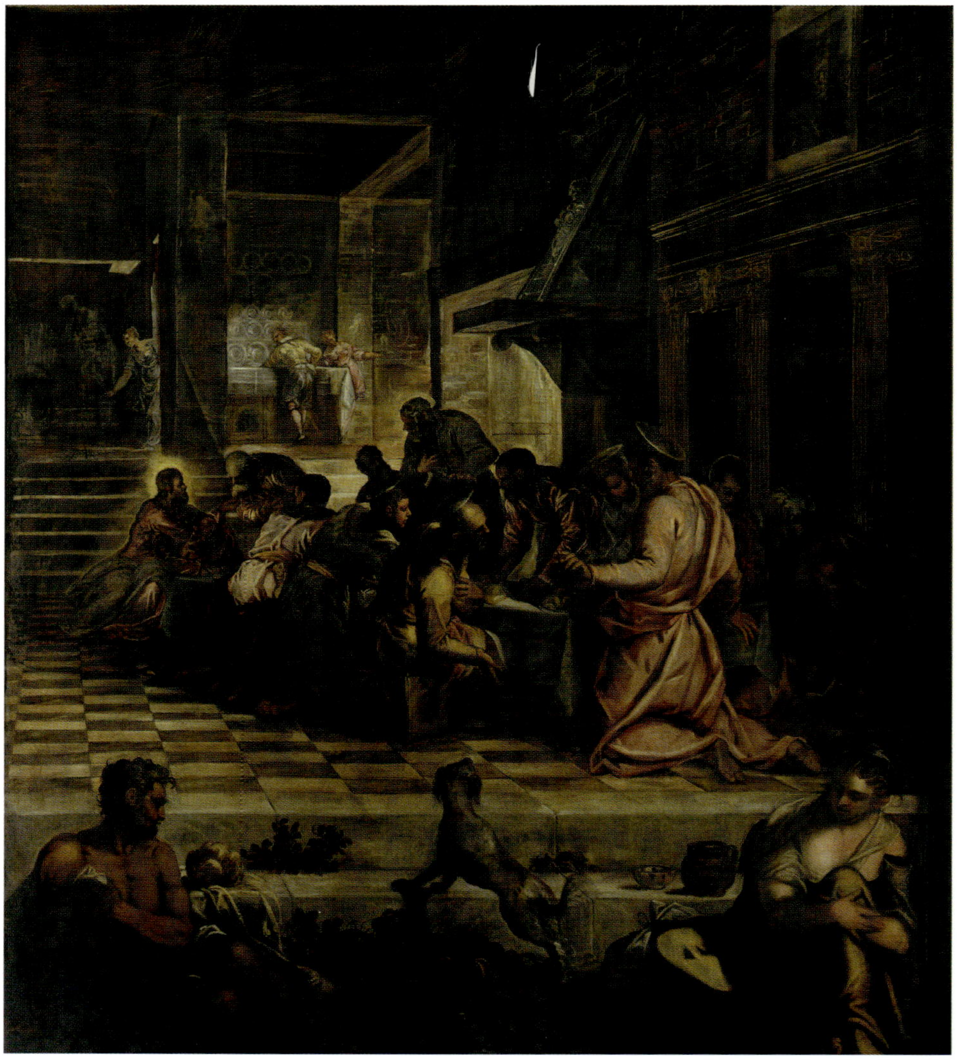

149

Humanae Salvationis (Mirror of Human Salvation), which figures three Old Testament comparisons for each New Testament subject (**32**). Similar, if less extensive, cycles are to be found in the early modern period, particularly on altarpieces and wall paintings in churches.

An early example of a Last Supper altarpiece with typological scenes is the emotionally charged triptych by Dieric Bouts painted at the request of the Holy Sacrament brotherhood in the church of St Peter at Louvain in 1464–67 (**148** and pp. 128–9). The central Last Supper is accompanied by four Old Testament types in the wings: *Abraham and Melchizedek* and the *Passover meal* on the left, the *Gathering of Manna* and *Elijah fed by the Angel in the desert* (I Kings 19.5–7) on the right. For the first three scenes, Bouts followed the *Speculum Humanae Salvationis*: the story of Elijah was added by the patrons, the brothers of the Confraternity of the Holy Sacrament, as being another suitable Old Testament prefiguration. As we have seen, they had hired two theologians at the University of Louvain to instruct Bouts about the order and the details of the subjects he was to paint.[1]

This painting has an unusual history in modern times. The central panel has always remained in the church at Louvain, but the wings were sold to private collectors in the early nineteenth century and ended up in the public galleries in Munich and Berlin. The esteem in which Bouts's masterpiece was held can be judged from the fact that the wings were returned to Louvain by a special decree of the Versailles treaty of 1919, by which the Last Supper was once again united with its Old Testament prefigurations.

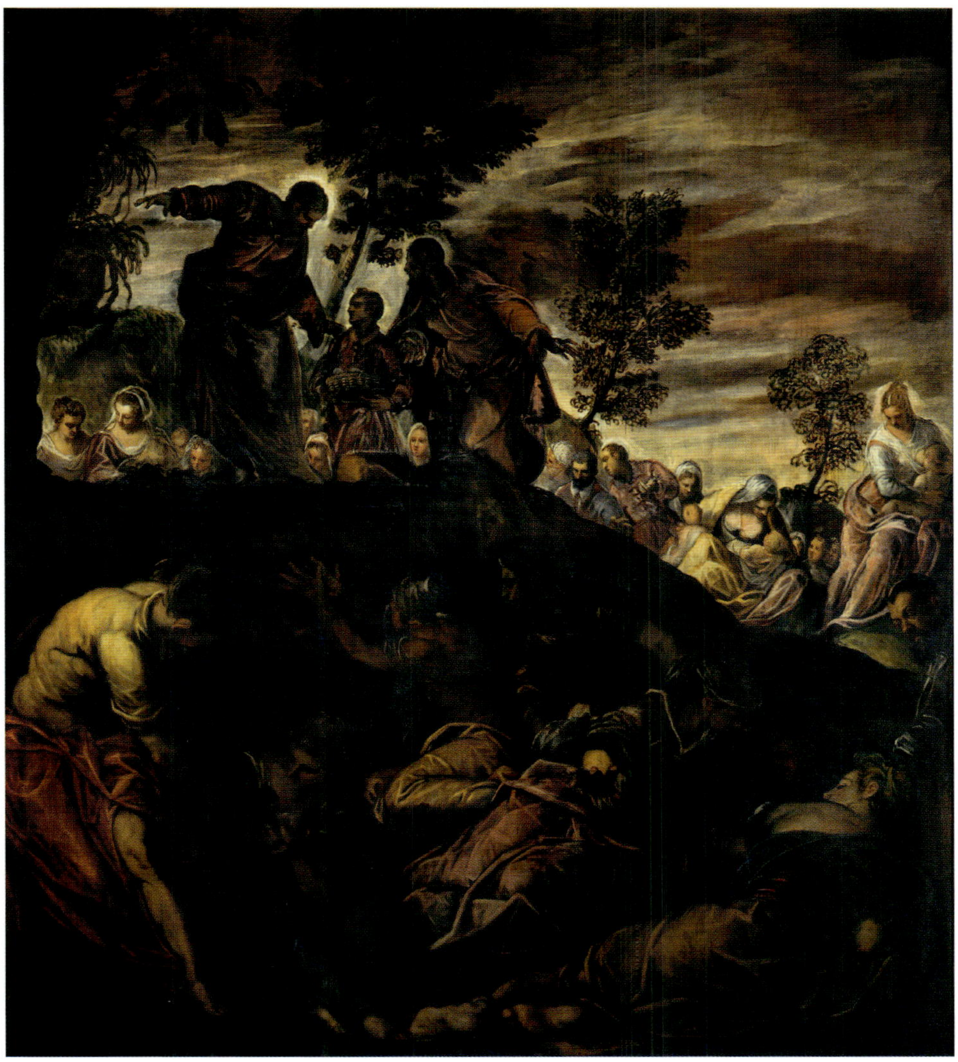

150

Tintoretto (Jacopo Robusti) (1518–94), typological canvases linked with the Last Supper in the upper church of the Scuola di San Rocco in Venice, 1576–81.

On the ceiling:

151. The fall of Manna.

152. Elijah fed by the Angel (I Kings 15.5–9).

153. Elisha multiplying the bread (2 Kings 4.42–44).

154. The Passover Meal.

151

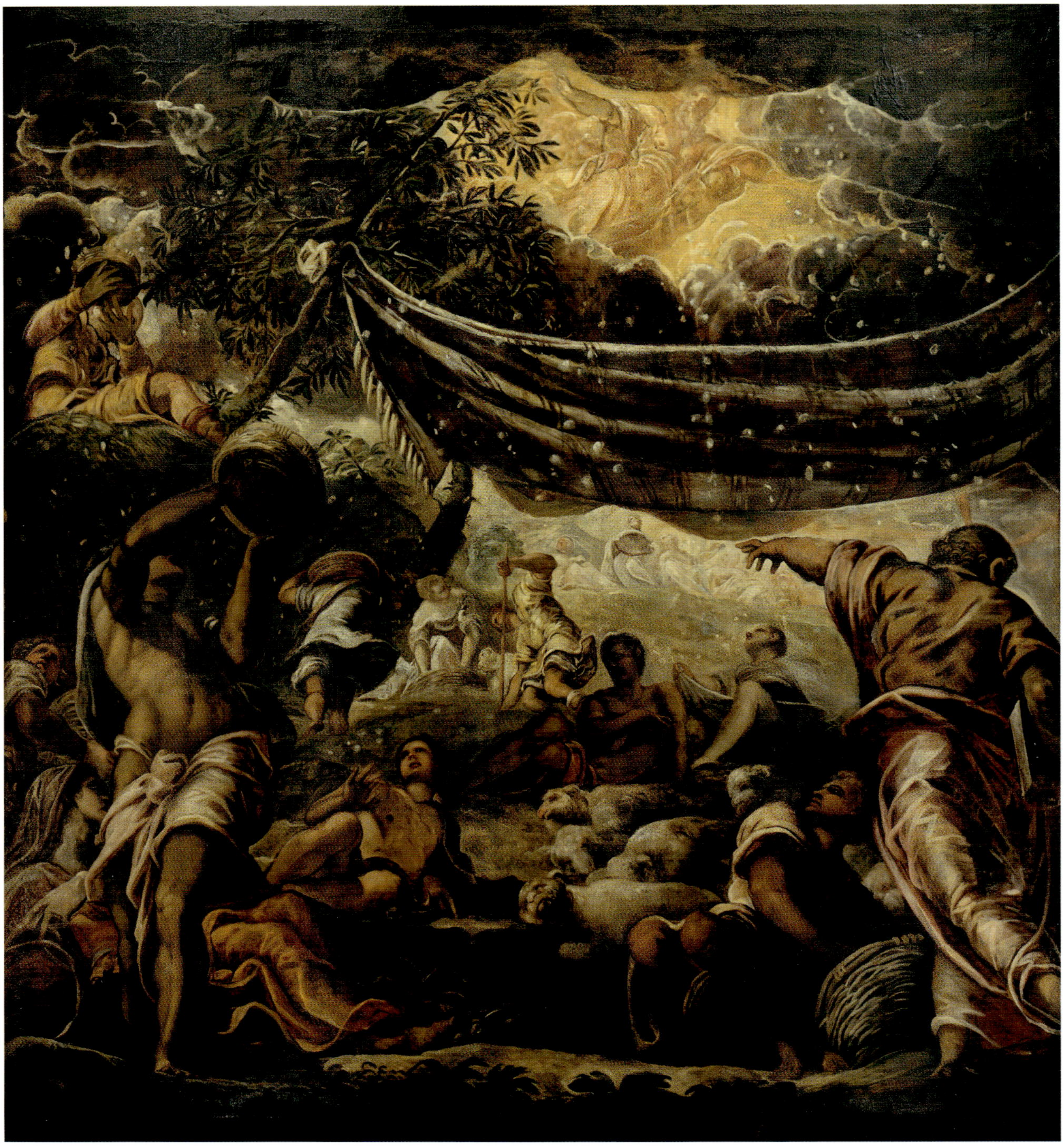

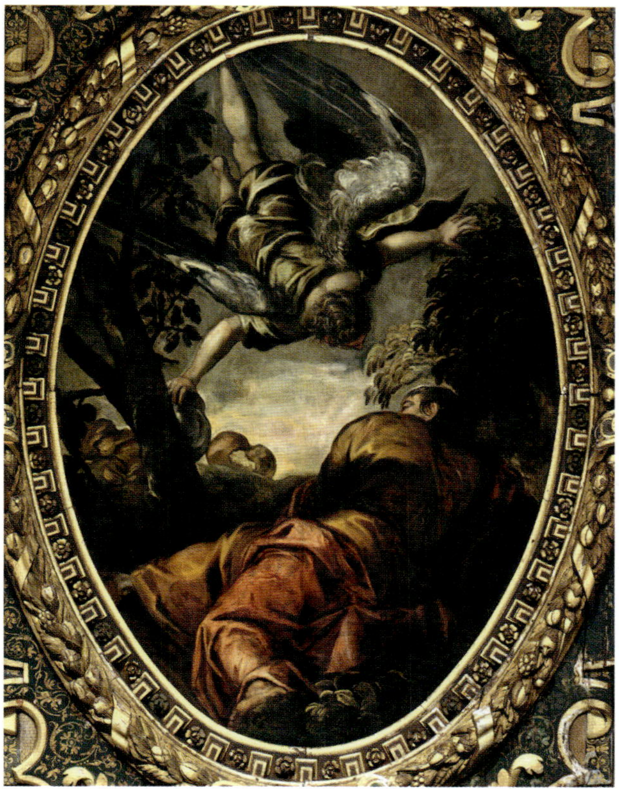

152

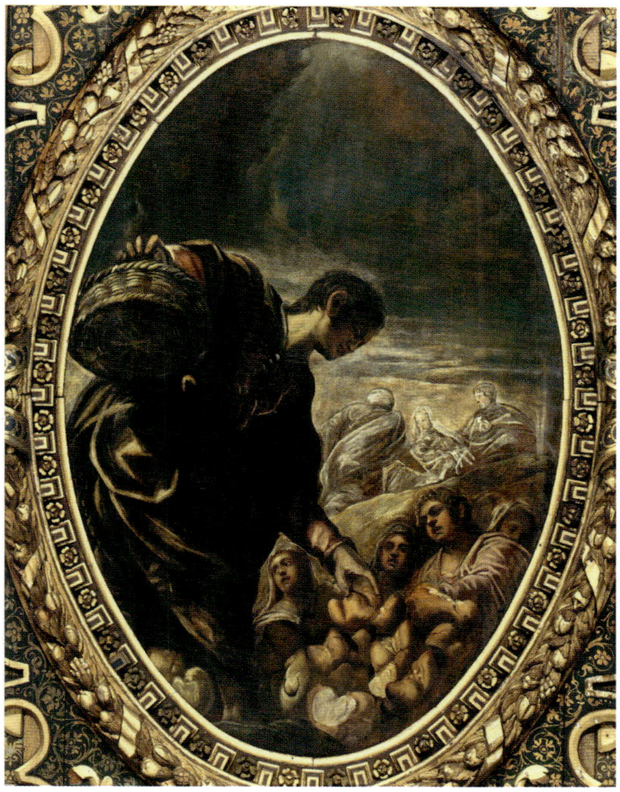

153

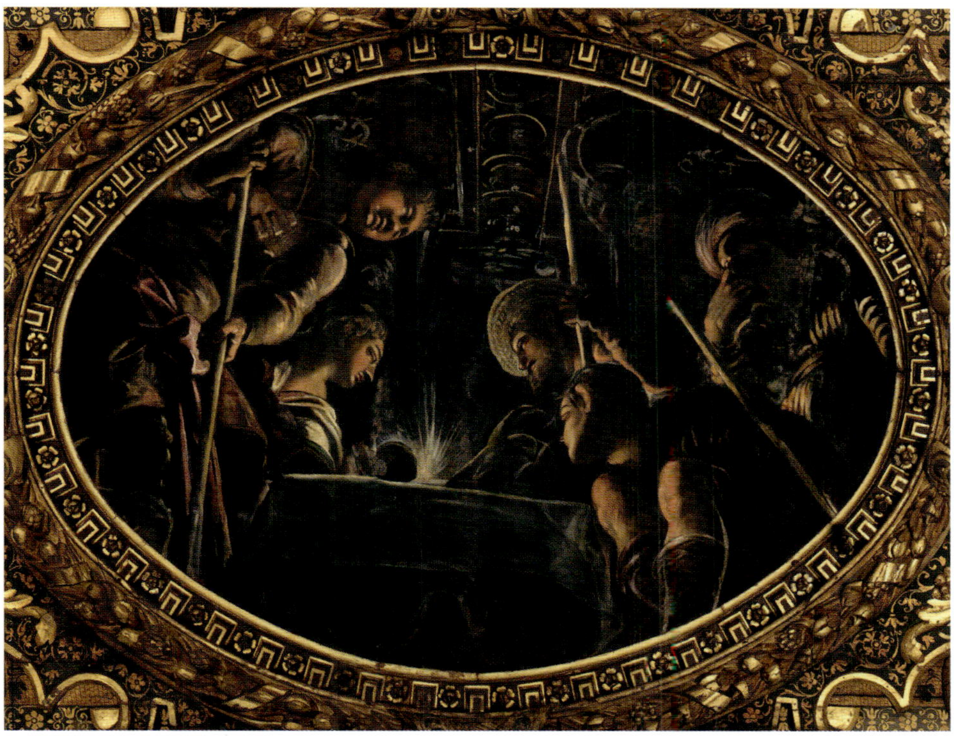

154

About a century after the Bouts altarpiece, Tintoretto painted his typological canvases for the upper church of the Scuola di San Rocco in Venice, a confraternity founded with the aim of helping the sick and needy, especially during epidemics (**149–54**). Under the influence of the Counter Reformation and its rules prescribing emotional emphasis for Christian art, Tintoretto, himself a profound believer, created many new and particularly dramatic interpretations of the traditional scenes. Of the thirty-one paintings in the upper church, seven illustrate biblical meals.[2]

The Last Supper with Christ administering the host to St Peter is on the wall opposite the *Multiplication of the Loaves and Fishes*, while five Old Testament types are figured on the ceiling above: the *Gathering of Manna*, *Elijah fed by the Angel*, *Elisha multiplying the bread* (2 Kings 4.42–44, a forerunner of the Multiplication of the Loaves and Fishes), *Abraham and Melchizedek* and the *Passover Meal*. All of these, except the rarer scene of Elisha, were common in this context, not least in the Bouts altarpiece. Elisha also appears in earlier typological cycles, such as the mid-thirteenth-century *Bible moralisée*.[3] However inventive Tintoretto showed himself to be in the originality of his compositions, the choice of subjects follows ancient traditions.

PICTORIAL TRADITION VS INNOVATION: VIEWERS AND PATRONS

Artists tended to copy or adapt from earlier compositions and a rapid look at the different scenes discussed will provide clear examples of both tradition and changes which, once adopted, become traditional. In pictures of the Last Supper Jesus usually sits at the head of the table in the earlier representations and then, in the later Middle Ages, almost always in the centre. Often such changes are due to new readings of the biblical text. In the *Multiplication of the Loaves and Fishes*, the boy mentioned in St John's Gospel as bringing 'five barley loaves and two fish' first appears in the illustrations in the early fourteenth century (**83**). After that he remains a central feature of the scene, one of the many examples of an innovation, once accepted, becoming routine.

Looking through the illustrations can provide a reasonable overview of stylistic development and iconographical differences, but it must be admitted that the size, material and settings of the originals are obscured by the uniformity of the reproductions. Whether we are considering a very small manuscript illumination or a huge wall painting, we are faced with the questions 'who was it made for?' and 'what was the relationship to the viewer?' Early Christian imagery was developed to aid an evangelising religion and we have seen its dependence on scriptural exegesis and typology. Yet this does not fully explain the impact on the viewer.[4] We have discussed several fifth-century mosaics of Old Testament subjects in the nave of Santa Maria Maggiore in Rome, but not considered the question of how they could have been seen at such great height. Would the members of the congregation have understood the narrative, let alone the typological interpretations? It is thought that the clergy probably explained the contents of church imagery in sermons and at other times, but precise evidence is lacking. When it comes to the meals depicted on the walls of monastic refectories we are on safer ground, as the monks would clearly have had a close understanding of the imagery.

Most problematic are the illuminated manuscripts. How and by whom were the images viewed and experienced? The subjects we have discussed appear in biblical cycles in Bibles, Gospels and psalters; in Gospel lectionaries they were selected to illustrate the readings on particular days. They would have been seen by relatively few viewers, but one may presume that their imagery also appeared in larger-scale versions, such as wall paintings, sculpture and stained glass. These were all more subject to damage and destruction and have a lower survival rate than manuscripts, which were protected by their wooden covers and preserved in monastic and other libraries.

From the fourteenth century onwards, paintings on panel, particularly altarpieces, are increasingly numerous. These could be seen by many in churches and chapels and by a more select audience in aristocratic households.

Consideration of the different classes of viewer raises the related question of patronage. Which institution or individual commissioned a particular work? In the earlier Middle Ages the majority of illuminated manuscripts were produced in monasteries, but little is known of individual patrons. We are exceptionally well informed from the monastic records about the giant Bible of c.1135 from the abbey of Bury St Edmunds. It was illuminated by Master Hugo, a lay artist, at the instructions of Prior Talbot, but we have no idea who suggested including the extremely rare scene of Moses expounding the law of the unclean beasts (**64**).

Several of the outstanding medieval manuscripts are linked with the names of their patrons, such as the *Codex Egberti*, the Gospel lectionary dedicated to Egbert, archbishop of Trier from 977 to 993, which we have discussed several times in this survey (**91**, **96**, **140**).[5] He was famous in his time for his artistic patronage, particularly of illuminated manuscripts and goldsmiths' work, and the frontispiece of the Egbert Codex shows two Reichenau monks, Keraldus and Heribertus, presenting the book to the much larger seated figure of the archbishop. Yet the script and the style of some of the miniatures have been attributed to Trier rather than Reichenau and this has raised discussions as to its place of origin. What remains beyond dispute is that, with its fifty-one Gospel illustrations, this manuscript contains a longer cycle of the Life of Christ than anything extant which had gone before it. Even with all the available evidence it remains unclear as to the extent of Egbert's influence, if any, on the choice of illustrations.

For the later periods we have considered the recorded patronage of the Confraternity of the Holy Sacrament at St Paul's Church, Louvain, in the case of Dieric Bouts's Last Supper altarpiece, and of the Scuola di San Rocco in Venice for Tintoretto's canvases, but such evidence is relatively rare. The class of secular patrons of the sixteenth and seventeenth centuries is reflected in the bourgeois settings and princely banquets, even where the patrons remain unknown.

Occasionally the individual patrons are portrayed, as on the wall painting of the *Wedding at Cana* in the Chapel of San Nicola at Tolentino, where two couples are shown kneeling below the tables (**73** and p. 76). Yet the principal patrons of these paintings of the Life of Christ are the Augustinian friars who commissioned them in about 1330 to support their proposal for the canonisation of San Nicola, who had been a member of their order. Presumably they laid down the subjects to be painted with reference to the biblical stories and their traditional compositions, leaving the artist, Pietro da Rimini, to provide the dramatic and emotional impact. What, if anything, the input of the kneeling donors was, apart presumably from their financial support, remains totally unknown.

The same sort of problem arises over Gerard David's more intimate setting of the same subject dating from about 1500 (**76**).[6] The painting formerly belonged to the Confraternity of the Holy Blood in the upper Church of St Basil at Bruges and a Dominican member of the Confraternity is shown looking into the room on the left. Within the room, kneeling on the left with his son and facing his wife, is the donor, who is wearing the costume of the Confraternity. He has been identified as Jan de Sedano, a Spanish merchant resident in Bruges, who is recorded as a member of the Confraternity and as a patron of Bouts. This picture of the wedding is highly unusual in that nearly all the seated diners are women. There is no explanation for this and, again, there is no clear answer as to whether the responsibility lies with Dominicans, the owners, or Sedano, the donor. The servants with the water jugs and wine flagons are standard for the scene, but there are other unusual features, such as the floral tapestry, symbol of fertility, behind the bride. The issue of the point at which the patron's demands end and the artist's contribution begins remains unresolvable.

TABLE SETTING AND FOOD DISPLAYED

Apart from a few notable exceptions, such as the water jars at the Wedding at Cana, the Bible makes hardly any mention of the table setting. In general terms the bowls, platters, goblets and cups remain standard in the illustrations. There is, for example, very little difference in the setting for the Last Supper between the Gospels of Henry the Lion of the 1180s and the Luttrell Psalter almost two centuries later (**130**, **137**). The latter has introduced spoons, which remain a rarity, while forks do not appear at all on the table until the sixteenth century. The lack of cutlery indicates the prevalence of eating with fingers from communal dishes and bowls, which is quite often shown in the illustrations (**51**, **52**, **119**, **130**, **131**). This in turn emphasised the importance of sharing and of the close relationship forged by the diners at communal meals. Indeed, the increasing use of cutlery and individual plates at the expense of shared eating has been interpreted as a sign of the growing autonomy of the individual in society.[7]

Increasingly also, there is a greater stress on the display of diverse contemporary artefacts of ceramics, glass and silver, as in the example of the maiolica jugs at Tolentino (**74**). It was usual to show all the diners seated on one side of the table, allowing the servants to bring the food from the other side and giving the viewer a clear sight of the meal and its participants. This arrangement also strengthened the visual link between table and altar, which could be further emphasised by the careful depiction of the covering cloth. Tables covered with richly decorated silver vessels also served to indicate the social class of the diners in the late medieval and early modern periods. By the time of Veronese's great banquet pictures, all the tables are weighed down by the wealth of plates, dishes, goblets, jugs and aristocratic silver ware (**78**).

As to the food itself, we have seen that the Bible provides only a few instances of precise description. Abraham's meal for the three visitors is fully described: the freshly baked loaves came with butter and milk, the calf selected had to be good and tender. Esau gives up his birthright to his brother Jacob in exchange for a plate of lentil soup, well known as the food of the poor in the ancient Near East, while Ruth dips her bread into sour wine as she eats her meal in the barley field with her fellow workers. Even more rarely are actual items of food mentioned in the Gospels, apart from the bread and wine of the Eucharist. A rare example of such precision is to be found in the parable of the king's son's wedding, described by the king himself: 'I have prepared my dinner, my oxen and fat calves have been slaughtered and everything is ready' (Matt. 22).

Bread – the basic food in classical and medieval times – wine and fish dominate in the images. Otherwise chicken or different fowl are most common, reflecting actuality both in the Middle East of biblical times and in the West in subsequent centuries.[8] More occasionally there is calf, which, like the fowl, is often shown being carved on a trencher – a flat platter of hardened bread or wood. Pies, which have a long history, are frequently depicted from the later Middle Ages, as is fruit (**138**). Sugar, increasingly imported into Europe and predominant in upper-class banquets from the fifteenth century, appears, for example, in the guise of a sugar ball sweet in Veronese's *Wedding at Cana* (**78**). Yet the items of identifiable food remain minimal. There is no representation of stews, vegetables, cheese or eggs in the biblical text or its illustrations.

THE BROADER CONTEXT

Given our need for food and our desire for table fellowship, it is hardly surprising that the description of meals is as central to secular literature as it is to the Bible. For the classical period, there is the striking contrast between Plato's *Symposium*, for which the meal is an occasion for philosophical discourse, and the wild parties epitomised by Petronius' *Satyricon*, written in Nero's reign 54–68 CE. Almost a quarter of this long text is devoted to Trimalchio's feast, describing the endless series of courses provided by this *nouveau riche* host. Early on, dancers bring in a dish with fat fowls and sow's bellies 'and a hare got up with wings to look like Pegasus', with spice sauce, by which time all the guests were already drunk.[9] A middle way between these two extremes is supplied by Athenaeus, whose lengthy volume *The Learned Banqueters* (second century CE) imitates the philosophical discussion of Plato's *Symposium* while also providing a detailed description of an extraordinarily extravagant dinner and drinkers' party.

For the Middle Ages, King Arthur, whose legends were collected in the twelfth century, was famously known for his round table and there are more than twenty meals recorded at his court in the Arthurian romance *Sir Gawain and the Green Knight* of c.1400. Chaucer's *Canterbury Tales* have numerous meals taking place at key moments in the narrative. In The Franklin's Tale, for instance, it is at a dinner that the handsome squire Aurelius approaches the heroine, Dorigen, during her husband's absence. Yet these are all brief references. Longer descriptions of meals occur in the records of wedding celebrations, particularly in Renaissance Italy. The celebration at Pesaro for the marriage of Costanzo Sforza and Camilla d'Aragona in May 1475, for example, went on for five days and included a banquet beginning at 9 a.m. and lasting seven hours. The 100 guests ate their way through nine courses, each presented as a gift from a specified Roman god or goddess and described in mouthwatering detail.[10]

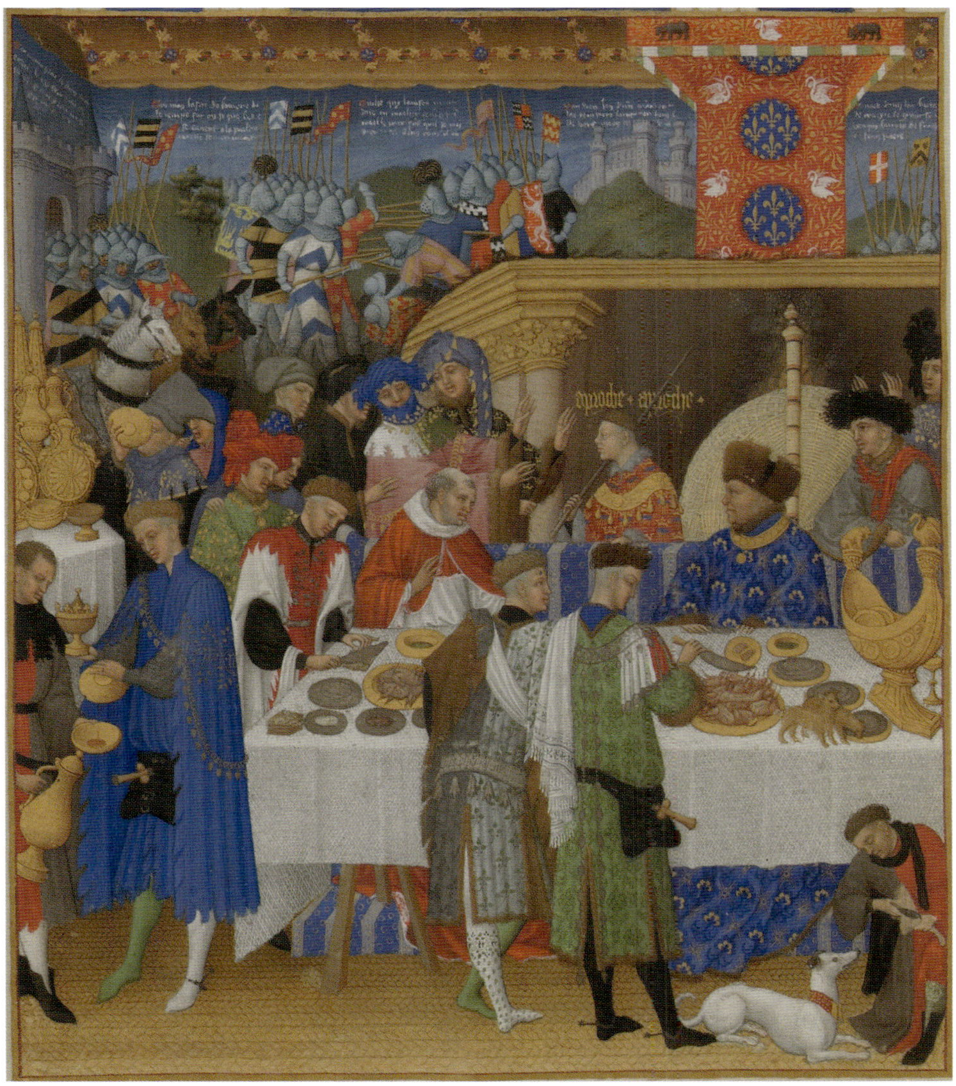

155. Illustration for the month of January in the calendar of a Book of Hours, the *Très Riches Heures* of the duc de Berry, 1413–16, by the Limbourg Brothers. Feasting is the usual occupation shown for January in such calendars. Chantilly, Musée Condé, MS 65, fol. 1v.

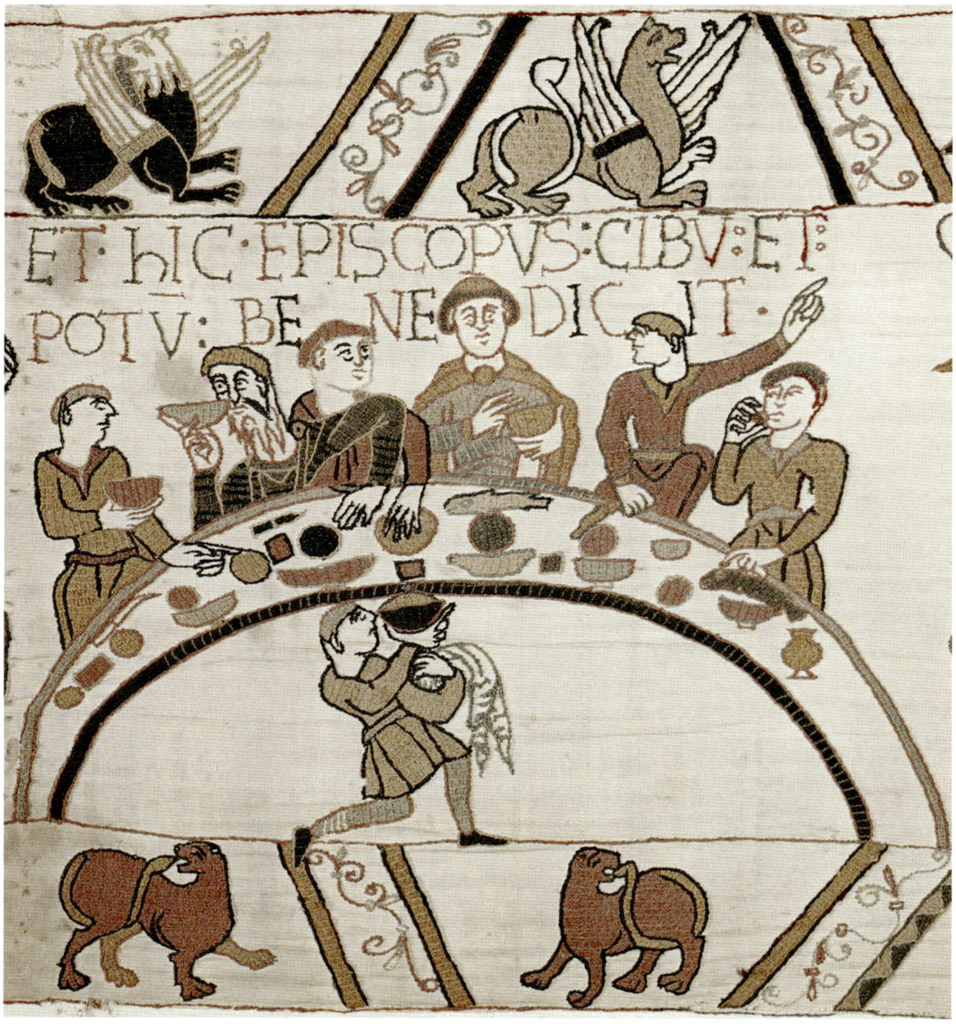

156. Bishop Odo saying grace as he dines with William the Conqueror before the Battle of Hastings. The Bayeux tapestry, an embroidery on linen, probably English, dating from about 1080.

As to wilder, self-indulgent parties, it was not until François Rabelais' *Gargantua and Pantagruel* (1535–52) that there was a rival to Petronius. Rabelais was a former Benedictine monk attacking what he saw as debased monastic communities, and the dishes he describes include the swan into which Zeus metamorphosed to seduce Leda and the genitals of the bull beloved of Queen Pasiphae (Book V, ch. 32).

When it comes to depictions of secular meals, there are plenty in classical times from fifth-century BCE painted vases to Pompeian wall paintings of the first century CE.[11] Yet from the Early Christian period they are far outnumbered by the illustrations of biblical meals. Indeed, the only commonly represented meal appears in the calendars of prayer books, notably psalters and books of hours, where eating is the activity illustrating either December or January. The labours of the months had long been represented in the form of rural occupations but from the twelfth century single figures shown eating regularly illustrate December or January, both on cathedral sculpture and in illuminated manuscripts. From about 1300 framed miniatures depicting group meals become the norm. The East Anglian Queen Mary Psalter of about 1310–20 (BL Royal 2.B.VII) shows a king and queen with guests at dinner with servants and musicians, and the setting becomes ever more splendid in subsequent periods. One of the best-known examples is the scene of January in the Limbourg brothers' *Très Riches Heures* of the duc de Berry of 1413–16, in which both the food and the silver gilt vessels are more luxurious than those in the depictions of biblical meals (**155**).

These feasting illustrations to the month of January in the calendars of religious manuscripts are the most commonly surviving depictions of royal and aristocratic meals, but such scenes also occur in other contexts. In the Bayeux tapestry – actually an embroidery, dating from about 1080 – Bishop Odo of Bayeux, seated next to William the Conqueror, is saying grace as they dine before the battle of Hastings (**156**).[12] At the side, meat is being roasted on a spit while other food is being brought to the table. Such wealth of detail on the preparation of the meal contrasts with the more abstemious depictions of biblical meals in the Middle Ages. For the early modern period, the tavern scenes of seventeenth-century Dutch artists such as Jan Steen have the same emphasis on crowded rooms and laden tables, but the diners are clearly peasants or bourgeois, as opposed to the aristocratic guests at Veronese's biblical banquets.

Meals are frequently described in secular literature but these are rarely illustrated. The only surviving manuscript of *Sir Gawain and the Green Knight* opens with a picture of Gawain taking up the challenge of the Green Knight, whose severed head is on the dinner table.[13] On a larger scale, Botticelli's panel painting of Boccaccio's tale of Nastasia degli Onesti (Prado, Madrid, 1493) includes a scene of outdoor dining in which, as in the biblical illustrations, the emphasis is on the story rather than on the food on the table.

GLUTTONY AND ABSTINENCE

Having discussed the forbidden foods of the Jews (p. 64), it should also be said that most major religions have codified traditions governing food customs. Among Muslims there are set periods of fasting and forbidden foods; the cow is venerated by Hindus and devout Buddhists tend to be vegetarian. The strict rules governing food laid down in the Hebrew Bible were abandoned by the Christians. Yet, as Christian ritual developed, there were calls for abstinence and days of fasting were increasingly adopted. The constitution of Western monasticism, codified in the sixth-century rule of St Benedict, emphasised the need for simplicity and abstinence governing the intake of food. An illustration in a late twelfth-century French manuscript shows two Cistercian monks seated at a table on which the only foodstuffs shown are green vegetables.[14] Above all, there was the idea of food as temptation, typified by Eve's fruit and the fear of Gluttony, one of the seven deadly sins as defined by Gregory the Great in his *Moralia in Job* (31.45).

Two centuries earlier, the renowned theologian John Cassian (c.360–c.425) was one of the first to systematically treat a list of eight vices which later developed into the seven deadly sins.[15] In the same period the Latin poet Prudentius (348–410) wrote his *Psychomachia*, which embodied Christian asceticism as an allegory of spiritual warfare between virtues and vices that battled for man's soul. In this context, Abstinence defeated Gluttony (*Gula*) and the contrast between the two remained a constant theme among Early Christian and medieval theologians.[16] To take only one example, Robert Grosseteste, theologian and scientist before he became bishop of Lincoln in 1235, devoted two of his *Dicta* (Sayings) to the subject.[17] These sayings on matters of moral theology were gathered from his lectures at the Oxford schools in about 1220–30, the early years of the university. Dictum 36 deals with Fasting, quoting Augustine's *Commentary on the Gospel of St John* (17.4) on the need to abstain from unreasonable and illicit pleasure. The fear of gluttony and the need for abstinence is a constant theme supported by numerous biblical references. Frequently, also, the message is extended to cover other lessons of morality. 'Why do we fast. Is it not to share your bread with the hungry and bring the homeless poor into your house?' (Isaiah 58.7).

Illustrated manuscripts of Prudentius' *Psychomachia* dating from the ninth to the thirteenth century, as well as the sculptures on Gothic cathedrals, show Virtues and Vices as single female figures engaged in battle, with the victor usually standing in triumph over the body of the vanquished.[18] In the later Middle Ages, when other texts dealing with virtues and vices were more often illustrated, Gluttony and Abstinence were increasingly shown in the setting of a meal. An amusing example is an illustration entitled Temperance and

Intemperance in a French translation of the Roman author Valerius Maximus, *Memorable Deeds and Sayings*. Written in about 30 CE and dedicated to the Emperor Tiberius, it is an anthology of moralising anecdotes, several of them contrasting virtues and vices. Here we are dealing with a printed edition of the French text, produced at Ghent or Bruges in about 1477, to which hand-painted illustrations and marginal decorations were added, as was often the case in the early decades after the invention of printing (**157**).[19] The temperate diners, well dressed and upright, are eating from an orderly set table, in contrast with the intemperate, who are slovenly and drunk, slumped at their table, which is covered with spilt wine and scattered loaves. As a further distinction, their table is round, in contrast to the oblong table of the upright group, demonstrating how far round tables had fallen out of fashion. On the left two men are discussing the moral of the story, while among the marginal decoration a woman pouring wine is doubtless intended to be linked with the main illustration.

A rather different picture, more specifically of Gluttony, appears in a French manuscript of *Le miroir du monde*, another moralising treatise dealing at length with the seven cardinal sins and dated to about 1470–80 (**158**).[20] This is a rare example of an artist following lengthy written instructions that have survived in the text. In the foreground the female embodiment of Sobriety, holding a bird, points at a youth seated at a small table and vomiting during his meal. This narrative is continued in the contrast of the upright lion at the woman's feet facing the hellmouth dragon swallowing the soul of Gluttony. Meanwhile, the diners in the top half of the miniature are identified as Dives, the rich man, with his family

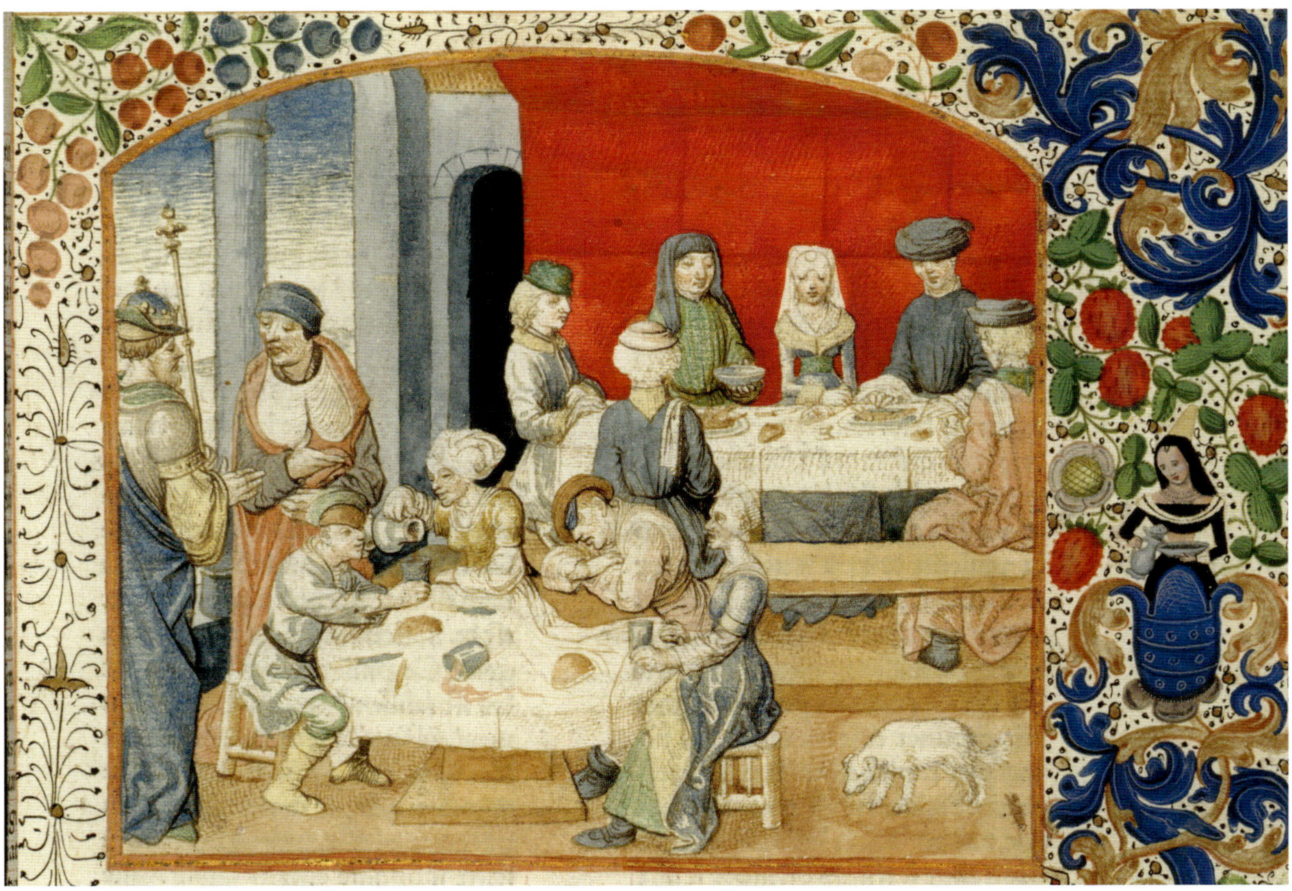

157. Gluttony and Abstinence, painted illustration in a printed text of Valerius Maximus, *Memorable Deeds and Sayings* (French version), Ghent or Bruges 1477. Interestingly, the Abstinence table is oblong, in contrast with the round one for Gluttony. Paris, Bibliothèque Nationale. Rés.Z.200, fol. 85.

158. Gluttony and Sobriety in the foreground together with the Parable of Dives and Lazarus above and on the left. Miniature in a manuscript of *Le miroir du monde*, a French moralising treatise of about 1470–80. Brussels, Bibliothèque Royale, MS 10204, fol. 297v.

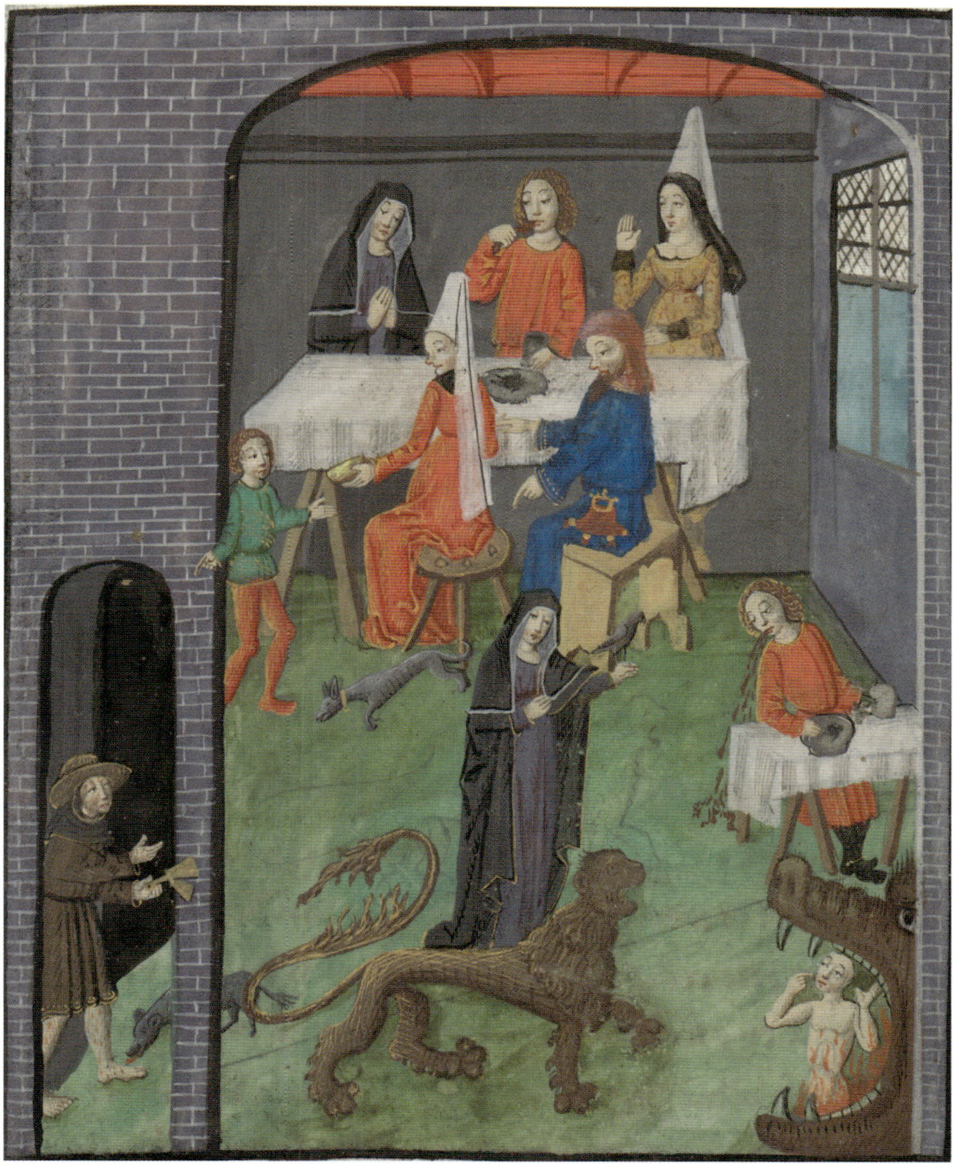

and guests, while Lazarus, the beggar, as usual covered in sores (compare **107–13**), is standing at the door. The biblical parable has been introduced here as a further illustration of the classical contrast of virtues and vices.

Robert Grosseteste followed his dictum on Fasting with one on convivial meals and banquets (Dictum 37). Warnings about the dangers of Gluttony are kept in mind; there must be no overeating or drunkenness. St Paul is quoted: 'do not get drunk on wine, for that is debauchery, but be filled with the Spirit' (Ephesians 5.18). Having given that warning, he emphasises the need to eat and drink with friends as basic to Christian fellowship. The message of this saying is: invite your friends for an enjoyable meal. As we have seen, communal meals forge social bonds, not least when the diners eat with their fingers food taken from shared bowls.

In discussing the most frequently depicted biblical meals we have usually had to conclude that there is not much information on the food itself. The act of dining together is always of central importance; the food itself is rarely mentioned. The significance of these meals is to provide a setting for key events and for the moral lessons to be learnt. The importance of the Parable of Dives and Lazarus does not depend on knowing exactly what was on the rich man's table. It is the tale's moral that still reverberates today.

NOTES

INTRODUCTION

1. New York, Morgan Library, M.736. S.C. Cockerell and J. Plummer, *Old Testament Miniatures*, London n.d.
2. Most of these have an entry with a bibliography and illustrations in the *Lexikon der Christlichen Ikonographie*, ed. E. Kirschbaum, 4 vols, Rome, Freiburg 1968–72.
3. F.E. Whelan, 'Urbanus Magnus: A Twelfth-Century Courtesy Text and Three Oxford Manuscripts', *Bodleian Library Record*, 27, 2014, pp. 12–55, esp. p. 26.

BREAD, WINE, FISH AND TABLE FELLOWSHIP

1. M. Broshi, 'The Diet of Palestine in the Roman Period', in *Bread, Wine, Walls and Scrolls*, London 2001, p. 121.
2. Edward Hyams, *Dionysus. A Social History of the wine-vine*, London 1965; Athalya Brenner and J. van Heuten (ed.), *Food and Drink in the Biblical Worlds* (Semeia 86), Atlanta GA 1999, esp. pp. 19–32.
3. F.J. Dölger, *Ichtheus. Das Fischsymbol in Früchristlicher Zeit*, 1, Münster 1928. A. McGowan, *Ascetic Eucharists. Food and Drink in Early Christian Ritual Meals*, Oxford 1999, pp. 127–43. For a summary, see the entry for Fish in *The Encyclopedia of Christianity*, 2, Grand Rapids MI 2001, p. 321.
4. R. Barthes, 'Pour une psycho-sociologie d'alimentation contemporaine', *Annales*, 16 (5), 1961, pp. 977–86 at 979, reprinted in *Food and Drink in History: selections from Annales*, vol. 5, ed. R. Forster and O. Ranum, Baltimore, London 1979, pp. 166–73.
5. See J. Brumberg-Kraus, 'Not by bread alone', in *Food and Drink in the Biblical Worlds*, ed. Athalya Brenner and J. van Heuten (Semeia 86), Atlanta GA 1999, as in n.5, pp. 165–91; for a somewhat different view, especially on the importance of Acts 2.46 as evidence for the place of communal meals in the Early Christian period, see G. Vermes, *Christian Beginnings. From Nazareth to Nicaea (AD 30–325)*, London 2012, p. 75.

THE OLD TESTAMENT

1. For a summary with further references, see C.M. Kauffmann, *Biblical Imagery in Medieval England 700–1550*, London, Turnhout 2003, pp. 79–89.
2. For a recent discussion of this point, see John Harvey, *The Bible as Visual Culture. When Text Becomes Image*, Sheffield 2013, esp. pp. 6–13.
3. For an exemplary survey see J.B. Trapp, 'The Iconography of the Fall of Man', in *Approaches to Paradise Lost*, ed. C.A. Patrides, London 1968, pp. 223–65, this example at p. 228 and fig. 2.
4. See respectively, Trapp, as in n. 11, 3: W. Tronzo, *The Via Latina Catacomb*, University Park PA 1986, p. 52.

5. All the illustrations are reproduced and discussed in K. Weitzmann and M. Bernabò, *The Byzantine Octateuchs*, Princeton 1999. See also J. Lowden, *The Octateuchs. A Study in Byzantine Manuscript Illumination*, University Park PA 1992.
6. A.S. Cohen and A. Derbes, 'Bernward and Eve at Hildesheim', *Gesta*, 40, 2001, pp. 19–38, esp. p. 24.
7. L. Ginzberg, *The Legends of the Jews*, University Park PA 1947, 1, pp. 73–5; 5, pp. 97–8, n. 7. The appearance of the fig and the apple in Jewish commentaries is discussed by Weitzmann and Bernabò (as in n. 5), pp. 34–6.
8. H.-G. Leder, 'Arbor Scientiae. Die Tradition vom Paradiesischen Apfelbaum', *Zeitschrift für die Neutestamentliche Wissenschaft*, 52, 1961, pp. 156–89, at p. 166.
9. J. O'Reilly, 'The Trees of Eden in Medieval Iconography', in *A Walk in the Garden. Biblical, Iconographical and Literary Images of Eden*, ed. P. Morris and D. Sawyer, Sheffield 1992, pp. 167–204.
10. N. Zimmermann, *Werkstattgruppen Römischer Katakombenmalerei*, Münster 2002, p. 109, pl. XXIII.
11. Leder, as in n. 8, pp. 176–84.
12. M. Schapiro, 'The Apple of Cézanne', in his collected essays, *Modern Art 19th and 20th centuries*, London 1978, esp. p. 35, n. 36.
13. Leder, as in n. 8, pp. 184–8.
14. Homily 4: 'Tribus occurrit et unum adorat'. For the original text with a French translation, see Origène, *Homélies sur la Genèse*, transl. L. Doutreleau, Paris 1976, pp. 145–51.
15. 'Cui deus refulget trinitatem videt'. *De Abraham. Tutte le Opere di Sant' Ambrogio*, 2/II, Milan, Rome 1984, I.5.33.
16. *Lexikon der Christlichen Ikonographie* (as in Introduction, n. 2), vol. 1, col. 25, 2.
17. For the sequence of Genesis scenes in the nave mosaics at Santa Maria Maggiore, see C. Cecchelli, *I Mosaici della Basilica di S. Maria Maggiore*, Turin 1956.
18. C.O. Nordström, *Ravenna-Studien*, Stockholm 1953, p. 114.
19. K. Weitzmann and H.L. Kessler, *The Cotton Genesis. British Library Codex Cotton Otho.B.VI*, Princeton 1986, pp. 79–80, 216.
20. B.F. Davidson, *Raphael's Bible. A Study of the Vatican Logge*, University Park PA 1985, pp. 68, 38.
21. *Moritz Oppenheim. The First Jewish Painter*, exhibition catalogue, Israel Museum Jerusalem, 1983, pp. 7–29, 81–2, nos 3–14.
22. B. Narkiss, *El Pentateuco Ashburnham. La Ilustración de Códices en la Antigüedad Tardiá*, Valencia 2007 (with English translation). D.H. Verkerk, 'Moral Structure in the Ashburnham Pentateuch', in *Image and Belief*, ed. C. Hourihane, Princeton 1991, pp. 71–89.
23. Tertullian, *Contra Marcion*, ed. with French translation R. Braun, Paris 1994, III.24.7–9, p. 209. *Tutte le opere di Sant Ambrogio (edizione bilingua)*, Milano 1982, vol. 3, *De Jacob et vita beata*, II.2.8, pp. 280–3.
24. A. Ferrua, *The Unknown Catacomb. A Unique Discovery of Early Christian Art*, New Lanark 1991, figs 150, 154.
25. Justin Martyr, *Dialogus cum Tryphone*, CXI.4. See J. Daniélou, *The Bible and the Liturgy*, London 1979, ch. 10.
26. John's somewhat different version is discussed in connection with the Last Supper, see below, p. 137.
27. M. Niesner, *Das Speculum Humanae Salvationis der Stiftsbibliothek Kremsmünster*, Cologne 1995, pp. 8–25. For an English summary dealing with the woodcut illustrations, see A. Wilson and J.L. Wilson, *A Medieval Mirror. Speculum Humanae Salvationis*, Berkeley 1984.
28. K. Kogman-Appel, *Illuminated Haggadot from Medieval Spain*, University Park PA 2006; Marc M. Epstein, *The Medieval Haggadah. Art, Narrative and Religious Imagination*, New Haven, London 2011.
29. J. Wilpert, *Die Malereien der Katakomben Roms*, Freiburg im Breisgau 1903, pl. 242.2.
30. K. Corrigan, *Visual Polemics in ninth-century Byzantine Psalters*, Cambridge 1992, p. 50.
31. For a discussion of the Hebrew text, see *Ruth. A New Translation* (The Anchor Bible), New York 1975, p. 102.
32. For these illustrations, see M. Levi D'Ancona, 'Figurazione del Libro di Ruth nella Bibbia', in *Il Codice Miniato*, ed. M. Ceccanti, Florence 1992, pp. 3–18.
33. W.O.E. Oesterley, *Sacrifices in Ancient Israel. Their Origins, Purposes and Development*, London 1937, pp. 168–71.
34. K. Weitzmann, ed. H. Kessler, *Studies in Classical and Byzantine Manuscript Illumination*, Chicago 1971, p. 59.
35. Jeremy P. Gray, 'The Iconography of the Illuminated Medieval Manuscripts of Gregory's "Moralia in Job"', unpublished PhD dissertation, Courtauld Institute, University of London 1992.
36. W. Cahn, *Romanesque Bible Illumination*, Ithaca NY 1982, pp. 198–9, 265.
37. J. Williams, *A Corpus of the Illustrations of the Commentary on the Illustrated Beatus*, 5 vols, London 1994–2003.
38. Cahn, pp. 76, 292–3.
39. K. Fugelso, 'Dante as Auctor in Musée Condé MS 597', *Gesta*, 49, 2010, pp. 1–16 at p. 6.
40. M. Harris, *Cows, Pigs, Wars and Witches. The Riddles of Culture*, London 1977, esp. pp. 31–8. See also G. Feeley-Harnik, *The Lord's Table. The Meaning of Food in Early Judaism and Christianity*, Washington/London, 2nd ed. 1994, pp. 1–24; R. Alter, 'A New Theory of Kashrut', *Commentary*, 68 (2), 1979, pp. 46–52. J. Soler, 'The Semiotics of Food in the Bible', in *Food and Drink in History: Selections from Annales*, ed. R. Forster and O. Ranum, vol. 5, Baltimore, London 1979, pp. 126–38.
41. For a general discussion of the biblical texts, see K. Albala (ed.), *The Food History Reader. Primary Sources*, London 2014, pp. 171–90.
42. Weitzmann and Barnabo, as in n. 5, pp. 188–9.
43. R.M. Thomson, *The Bury Bible*, Woodbridge 2001, p. 25.

THE NEW TESTAMENT

1. G. Vermes, *Christian Beginnings. From Nazareth to Nicaea*, London 2012, pp. 52–4.
2. For a recent discussion of these points, see K. Albala and T. Eden, *Food and Faith in Christian Culture*, New York 2011, esp. pp. 7–19.
3. P. Payan, *Joseph. Une image de la paternité dans L'Occident medieval*, Aubrier 2006. For the *Meditations*, see below n. 11.
4. It was reproduced by J. Wilpert, *Die Malereien der Katakomben Roms*, Freiburg im Breisgan, 1903, II pl. 57, but can no longer be traced.

5. For the fullest corpus of reproductions of this and the other scenes discussed, see G. Schiller, *Iconography of Christian Art*, vols 1 and 2, New York 1971.
6. P. Williamson, *Medieval Ivory Carvings. Early Christian to Romanesque*, London 2010, no. 39, pp. 160–3.
7. For this and the other Ottonian manuscripts to be discussed, see H. Mayr-Harting, *Ottonian Book Illumination*, 2 vols, London 1991.
8. L. Jacobus, *Giotto and the Arena Chapel*, London, Turnhout 2008, p. 141.
9. J. Gardner, 'The Cappellone di San Nicola at Tolentino', in *Italian Church Decoration of the Middle Ages and early Renaissance*, ed. W. Tronzo, Baltimore 1989, pp. 101–17. *San Nicola da Tolentino nell'arte. Corpus iconografico*, Tolentino, Milano 2005, esp. chapter by A. Dunlop, pp. 47–63.
10. See H. Blake, 'The Archaic Maiolica of north-central Italy: Montalcino, Assisi and Tolentino', in *Faenza. Bollettino del Museo Internazionale delle Ceramiche in Faenza*, 66, 1980, pp. 91–152, esp. 100–2. I am grateful to John Mallet for this reference.
11. I. Ragusa and R.B. Green, *Meditations on the Life of Christ. An Illustrated Manuscript of the Fourteenth Century*, Princeton 1961, pp. 124–31. For a recent discussion of the origin of the *Meditations* and of the other illustrated copies, see H. Flora, *The Devout Belief of the Imagination: The Paris Meditationes Vitae Christi and Female Franciscan Spirituality in Trecento Italy*, Turnhout 2009.
12. See K. Albala, *The Banquet. Dining in the Great Courts of Late Renaissance Europe*, Urbana, Chicago 2007, esp. ch. 1.
13. *Les Noces de Cana de Véronèse. Une oeuvre et sa restauration*, Paris, 1992–93, for a general discussion. Aretino's influence is emphasised by P. Fehl, 'Veronese's decorum: Notes on the Marriage at Cana', in *Art the Ape of Nature. Studies in Honor of H.W. Janson*, ed. M. Barasch and L.F. Sandler, New York 1981, pp. 341–65.
14. S. Loffredo, *I Santuari di Tabgha*, Jerusalem 1975.
15. A. Grabar, *Les Peintures de l'Evangéliaire de Sinope*, Paris 1948, p. 9, pl. 3.
16. P. Binski and A. Massing, ed., *The Westminster Retable*, London, Turnhout 2009, p. 50, 1b. See also p. 29, 15 for a comparison with the Queen Mary Psalter illustration.
17. Chantilly, Musée Condé, MS 65, f.168v. M. Meiss, *French Painting in the time of Jean de Berry. The Limbourgs and their Contemporaries*, London 1974, p. 163, pl. 592.
18. U. Hoff and M. Davies, *Les Primitifs Flamands. National Gallery of Victoria*, Melbourne, Brussels 1971, pp. 1–26, pls 1–45 (English text).
19. C. Ishikawa, *The Retablo de Isabel la Católica by Juan de Flandes and Michel Sittow*, Turnhout 2004.
20. E.A. Safarik, *Domenico Fetti*, Milan 1990, pp. 133–43, no. 32.
21. S. Haskins, *Mary Magdalen. Myth and Metaphor*, New York, London 1993, esp. pp. 3–26, 94–7.
22. J. Mitchell, 'The High Cross and Monastic Strategies in Eighth-century Northumbria', in *New Offerings, Ancient Treasures. Studies in Medieval Art for George Henderson*, ed. P. Binski and W. Noel, Stroud 2001, pp. 88–114.
23. Williamson, as in n. 6, p. 197, no. 48.
24. O. Pächt, C.R. Dodwell, and F. Wormald, *The St Albans Psalter*, London 1960, p. 87.
25. M. Boskovits, *Giovanni da Milano*, Firenze 1966.
26. R. Haussherr, in *Kunstchronik*, 24, 1971, pp. 177–212. C. Sterling, 'Observations on Moser's Tiefenbronn Altarpiece', *Pantheon*, 30, 1972, pp. 19–32.
27. A. Blunt, *The Paintings of Nicolas Poussin. A Critical Catalogue*, London 1966, cat. Nos 105–18, pp. 73–9; E. Cropper and C. Dempsey, *Nicolas Poussin. Friendship and the Love of Painting*, Princeton 1996, pp. 116–18.
28. A. Blunt, 'The Triclinium in Religious Art', *JWCI*, 2, 1938–9, pp. 271–6.
29. P. Fehl, 'Veronese and the Inquisition', *Gazette des Beaux-Arts*, 58, 1961, pp. 325–54.
30. S.L. Wailes, *Medieval Allegories of Jesus' Parables*, Berkeley, London 1987, see esp. nos 16 (p. 153), 17 (p. 161), 36 (p. 236), 38 (p. 253).
31. C.M. Kauffmann, *Romanesque Manuscripts 1066–1190*, London 1975, p. 74, no. 35.
32. Augustine, *Questions on the Gospels*, II, no. 30.
33. F.W.H. Hollstein, *German Engravings, Etchings and Woodcuts*, vol. 19, ed. F. Anzelewsky, Amsterdam 1976, 172.2.
34. M. Gibson, T.A. Heslop, and R.W. Pfaff, ed., *The Eadwine Psalter. Text, Image, and Monastic Culture in Twelfth-Century Canterbury*, University Park PA 1992, pp. 25–61, esp. p. 37, pl. 11.
35. G.B. Guest, 'The Prodigal Journey: Ideology of Self and City in the Gothic Cathedral', *Speculum*, 81, 2006, pp. 35–75.
36. L.R. Muir, *The biblical drama of medieval Europe*, Cambridge 1995, pp. 121–3.
37. For a facsimile edition, see R. Kroos et al., *Das Goslaer Evangeliar*, with a commentary volume, Graz, Goslar 1991, pp. 62–6. For a survey of images of the Prodigal Son, see E. Vetter, *Der Verlorene Sohn*, Düsseldorf 1955.
38. B. Haeger, 'The Prodigal Son in 16th and 17th century Netherlandish Art', *Simiolus*, 16, 1986, pp. 128–38, esp. p. 5, engraving after Maerten de Vos, c.1600. For an English version of about 1600, see T. Hamling, *Decorating the Godly Household. Religious Art in Post-Reformation Britain*, New Haven 2010, pp. 155, 101.
39. For the medieval illustrations of Dives and Lazarus, see U. Wolf, *Die Parabel vom reichen Prasser und armen Lazarus in der mittelalterlichen Buchmalerei*, Munich 1989; K.D. Sievers, *Die Parabel vom reichen Mann und armen Lazarus im Spiegel bildlicher Uberlieferung*, Kiel 2005.
40. D. Grivot and G. Zarnecki, *Gislebertus Sculptor of Autun*, London 1961, pp. 146–7.
41. St Ambrose, 'De Virginibus', 3.25, in *Tutte le Opere di Sant' Ambrogio*, 14/1 *Verginità*, Milan, Rome 1989, pp. 230–1.
42. Grabar, as in n. 15, p. 9, pl. I.
43. K.M.D. Dunbabin, 'Triclinium and Stibadium', in *Dining in a Classical Context*, ed. W.J. Slater, Ann Arbor 1991, pp. 121–48.
44. This, and several of the other examples under consideration, are discussed in E. Bairati, *Salomé*, Nuovo 1998, p. 51 and passim.
45. L. Seidel, 'Salome and the Canons', *Womens' Studies*, 11, 1984, pp. 29–68, esp. 39f.
46. N.J. Morgan, *Early Gothic Manuscripts 1190–1250*, London 1982, p. 68, no. 23.
47. A. Watson, 'Tumblers', *The Reliquary and Illustrated Archaeologist*, 1903, pp. 106–202. The image in the Munich Psalter is discussed in connection with tumblers and Saracen dancers by Torsten Hausamann, *Die Tanzende Salomé*, Zurich 1980, pp. 338–43, 357–9, but without illustrations. The closest comparisons are with fourteenth-century English manuscripts such as the Carmelite missal of c.1330, BL MS Add. 29704; see K.L. Scott, *Later Gothic Manuscripts 1390–1490*, no. 2, fig. 11. Thanks are due to Richard Barber for perceptive help.
48. J. Lubbock, *Storytelling in Christian Art from Giotto to Donatello*, New Haven, London 2006, pp. 190–203.
49. See J. Ruda, *Fra Filippo Lippi, Life and Work*, London 1993, pl. 155.
50. J.K. Cadogan, *Domenico Ghirlandaio. Artist and Artisan*, New Haven, London 2000, p. 82.
51. L. Burchard, 'Rubens' Feast of Herod at Port Sunlight', *Burlington Magazine*, 95, 1953, pp. 383–7.
52. D. Rigaux, *A la Table du Seigneur. L'Eucharisties chez les Primitifs Italiens 1250–1497*, Paris 1989, p. 54.

53. E. Saxon, *The Eucharist in Romanesque France*, Woodbridge 2006, pp. 13–47 for the early commentaries.
54. For the development of Eucharistic theology 1150–1350, see especially M. Rubin, *Corpus Christi. The Eucharist in late Medieval Culture*, Cambridge 1991.
55. For a summary of these early examples, see K. Wessel, *The Last Supper*, Recklinghausen 1967. More generally, see Schiller, n. 5 above, vol. II, pp. 24–41, 332–48. Another early example is on a late fifth-century ivory diptych in Milan Cathedral Treasury: see W.F. Volbach, *Elfenarbeiten der Spätantike und des frühen Mittelalter*, 3rd edition, Mainz 1976, p. 84 no. 119, pl. 63.
56. F. Wormald, *The Miniatures in the Gospels of St Augustine*, Cambridge 1954, pp. 11–12, pls I and IV.
57. S. Neilson Blum, *Early Netherlandish Triptychs. A Study in Patronage*, Berkeley 1969, pp. 59–70. M. Smeyers, 'Dirk Bouts and the Last Supper', in *Dirk Bouts (c.1410–1475)*, exh. cat., Leuven 1998, pp. 35–58.
58. L. Steinberg, *Leonardo's Incessant Last Supper*, New York 2001, esp. pp. 31–53. R. King, *Leonardo and the Last Supper*, London 2012, esp. pp. 200–19.
59. J.E. Jung, 'Peasant Meal or Lord's Feast? The Social Iconography of the Naumburg Last Supper', *Gesta*, 42, 2003, pp. 39–61.
60. See above, nn. 27–8.
61. M. Brown, *The Luttrell Psalter. A Facsimile*, London 2006, pp. 5–7.
62. G. Feeley-Harnick, op. cit., see above, Part I, n. 40.
63. M. Levi D'Ancona, *The Garden of the Renaissance. Botanical Symbolism in Italian Painting*, Florence 1977, pp. 52, 89, 159, 205, 209, 272.
64. A. Lymberopoulou in *Eat, Drink and be Merry: Food and Wine in Byzantium*, ed. L. Brubaker and K. Linardou, Aldershot 2007, pp. 223–32.
65. C.C. Young, 'Crayfish at the Last Supper', in *I Gamberi alla Tavola del Signore*, ed. L. Romeri, Trento 2000, pp. 45–56.
66. These commentaries are discussed in *Incontrarsi a Emmaus*, exh. Padua, Palazzo del Monte di Pietà, ed. G.M. Canova, 1997, pp. 27–35.
67. Pächt, op. cit. at n. 24, pp. 73–9. For the Peregrinus play, see K. Young, *The Drama of the Medieval Church*, I, Oxford 1933, pp. 450–91.
68. For example, in an English Psalter of c.1210 (BL Royal I.D.x, f.7v) and a Lectionary from the Ste Chapelle in Paris (BnF. MS lat.17326). For a detailed discussion of this theme, see K. Gerry, 'The Reappearance of the Disappearing Christ in an Early Thirteenth-Century Psalter from Oxford', *Art & Nature. Studies in Medieval Art and Architecture*, Courtauld Institute, London 2009, pp. 115–29.
69. O. Demus, *The Mosaics of Norman Sicily*, London 1950, pp. 117, 289, pl. 73.
70. A. Heimann, 'The Capital Frieze and Pilasters of the Portail Royal, Chartres', *JWCI*, 31, 1968, pp. 73–102.
71. A. Pigler, *Barockthemen*, Budapest 1956, I, pp. 346–54.
72. G.P. Bellori, *The Lives of the Modern Painters, Sculptors and Architects*, translated by A.S. Wohl, Cambridge 2005, p. 185.
73. D. Davies and E. Harris, *Velázquez in Seville*, exh. National Gallery of Scotland, 1996, pp. 45–9, 134–5, no. 22.

CONTEXTS AND CONCLUSIONS

1. S.N. Blum, *Early Netherlandish Triptychs. A Study in Patronage*, Berkeley, Los Angeles 1969, p. 66.
2. E. Brunet, *The Bible according to Tintoretto*, Venice 2012, pp. 88–105.
3. Oxford, Bodleian Library, MS Bodley 207b, f. 179v.
4. For an illuminating general discussion, see J. Elsner, *Art and the Roman Viewer. The Transformation of Art from the Pagan World to Christianity*, Cambridge 1995, pp. 1–14.
5. H. Mayr-Harting, *Ottonian Book Illumination*, II, London 1991, pp. 60–81. For a facsimile, see G. Franz, *Der Egbert Codex*, Darmstadt 2005. More generally on Egbert's artistic activity: T. Head, 'Art and Artifice in Ottonian Trier', *Gesta*, 36, 1997, pp. 55–82.
6. H. Adhémar, *Le Musée Nationale du Louvre, Paris. Les Primitifs flamands*, I, 1962, no. 89, pp. 101–13 (English text).
7. T. Scully, *The Art of Cookery in the Middle Ages*, Woodbridge 1995.
8. M. Broshi, *Bread, Wine, Walls and Scrolls*, Sheffield 2001, pp. 121–43.
9. Petronius, *Satyricon*, with an English translation by M. Heseltine revised by E.H. Warmington, Cambridge MA 1975, pp. 53–183, at p. 75.
10. J. Bridgeman ed., *A Renaissance Wedding*, London, Turnhout 2013, pp. 57–96.
11. P. Roberts, *Life and Death in Pompeii and Herculaneum*, London 2013, pp. 226–30, 263, 266–7.
12. F. Stenton, ed., *The Bayeux Tapestry. A Comprehensive Survey*, London 1957, p. 171, pl. 49; R. Gameson, ed., *The Study of the Bayeux Tapestry*, Woodbridge 1997, pp. 157–211.
13. BL, Cotton Nero A.X. c.1400. See N. Perkins and A. Wiggins, *The Romance of the Middle Ages*, exh. Bodleian Library, Oxford 2012, p. 11, 1.
14. Troyes, Bibliothèque municipal, MS 392, fol. 73. L. Morel-Payen, *Les plus beaux manuscrits et les plus belles reliures de la Bibliothèque de Troyes*, Troyes 1935, p. 87.
15. M.W. Bloomfield, *The Seven Deadly Sins*, East Lansing MI 1967, ch. 3; John Cassian, *The Institutes*, transl. B. Ramsey, New York 2000, Book 5.
16. K. Albala and T. Eden, ed., *Food and Faith in Christian Culture*, New York 2011, pp. 7–19; C.W. Bynum, *Holy Feast and Holy Fast. The Religious Significance of Food to Medieval Women*, Berkeley, Los Angeles 1987, Introduction.
17. R.W. Southern, *Robert Grosseteste*, Oxford 1986, on Grosseteste generally. On the *Dicta*, J. Flood, J.R. Ginther and J.W. Goering, ed., *Robert Grosseteste and his Intellectual Milieu*, Toronto 2013, pp. 64–86. For an English translation of the text, see Robert Grosseteste, *The Complete Dicta in English*, Lincoln 2003, vol. 3, pp. 33–6, vol. 4, pp. 5–7. I am grateful to Lesley Smith for the reference to Grosseteste.
18. A. Katzenellenbogen, *Allegories of the Virtues and Vices in Mediaeval Art*, New York 1964.
19. Paris, BnF, Rés.Z.200, f.85. *Miniatures flamands 1404–1482*, exh. cat. Bibliothèque nationale de France, 2012, no. 121.
20. Brussels, Bibliothèque Royale, MS 10204, f.297v. F. Lyna, *Les Principaux Manuscrits à peintures de la Bibliothèque Royale de Belgique*, III (1), Brussels 1989, pp. 353–9.

GLOSSARY

Altarpiece	A devotional painting or sculpture placed on or behind the altar.
Carolingian	Describes French history of the ninth century, taking its name from Charlemagne, king of France, crowned Holy Roman Emperor in 800.
Gospel lectionary	A selection of passages from the Gospels, arranged in order of the liturgical year, to be sung at Mass.
Haggadah	Hebrew service book for the Jewish festival of Passover Eve (Seder).
Hours, book of	Prayer book of the laity, the most popular book of the later Middle Ages. Its central content was the Hours of the Blessed Virgin Mary, to be recited at eight specified hours per day.
Octateuch	Byzantine manuscript of the first eight books of the Bible. There are five related illustrated copies from the period c.1075–1275.
Ottonian	The three German emperors of the Saxon dynasty named Otto ruled from 936 to 1002, but the term is more generally used to cover German history of the tenth and eleventh centuries.
Pentateuch	The first five books of the Bible; the Jewish Torah, covering Genesis to Deuteronomy.
Psalter	The Old Testament Book of Psalms, with added prayers, became the principal prayer book of the Christian Church for both clergy and laity. Copies illustrated with the Life of Christ were popular from the eleventh to the fourteenth centuries.
Typology	The interpretation of the Old Testament in terms of, and parallel to, the New Testament.
Vulgate	The Latin text of the Bible translated from the Greek by St Jerome in c.380–404. This was the norm in the Middle Ages.

BIBLIOGRAPHY: FOOD HISTORY

Albala, Ken, *The Banquet. Dining in the great courts of late Renaissance Europe*, Urbana 2007

Albala, Ken, ed., *The Food History Reader. Primary Sources*, London 2014

Albala, Ken, & T. Eden, eds, *Food and faith in Christian culture*, New York 2011

Astell, Ann, *Eating beauty. The Eucharist and the spiritual arts of the Middle Ages*, Ithaca NY 2006

Barthes, Roland, 'Towards a psychopsychology of contemporary food consumption', in R. Forster & O. Ranum, eds, *Food and drink in history. Selections from Annales Economies, Societés, Civilisations*, vol. 5, Baltimore/London 1975

Bendiner, Kenneth, *Food in painting, from the Renaissance to the present*, London 2004

Bober, Phyllis P., *Art, culture and cuisine. Ancient and medieval gastronomy*, Chicago 1999

Brenner, Athalya, ed. *Food and drink in the Biblical Worlds* (Semeia 86), Atlanta 1999

Broshi, Magen, *Bread, wine, walls and scrolls*, Sheffield 2001

Brothwell, Don, & Patricia Brothwell, *Food in Antiquity. A survey of the diet of early peoples*, London 1998

Brubaker, Leslie, & K. Linardou, eds, *Eat, drink and be merry (Luke 12.19) – food and wine in Byzantium*, Aldershot 2007

Bynum, Caroline W., *Holy feast and holy fast. The religious significance of food to medieval women*, Berkeley 1987

Cosman, Madeleine P., *Fabulous feasts. Medieval cookery and ceremony*, New York 1976

Douglas, Mary, *Purity and Danger. An analysis of concepts of pollution and taboo*, London 1966

Feeley-Harnik, Gillian, *The Lord's table. The meaning of food in early Judaism and Christianity*, Washington/London 1944

Frankel, Rafael, *Wine and oil production in antiquity in Israel and other Mediterranean countries*, Sheffield 1999

Garnsey, Peter, *Food and Wine in Classical Antiquity*, Cambridge 1999

Goody, Jack, *Cooking, cuisine and class: a study in comparative sociology*, Cambridge 1982

Gowers, Emily, *The loaded table. Representations of food in Roman literature*, Oxford 1993

Grimm, Veronika, *From feasting to fasting, the evolution to sin. Attitudes to food in late Antiquity*, London/New York 1996

Henisch, Bridget A., *Fast and feast. Food in medieval society*, Philadelphia 1985

Hyams, Edward, *Dionysus: a social history of the wine vine*, London 1965

McGowan, Andrew, *Ascetic Eucharists: food and drink in Early Christian ritual meals*, Oxford 1999

Riley, Gillian, *A feast for the eyes*, National Gallery London (exh. cat.) 1997

Scully, Terence, *The art of cookery in the Middle Ages*, Woodbridge 1995

Slater, William J., *Dining in a Classical context*, Ann Arbor 1991

Strong, Roy, *Feast: a history of grand eating*, London 2002

The Cambridge World History of Food, ed. K.F. Kiple & K.C. Ornelas, Cambridge 2000

Vamosh, Miriam Feinberg, *Food at the Time of the Bible*, Herzlia n.d.

Varriano, John L., *Tastes and temptations: food and art in Renaissance Italy*, Berkeley 2009

Varriano, John L., *Wine: a cultural history*, London 2010

Visser, Margaret, *The rituals of dinner: the origins, evolution, eccentricities and meaning of table manners*, New York/London 1992

Wilkins, John M., & S. Hill, *Food in the ancient world*, Oxford 2006

PHOTOGRAPHIC ACKNOWLEDGEMENTS

AUSTRALIA

© National Gallery of Australia, Canberra **85**

AUSTRIA

Stiftsbibliothek Kremsmünster CC 243 **32**
ÖNB/Wien (Cod.theol.gr.1 fol. 1r) **13**
ÖNB/Wien (Cod.1855 fol. 59r) **66**

BELGIUM

Antwerp
© Museum Mayer van den Bergh, Antwerpen **106**

Brussels
© Musées Royaux des Beaux-Arts de Belgique, Bruxelles/photo: F. Maes (KMSKB) **55**
© KBR Bibliothèque Royale de Belgique **111**; **158**

Louvain
© 2016. Photo Scala, Florence: St Peter's Church, Louvain **34**; **127**; **148**

BOSNIA HERZEGOVINA

The National Museum of Bosnia and Herzegovina **36**

BRITISH ISLES

ENGLAND

Bristol
© Bristol Museum and Art Gallery, UK / Purchased with the assistance of the Friends of Bristol Art Gallery, 1958. / Bridgeman Images **105**

Cambridge
The Master and Fellows of Corpus Christi College, Cambridge **64**; **126**
By permission of the Master and Fellows of Pembroke College, Cambridge **99**

London
© The British Library Board **31**; **43**; **44**; **49**; **54**; **57**; **83**; **137**
© The Trustees of the British Museum **10**; **101**; **112**
Lambeth Palace Library, Ms 3. 6r **16**
© The National Gallery, London. Bought with a contribution from The Art Fund, 1964 **62**
© The National Gallery, London. Presented by the Hon. George Vernon, 1839 **145**
The Samuel Courtauld Trust, The Courtauld Gallery, London **11**
© Victoria and Albert Museum, London **35**; **69**; **81**; **89**

Manchester
Copyright of The University of Manchester **39**

Oxford
The Bodleian Libraries, The University of Oxford **9**

Winchester
© The Dean & Chapter of Winchester 2015. Reproduced by kind permission of The Dean & Chapter of Winchester **50**

IRELAND
© National Gallery of Ireland, Dublin **146**

SCOTLAND
Bridgewater Collection Loan, Scottish National Gallery, Edinburgh **95**; **136**
Scottish National Gallery, Edinburgh **122**
Ruthwell Cross, Creative Commons, Photo: Doug Sim **88**

FRANCE

© Adrian Fletcher, paradoxplace.com **110**; **144**
Bibliothèque Nationale de France **21**; **23**; **33**; **52–3**; **58**; **75**; **80**; **114**; **115**; **157**
© Douai, Musée de la Chartreuse – Photo: Hugo Maertens **47**
© Henri Gaud, Gaud Phototèque **103**
© 2016. Photo Scala, Florence: Bayeux Tapestry **156**

Réunion des Musées Nationaux
Paris, musée du Louvre. Photo © RMN-Grand Palais (musée du Louvre)/Droits réservés **76**; **78**
Paris, musée du Louvre. Photo © RMN-Grand Palais (musée du Louvre)/Adrien Didierjean **147**
Chantilly, musée Condé. Photo © RMN-Grand Palais (domaine de Chantilly)/René-Gabriel Ojéda **17**; **61**; **84**; **155**

Toulouse
Toulouse, Musée des Augustins. Photos: Daniel Martin **117**; **118**

GERMANY

Aachen
© Domkapitel Aachen (Photos: Ann Münchow) **107**; **116**

Bad Wildungen
Conrad von Soest painting, Church of St Nicholas. Photo: www.zeno.org **67**

Berlin
Gemäldegalerie Staatliche Museen zu Berlin Preußischer Kulturbesitz Photo: Jörg P. Anders **94**

Goslar
Stadtarchiv Goslar, B 4387, fol. 71r **104**

Hamburg
© Photo: Elke Walford © 2016. Photo Scala, Florence/bpk, Bildagentur fuer Kunst, Kultur und Geschichte, Berlin **26**; **65**

Hildesheim
Dommuseum Hildesheim. Photo: Florian Monheim **8**
Dommuseum Hildesheim. Photo: Frank Tomio **109**
Dommuseum Hildesheim. Photo: Bayerische Staatsbibliothek Munich **129**
Dombibliothek Hildesheim **90**; **141**; **142**; **143**

Munich
Bayerische Staatsbibliothek München:
Clm 835, fol. 106v, urn:nbn:de:bvb:12-bsb00012920-3 **60**
Clm 4453, fol. 163r, urn:nbn:de:bvb:12-bsb00096593-3 **82**
Clm 15903, fol. 22v, urn:nbn:de:bvb:12-bsb00070697-0 **71**
Clm 835, fol. 66r, urn:nbn:de:bvb:12-bsb00012920-3 **119**
Clm 23338, fol. 154v, urn:nbn:de:bvb:12-bsb00095112-3 **98**

Naumburg
Bildarchiv Naumburg, Photo: Matthias Rutkowski **132**

Nuremberg
© Germanisches Nationalmuseum **70**; **100**; **108**
University Library Erlangen-Nürnberg **59**

Stuttgart
Stuttgart, Württembergische Landesbibliothek, Cod. bibl. fol. 23, f. 91v **41**

Tiefenbronn
© Erich Lessing / lessingimages.com **93**

Trier
Stadtbibliothek Weberbach **91**; **96**; **140**

Ulm
Museum der Brotkultur, Ulm **113**

Wolfenbüttel
Herzog August Bibliothek **130**

ISRAEL

Sepphoris Synagogue, lower Galilee. Photo: Hanan Isachar/Alamy **1**
The Israel Museum, Jerusalem. Photo © The Israel Museum, Jerusalem by Ardon Bar-Hama **37**; **38**
Church of the Multiplication, Tabgha, Israel / Bridgeman Images **79**

ITALY

Assisi

Church of San Francesco © 2016. Photo Scala, Florence **133**

Bologna

Museo Medievale; Photo: © Michael Kauffmann **74**

Carisolo

Church of Santo Stefano, Creative Commons, Photo, 2009: Laurom **139**

Florence

Ognissanti Monastery © 2016. Photo Scala, Florence **138**
Santa Croce Sacristy © 2016. Photo Scala, Florence **92**
Santa Maria Novella © 2016. Photo Scala, Florence **121**

Mantua

Palazzo Ducale © 2016 Photo Scala, Florence – courtesy of the Ministero Beni e Att. Culturali **87**

Milan

Pinacoteca di Brera © Photo Scala, Florence – courtesy of the Ministero Beni e Att. Culturali **135**
Santa Maria delle Grazie © Photo Scala, Florence – courtesy of the Ministero Beni e Att. Culturali **128**

Padua

Baptistery of St John © Photo Scala, Florence **18**
Scrovegni Chapel © 2016. DeAgostini Picture Library/Scala, Florence **72**
Scrovegni Chapel © 2016. A. Dagli Orti/Scala, Florence **131**

Ravenna

Church of S. Apollinare Nuovo © 2016. Photo Scala, Florence – courtesy of the Ministero Beni e Att. Culturali **123**
Church of San Vitale © 2016. Photo Scala, Florence **15**

Rome

Church of Santa Sabina. Photo: courtesy rome101.com **40**
Basilica of Santa Maria Maggiore © 2016 Photo Scala, Florence **2**; **14**
Catacombs of St Callixtus © 2016. Photo Scala, Florence **4**
Marcellinus & Peter catacombs © 2016. DeAgostini Picture Library/Scala, Florence **5**; **6**
St Peter's Basilica (Treasury Museum)© 2016 Photo Scala, Florence **7**
Raphael School, Vatican, Logge © 2016. Photo Scala, Florence **27**
© 2017 Biblioteca Apostolica Vaticana **22**; **24**; **51**
Thermae Museum: Creative Commons, Photo: Marie-Lan Nguyen, 2007 **3**

Sant'Angelo in Formis

Capua, Sant'Angelo in Formis © 2016. Photo Scala, Florence **125**

Siena

Baptistery, Siena Cathedral © 2016. Photo Opera Metropolitana Siena/Scala, Florence **120**

Tolentino

Basilica of St Nicholas © 2016. DeAgostini Picture Library/Scala, Florence **73**

Veneto

Rossano, Museo Diocesaro d'Arte Sacra © 2016. DeAgostini Picture Library/Scala, Florence **124**

Venice

Accademia © 2016. Photo SCALA, Florence – courtesy of the Ministero Beni e Att. Culturali **97**
Church of San Giorgio Maggiore © 2016. Photo Scala, Florence **134**
San Marco Basilica © 2016. Photo Scala, Florence **12**; **45**
Santa Maria della Salute © 2016. Photo Cameraphoto/Scala, Florence **77**
Scuola di San Rocco © 2016. Photo Scala, Florence **149–54**

RUSSIA

The State Hermitage Museum, St. Petersburg, Photograph © The State Hermitage Museum. Photo by Vladimir Terebenin **19**

SPAIN

Madrid

Prado Museum © Photo MNP/Scala, Florence **28**; **29**
Royal Palace © 2016. Photo Album/Scala, Florence **86**

Valladolid

Biblioteca Histórica, Universidad de Valladolid **56**

USA

The Pierpont Morgan Library, New York. MS M.521, recto. Purchased by J. P. Morgan in 1911 **102**
The Pierpont Morgan Library, New York. MS M.638, folio 4r. Purchased by J. P. Morgan in 1916 **25**
The Pierpont Morgan Library, New York. MS M.638, folio 9v. Purchased by J. P. Morgan in 1916 **46**
The Pierpont Morgan Library, New York. MS M.638, folio 17v. Purchased by J. P. Morgan in 1916 **48**

INDEX OF MANUSCRIPTS

Numbers in **bold** refer to illustrations

GENERAL INDEX